Joyful Path of
Good Fortune

Also by Geshe Kelsang Gyatso

Meaningful to Behold
Clear Light of Bliss
Heart of Wisdom
Universal Compassion
Guide to Dakini Land
The Bodhisattva Vow
Heart Jewel
Great Treasury of Merit
Introduction to Buddhism
Understanding the Mind
Tantric Grounds and Paths
Ocean of Nectar
Essence of Vajrayana
Living Meaningfully, Dying Joyfully
Eight Steps to Happiness
Transform Your Life
The New Meditation Handbook
How to Solve Our Human Problems
Mahamudra Tantra

Profits received by Tharpa Publications from the
sale of this book will be donated to the
NKT-International Temples Project
Part of the New Kadampa Tradition
[Reg. Charity Number 1015054 (England)]
a Buddhist Charity, Building for World Peace
www.kadampa.org/temples.htm

GESHE KELSANG GYATSO

Joyful Path of Good Fortune

THE COMPLETE
BUDDHIST PATH TO
ENLIGHTENMENT

THARPA PUBLICATIONS
Ulverston, England
Glen Spey, New York

First published in 1990
Second edition revised and reset 1995
Reprinted 1997, 2001, 2003, 2006

The right of Geshe Kelsang Gyatso
to be identified as author of this work
has been asserted by him in accordance with
the Copyright, Designs, and Patents Act 1988.

Tharpa Publications
Conishead Priory
Ulverston, Cumbria
LA12 9QQ, England

Tharpa Publications
47 Sweeney Road
P.O. Box 430, Glen Spey,
NY 12737, USA

Cover painting of Atisha
by the Tibetan artist Chating Jamyang Lama.
Line illustrations by Gen Kelsang Wangchen and Kelsang Pema.

Library of Congress Control Number: 2001092513

British Library Cataloguing in Publication Data
A catalogue record for this book is
available from the British Library.

ISBN-13 978 0 948006 45 6 – hardback
ISBN-10 0 948006 45 5 – hardback
ISBN-13 978 0 948006 46 3 – paperback
ISBN-10 0 948006 46 3 – paperback

Set in Palatino by Tharpa Publications
Printed on Wentworth Opaque, acid-free 250-year longlife paper
and bound by Cromwell Press, Trowbridge, Wiltshire, England.

Contents

Illustrations

Acknowledgements

In 1981 Venerable Geshe Kelsang Gyatso gave extensive teachings on the stages of the path to enlightenment to the fortunate students of Manjushri Kadampa Meditation Centre in Ulverston, England. Those teachings form the basis of this present book. We would like to express our very deepest gratitude to the author for making these precious spiritual instructions widely available in English; instructions which if put into practice sincerely will bring peace and joy to many beings.

We also thank all the dedicated, senior Dharma students who assisted the author with the rendering of the English and who prepared the final manuscript for publication.

Through the merits created in producing this work, may all living beings find the happiness they seek.

Roy Tyson,
Administrative Director,
Manjushri Kadampa
Meditation Centre,
October 1997.

Preface

Although there are countless living beings, humans and non-humans, all are included within three kinds: those who seek mainly worldly happiness, those who seek mainly the attainment of liberation from samsara, and those who seek mainly the attainment of full enlightenment.

In the scripture known as the *Stages of the Path* (Tib. *Lamrim*) the first kind of being is called 'a person of initial scope' because his or her mental scope or capacity is at the initial stage of development. The second kind of being is called 'a person of intermediate scope' because his or her mental capacity is more extensive than the first being but less developed than the third being. The third kind of being is called 'a person of great scope' because such a person has progressed from the initial scope through the intermediate scope so that his or her mental capacity has become great.

The actual practice of the stages of the path fulfils the wishes of all three kinds of being. The practice of the stages of the path of a person of initial scope, which is explained in the first part of this book, brings us the happiness of humans and gods. The practice of the stages of the path of a person of intermediate scope, which is explained in the second part of this book, brings us the happiness of liberation. The practice of the stages of the path of a person of great scope, which is explained in the third part of this book, brings us the ultimate happiness of full enlightenment. Thus the main function of the Lamrim instructions is to fulfil the *Bold* needs and wishes of all living beings.

The instructions of Lamrim form the main body of Buddhadharma. They arose from the omniscient wisdom of Atisha (AD 982–1054), and the tradition has continued to this day.

Buddha Shakyamuni

It is wonderful and a sign of great fortune that these precious teachings are now beginning to flourish in western countries. I received these teachings from my Spiritual Guide, Trijang Dorjechang, who was an emanation of Atisha; thus the explanations given in this book, *Joyful Path of Good Fortune*, actually come from him and not from myself. Nevertheless, I have worked with great effort over a long period of time to complete this book.

The practice of Lamrim is very important because everyone needs to cultivate peaceful states of mind. By listening to or reading these teachings we can learn how to control our mind and always keep a good motivation in our heart. This will make all our daily actions pure and meaningful. By controlling our mind we can solve all our daily problems, and by gradually improving our daily practice of Lamrim we can advance from our present stage to the stage of a Bodhisattva. By progressing further we can become a fully enlightened being. This is the essential meaning of our human life. Such a great attainment will be the result of our practice of Lamrim.

Geshe Kelsang Gyatso,
Tharpaland,
November 1988.

PART ONE

Foundations and the Initial Scope

The Stages of the Path

The great Buddhist monastic universities of Nalanda and Vikramashila each developed their own discourse style. According to the tradition of Nalanda, whenever a Spiritual Guide teaches Dharma he or she begins by explaining three purities. Whenever we listen to, read, or teach Dharma these three purities are necessary: a pure mind on the part of the student, pure speech on the part of the Spiritual Guide, and pure Dharma. The mind of the student is pure if he or she is free from holding wrong views, has faith in the Spiritual Guide and in the Dharma that is taught, and has a correct motivation. The speech of the Spiritual Guide is pure if it is unmistaken and clear, if he or she received it from an authentic Spiritual Guide, and if the oral transmission and lineage teachings have blessings. The Dharma is pure if it reveals the entire path that leads to enlightenment, presents each point unmistakenly, and has been handed down in an unbroken lineage from Buddha Shakyamuni. The Dharma that is explained here, the Lamrim, is pure because it possesses these three necessary conditions. Therefore, our task as readers is to make sure that our own mind is pure while we read, contemplate, and meditate on the meanings that are explained. Principally, we need to develop a good motivation by thinking:

> Now I have a supreme opportunity to attain Buddhahood and lead others to the same state. To become enlightened I need to practise all the stages of the path. Therefore, I am going to study these instructions and put them into practice.

If we read Lamrim with such a pure intention we shall increase our collection of merit moment by moment. There is nothing more meaningful that we can do with our lives. For myself, the author, there is no greater meaning in my life than to teach and explain pure Dharma.

According to the tradition of Vikramashila, whenever a Spiritual Guide teaches Dharma he or she begins by explaining three things:

(1) The pre-eminent qualities of the author of the root texts upon which the teachings are based
(2) The pre-eminent qualities of the teachings presented in those texts
(3) How to listen to and teach Dharma

There are great benefits to be derived from receiving these explanations before studying the actual instructions on the stages of the path. From knowing the excellences of the author we shall easily understand that the Dharma he or she teaches must be authentic. From knowing the pre-eminent qualities of Lamrim we shall naturally develop interest, respect, and confidence in it. From knowing how to listen to and read the instructions, and how they should be taught, we shall be able to take the greatest advantage of opportunities such as the one we now have; and eventually we shall be able to benefit others greatly by giving the instructions to them.

All the explanations presented in this book are contained within four parts:

1 Explanation of the pre-eminent qualities of the author, showing that the instructions of Lamrim are authentic
2 Explanation of the pre-eminent qualities of Lamrim to inspire faith and respect for the Lamrim instructions
3 Explanation of how to listen to and teach Dharma
4 Explanation of the actual instructions of the stages of the path to enlightenment

The Qualities of the Author

The Lamrim instructions were originally taught by Buddha Shakyamuni. They were handed down in two separate lineages: the wisdom lineage of Nagarjuna and the method lineage of Asanga. The wisdom lineage, or profound path, passed from Buddha Shakyamuni to Manjushri, from Manjushri to Nagarjuna, and then through further Teachers to Atisha. The method lineage, or vast path, passed from Buddha Shakyamuni to Maitreya, from Maitreya to Asanga, and then through further Teachers to Atisha. Both these lineages include instructions on method and wisdom, but they differ in emphasis.

The author of Lamrim is Atisha because it was he who first combined all the instructions of these two great Mahayana lineages in his work, *Lamp for the Path to Enlightenment*, and gave his presentation the abbreviated title, *Lamrim*. He united the two traditions in a way that made both of them easier to understand and practise, and this work is the prototype for all subsequent Lamrim texts.

Atisha's life and work are explained in three parts:

1 Atisha's birth into a royal family and his early life
2 Atisha's attainments of knowledge and spiritual realizations
3 Atisha's work of spreading Buddhadharma in India and Tibet

ATISHA'S BIRTH INTO A ROYAL FAMILY AND HIS EARLY LIFE

Atisha was born in AD 982 as a prince in East Bengal, India. His father's name was Kalyanashri (Glorious Virtue) and his mother's name was Prabhavarti Shrimati (Glorious Radiance). He was the second of three sons and when he was born he was given the name Chandragarbha (Moon Essence). The name Atisha, which means Peace, was given to him later by the Tibetan king Jangchub Ö because he was always calm and peaceful.

When he was still a child Chandragarbha's parents took him to visit a temple. All along the way thousands of people gathered to see if they could catch a glimpse of the prince. When he saw them Chandragarbha asked 'Who are these people?' and his parents replied 'They are all our subjects.' Compassion arose spontaneously in the prince's heart and he prayed 'May all these people enjoy good fortune as great as my own.' Whenever he met anyone the wish arose naturally in his mind, 'May this person find happiness and be free from suffering.'

Even as a small boy Chandragarbha received visions of Tara. Sometimes, while he was on his mother's lap, blue upali flowers would fall from the sky and he would begin to speak, as if to the flowers. Yogis later explained to his mother that the blue flowers she had seen were a sign that Tara was appearing to her son and speaking to him.

When the prince was older his parents wanted to arrange a marriage for him, but Tara advised him 'If you become attached to your kingdom you will be like an elephant when he sinks into mud and cannot lift himself out again because he is so huge and heavy. Do not become attached to this life. Study and practise Dharma. You have been a Spiritual Guide in many of your previous lives and in this life also you will become a Spiritual Guide.' Inspired by these words Chandragarbha developed a very strong interest in studying and practising Dharma and he became determined to attain all the realizations of Buddha's teachings. He knew that to accomplish his aim he would need to find a fully qualified Spiritual

Guide. At first he approached a famous Buddhist Teacher called Jetari, who lived nearby, and requested Dharma instructions on how to find release from samsara. Jetari gave him instructions on refuge and bodhichitta, and then told him that if he wanted to practise purely he should go to Nalanda and learn from the Spiritual Guide Bodhibhadra.

When he met Bodhibhadra the prince said 'I realize that samsara is meaningless and that only liberation and full enlightenment are really worthwhile. Please give Dharma instructions that will lead me quickly to the state beyond sorrow.' Bodhibhadra gave him brief instructions on generating bodhichitta and then advised 'If you wish to practise Dharma purely you should seek the Spiritual Guide Vidyakokila.' Bodhibhadra knew that Vidyakokila was a great meditator who had gained a perfect realization of emptiness and was very skilful in teaching the stages of the profound path.

Vidyakokila gave Chandragarbha complete instructions on both the profound path and the vast path and then sent him to study with the Spiritual Guide Avadhutipa. Avadhutipa did not give guidance immediately but told the prince to go to Rahulagupta to receive instructions on *Hevajra* and *Heruka Tantras* and then to return to him to receive more detailed instructions on Secret Mantra. Rahulagupta gave Chandragarbha the secret name Janavajra (Indestructible Wisdom) and his first empowerment, which was into the practice of Hevajra. Then he told him to go home and obtain the consent of his parents.

Although the prince was not attached to worldly life it was still important for him to have his parents' permission to practise in the way he wished. Thus he returned to his parents and said 'If I practise Dharma purely, then, as Arya Tara has predicted, I shall be able to repay your kindness and the kindness of all living beings. If I can do this my human life will not have been wasted. Otherwise, even though I may spend all my time in a glorious palace, my life will be meaningless. Please give me your consent to leave the kingdom and dedicate my whole life to the practice of Dharma.'

Chandragarbha's father was unhappy to hear this and wanted to prevent his son from giving up his prospects as future king, but his mother was delighted to hear that her son wished to dedicate his life to Dharma. She remembered that at his birth there had been marvellous signs, such as rainbows, and she remembered miracles like the blue upali flowers falling from the sky. She knew that her son was no ordinary prince and she gave her permission without hesitation. In time, the king also granted his son's wish.

Chandragarbha returned to Avadhutipa and for seven years he received instructions on Secret Mantra. He became so accomplished that on one occasion he developed pride, thinking 'Probably I know more about Secret Mantra than anyone else in the whole world.' That night in his dream Dakinis came and showed him rare scriptures that he had never seen before. They asked him 'What do these texts mean?', but he had no idea. When he awoke, his pride was gone.

Later, Chandragarbha began to think that he should imitate Avadhutipa's way of practising and strive as a layman to attain enlightenment quickly by practising Mahamudra depending upon an action mudra; but he received a vision of Heruka who told him that if he were to take ordination he would be able to help countless beings and spread Dharma far and wide. That night he dreamt that he was following a procession of monks in the presence of Buddha Shakyamuni, who was wondering why Chandragarbha had not yet taken ordination. When he awoke from his dream he resolved to become a monk. He received ordination from Shilarakshita, and was given the name Dhipamkara Shrijana.

From the Spiritual Guide Dharmarakshita, Dhipamkara Shrijana received extensive instructions on the *Seven Sets of Abhidharma* and the *Ocean of Great Explanation* – texts written from the point of view of the Vaibhashika system. In this way he mastered the Hinayana teachings.

Still not satisfied, Dhipamkara Shrijana went to receive detailed instructions at Bodh Gaya. One day he overheard a conversation between two ladies who were in fact emanations of Arya Tara. The younger asked the elder 'What is the principal method for attaining enlightenment quickly?' and the elder replied 'It is bodhichitta.' Hearing this, Dhipamkara Shrijana became determined to attain the precious bodhichitta. Later, while he was circumambulating the great stupa at Bodh Gaya, a statue of Buddha Shakyamuni spoke to him, saying 'If you wish to attain enlightenment quickly you must gain experience of compassion, love, and the precious bodhichitta.' His desire to realize bodhichitta then became intense. He heard that the Spiritual Guide Serlingpa, who was living far away in a place called Serling, in Sumatra, had attained a very special experience of bodhichitta and was able to give instructions on the *Perfection of Wisdom Sutras*.

It took Dhipamkara Shrijana thirteen months to sail to Sumatra. When he arrived there he offered Serlingpa a mandala and made his requests. Serlingpa told him that the instructions would take twelve years to transmit. Dhipamkara Shrijana stayed in Sumatra for twelve years and finally gained the precious realization of bodhichitta. Then he returned to India.

ATISHA'S ATTAINMENTS OF KNOWLEDGE AND SPIRITUAL REALIZATIONS

By relying upon his Spiritual Guides Atisha gained special knowledge of the three sets of Buddha's teachings – the set of moral discipline, the set of discourses, and the set of wisdom; and of the four classes of Tantra. He also mastered arts and sciences such as poetry, rhetoric, and astrology, was an excellent physician, and was very skilled in crafts and technology.

Atisha also gained all the realizations of the three higher trainings: training in higher moral discipline, training in higher concentration, and training in higher wisdom. Since all the stages of Sutra, such as the six perfections, the five paths, the ten grounds; and all the stages of Tantra, such as generation stage and completion stage, are included within the three higher trainings, Atisha therefore gained all the realizations of the stages of the path.

There are three types of higher moral discipline: the higher moral discipline of the Pratimoksha vows, or vows of individual liberation; the higher moral discipline of the Bodhisattva vows; and the higher moral discipline of the Tantric vows. The vows to abandon two hundred and fifty-three downfalls, undertaken by a fully ordained monk, are amongst the Pratimoksha vows. Atisha never broke any one of these. This shows that he possessed very strong mindfulness and very great conscientiousness. He also kept purely the Bodhisattva vow to avoid eighteen root downfalls and forty-six secondary downfalls, and he kept purely all his Tantric vows.

The attainments of higher concentration and higher wisdom are divided into common and uncommon. A common attainment is one that is gained by practitioners both of Sutra and Tantra, and an uncommon attainment is one that is gained only by practitioners of Tantra. By training in higher concentration Atisha gained the common concentration of tranquil abiding and, based on that, clairvoyance, miracle powers, and the common virtues. He also attained uncommon concentrations such as the concentrations of generation stage and completion stage of Secret Mantra. By training in higher wisdom Atisha gained the common realization of emptiness, and the uncommon realizations of example clear light and meaning clear light of Secret Mantra.

ATISHA'S WORK OF SPREADING BUDDHADHARMA
IN INDIA AND TIBET

Atisha mastered the teachings of both Hinayana and Mahayana and was held in respect by Teachers of both traditions. When non-Buddhists debated with him and were defeated they would convert to Buddhism. Atisha was like a king, the crown ornament of Indian Buddhists, and was regarded as a second Buddha.

Before Atisha's time the thirty-seventh king of Tibet, Trisong Detsen (AD circa 754–97), had invited Padmasambhava, Shantarakshita, and other Buddhist Teachers to Tibet, and through their influence pure Dharma had flourished; but some years later a Tibetan king called Lang Darma (AD circa 836) destroyed the pure Dharma in Tibet and abolished the Sangha. Until that time most of the kings had been religious, but it was a dark age in Tibet during Lang Darma's evil reign. About seventy years after his death Dharma began to flourish once again in the upper part of Tibet through the efforts of great Teachers such as the translator Rinchen Sangpo, and it also began to flourish in the lower part of Tibet through the efforts of a great Teacher called Gongpa Rabsel. Gradually, Dharma spread to central Tibet.

At that time there was no pure practice of the union of Sutra and Tantra. The two were thought to be contradictory, like fire and water. When people practised Sutra they abandoned Tantra, and when they practised Tantra they abandoned Sutra, including even the rules of the Vinaya. False teachers came from India wishing to procure some of Tibet's plentiful gold. Pretending to be Spiritual Guides and Yogis they introduced perversions such as black magic, creating apparitions, sexual practices, and ritual murder. These malpractices became quite widespread.

A king called Yeshe Ö and his nephew Jangchub Ö, who lived in Ngari in west Tibet, were greatly concerned about what was happening to the Dharma in their country. The king wept when he thought of the purity of Dharma in former times compared with the impure Dharma now being practised. He was grieved to see how hardened and uncontrolled the minds of the people had become. He thought 'How wonderful it would be if pure Dharma were to flourish once again in Tibet to tame the minds of our people.' To fulfil this wish he sent Tibetans to India to learn Sanskrit and train in Dharma, but many of these people were unable to endure the hot climate. The few who survived learnt Sanskrit and trained very well in Dharma. Amongst them was the translator Rinchen Sangpo, who received many instructions and then returned to Tibet.

Since this plan had not met with much success Yeshe Ö decided to invite an authentic Teacher from India. He sent a group of Tibetans to India with a large quantity of gold, and gave them the task of seeking out the most qualified Spiritual Guide in India. He advised them all to study Dharma and gain perfect knowledge of Sanskrit. These Tibetans suffered all the hardships of climate and travel in order to accomplish his wishes. Some of them became famous translators. They translated many scriptures and sent them to the king, to his great delight.

When these Tibetans returned to Tibet they informed Yeshe Ö, 'In India there are many very learned Buddhist Teachers, but the most distinguished and sublime of all is Dhipamkara Shrijana. We would like to invite him to Tibet, but he has thousands of disciples in India.' When Yeshe Ö heard the name 'Dhipamkara Shrijana' he was pleased, and became determined to invite this Master to Tibet. Since he had already used most of his gold and more was now needed to invite Dhipamkara Shrijana to Tibet, the king set off on an expedition to search for more gold. When he arrived at one of the borders a hostile non-Buddhist king captured him and threw him into prison. When the news reached Jangchub Ö he considered 'I am powerful enough to wage war on this king, but if I do so many people will suffer and I shall have to commit many harmful, destructive actions.' He decided to make an appeal for his uncle's release, but the king responded by saying 'I shall release your uncle only if you either become my subject or bring me a quantity of gold as heavy as your uncle's body.' With great difficulty Jangchub Ö managed to gather gold equal in weight to his uncle's body, less the weight of his head. Since the king demanded the extra amount, Jangchub Ö prepared to go in search of more gold, but before he set out he visited his uncle. He found Yeshe Ö physically weak but in a good state of mind. Jangchub Ö spoke through the bars of the prison, 'Soon I shall be able to release you for I have managed to collect almost all the gold.' Yeshe Ö replied 'Please do not treat me as if I were important. You must not give the gold to this hostile king. Send it all to India and offer it to Dhipamkara Shrijana. This is my greatest wish. I shall give my life joyfully for the sake of restoring pure Dharma in Tibet. Please deliver this message to Dhipamkara Shrijana. Let him know that I have given my life to invite him to Tibet. Since he has compassion for the Tibetan people, when he receives this message he will accept our invitation.'

Jangchub Ö sent the translator Nagtso together with some companions to India with the gold. When they met Dhipamkara Shrijana they told him what was happening in Tibet and how the people wanted to invite a Spiritual Guide from India. They told him how much gold the king had sent as an offering and how many Tibetans had died for the sake of restoring pure Dharma. They told him how Yeshe Ö had sacrificed his life to bring him to Tibet. When they had made their request Dhipamkara Shrijana considered what they had said and accepted their invitation. Although he had many disciples in India and was working very hard there for the sake of Dharma, he knew that there was no pure Dharma in Tibet. He had also received a prediction from Arya Tara that if he were to go to Tibet he would benefit countless living beings. Compassion arose in his heart when he thought how many Tibetans had died in India, and he was especially moved by the sacrifice of Yeshe Ö.

Dhipamkara Shrijnana had to make his way to Tibet in secret, for had his Indian disciples known that he was leaving India they would have prevented him. He said that he was making a pilgrimage to Nepal, but from Nepal he passed into Tibet. When his Indian disciples eventually realized that he was not going to return they protested that the Tibetans were thieves who had stolen their Spiritual Guide!

Since it was customary in those days, as it is today, to greet an honoured guest in style, Jangchub Ö sent an entourage of three hundred horsemen with many eminent Tibetans to the border to welcome Atisha and offer him a horse to ease the difficult journey to Ngari. Atisha rode at the centre of the three hundred horsemen, and by means of his miracle powers he sat one cubit above his horse's back. When they saw him, those who previously had no respect for him developed very strong faith, and everyone said that the second Buddha had arrived in Tibet.

When Atisha reached Ngari, Jangchub Ö requested him: 'O Compassionate Atisha, please give instructions to help the Tibetan people. Please give advice that everyone can follow. Please give us special instructions so that we can practise all the paths of Sutra and Tantra together.' To fulfil this wish Atisha composed and taught *Lamp for the Path to Enlightenment*. He gave these instructions first in Ngari and then in central Tibet. Many disciples who heard these teachings developed great wisdom.

While he had been in India Atisha had received a prediction from Arya Tara, 'When you go to Tibet, a layman will come to receive instructions from you, and this disciple will cause Dharma to flourish far and wide.' This prediction referred to Atisha's foremost disciple, Dromtonpa. At first Atisha taught Lamrim mainly to Dromtonpa, and to other disciples he gave instructions on Secret Mantra. When Dromtonpa asked him 'Why do you give Lamrim mainly to me and not to others?', Atisha replied that he was especially worthy to receive Lamrim teachings. After Atisha's death Dromtonpa was regarded as his representative and respected as his equal. Dromtonpa taught Lamrim extensively in Tibet.

Three lineages of Lamrim instructions were passed down from Dromtonpa. Kadam Shungpawa passed from Dromtonpa to Geshe Potowa to Geshe Sharawa, and through further Teachers to Je Tsongkhapa. Kadam Lamrimpa passed from Dromtonpa to Geshe Gonbawa to Geshe Neusurpa, and through further Teachers to Je Tsongkhapa. Kadam Männgagpa passed from Dromtonpa to Geshe Chengawa to Geshe Jayulwa, and through further Teachers to Je Tsongkhapa. Up to the time of Je Tsongkhapa these three lineages are called 'Old Kadam lineages'. The three lineages from the time of Je Tsongkhapa to the present day are called 'New Kadam lineages'. All three are still practised today. Practitioners of the three schools are differentiated in terms of the extent of their philosophical studies. Kadam Shungpawas study very extensively, Kadam Lamrimpas study less extensively, and Kadam Menngagpas study least extensively. However, they all have Lamrim as their main practice and integrate all their philosophical studies into their practice of Lamrim.

The great Spiritual Guide, Ngawang Chogden, is an example of a Kadam Shungpawa. He studied philosophy for many years in central Tibet, and when he had qualified as a Geshe he returned home to Kham in eastern Tibet. There he received instructions from Jamyang Shaypa and came to know the entire Lamrim. He then realized that all Buddha's teachings are to be taken as reliable personal advice and put into practice. He saw that all his philosophical studies were part of Lamrim, not separate from it. He thought 'When I was a student in central Tibet I was actually studying Lamrim, but I had not received complete instructions and so I could not see how to put all my studies into practice. However, now I can put them to good use by integrating them into my practice of Lamrim.'

Kadam Lamrimpas of the present day study texts such as Je Tsongkhapa's *Great Exposition of the Stages of the Path* and *Middling Exposition of the Stages of the Path*. Kadam Menngagpas of the present day study a few short texts such as the first Panchen Lama's *Blissful Path* and the second Panchen Lama's *Quick Path*. Although these texts are brief they include all the practices of Lamrim.

All three lineages passed to Je Tsongkhapa. After writing *The Three Principal Aspects of the Path*, which he received together with its title directly from Manjushri, Je Tsongkhapa went into intensive retreat on Lamrim at Reting Monastery. While he was there he wrote a praise to all the Lamrim lineage Gurus called *Opening the Door to the Supreme Path*. At this monastery there was a very precious statue of Atisha. In front of this statue Je Tsongkhapa made requests and offered praises to Buddha Shakyamuni and all the Lamrim lineage Gurus, and received visions of Atisha, Dromtonpa, Geshe Potowa, and Geshe Sharawa. They remained with him for one month and talked to him as one person to another. After one month Dromtonpa, Geshe Potowa, and Geshe Sharawa absorbed into Atisha, who then touched Je Tsongkhapa's crown with his right hand and said 'You must work for the sake of Buddhadharma and I will help you.' Je Tsongkhapa then wrote his *Great Exposition of the Stages of the Path*, the king of all Lamrim texts. Later he wrote his *Middling Exposition of the Stages of the Path*, and finally he wrote his *Condensed Exposition of the Stages of the Path* for those who are unable to study the longer texts.

Since the time of Je Tsongkhapa many other Lamrim texts have been composed. Amongst these are eight major texts known as the *Eight Great Guides of Lamrim*. These are Je Tsongkhapa's three texts mentioned above; the first Panchen Lama's *Blissful Path*, and the second Panchen Lama's *Quick Path*, which present the main Lamrim instructions in conjunction with Secret Mantra; the third Dalai Lama's *Essence of Refined Gold*, and the fifth Dalai Lama's *Instructions Received from the Mouth of Manjushri*, a commentary to *Essence of Refined Gold*, which teach only the Sutra instructions of Lamrim; and *Essence of Well-spoken Advice* by the great Lama, Dagpo Ngawang Dragpa.

The Qualities of the Teaching

This has two divisions:

1 The pre-eminent characteristics of Lamrim
2 The pre-eminent attributes of Lamrim

THE PRE-EMINENT CHARACTERISTICS OF LAMRIM

Lamrim possesses three pre-eminent characteristics that are not possessed by other texts. These are:

1 The Lamrim teaching is the condensation of all Buddhadharma
2 The instructions of Lamrim are easy to put into practice
3 The presentation of the instructions of Lamrim is superior to other traditions

These three characteristics are exclusive to Lamrim. They are not possessed even by the king of Tantras, the *Guhyasamaja Tantra*, or the king of Sutras, the *Perfection of Wisdom Sutras*. Other texts do not include all the subjects and practices of all other scriptures, and they cannot be practised easily and by everyone. For example, if we receive empowerments and instructions on *Guhyasamaja Tantra* and make this our daily practice, but do not combine it with Lamrim, we shall not be able to include every other practice within it. Furthermore, the instructions themselves are not easy to understand. Similarly, Maitreya's *Ornament for Clear Realization* is difficult to understand, even if we receive commentaries on it; and when we have understood the commentaries it remains hard to understand how all other Dharma practices are included within it. Unless we receive complete teachings on Lamrim it is difficult to put such advanced teachings into practice. We may become learned, but we shall not know how to control our disturbed states of mind. Desirous attachment, anger, jealousy, and other delusions will remain as strong as ever. With such turbulent states of mind we cannot find stable, pure happiness for ourself, let alone for others; and the studies we engage in, no matter how advanced, will not bring real benefit.

All other Buddhist scriptures are either a part or a preliminary of Lamrim. For example, the *Perfection of Wisdom Sutras* are part of Lamrim. They are the source of the main Lamrim instructions, the Sutra instructions. Explicitly, the *Perfection of Wisdom Sutras* teach the stage of superior seeing according to Sutra, at which stage our object of meditation is emptiness. All the stages of the path that have emptiness as their object of meditation are the stages of the profound path. Therefore, explicitly, the *Perfection of Wisdom Sutras* teach the stages of the profound path according to Sutra. Implicitly, they teach the stages of the vast path according to Sutra.

All the stages of the path of Sutra and Tantra are divided into the stages of the profound path and the stages of the vast path. All Buddha's scriptures, and all the philosophical texts composed after his time, such as Nagarjuna's *Six Collections of Reasonings* and Asanga's *Five Sets on the Spiritual Grounds*, are included within either the stages of the profound path or the stages of the vast path. Maitreya's *Ornament for Clear Realization* is included within the vast path, and Chandrakirti's *Guide to the Middle Way* is included within the profound path. Atisha's Teacher Vidyakokila was very skilful in teaching the stages of the profound path, and Atisha's Teacher Serlingpa was very skilful in teaching the stages of the vast path. Lamrim combines these two Lamas' instructions in a way that enables us more easily to understand and practise them, and is therefore superior to other traditions.

When we begin to study philosophical texts such as those mentioned above we may at first think that we are studying different scriptures not to be found in Lamrim, and we may even think that because they are more difficult to understand they are intended for more intelligent students. In fact, all these philosophical texts are to be studied only as part of our main practice, the practice of Lamrim. If we were to try engaging in philosophy and logic on their own, without integrating them into our practice of Lamrim, we would lose their main point; for without continuous practice of Lamrim we shall not gain control over our mind and we shall not be able to help others overcome their problems.

If we have not studied the complete Lamrim these three pre-eminent characteristics will not be obvious; but if we meet someone actually putting the whole Lamrim into practice we may understand its supreme characteristics from this person's example alone, without having to study all the instructions for ourself. Unfortunately, such a person is extremely rare. Even studying the whole Lamrim will not bring a full appreciation of all its qualities. Just as we need to savour a cup of tea to gain a full appreciation of its good qualities, which cannot be gained merely by reading the advertisements, so we need to put the complete Lamrim into practice to gain a full appreciation of its excellence.

THE PRE-EMINENT ATTRIBUTES OF LAMRIM

Through gaining experience of Lamrim:

1 We shall understand that none of Buddha's teachings are contradictory
2 We shall take all Buddha's teachings as personal advice and put them into practice
3 We shall easily realize Buddha's ultimate intention
4 We shall naturally become free from the great fault and from all other faults.

WE SHALL UNDERSTAND THAT NONE OF BUDDHA'S
TEACHINGS ARE CONTRADICTORY

By studying and practising the complete Lamrim we shall see that there are no contradictions between Hinayana and Mahayana scriptures, between Sutra and Tantra, or between root texts and their commentaries. From a superficial reading of the scriptures it may appear that there are contradictions. For instance, some Hinayana scriptures emphasize meditation on the uncleanliness and repulsiveness of the body and on the impurities of the environment, whereas Tantric scriptures teach us to regard our body as the body of a Deity and our environment as pure. Hinayana scriptures teach us how to attain liberation for ourself alone, whereas Mahayana scriptures teach us how to attain full enlightenment for the benefit of others. Some scriptures advise against eating meat, whereas others encourage us to practise the yoga of eating whereby even the action of eating meat is transformed into a pure action. By studying the entire stages of the path we shall see how such differences are reconciled because we shall understand that each instruction is a method for solving a specific problem and is to be applied at a specific time. For example, the meditation on the uncleanliness and repulsiveness of the body reduces attachment, whereas the meditation on our body as the body of a Deity eliminates ordinary appearance which is the cause of samsara.

If a sick man goes to the doctor to be cured of a fever his doctor may advise him not to eat meat. If the same man returns to his doctor later because he is suffering from anaemia his doctor may this time advise him to eat meat. If the sick man ignores his doctor's advice on the grounds that he has prescribed contradictory cures, he will not become well. A doctor gives different cures for different diseases. In the same way, Buddha gave different instructions for different afflictions. Not one remedy is superfluous or redundant. For our own sake we need to apply each different instruction at different times; and if we are to help others whose situation and experiences differ from our own we need to know all the methods and when and how to apply them.

If we know how to practise the whole Lamrim we shall know how to practise all other scriptures. Whenever we receive any other teaching we shall know where to place it within Lamrim. In this way each new instruction we receive will amplify and reinforce those we have already learnt. Suppose someone is given a handful of rice that he or she cannot use immediately. If that person has nowhere to store the rice he will not be able to put it to good use and will have to throw it away, but if he has built a storeroom to hold bags of different cereals he will be able to put the rice in the appropriate bag and increase his store. When the time is right he will be able to put the rice to good use. Lamrim is like such a storeroom. For example, Hinayana teachings can be stored amongst the stages of the path of a person of intermediate scope, Mahayana teachings can be stored amongst the stages of the path of a person of great scope, Vajrayana teachings can be stored amongst the stages of Secret Mantra within Lamrim, teachings on dependent relationship and the middle way can be stored within the stage of superior seeing, and so forth. Without studying the entire Lamrim we may receive many different instructions and still be wondering what to do, like a person standing with a handful of rice wondering where to put it. If we are like this, we shall waste most of the instructions we receive.

While the great Tibetan Master Kyabje Phabongkha was living in Kham in eastern Tibet, a Geshe arrived there from one of the great Gelug monasteries and went to receive practical instructions from a Nyingma Lama. The local people concluded that the Gelugpas had no practice since such a great Geshe needed to go looking for one. When Kyabje Phabongkha heard of this he said that it was a great shame that this Geshe had wasted so many years of instruction by failing to realize that all his previous study was to be put into practice. It was possible for the Geshe to lose so much time only because he had not built the storeroom of Lamrim within his own mind.

WE SHALL TAKE ALL BUDDHA'S TEACHINGS AS PERSONAL ADVICE AND PUT THEM INTO PRACTICE

By studying the complete Lamrim we shall see that there are no contradictions between any of Buddha's teachings and that all of them are to be put into practice. Knowing this we shall take each instruction as personal advice and gain experience for ourself, thus discovering that every instruction is perfect and reliable.

When we practise Buddha's teachings we should do so without omitting or adding anything. In *Sublime Continuum of the Great Vehicle* Maitreya says:

In this world there is no one more skilled than
  Buddha.
His omniscient mind directly perceives all objects to
  be known, without exception.
Therefore we should practise whatever Buddha
  taught.
If we impose our own interpretations or omit
  anything we are destroying Buddhadharma.

Pure Buddhist instructions are only those that have been received through a pure, unbroken lineage from Buddha Shakyamuni. Lamrim has all of these instructions and is the very method for putting them into practice.

WE SHALL EASILY REALIZE BUDDHA'S ULTIMATE INTENTION

Buddha's ultimate intention is that all living beings attain full enlightenment by gaining all the realizations of the stages of the path. These are included within five: the realizations of the three principal aspects of the path – renunciation, bodhichitta, and the correct view of emptiness; and the realizations of generation stage and completion stage of Secret Mantra. To realize Buddha's ultimate intention is to gain all these realizations and thus fulfil the greatest wish he has for us.

The three pre-eminent attributes explained so far can be differentiated by contemplating the analogy of a painter. Just as a painter knows that all his implements are necessary if he is to paint a picture, and he knows the specific function of each of them, so practitioners of Lamrim understand that all Buddha's teachings are necessary if they are to attain enlightenment, and that there are no contradictions between any of the teachings. Just as a painter proceeds by putting all his tools to use in painting his picture, so practitioners of Lamrim understand that each and every one of Buddha's instructions must be taken as personal advice and put to use in their lives. Just as by making use of his tools a painter eventually completes his work and fulfils the wish of his patron or employer, in a similar way practitioners of Lamrim will attain enlightenment and thereby fulfil Buddha's ultimate intention.

In *Condensed Exposition of the Stages of the Path* Je Tsongkhapa says that if we listen to or teach Lamrim only once, we receive the benefits of having heard or taught the entire Buddhadharma. Similarly, if we practise the whole Lamrim we shall be practising, directly or indirectly, all Buddha's teachings. Therefore we do not need to feel dissatisfied with Lamrim or search for other instructions to practise.

WE SHALL NATURALLY BECOME FREE FROM THE GREAT FAULT AND FROM ALL OTHER FAULTS

The great fault is the fault of rejecting Dharma as a result of wrongly discriminating between Buddha's scriptures. If we think that some scriptures are good and others are bad, or if we think that some are reasonable and others are not, we shall incur the great fault of rejecting Dharma. We are also rejecting Dharma if out of sectarianism we maintain that some scriptures are unnecessary for higher practitioners, thinking, for example, that some scriptures are for Bodhisattvas and others are only for those who have a more limited aspiration. By studying and practising the complete Lamrim we are prevented from making this mistake. When we understand the real purpose of each instruction and see that none of them is contradictory, and when we practise the instructions for ourself, proving by experience that each one is correct and reliable, we shall never reject or belittle any of them.

By studying and practising the complete Lamrim we shall also overcome every other fault because each instruction is a perfect opponent and all faults find their opponents within Lamrim. For example, the stage of training our mind in faith and respect for our Spiritual Guide destroys faulty attitudes of anger or disrespect towards our Teacher and frees us from regarding him or her as an ordinary person. All the other stages of training the mind function in a similar way to eliminate mistaken states of mind and the actions they induce.

It is quite easy to learn what are the pre-eminent qualities of Lamrim, but it is rare to find someone who has realized these by direct experience. To gain such experience we need to put every instruction into practice. If we realize that Lamrim is to be practised in its entirety, our realizations and insights will increase and we shall gradually become familiar with virtuous habits of mind. Our state of mind next year will be better than our state of mind this year. Eventually we shall gain the highest realizations. If we always remember the pre-eminent qualities of Lamrim we shall never feel discouraged, and we shall generate joyous effort in bringing the methods to bear upon the problems we experience in our daily lives.

Listening to and Teaching Dharma

EXPLANATION OF HOW TO LISTEN TO AND TEACH DHARMA

Traditionally, disciples learn Dharma by first listening to oral instructions from their Spiritual Guide. Since listening is the basis for contemplating and meditating on Dharma it is especially important to listen well – with an open and attentive mind and in such a way as to be able to remember the instructions and reflect upon them once the discourse has ended. Whenever we have the opportunity to receive oral discourses on Dharma we should apply these instructions on how to listen. They can easily be adapted to our situation as a reader. The great meditator, Ngawang Dragpa, said:

> This instruction on how to listen to and teach Dharma is a method for transforming listening and teaching into the spiritual path. It is also a supreme instruction to give as a preliminary to teachings. Therefore, keep it in your heart.

The instructions are in three parts:

1 How to listen to Dharma
2 How to teach Dharma
3 The concluding stage common to the Teacher and the student

HOW TO LISTEN TO DHARMA

This has three parts:

1 Considering the benefits of listening to Dharma
2 Developing respect for Dharma and its Teacher
3 The actual way of listening to Dharma

RING THE BENEFITS OF LISTENING TO DHARMA

nplate some of the countless benefits of listening
we shall naturally enjoy listening to and reading
the instructions, and we shall do so with an especially keen
interest. The result of listening and reading in such a positive
frame of mind is that we shall actually experience all the
benefits we have contemplated. In *Collection of Many Special
Verses* by Buddha Shakyamuni, called *Tshom* in Tibetan, it
says:

By listening you will know all Dharmas.
By listening you will cease all non-virtuous actions.
By listening you will abandon all that is meaningless.
By listening you will attain liberation.

Here the term 'Dharmas' refers specifically to the meaning
of Dharma instructions. The meaning of Dharma reveals
what objects are to be abandoned, what objects are to be practised, and so forth. By listening to Dharma instructions we
shall understand the meaning of Dharma clearly and we
shall gradually gain Dharma realizations. Every pure Dharma
realization arises in dependence upon meditation, and successful meditation depends upon receiving correct instructions. As explained, all the instructions of Sutra and Tantra
are included within the three sets of Buddha's teachings. By
receiving and practising the instructions on the set of moral
discipline we shall cease non-virtuous actions. By receiving
and practising the instructions on the set of discourses, where
Buddha explains how to attain concentration, we shall abandon all meaningless activities and distractions, the obstacles
to concentration. By receiving and practising the instructions
on the set of wisdom we shall attain liberation.

In *Stories of Rebirth* Aryasura mentions the following benefits of listening:

Listening is a lamp that dispels the darkness of
ignorance.
Listening is the best wealth that cannot be stolen by
thieves.

Listening is a weapon that destroys our enemy of
confusion.

Listening is our best friend from whom we receive
our best advice.

Listening is a relative and friend who remains loyal
even when we are impoverished.

Listening is a harmless medicine that cures the
disease of delusion.

Listening is the supreme opponent that destroys great
faults.

Listening is the best treasure because it is the
foundation of all fame and resources.

Listening is the best gift that we can offer to our
friends.

Listening is the best means of pleasing many people.

Listening is a lamp that dispels the darkness of ignorance
Nothing is more important than to remove ignorance, which
is the main cause of all our suffering and the root from which
all other delusions arise. Ignorance is an inner darkness that
is removed by the illuminating lamp of listening to Dharma.

Listening is the best wealth that cannot be stolen by thieves
Whenever we accumulate ordinary wealth and material
resources our life becomes full of practical problems and
anxieties. We live in fear of losing our wealth, and to maintain it we have to work hard, even sometimes having to
deceive others. We have to pay taxes and spend time and
energy working out how to use our wealth and where to
invest it. However the wealth of listening to Dharma never
causes problems. It can never be lost even when we offer it
freely to others. The more we give away, the richer we
become. After death it is the only wealth that we can carry
with us. Unlike worldly wealth it benefits all future lives as
well as this one.

The Tibetan Teachers are living examples of the great
value of listening to Dharma. When they were forced to flee
Tibet they left everything behind, including even their begging bowls; but nothing could force them to part with their

wealth of listening to Dharma. This will always remain with them. It is the very wealth that they are now giving to their western students, the only wealth that can survive death and external destruction.

Listening is a relative and friend who remains loyal even when we are impoverished When we experience severe misfortune and great suffering there is very little that our friends and relatives can do. At such times only the spiritual advice that we have received will come to our aid. Remember the example of Yeshe Ö, who was able to confront death with equanimity by relying upon the good advice and encouragement he had received from his Spiritual Guides. If we listen to or read many Dharma instructions we too can transform the difficulties we experience into the spiritual path and use them to increase our wisdom. Our problems are opportunities to observe and contemplate the law of actions and their effects, the law of karma. They are opportunities to contemplate suffering and its causes, and to practise patience and joyful perseverance. At such times, if we apply the Dharma that we have heard and read we shall find that it is a true friend enabling us to maintain our practice uninterruptedly and with joy.

Our ordinary friends and relatives are of no help when we experience great suffering. Sometimes they even abandon us in our greatest need. While Lama Kachen Yeshe Gyaltsen was practising meditation in his cave, he was as poor as Milarepa. One day he was travelling to Tashi Lhunpo Monastery and on his way he saw one of his uncles. His uncle, noticing how impoverished his nephew seemed to be, pretended not to know him. Later, Lama Kachen Yeshe Gyaltsen was promoted to the position of tutor to the eighth Dalai Lama. Thinking that his nephew must now be very wealthy this uncle went to visit him and declared 'Hello, nephew, I am your uncle.'

Once, a man who was at first very poor and without friends or relatives became rich by engaging in business. People began to visit him, pretending to be his friends or claiming to be his relatives. One day this man invited all his new friends and relatives to dinner. In the middle of the table he placed a huge sack containing all the money he had accumulated. When his guests arrived he made solemn prostrations to the sack and recited these words of praise: 'O Lord Money, through your great kindness I now have many friends and relatives when previously I had none. Therefore, I make prostrations to you.'

Ordinary friends and relatives can change their feelings and attitudes towards us largely depending upon whether or not we possess wealth and good fortune, but our friend of listening to Dharma will not let us down. It comes to our aid when we are prosperous and it comes to our aid when we are poor. It is the only friend that will endure death with us and support us in all our future lives until we attain enlightenment.

In one Sutra, Buddha says:

By listening you will develop strong faith in Dharma.
By listening your mind will be attracted to Dharma
    and you will experience powerful results.
By listening your wisdom will increase and your
    confusion will be eliminated.

To hear just these three lines Prince Chandra offered a thousand gold coins. In the past, those who were intent upon spiritual paths considered receiving instructions so precious that even a gift of their own flesh was not too dear a price to pay.

In a dream, the first Panchen Lama once heard Je Tsong-khapa say:

If you wish to benefit yourself and others you should not be satisfied with what you have learnt. You should take as your example those Bodhisattvas on the third spiritual ground who are still not satisfied that they have heard enough.

We need to listen to and read Dharma instructions many times. Our listening and reading are not complete until we have gained all the realizations of the stages of the path to enlightenment.

DEVELOPING RESPECT FOR DHARMA AND ITS TEACHER

In *Sutra on the Essence of Grounds* Buddha says:

> You should listen to Dharma with exceptional faith and respect, not seeing the Teacher as faulty or being displeased with him. When you listen to Dharma you should view the Teacher as Buddha.

In *Five Sets on the Spiritual Grounds* Arya Asanga advises us to practise five inattentivenesses whenever we listen to Dharma:

(1) If our Teacher has broken his or her moral discipline we should not pay attention to the fault or judge that his moral discipline is weak. There is no benefit to be derived from paying attention to such a fault. On the contrary, it would be to our own disadvantage, for if we become preoccupied with our Teacher's apparent failure we shall not be able to appreciate his or her instructions and advice. Instead of taking them to heart we shall spend our whole time accumulating negative karma.

(2) If our Teacher is from a lower social class we should not pay attention to this or consider it an inferiority. Otherwise we shall spend all our time cultivating pride and we shall not be able to listen properly.

(3) If our Teacher is ugly or physically unattractive we should not consider his or her physical appearance. There is no value in contemplating our Teacher's ugliness. If we do so we shall only make it harder for ourself to develop faith. Our Teacher's physical appearance is unimportant; what matters is the Dharma he or she teaches.

(4) If our Teacher's manner of speech is displeasing, the language unrefined, or the way of presenting the instructions rough and clumsy, we should not pay attention to the style. What matters are the meanings our Teacher conveys.

(5) If our Teacher says things that are unpleasant to hear, such as words of blame or criticism, we should

not think that he or she is at fault. If we do so we shall develop many misunderstandings and non-virtuous states of mind.

In addition to these five we should practise inattentiveness to any other fault we think we see in our Teacher. For example, if our Teacher is not famous and seems to be very ordinary we should disregard fame and ordinary appearance. It is enough for us that we receive correct instructions. What benefit would there be in our receiving Dharma from someone famous throughout the world if his or her instructions were incorrect? By paying attention to faults we think we see in our Teacher we lose all the benefits of listening to Dharma and we bring only disadvantages upon ourself.

Just as we need to increase respect for our Teacher, so we need to increase respect for the Dharma he or she teaches. If we regard our Teacher's instructions as the actual Dharma Jewel, the supreme method for gaining temporary and ultimate happiness, we shall naturally feel respect.

THE ACTUAL WAY OF LISTENING TO DHARMA

This has two parts:

1 Abandoning three faults
2 Cultivating six recognitions

ABANDONING THREE FAULTS

Whenever we listen to or read Dharma we need to abandon three faults that prevent us from receiving the benefits of listening or reading:

1 The fault of being like a pot turned upside-down
2 The fault of being like a bad-smelling pot
3 The fault of being like a leaky pot

The first fault is to be like a pot turned upside-down. We are physically present at a discourse, or we have adopted the posture of reading a book, but we are so inattentive and distracted that no matter how many instructions are poured in through our ears or how many pages we manage to turn, no Dharma actually enters the vessel of our mind.

The second fault is to be like a bad-smelling pot. We listen or read attentively, without letting our mind wander, but our motivation is incorrect. Just as good food becomes contaminated when we put it into a bad-smelling pot, so Dharma is wasted on us when we listen with an incorrect motivation.

The third fault is to be like a leaky pot. We listen or read attentively and with a good motivation, but we quickly forget what we have been taught. If we cannot remember Dharma, how can we put it into practice?

There are two methods we can use to improve our ability to remember Dharma. The first is to make an effort to recall what we have heard or read soon after a discourse has finished or after we have finished reading a chapter of a Dharma book. We can do this several times at intervals. If we gain greater understanding or a new feeling from remembering and contemplating what we have learnt, we should deepen this experience by doing meditation. In this way our practice will become very powerful.

The second method is to discuss Dharma with our Dharma friends, asking them questions and explaining what we have understood. This is an excellent way to increase our understanding, remove doubts, and place Dharma firmly within our minds.

CULTIVATING SIX RECOGNITIONS

Whenever we listen to or read Dharma we should cultivate six recognitions:

1 Regarding ourself as a sick person because we suffer from desirous attachment, hatred, ignorance, and other diseases of the mind.
2 Regarding Dharma as supreme medicine for our mental sickness.
3 Regarding our Dharma Teacher as a supreme doctor.
4 Regarding putting Dharma into practice as the way to become cured of our mental disease.

5 Developing conviction in Buddha Shakyamuni as a holy being who is completely reliable.

6 Developing a strong wish that Dharma will flourish and remain for a long time.

If we have these six recognitions we shall not waste a moment while we are listening to or reading the instructions, and our subsequent contemplations and meditations will become much more powerful. Our actions of listening and reading will accumulate great merit and become strong causes of our enlightenment.

HOW TO TEACH DHARMA

This has four parts:

1 Considering the benefits of teaching Dharma
2 Increasing faith and respect for Dharma and its Teacher
3 The attitudes to cultivate and the way to conduct oneself whilst teaching Dharma
4 Recognizing whom should be taught and whom should not be taught

CONSIDERING THE BENEFITS OF TEACHING DHARMA

In *Treasury of Abhidharma* Vasubandhu says that when we give Dharma instructions our mind should not be polluted with delusions and we should teach Dharma in accordance with the instructions given by Buddha.

If we teach Dharma in order to receive gifts or veneration from our students, or to become well known for our grasp of Buddha's teachings, we shall be misusing the precious Dharma, treating it as a mere commodity. On the other hand, if we practise the generosity of giving Dharma with a good motivation the benefits are limitless. Twenty of these benefits are mentioned in *Exhortation to Superior Intentions Sutra*. We shall attain:

(1) A special mindfulness that never forgets Dharma
(2) A special wisdom that comes from listening to Dharma
(3) A special wisdom that comes from contemplating Dharma
(4) A special wisdom that comes from meditating on Dharma
(5) A special wisdom on the paths of accumulation and preparation
(6) A special wisdom on the paths of seeing and meditation
(7) Freedom from attachment
(8) Freedom from hatred
(9) Freedom from ignorance
(10) Freedom from demonic interference
(11) The Buddhas will be delighted with us
(12) The Deities will cause our physical strength and power to increase
(13) The Deities will give us protection
(14) External enemies will not be able to harm us
(15) Our relationships with friends and relatives will improve
(16) Our speech will become very influential
(17) We shall become confident in explaining Dharma to others
(18) We shall be praised and respected by those who are wise
(19) People will trust what we say
(20) We shall always be happy

The first six benefits are effects similar to the cause. They are future experiences similar to the experiences gained by others as a result of our giving Dharma to them. For example, when we teach Dharma the mindfulness and wisdom of those who listen increase, and as a result our own mindfulness and wisdom increase. The next four benefits are effects of separation, or freedom, from four faults; the next nine benefits are environmental effects; and the remaining benefit is a ripened effect.

The various effects of actions will be explained in more detail below. At this point it is sufficient to know that there are two types of effect similar to the cause: experiences that are effects similar to the cause, and tendencies that are effects similar to the cause. The six effects similar to the cause which are mentioned above are all the first type. Tendencies that are effects similar to the cause are not mentioned explicitly but they are implied. For example, as a result of our giving Dharma, in the future we shall be happy to give Dharma teachings, happy to listen to Dharma, and happy to study and practise Dharma.

Before we can teach Dharma we need to have studied many instructions and gained personal experience by putting them into practice. When the time comes for us to teach we should contemplate all the benefits of teaching Dharma. Then we shall develop enthusiasm and consider ourself extremely fortunate to be able to create so much good karma by giving the instructions to others. Provided that those who receive the instructions actually want to put them into practice, giving Dharma is much more beneficial than giving material wealth. Material wealth can help for only one short lifetime, whereas the gift of Dharma will help in this life and in all future lives.

INCREASING FAITH AND RESPECT FOR DHARMA AND ITS TEACHER

Whenever we give Dharma to others we remember the kindness of Buddha Shakyamuni, and the pre-eminent qualities of Dharma, thinking:

If I now have any ability to teach Dharma it is entirely through the kindness of Buddha. The Dharma I am giving is the supreme gift of temporary and ultimate benefit to others.

THE ATTITUDES TO CULTIVATE AND THE WAY TO CONDUCT
OURSELF WHILST TEACHING DHARMA

When we teach Dharma we do so out of love and compassion, thinking:

These people have not gained experience of Dharma, therefore they have problems without freedom or control. How wonderful it would be if they could overcome these and enjoy the supreme bliss of enlightenment! I will now explain Dharma to help them eliminate their problems and attain ultimate happiness.

With a motivation like this we teach, recognizing:

(1) All living beings experience mental pain because they are afflicted with the disease of delusions.
(2) Dharma is medicine for those who receive it.
(3) I myself am a spiritual doctor.
(4) The kindness of Buddha Shakyamuni is the source of my own ability to teach and others' ability to receive Dharma.
(5) How wonderful it will be if with the help of my own teaching and practice Dharma flourishes in this world for a very long time.

When we teach Dharma we should be clean and appropriately dressed because this will be appreciated by those who listen and it helps them to develop respect. Out of respect for Dharma the Teacher should have a raised seat. At the first meeting of Buddha Shakyamuni's disciples after his passing away, five hundred Foe Destroyers took off their saffron robes and placed them one upon the other to make a throne for Ananda. By laying down their robes in this way, the disciples were honouring Dharma. The Teacher may be very humble in his or her own mind but should sit on a raised seat to acknowledge the pre-eminence of Dharma. This holds even if the Teacher has taken the eight Mahayana precepts, which include the precept of avoiding sitting on raised or luxurious seats.

Before sitting the Teacher makes three prostrations, imagining that his or her own principal Spiritual Guide is on the seat surrounded by all the lineage Gurus of the instructions he is about to give. He imagines that the lineage Gurus absorb into his principal Spiritual Guide, who then comes to the crown of his head and descends to his heart. The Teacher then sits and prepares to teach. Traditionally, before the discourse the Teacher and disciples eliminate obstacles by reciting mantras or reciting the *Heart Sutra* and applying the method for overcoming hindrances. They then perform the six preparations to accumulate merit and purify negativity, both of which are necessary if the disciples are to gain the realizations of the Dharma that is to be taught. The Teacher and disciples then offer the mandala and request the lineage Gurus to bestow blessings and inspiration to gain the realizations. To develop the best motivation the Teacher leads the recitation of the prayer of going for refuge and generating bodhichitta. If we are unable to make all of these preparations we must at least offer the mandala and recite a prayer of going for refuge and generating bodhichitta. Generating bodhichitta has the same effect as reciting the *Heart Sutra*. The Teacher recites:

> *I and all sentient beings, until we achieve enlightenment,*
> *Go for refuge to Buddha, Dharma, and Sangha.*
> *Through the virtues I collect by teaching Dharma,*
> *May I become a Buddha for the benefit of all.*

The students recite:

> *I and all sentient beings, until we achieve enlightenment,*
> *Go for refuge to Buddha, Dharma, and Sangha.*
> *Through the virtues I collect by listening to Dharma,*
> *May I become a Buddha for the benefit of all.*

As the Teacher explains Dharma he or she should have a pleasant, smiling expression. To bring out the meaning more clearly he or she should elaborate by skilfully applying logical reasoning, quoting readily from the scriptures, and using vivid examples that are relevant to the experience of those who listen.

RECOGNIZING WHOM SHOULD BE TAUGHT AND WHOM SHOULD NOT BE TAUGHT

In the *Vinaya Sutras* Buddha says that in general Dharma should be taught only when it is requested. Nevertheless, if a request is made by someone who has no faith in Dharma and no real wish to practise, the instructions should not be given. On the other hand, if no request has been made but someone has a sincere wish to practise, Dharma can be taught.

THE CONCLUDING STAGE COMMON TO THE TEACHER AND THE STUDENT

When a teaching has finished, the Teacher and the students dedicate the merit they have gained to their attainment of enlightenment for the sake of all other living beings. If there is time a mandala can be offered in thanks to the Teacher, but there is no fault if this is omitted.

Preparing for Meditation

**EXPLANATION OF THE ACTUAL INSTRUCTIONS OF THE
STAGES OF THE PATH TO ENLIGHTENMENT**

This explanation is in two parts:

1 How to rely upon a Spiritual Guide, the root of
spiritual paths
2 How to take the essence of our human life

**HOW TO RELY UPON A SPIRITUAL GUIDE,
THE ROOT OF SPIRITUAL PATHS**

This has two parts:

1 How to train the mind during the meditation
session
2 How to train the mind during the meditation
break

The instructions for each of the stages of the path are divided
into these two parts. The meditation session is the time we
spend in formal meditation on Lamrim and the meditation
break is all the rest of our time spent engaging in various
activities. The instructions provide guidance for all times so
that we can be putting them into practice every moment of
our lives. Since most of our time is spent out of meditation
it is important to put effort into training our mind while we
are involved in work and other activities, just as we put effort
into training our mind during our meditation sessions. If we
practise continuously, transforming all that we do into the
spiritual path, our meditations will become more successful
and our whole life will become meaningful.

Maitreya

Vasubandhu

Asanga

HOW TO TRAIN THE MIND DURING THE
MEDITATION SESSION

All Lamrim meditations have three stages:

1 Preparing for meditation
2 The actual meditation
3 Concluding the meditation

The following sections will explain how to prepare for a meditation session, how to do an actual meditation, and how to conclude the meditation session. This explanation will be given by taking as our example the actual meditation on relying upon a Spiritual Guide, the first Lamrim meditation. Since the first stage, preparing for meditation, and the third stage, concluding the meditation, are the same for all Lamrim meditation sessions, the explanation of these will be given only once. For subsequent meditations only the second stage, the actual meditation, will be explained.

PREPARING FOR MEDITATION

The success of our meditation depends upon our making six preparations. Just as we need to prepare carefully for an examination or a dinner party if it is to be a success, so we need to prepare carefully for meditation if we are to experience good results. The six preparatory practices are:

1 Cleaning the meditation room and setting up a shrine with representations of Buddha's body, speech, and mind.
2 Arranging suitable offerings.
3 Sitting in the correct meditation posture, going for refuge, generating and enhancing bodhichitta.
4 Visualizing the Field for Accumulating Merit.
5 Accumulating merit and purifying negativity by offering the practice of the seven limbs and the mandala.
6 Requesting the Field for Accumulating Merit in general and the Lamrim lineage Gurus in particular to bestow their blessings.

CLEANING THE MEDITATION ROOM AND SETTING UP A SHRINE WITH REPRESENTATIONS OF BUDDHA'S BODY, SPEECH, AND MIND

CLEANING THE MEDITATION ROOM

Usually when we clean our room or our house we do it to make ourself feel more cheerful and energetic, or we make a special effort to clean it because we are expecting important guests. However, when we clean our room before doing meditation we should do it with a motivation that brings the greatest merit. We clean our room in order to invite all the holy beings so that we can accumulate merit and purify negative karma by offering them the practice of the seven limbs and the mandala. It is far more appropriate and worthwhile to put effort into cleaning our room when enlightened beings are to be our guests!

Five good results come from cleaning our meditation room with this motivation:

(1) Our mind becomes clearer
(2) The minds of others who enter our room become clearer
(3) The Deities are delighted to enter our room
(4) We create the cause to be reborn with a beautiful form
(5) We create the cause to be reborn in a pure environment such as a Pure Land

While we are cleaning we should regard all the dust and dirt as the filth of our own non-virtuous actions and delusions, thinking 'This is the dirt of my ignorance – I am removing it. These are the stains of my destructive deeds – I am eliminating them.' If we have an especially strong emotional problem, such as strong desirous attachment, we can concentrate on it and clean vigorously, thinking 'This is the grime of my attachment. I am extracting it from my mind.'

There was once a monk called Lam Chung who lived at the time of Buddha Shakyamuni. Before he became a monk he had already gained the reputation of being dull and unteachable.

He was sent to school but soon expelled because the teachers said he was unable to remember any of his lessons. Later his parents sent him to a Brahmin to learn the Vedic scriptures. Again he was unable to remember or understand anything he was taught and was once again expelled.

Thinking that a monastic situation might be more to his liking, his parents sent Lam Chung to his elder brother, Arya Lam Chen, who ordained him as a monk. Lam Chen took responsibility for his younger brother's education and began by teaching him one verse of Dharma. Lam Chung studied this verse for three months but never mastered it! If he memorized it in the morning he would forget it by the evening, and if he memorized it at night he would forget it by the following morning. He tried studying out of doors, hoping this would be helpful for his mind, but with no success. He recited the verse so often while he was in the hills that even the shepherds minding their flocks came to memorize and understand it, but poor Lam Chung still could not master it. The shepherds themselves tried teaching him, but still Lam Chung was unable to learn it. As a result of his repeated failure even his older brother Lam Chen was compelled to dismiss him.

Lam Chung felt utterly depressed and cried as he walked slowly along the road. He thought to himself 'Now I am neither a monk nor a lay person. How miserable I am!' Through the power of his clairvoyance Buddha saw all that had taken place with Lam Chung and went to meet him. He asked him why he was crying and Lam Chung replied 'I am so stupid I cannot memorize even one verse of scripture. Now even my own brother has given up on me.'

Buddha told him not to worry. As a method to purify his mind of past negativities he taught Lam Chung just a few words of Dharma and appointed him as the sweeper at the temple. Lam Chung was very happy with his new position. He swept the temple with great dedication, reciting as he did so the few words that Buddha had taught him.

He swept and swept for a long time, but through the power of Buddha, whenever Lam Chung swept the right side of the temple more dust would appear on the left side, and whenever he swept the left side of the temple more dust would appear on the right side. Nevertheless he continued to sweep, and purify, just as Buddha had instructed. The situation remained like this for a long time until, all of a sudden, Lam Chung was struck by the realization that the dust he was constantly sweeping lacked true, independent existence. This was a profound realization and through it he gained a direct understanding of emptiness, the ultimate nature of reality. By meditating on this emptiness continuously he was soon able to attain complete liberation from suffering. He had become a glorious Foe Destroyer.

Buddha saw that the purification techniques he had given Lam Chung had been profoundly successful and decided to proclaim Lam Chung's new qualities publicly. He directed his disciple Ananda to inform a certain community of nuns that from then on their new Spiritual Guide was to be Lam Chung. The nuns were very upset and felt, 'How can we accept as our Abbot a monk who is so stupid that he could not even remember one verse of the teachings over months and months?' They decided that if they exposed Lam Chung's inadequacies in public they would not have to accept him as their Teacher. So they spread the word in a nearby town that a monk who was as wise as Buddha himself would be coming soon to give teachings, and that all those who attended would certainly attain great realizations. To increase his expected humiliation the nuns even erected a large, ostentatious throne without any steps leading up to its elevated seat.

When the day of the scheduled teachings arrived, Lam Chung made his way to the nuns' community where over one hundred thousand people had gathered, some to listen and others to see him humiliated. When he saw the large throne without steps he realized that it had been constructed in this way to make him look foolish. Without hesitation he stretched out his hand so that it seemed like an enormous elephant's trunk and with it he reduced the throne until it was just a small speck. Then he returned the throne to its former size and, to the increasing amazement of the gathering, flew up to the top of it! After a brief period of meditation he flew into the sky and circled the gathering before returning to the throne. Seated once more he said: 'Listen carefully. I shall now give a week-long discourse on the meaning of one verse of Dharma. This is the same verse that in the past I could not remember or understand even after three months of trying.'

When the seven days of teaching were complete, many thousands in the audience had attained a direct realization of emptiness, while others attained the elevated states of a Stream Enterer, a Once Returner, a Never Returner, and a Foe Destroyer. Others who were present were able to develop the precious bodhichitta, and those who came to test him increased their faith in the Three Jewels. Afterwards Buddha himself prophesied that among all his disciples Lam Chung would possess the greatest skill in taming the minds of others. Even today we can see pictures of Lam Chung, who is one of the sixteen Foe Destroyers often depicted in Buddhist art.

SETTING UP A SHRINE WITH REPRESENTATIONS OF BUDDHA'S BODY, SPEECH, AND MIND

Facing our meditation seat, on a higher level, we set up a shrine with a picture or statue of Buddha Shakyamuni at the centre. If we have them we can place a scripture to Buddha's right and a stupa or a picture of a stupa to his left. The statue or picture of Buddha represents his body, the scripture represents his speech, and the stupa represents his mind. In addition we can place on our shrine other statues or pictures of Buddhas, Bodhisattvas, and Spiritual Guides.

With our present, ordinary state of mind we cannot perceive the actual body, speech, and mind of Buddha; but if we regard the image of Buddha as an actual Buddha and make prostrations, offerings, and requests to it, our actions will have the same merit or value as if we had performed them in the presence of the living Buddha. Buddha Shakyamuni said:

Now my four disciples and others make offerings to me directly. In the future many people will make offerings with faith to an image representing my form. These actions have the same meaning.

Since both actions have equal merit and their ripened effects are the same, we would not gain any greater benefit if we were to meet the actual Buddha and make offerings to him than we would if we were to make offerings with faith to his image. We can gain conviction of this if we follow three lines of reasoning. First, since an offering is, by definition, that which delights the Buddhas, we can be sure that every time we make an offering to the image of Buddha all the Buddhas of the three times and ten directions are overjoyed. Second, since Buddhas possess clairvoyance, such as clairvoyance of divine eye, clairvoyance of divine ear, and clairvoyance of knowing others' minds, we can be sure that every time we make an offering to the image of Buddha all the Buddhas behold our offerings by means of their clairvoyance of divine eye; that every time we sing praises to Buddha all the Buddhas hear our praises by means of their clairvoyance of divine ear; and that every time we make offerings or praises inwardly these are known to all the Buddhas by means of their clairvoyance of knowing others' minds. Third, since a Buddha's body is not obstructed by material objects we can be sure that the Buddhas come into our presence whenever we make prostrations or offerings with faith, regardless of the fact that our minds are so clouded by delusions that we cannot see them.

It is taught in some philosophical scriptures that no place exists where there is no Buddha. According to Secret Mantra the mind and body of a Buddha are the same nature, and so everything that is pervaded by a Buddha's omniscient mind is also pervaded by his divine body. Since the mind and body of ordinary beings are different in nature, their bodies cannot go everywhere their minds go. For example, if we think of India our mind goes there but our body does not. A Buddha's body spontaneously goes wherever his or her mind goes.

Therefore, whenever a Buddha hears our prayers his body comes into our presence. We do not see it because our mind is like a window with the blind pulled down.

On one occasion while Atisha was with his disciples in Tibet he suddenly broke into smiles and laughter. When his disciples asked him why he was so happy he replied 'Right now in Magadha, in India, my disciples are making offerings to me in front of my statue, and they are singing beautiful songs.' If through his clairvoyance Atisha was able to take delight in the songs of his disciples, can there be any doubt that the Buddhas receive our praises, offerings, and requests whenever we make them with faith?

We receive great benefit from making prostrations, offerings, and requests every day in front of the image of Buddha on our shrine. If we are very busy, even just looking at the image with faith and with our hands pressed together in respect is prostration, and creates a strong potentiality for us to see actual Buddhas in the future. In one of his previous lives Shariputra entered a temple where there were many paintings and statues of Buddhas. As he beheld them he wondered 'When shall I see the real Buddha face to face?' All night long he gazed at the images and longed to meet the real Buddha. As a result of the good karma he created on that occasion, in a later life he became one of the main disciples of Buddha Shakyamuni and attained liberation in that life.

With our present impure mind the only way we can perceive Buddha is in the form of someone like our Spiritual Guide, or as an image, like the image we have on our shrine. Due to our karmic obstructions we perceive these forms as impure, but our impurities do not exist from their own side. As our mind becomes more virtuous we perceive Buddha's image differently. When our mind is pure we perceive the image of Buddha as Buddha's Emanation Body and not as a mere work of art. When we gain the concentration of the Dharma continuum we perceive the image of Buddha as Buddha's Supreme Emanation Body and we are able to receive instructions from it directly, just as Atisha received instructions from his statue of Arya Tara. Atisha brought this statue with him to Tibet and whenever he was asked an important question he would say 'First I shall consult the Lady Tara.' When we attain the first spiritual ground of a Bodhisattva we perceive the image of Buddha as Buddha's Enjoyment Body, and when we attain full enlightenment we perceive the image of Buddha as Buddha's Truth Body.

ARRANGING SUITABLE OFFERINGS

In front of the image of Buddha on our shrine we set up beautiful offerings, making sure that as we do so our mind is free from gross delusions, worldly concerns, and any bad or impure motivation. For example, we do not set up offerings with the thought 'I shall make these offerings look very beautiful so that people who enter my room can appreciate my good taste.'

We may arrange a row, or many rows, of seven offering substances: water for drinking, water for bathing, flowers, incense, light, perfume, and food. These can be offered as actual substances or as water. The seven substances represent the objects that delight the senses. In some Asian countries it used to be customary for hosts to offer these things to their guests whenever they entered the house. In the same spirit we can offer anything we find beautiful or welcoming.

When we are making offerings it is especially important to guard against feelings of greed or miserliness because these can easily enter our mind and destroy the virtue of our action. For example, we may buy some delicious cream cakes to offer to Buddha but on our way home we may feel a strong impulse to eat one. Even if we manage to resist this temptation we may still feel a sense of loss as we lay the cakes out on the shrine, and we may find ourself thinking about how soon we can take them down. Again, we may find that when we are buying offerings we are tempted to select the cheapest kind, thinking that we can economize because the offerings are only going on the shrine. Thoughts like these destroy the merit of our offering.

If we offer water to represent the seven offering substances, and if the water we offer has eight good qualities,
we experience eight special benefits:

(1) Offering cool water causes us to develop pure
moral discipline.
(2) Offering delicious water ensures that we shall
always find delicious food and drink in future
lives.
(3) Offering light water causes us to experience the
bliss of physical suppleness.
(4) Offering soft water makes our mind calm and
gentle.
(5) Offering clear water makes our mind clear and
alert.
(6) Offering sweet-smelling water brings easy and
powerful purification of negative karma.
(7) Offering water that is good for the digestion
reduces our illnesses.
(8) Offering water that soothes the throat makes our
speech beautiful and powerful.

When we offer water to Buddha we should regard it as pure
nectar because that is how it is perceived by Buddha. We can
also arrange many sets of seven offering bowls filled with
pure water, symbolizing our future attainment of the seven
pre-eminent qualities of embrace of a Buddha.

The practice of offering is a very important preparation
since it creates a vast amount of merit and makes our mind
very strong. One of its special beauties is that everyone can
do it easily because seven offering bowls are not hard to find
and we can easily obtain water. Furthermore, when we offer
water there is no danger of developing greed or miserliness
as there is when we offer other substances. Therefore, this is
one practice that we can perform very purely right from the
beginning.

If people who are not religious come into our room and
see our shrine and ask us why we are offering things in front
of an image, we can answer them by pointing out that in

every country it is customary to offer flowers in front of the pictures and statues of important citizens, and that many people offer flowers in front of the portraits and photographs of their loved ones.

SITTING IN THE CORRECT MEDITATION POSTURE, GOING FOR REFUGE, GENERATING AND ENHANCING BODHICHITTA

SITTING IN THE CORRECT MEDITATION POSTURE

When we practise meditation we need to have a comfortable seat and a good posture. The most important feature of the posture is to keep our back straight. To help us do this, if we are sitting on a cushion we make sure that the back of the cushion is slightly higher than the front, inclining our pelvis slightly forward. It is not necessary at first to sit cross-legged, but it is a good idea to become accustomed to sitting in the posture of Buddha Vairochana. If we cannot hold this posture we should sit in one which is as close to this as possible while remaining comfortable.

The seven features of Vairochana's posture are:

(1) The legs are crossed in the vajra posture. This helps to reduce thoughts and feelings of desirous attachment.

(2) The right hand is placed in the left hand, palms upwards, with the tips of the thumbs slightly raised and gently touching. The hands are held about four fingers' width below the navel. This helps us to develop good concentration. The right hand symbolizes method and the left hand symbolizes wisdom – the two together symbolize the union of method and wisdom. The two thumbs at the level of the navel symbolize the blazing of inner fire.

(3) The back is straight but not tense. This helps us to develop and maintain a clear mind, and it allows the subtle energy winds to flow freely.

(4) The lips and teeth are held as usual, but the tongue touches against the back of the upper teeth. This

prevents excessive salivation while also preventing our mouth from becoming too dry.

(5) The head is tipped a little forward with the chin slightly tucked in so that the eyes are cast down. This helps prevent mental excitement.

(6) The eyes are neither wide open nor completely closed, but remain half open and gaze down along the line of the nose. If the eyes are wide open we are likely to develop mental excitement and if they are closed we are likely to develop mental sinking.

(7) The shoulders are level and the elbows are held slightly away from the sides to let air circulate.

A further feature of Vairochana's posture is the preliminary breathing meditation, which prepares our mind for developing a good motivation. When we sit down to meditate our mind is usually full of disturbing thoughts, and we cannot immediately convert such a state of mind into the virtuous one we need as our motivation. A negative, disturbed state of mind is like pitch-black cloth. We cannot dye pitch-black cloth any other colour unless we first remove all the black dye and make the cloth white again. In the same way, if we want to colour our mind with a virtuous motivation we need to clear away all our negative thoughts and distractions. We can accomplish this temporarily by practising breathing meditation.

When we have settled down comfortably on our meditation seat we begin by becoming aware of the thoughts and distractions that are arising in our mind. Then we gently turn our attention to our breath, letting its rhythm remain normal. As we breathe out we imagine that we are breathing away all disturbing thoughts and distractions in the form of black smoke that vanishes in space. As we breathe in we imagine that we are breathing in all the blessings and inspiration of the holy beings in the form of white light that enters our body and absorbs into our heart. We maintain this visualization single-pointedly with each inhalation and exhalation for twenty-one rounds, or until our mind has become peaceful and alert. If we concentrate on our breathing in this way, negative thoughts and distractions will temporarily disappear because we cannot concentrate on more than one object at a time. At the conclusion of our breathing meditation we should think 'Now I have received the blessings and inspiration of all the holy beings.' At this stage our mind is like a clean white cloth which we can now colour with a virtuous motivation such as compassion or bodhichitta.

GOING FOR REFUGE

Once we are seated in the meditation posture and have generated a peaceful and alert state of mind, we can go for refuge and generate bodhichitta. We begin by going for refuge.

The objects to which we go for refuge are the Three Jewels: the Buddha Jewel, the Dharma Jewel, and the Sangha Jewel. There now follows an extensive description of the Three Jewels as they are to be visualized whenever we do Lam-rim meditation. Since it takes repeated practice to become familiar with the whole visualization, we should at first concentrate on visualizing the central figure of Buddha Shakyamuni. In time this will become clear and we shall be able to extend the scope of the visualization. There is no need to feel discouraged if visualization seems difficult at first because it will definitely become easier as we become more familiar with the objects. Everyone can easily visualize someone they know very well. For example, if we close our eyes and try to visualize our mother we shall be able to visualize her clearly. Visualizations are not switched on like the picture on a television screen, but with repeated acquaintance we can learn how to establish extensive visualizations quickly and hold them firmly in our mind. In the beginning we should be satisfied with just a vague image, remembering that the most important thing is to develop strong faith that the holy beings are actually present before us, full of life and looking at us with great kindness, ready to receive our offerings and respond to our prayers.

In the space in front of us, level with our eyebrows and at a distance from us of about one arm's length, is a high, spacious throne. It is square and adorned with jewels such as diamonds, emeralds, and lapis lazuli. On it there are five smaller thrones, one in the centre raised higher than the others and one in each of the four cardinal directions. The thrones are supported by snow lions, two at each corner. Covering the entire surface of the central throne, which faces east towards where we are sitting, is an eight-petalled lotus of various colours. The petals in the cardinal directions are red and the others are: south-east, yellow; south-west, green; north-west, yellow; north-east, black. The centre of the lotus is a flat, green disc surrounded by yellow anthers. Above this is a white moon disc, and above that a yellow sun disc. Upon this sits our principal Spiritual Guide in the aspect of the Conqueror Buddha Shakyamuni. His body is the colour of gold and he is in the posture known as 'Buddha Shakyamuni Conquering the Demons'. His legs are in the vajra posture. His right arm is held with the elbow at the hip and the forearm on the right thigh extending to his knee so that his fingers touch the sun disc. This gesture indicates that he has conquered the Devaputra demon. His left hand is held palm upwards below his navel in the gesture of meditative equipoise, and holds a precious bowl made of lapis lazuli containing three nectars indicating that he has conquered the demon of uncontrolled death, the demon of contaminated aggregates, and the demon of the delusions. He wears the three robes of an ordained person and his body is adorned with the thirty-two major signs and eighty minor indications of a Buddha. Buddha Shakyamuni is the main object of refuge because he is the founder of this present doctrine of Dharma.

We do not imagine the body of Guru Buddha Shakyamuni as if it were hollow or two-dimensional like a painting, or as if it were composed of any material substance like a statue or like the body of a human being with flesh, bones, inner organs, and so forth. Buddha's body is composed of light, clear and translucent. It radiates an aura of light of five colours: white, yellow, red, green, and blue. It is the body of a real person, an enlightened being. As we behold Guru Buddha Shakyamuni in front of us we let his appearance remind us of all the good qualities of his enlightened mind: his wisdom clearly and directly perceiving all objects to be known; his compassion towards every single living being without exception, like a mother towards her only child; and his perfect skilful means, whereby he works unceasingly to bring all living beings to the unsurpassed happiness of full enlightenment.

At Guru Buddha Shakyamuni's heart is a lotus, and above that a sun disc. Upon this sits Conqueror Vajradhara. His body is deep blue with one face and two arms. His right hand holds a golden, five-pronged vajra, and his left hand holds a bell of white silver. He wears eight jewelled ornaments: a crown, earrings, three necklaces of different lengths, bracelets, anklets, and a jewelled waistband. His body is adorned with skirts and other garments of silk. He sits in the vajra posture embracing his consort, Vajradhatu Ishvari, whose body is also deep blue and adorned with similar garments and ornaments. She is in the lotus posture.

At Vajradhara's heart is a blue seed-letter HUM radiating light of five colours profusely in all directions. This blue HUM is the concentration being, representing Buddha's Truth Body; Vajradhara is the wisdom being, representing Buddha's Enjoyment Body; and Guru Buddha Shakyamuni is the commitment being, representing Buddha's Emanation Body. By visualizing these three beings we are gaining familiarity with the three bodies of a Buddha and creating the cause actually to perceive them in the future. By regarding our main Spiritual Guide as in essence one with these three beings we receive inspiration more quickly.

From the heart of Guru Buddha Shakyamuni light radiates to his right where he emanates as Maitreya seated on a throne, lotus, and moon disc. Maitreya is in the aspect of the Enjoyment Body, adorned with ornaments and silk garments. He sits in the half-vajra posture. His body is red-yellow, with one face and two hands held at the level of his heart in the gesture of turning the Wheel of Dharma. Between the thumb and index finger of each hand he holds the stem of a naga tree. Beside his right ear the flower of one of the stems blooms and supports a golden wheel. Beside his left ear the flower of the other stem blooms and supports a long-necked vase.

In front of Maitreya, on a lotus and moon disc, sits Arya Asanga. His legs are crossed in such a way that his left leg extends from under his right thigh with the sole of his foot facing outwards, and his right leg, crossed over his left, extends several inches beyond his left knee. His right hand is in the gesture of expounding Dharma and his left hand is in the gesture of meditative equipoise. He wears the three robes of an ordained person and a Pandit's hat. To his left is a spherical vessel. All the lineage Gurus of the vast path form a circle starting with Asanga and going clockwise around the central figure of Maitreya.

From the heart of Guru Buddha Shakyamuni light radiates to his left where he emanates as Manjushri seated on a throne, lotus, and moon disc. His body is the same colour as Maitreya's and he has the same posture except that he holds the stems of upali flowers. The flower that blooms beside his right ear supports a wisdom sword, and the flower that blooms beside his left ear supports a text of the *Perfection of Wisdom Sutra in Eight Thousand Lines*. This posture is known as 'Manjushri Turning the Wheel of Dharma'.

In front of Manjushri sits Nagarjuna in the half-vajra posture, wearing the robes of an ordained person. His hands are in the gesture of expounding Dharma. He has a small crown-protrusion and, arched over his head without touching it, is a canopy of seven snakes. All the lineage Gurus of the profound path form a circle starting with Nagarjuna and going counter-clockwise around the central figure of Manjushri.

To the right of the lineage Gurus of the vast path sit the lineage Gurus of Kadam Lamrimpa, and to the left of the lineage Gurus of the profound path sit the lineage Gurus of Kadam Shungpawa. Behind the lineage Gurus of the vast path sit the lineage Gurus of Kadam Menngagpa. Each of these Kadampa Gurus sits on a lotus and moon disc.

From the heart of Guru Buddha Shakyamuni light radiates behind him where he emanates as Buddha Vajradhara seated on a throne, lotus, and moon disc. Surrounding him are all the lineage Gurus of Secret Mantra from Tilopa down to our present Spiritual Guide.

From the heart of Guru Buddha Shakyamuni light radiates in front of him where he emanates as our principal Spiritual Guide. We visualize him or her as radiant and youthful without any physical imperfections. His right hand is in the gesture of expounding Dharma, indicating that he dispels his disciples' ignorance. His left hand is in the gesture of meditative equipoise holding a life vase, indicating that he destroys the power death has over his disciples. These two, ignorance and death, are the greatest obstacles to our spiritual development. Ignorance prevents us from understanding Dharma, especially the instructions on superior seeing, which is the very antidote to ignorance; and death destroys the very life that is the basis for practising Dharma. Surrounding our main Spiritual Guide we visualize all the other Spiritual Guides who have taught us pure Dharma directly in this life.

In front of these groups of Gurus we visualize the Deities of Highest Yoga Tantra. On the right is Vajrabhairava, on the left Heruka, and in the centre Guhyasamaja, Vajrayogini, or whoever is our personal Deity of Highest Yoga Tantra. In front of these in successive rows are: Deities of Yoga Tantra, such as the assembly of Sarvavid, the main Deity of Yoga Tantra; Deities of Performance Tantra, such as the assembly of Vairochana Deities; Deities of Action Tantra, such as Amitayus, Green Tara, and White Tara; Buddhas of Sutra, such as the one thousand Buddhas of the Fortunate Aeon, the thirty-five Confession Buddhas, and the eight Medicine Buddhas; Sanghas of Sutra, including Bodhisattvas such as the eight Great Sons, Solitary Realizers such as the twelve Solitary Realizers, and Hearers such as the sixteen Foe Destroyers; Sanghas of Tantra, such as the Heroes and Heroines of the Twenty-four Auspicious Places, and supramundane Dharma Protectors such as Mahakala, Dharmaraja, Vaishravana, and Kalindewi.

In this vast assembly all the Gurus, Deities, and Buddhas are the Buddha Jewel; and all the Bodhisattvas, Solitary Realizers, Hearers, Heroes, Heroines, and Dharma Protectors are the Sangha Jewel. In front of each of the holy beings is a small marble table supporting scriptures that they have composed. These scriptures are in the nature of wisdom light, and they represent the Dharma Jewel. When we visualize them we regard them as in essence the inner realizations of the holy beings. These inner realizations are the actual Dharma Jewel.

We construct this visualization gradually, making it as vast as we can imagine because the objects of refuge are countless, pervading the whole of space. Each one is an emanation of the main object of refuge, Guru Buddha Shakyamuni.

When we have established this visualization we imagine that we are surrounded by all the countless living beings who experience the sufferings of the six realms of samsara. We imagine them all in human form. Closest to us are our own parents, family, and friends. To generate compassion towards all of them we meditate:

Unceasingly, since time without beginning, I have been experiencing the various kinds of suffering. Again and again I have undergone the pains of each of the six realms of uncontrolled rebirth without freedom or choice. Now I have obtained a precious human life with all the necessary freedoms and endowments, and I have discovered Dharma. Now I have a rare opportunity to attain liberation by putting Dharma into practice.

Nevertheless, it remains very difficult to attain liberation because my mind is heavily burdened with delusions preventing me from gaining realizations. Furthermore, I cannot be sure how long this opportunity will last because the time of death is most uncertain. If I die today or in a few months' time I shall have no control over my death and rebirth. I could easily take rebirth in one of the lower realms where the suffering is unbearable. If I were fortunate enough to take my next rebirth as a human being I would still have to endure the sufferings of birth, sickness, old age, death, and all the other sufferings of human life. Even if I were to take rebirth as a god I would not be free from suffering. Therefore I must use this chance to attain liberation.

I am not the only one trapped in this pitiable condition of pain and dissatisfaction; how could I aim only for my own release? Every living being who wanders within the six realms of samsara has at some time in the past been my own dear mother, and every single one of them experiences the same sufferings that I experience. Therefore, I must work to liberate all of them. Since only the Three Jewels have the power to protect and help us, I will go for refuge from the depths of my heart in order to be able to free all other living beings from their suffering.

In this way we generate the causes of going for refuge and increase our wish to gain freedom from samsara for ourself and others. This way of going for refuge increases our realizations of renunciation and compassion. Compassion induces the superior intention 'I must work to liberate all beings.' Recognizing that we need to go for refuge if we are to fulfil this wish, we focus our attention on the groups of Gurus visualized in front of us and recite fifty times 'I go for refuge to the Gurus.' When we have finished this recitation we request the Gurus to bestow their blessings. We then visualize white light descending from their hearts and absorbing into our body and mind, purifying all our negative karma, especially the negative karma that we have created with respect to our Spiritual Guide by actions such as developing dislike or disrespect for him or her, disturbing him, physically harming him, telling him lies, going against his wishes, or getting angry with him. When this visualization is complete we should feel that all our negativities have been purified and our body is transformed into the nature of light.

We then recite the same line another fifty times and when we have finished we make requests and visualize golden nectar descending from the hearts of the Gurus and absorbing into our body and mind. This nectar causes our realizations, life span, merit, and virtues to increase.

Next we focus attention on the Buddhas and Deities and recite fifty times 'I go for refuge to the Buddhas.' When we have finished this recitation we request the Buddhas to bestow their blessings. We then visualize white light descending from their hearts and purifying all our negative karma, especially the negative karma that we have created with respect to the Buddhas by actions such as developing dislike for them, wishing to harm them physically, going against their wishes, selling statues of Buddhas for our own financial gain, or stepping over images of Buddhas thinking that they are insignificant. We then recite the same line another fifty times and when we have finished we make requests and visualize the golden nectar as before.

We continue the practice in the same way, reciting 'I go for refuge to Dharma', with our attention focused on the Dharma Jewel, and 'I go for refuge to the Sangha', with our attention focused on the Sangha Jewel. When we have finished all these rounds of recitation and meditation we then focus our attention on all the objects of refuge together, and recite as many times as we can the short prayer of going for refuge:

I and all sentient beings, until we achieve enlightenment,
Go for refuge to Buddha, Dharma, and Sangha.

We then make specific requests to the objects of refuge in accordance with their different ways of helping us. The Gurus help us by transforming our mind with inspiration and blessings; the Buddhas help us by guiding us to liberation and full enlightenment; the Deities help us by bestowing attainments; the Sangha help us by offering assistance in our Dharma practice; the Heroes and Heroines help us by bestowing spontaneous great bliss, thus enabling us to practise Secret Mantra; and the Protectors help us by dispelling hindrances to our Dharma practice. When we have made these special requests we visualize the light and nectar as before.

In the beginning, if we find it difficult to visualize the objects of refuge in this elaborate form we can imagine simply that the Three Jewels are present in the space before us, and then with faith recite the short prayer of going for refuge.

GENERATING BODHICHITTA

Having gone for refuge we now generate bodhichitta by meditating:

What will it be like when I become enlightened? I shall possess every good quality and I shall be completely free from all faults, all sufferings, and every kind of hindrance. I shall have perfect ability to help all other living beings. My emanations will be as numerous as living beings and I shall use them for the benefit of all. Just as there is one moon shining in the sky whose reflections fill all the lakes and waters of the world, when I become enlightened my emanations will cover and protect every living being.

When this meditation induces in our mind a strong intention to become enlightened for the sake of others, we hold this thought clearly and single-pointedly for as long as we can, acquainting ourself with it more and more closely. Then we recite the prayer of generating bodhichitta:

Through the virtues I collect by giving and other perfections,
May I become a Buddha for the benefit of all.

Bodhichitta is a mind that has two aspirations, both of which are expressed in this prayer. The main aspiration, to benefit others, is expressed by the words 'for the benefit of all'. The secondary aspiration, to accomplish the means to fulfil the main aspiration, is expressed by the words 'May I become a Buddha'.

Since bodhichitta is the main cause of full enlightenment Guru Buddha Shakyamuni is overjoyed whenever it arises in our mind. Therefore, after reciting the prayer we should imagine that in response Buddha emanates another form in the same aspect, which comes to the crown of our head and enters our body, purifying all our non-virtues and obstructions. We are transformed into a Buddha in the same aspect as Guru Shakyamuni. From our body we radiate light in all directions, reaching every single living being and purifying their non-virtues and obstructions. All living beings absorb into light and reappear as Buddhas in the same aspect as Guru Buddha Shakyamuni. Practising in this way is known as 'bringing the result into the path'. It is so called because we are strongly imagining that we have already attained the future result of our practice. The result itself is full enlightenment and an enlightened being's ability to help others attain the same state. This practice ripens our potentiality to attain Buddhahood more quickly. This potentiality is known as 'Buddha lineage' or 'Buddha seed'.

ENHANCING BODHICHITTA: THE PRACTICE OF THE FOUR IMMEASURABLES

Before beginning this practice we need to reduce our divine pride and remember that we have only been imagining that we have attained the future result of our practice, and that in reality we ourself and countless other living beings have yet to become enlightened beings.

To enhance our bodhichitta motivation we practise the four immeasurables:

(1) Immeasurable equanimity
(2) Immeasurable love
(3) Immeasurable compassion
(4) Immeasurable joy

These are called 'immeasurables' because we practise them taking as our observed object all living beings whose number is immeasurable. When we practise immeasurable equanimity we develop the wish for all living beings to gain the realization of equanimity, and we actively dedicate ourself to help them do this. When we practise immeasurable love and immeasurable compassion we develop the wish for others to experience only happiness and freedom from suffering, and we actively dedicate ourself to make this happen. When we practise immeasurable joy we develop the wish that others should never lose the enjoyments and happiness that they experience in the fortunate states of humans and gods, or the supreme joy of liberation, and we actively dedicate our-self to prevent them ever being separated from temporary or ultimate happiness.

Each of the four immeasurables has four parts: an immeasur-able wish, an immeasurable prayer, an immeasurable superior intention, and an immeasurable request.

Immeasurable equanimity Observing all the beings around us we meditate:

> *At some time in their past lives all living beings have been related to each other as a mother to her own dear child, but they do not remember this and so now they develop attach-ment, hatred, or indifference towards one another, feeling close to some and distant from others. Hatred and attachment motivate them to commit harmful actions and as a result they continue to experience problems. If everyone were to develop equanimity they would not be governed by attachment and hatred, and they would find freedom from suffering.*

Meditating in this way induces in our heart an immeasurable wish, 'How wonderful it would be if all living beings were to abide in equanimity, free from hatred and attachment, not feeling close to some and distant from others.' Meditating on this immeasurable wish induces an immeasurable prayer, 'May all beings abide in equanimity.' Praying in this way induces an immeasurable superior intention, 'I myself will make this happen.' Meditating on this intention compels us to make an immeasurable request, 'Please, O Buddhas and Spiritual Guides, bless me to do this.'

If we gaze at a perfectly cloudless, blue sky we shall not prefer the east to the west or the west to the east. In the same way, when we gain the realization of equanimity we shall not prefer some people to others. All beings will be equally important to us. Before we have this realization our gaze is, as it were, fixed upon uneven ground. Some areas look high and others look low.

Most of the personal problems we experience are caused by our own biased mind. We think that we, our family, and our friends are most important. We cherish those who are close to us and take their concerns to heart, but we neglect almost everyone else, thinking that their concerns are insignificant. When we gain equanimity we shall see all beings as equally precious and as a result we shall find that many of our own problems are overcome.

Equanimity is an equal concern for others and not a mere indifference. Indifference is as far away from equanimity as hatred and attachment. When we develop equanimity we shall experience great peace and happiness. Our mind is like a well-ploughed field where we can plant the seeds of compassion, love, and bodhichitta.

Immeasurable love Observing all the beings around us we meditate:

> *All these beings long for happiness, yet most of them do not know what the cause of happiness is, and those who do know cannot create it. Therefore, all of them lack what they desire.*

Meditating in this way induces in our heart an immeasurable wish, an immeasurable prayer, an immeasurable superior intention, and an immeasurable request:

> *How wonderful it would be if all living beings were to possess happiness and its cause.*
> *May all beings possess these.*
> *I myself will make this happen.*
> *Please, O Buddhas and Spiritual Guides, bless me to do this.*

When we have generated this immeasurable wish continuously and spontaneously, we have gained the realization of immeasurable love. Since living beings are countless, so are the benefits of immeasurable love. Even when our meditation goes badly and we do not experience any special feeling, we still receive many benefits from meditating on immeasurable love.

Immeasurable compassion Observing all the beings around us we meditate:

All these beings are afraid of suffering and wish to be free from it, yet in ignorance they continue to commit negative actions which are the very cause of suffering.

Meditating in this way induces in our heart an immeasurable wish, an immeasurable prayer, an immeasurable superior intention, and an immeasurable request:

How wonderful it would be if all living beings were free from suffering and its cause.
May they all be free from these.
I myself will make this happen.
Please, O Buddhas and Spiritual Guides, bless me to do this.

Immeasurable joy Observing all the beings around us we again meditate in order to generate an immeasurable wish, an immeasurable prayer, an immeasurable superior intention, and an immeasurable request:

How wonderful it would be if all living beings were never to lose the happiness of humans and gods or the supreme joy of liberation.
May they never be parted from these.
I myself will make this happen.
Please, O Buddhas and Spiritual Guides, bless me to do this.

GENERATING THE BODHICHITTA MOTIVATION FOR A SPECIFIC PRACTICE

Before engaging in our actual meditation we generate the motivation to do it solely for the sake of attaining full enlightenment for the benefit of others. For example, if we are going to meditate on how to rely upon our Spiritual Guide we motivate ourself:

I will now train my mind in faith and respect for my Spiritual Guide so that I can benefit others by building the foundation that supports all other realizations of the stages of the path to enlightenment.

This bodhichitta is called 'engaging' or 'practical' bodhichitta. It decides to engage in a specific practice as a means of actually accomplishing the goal of aspiring bodhichitta, which is the wish to become enlightened for the sake of all other living beings.

VISUALIZING THE FIELD FOR ACCUMULATING MERIT

There are two ways of visualizing the Field for Accumulating Merit. According to the first way we imagine that the objects of refuge gradually gather into Guru Buddha Shakyamuni who comes to the crown of our head and descends to our heart, and then we visualize the Field for Accumulating Merit in the empty space in front of us. The second way is easier. We simply impute the Field for Accumulating Merit upon our visualization of the objects of refuge.

The objects of refuge are now designated as the Field for Accumulating Merit because when we offer the practice of the seven limbs and the mandala the holy beings act as a field in which we plant and nourish our seeds of virtue. By making these offerings we create and increase our virtuous energy, purify our negative karma, and increase our potentiality to gain the realizations of the stages of the path. These results are the good harvest of our virtue.

We begin this practice by remembering all the details of the previous visualization, from Guru Buddha Shakyamuni at the centre to the outermost row of Dharma Protectors. In addition, to increase the protection of Dharma, we visualize a guardian in each of the four cardinal directions of the Field for Accumulating Merit. At the crown of each holy being we visualize a white OM, the seed-letter of Vairochana; at the throat a red AH, the seed-letter of Amitabha; at the heart a blue HUM, the seed-letter of Akshobya; at the navel a yellow SÖ, the seed-letter of Ratnasambhava; and at the secret place a green HA, the seed-letter of Amoghasiddhi. These seed-letters indicate that all the holy beings in the Field for Accumulating Merit are, in essence, the same as the five Buddha lineages.

We then renew our conviction that we are in the living presence of the holy beings. In this we are like a blind person who is led into a room where a discourse is being given and whose friend describes how all the people appear. The blind person believes what he or she is told without hesitation. He vividly imagines all the people as if he were really seeing them and he actually feels their living presence.

Next we recite the prayer inviting the Field for Accumulating Merit – inviting all the wisdom beings to come before us and unite with the commitment beings visualized in front of us:

You, Protector of all beings,
Great Destroyer of hosts of demons,
Please, O Blessed One, Knower of All,
Come to this place with your retinue.

From the hearts of all the holy beings light radiates, reaching all the Buddha Lands and bringing the wisdom beings into our presence where they become inseparably one with the visualized Field for Accumulating Merit.

Buddha Shakyamuni said 'Whenever anyone develops faith in me, I am present.' Therefore it is certain that if we recite the prayer of invitation with faith, the wisdom beings will come. Then we can abandon all doubts that the holy beings are actually present.

At the time of Buddha Shakyamuni there lived a young woman called Magadhabhatri who had immense faith in Buddha Shakyamuni and his disciples. She went abroad to another country to live with her non-Buddhist husband and his family. Although they were often visited by their venerable non-Buddhist teacher, this never satisfied Magadhabhatri, who was always talking about the good qualities of her own Teacher, Buddha Shakyamuni. By listening to this her mother-in-law developed great faith in Buddha and asked Magadhabhatri to invite him to visit them. When Magadhabhatri promised the family that Buddha and his retinue would be arriving the next day they could hardly believe her. They said that even if Buddha was already on his way it would be impossible for him to get there so quickly. Magadhabhatri climbed to the top of the house holding flowers and incense, and requested Buddha to come by reciting a prayer inviting the Field for Accumulating Merit.

Buddha heard her request through his powers of clairvoyance and he summoned his five hundred Foe Destroyer disciples, telling them that those with miracle powers could come with him the following day. One disciple, not wanting to be left behind, meditated all night to attain the necessary miracle powers so that he could fly along with Buddha!

Magadhabhatri's mother-in-law meanwhile told all the local people that Buddha Shakyamuni would be arriving that day with five hundred disciples: 'Magadhabhatri tells me that they are going to fly here miraculously from her father's land!' There was great surprise and excitement. Many groups of people gathered on the surrounding hills and gazed at the sky to see from which direction Buddha would come. For their benefit Buddha emanated eighteen forms in similar aspect to himself in each of the eighteen gateways of the town. Although only one Buddha entered Magadhabhatri's house, everyone in the town and surrounding area saw Buddha and developed very strong faith in him. From that time forth they engaged fully in the practice of Dharma.

ACCUMULATING MERIT AND PURIFYING NEGATIVITY BY OFFERING THE PRACTICE OF THE SEVEN LIMBS AND THE MANDALA

THE PRACTICE OF THE SEVEN LIMBS

The seven limbs are:

(1) Prostration
(2) Offering
(3) Confession

(4) Rejoicing
(5) Beseeching the Buddhas and Spiritual Guides not to pass away
(6) Requesting the Buddhas and Spiritual Guides to turn the Wheel of Dharma
(7) Dedication

The practices of prostration, offering, beseeching, and requesting accumulate merit; the practices of rejoicing and dedication multiply merit; and the practice of confession purifies negative karma. These seven practices are called 'limbs' because they support our meditation as limbs support a body. Without the use of limbs we cannot accomplish much in the way of physical actions. Similarly, without the limbs of accumulating merit and purifying negativity we cannot accomplish much in the way of meditation.

Each of the practices has a different function: prostration overcomes pride; offering overcomes miserliness; confession overcomes all three root delusions – desirous attachment, hatred, and ignorance; rejoicing overcomes jealousy; beseeching overcomes our wrong views and the negative karma we have created by committing negative actions towards the Buddhas and Spiritual Guides; requesting overcomes the negative action of abandoning Dharma; and dedication overcomes the power of our anger to destroy the merit of whatever good actions we dedicate.

PROSTRATION

The practice of prostration was taught by Buddha Shakyamuni, and it was one of the main practices of Naropa and Je Tsongkhapa. There are three types of prostration: physical, verbal, and mental. We make physical prostrations by paying respect with a physical action of our body, such as by making full-length or half-length prostrations, bowing our head, or pressing the palms of our hands together. We make verbal prostrations by paying respect with our speech, such as by reciting praises to the Buddhas and Bodhisattvas. We make mental prostrations by paying respect mentally, such as by developing faith in the Three Jewels. We can perform all three types of prostration together by making physical prostrations with faith whilst reciting praises or mantras.

To make physical prostrations we place the palms of our hands together with the thumbs tucked in and then touch, in turn, the crown of our head, the point between our eyebrows, our throat, and the point at the level of our heart. Then we bring our body to the ground either in half-length prostration with our palms, knees, and forehead touching the ground, or in a full-length prostration with our whole body stretched face downwards on the ground. Touching our crown and forehead creates the cause to attain the body of a Buddha. In particular, touching our crown creates the cause to attain the crown protrusion of a Buddha, and touching the point between our eyebrows creates the cause to attain the hair-curl of a Buddha. Touching our throat creates the cause to attain the speech of a Buddha, and touching the point at the level of our heart creates the cause to attain the mind of a Buddha.

According to Secret Mantra we begin by placing the two hands palms together at our heart. The five fingers of the right hand represent the five root winds and the five fingers of the left hand represent the five branch winds. Bringing the hands together represents the gathering of these subtle energy winds into the central channel. Touching the point at the level of our heart symbolizes the winds absorbing into the indestructible drop at the heart. When this is actually accomplished through meditation we gain the highest attainments of Secret Mantra, such as the realizations of example and meaning clear light.

If we recite the following mantra as we make our physical prostrations, the power of each prostration is multiplied by one thousand:

OM NAMO MANJUSHRIYE
NAMO SUSHRIYE
NAMO UTAMA SHRIYE SÖHA

NAMO means 'homage' and MANJUSHRIYE means 'Glorious Peaceful One'. A Buddha's mind is peaceful because it is completely free from the two obstructions: delusion-obstructions – delusions and their seeds; and obstructions to omniscience – the imprints of delusions. Any being who is completely free from these is a Buddha. SU means 'noble' or 'good'; and SHRI means 'glorious', and refers to the qualities of the Dharma Jewel. UTAMA SHRIYE means 'glorious and unsurpassed', and refers to the Sangha Jewel. Thus the meaning of the whole mantra is:

I pay homage to the Buddha Jewel,
I pay homage to the Dharma Jewel,
I pay homage to the Sangha Jewel.

We can also recite prayers as we physically prostrate. For example, we can recite the four verses of prostration from the *King of Prayers of Superior Excellent Deeds Sutra*:

However many Lions of Men there are
In the worlds of the ten directions and three times,
To all of them without exception
I prostrate with body, speech, and mind.

By the power of prayers of excellent deeds
All Conquerors appear clearly to my mind.
Bowing with bodies numerous as atoms of the world,
To all these Conquerors I prostrate.

Upon each atom are Buddhas numerous as atoms
Surrounded by all Buddha's Sons.
In this way I visualize the Conquerors
Filling the realms of space.

With inexhaustible oceans of praise
And the sound of infinite tongues
I proclaim the good qualities of all the Conquerors
And praise all those gone to bliss.

If we physically prostrate while reciting the first verse we are making prostrations with our body, speech, and mind. The second verse shows how to multiply physical prostrations by imagining that we have countless bodies prostrating simultaneously. The third verse shows how to make mental prostrations by generating faith and remembering the countless good qualities of Buddha, which go beyond our imagination. The fourth verse shows how to make verbal prostrations by offering praise to Buddha.

If we cannot recite these four verses, when we have finished reciting the mantra we can prostrate while reciting Buddha Shakyamuni's prayer:

Guru, Founder, Blessed One,
Tathagata, and Arhat,
Completely Perfect Buddha,
Great Victor, Shakyamuni, Lord,
To you we bow, go for refuge, and offer gifts.
O Please bless us.

As we offer this prayer we prostrate to Guru Buddha Shakyamuni who is our main Field of Merit. Then we prostrate to all five groups of Gurus, including Guru Buddha Shakyamuni in the centre, and to all the holy beings who are the Buddha Jewel, reciting: 'I prostrate to all the Buddhas such as the Yidams of all four classes of Tantra and the thousand Buddhas.' Then we prostrate to the Dharma Jewel, reciting: 'I prostrate to the holy Dharma, the actual protection.' Finally we prostrate to the holy beings who are the Sangha Jewel, such as the Bodhisattvas, Solitary Realizers, Hearers, Heroes, Heroines, and Dharma Protectors, reciting: 'I prostrate to the supreme Sangha.'

When we are making prostrations it is helpful to remember all the benefits. According to Sutra the ten main benefits are that in the future we shall obtain:

(1) A healthy and beautiful form
(2) Rebirth in an honoured family
(3) A great circle of assistants
(4) Offerings and respect from others
(5) Abundant resources
(6) The many benefits of listening to Dharma
(7) Strong faith in the Three Jewels

(8) A good and vast memory

(9) Great wisdom

(10) A deep and vast realization of concentration

There are also many other benefits. For example, prostration purifies negative karma and creates the cause to attain the Form Body of a Buddha.

OFFERING

There are two types of offering, ordinary and sublime. All material offerings are ordinary. They can be either actually arranged before our shrine or imagined, and they can be either owned or unowned. If we see a beautiful garden and mentally offer it to the Three Jewels, this is an owned offering because the garden belongs to someone. If we see wild flowers and mentally offer them, these are unowned offerings.

There are four types of sublime offering. Two are mentioned in *Sutra Requested by Sagaramati* – the offering of putting Dharma into practice and the offering of generating bodhichitta. Applying effort to learn Dharma, meditating on it, and explaining it to others are all examples of the sublime offering of putting Dharma into practice. Generating the minds of love and compassion are also sublime offerings.

The third type of sublime offering, mentioned in *White Lotus of Compassion Sutra*, is the offering of putting into practice whatever special instructions we have received from our Spiritual Guide. The great Yogi Milarepa said:

> I do not have wealth or possessions and so I cannot make material offerings, but I shall repay the kindness of my Spiritual Guide by putting the Dharma he teaches into practice.

The best offering that we can make to our Spiritual Guide is to practise the instructions he or she has given us. One Kadampa Teacher said:

> Any Spiritual Teacher who prefers material offerings to the practice of his disciples is not qualified and creates the cause to take rebirth in the lower realms.

The fourth type of sublime offering is the offering of our virtuous actions imagined as beautiful substances. For example, if we meditate on love we can mentally transform this virtue into a gem, or a flower, or a Pure Land, and offer it to the Three Jewels.

We can mentally arrange offerings by reciting prayers such as the one included in Yeshe Tsondru's Lamrim, *Essence of Nectar*, or the verses of offering from the *King of Prayers of Superior Excellent Deeds Sutra*:

Sacred flowers, sacred garlands,
Cymbals, balms, supreme parasols,
Supreme butter-lamps, and sacred incense,
I offer to all the Conquerors.

Superb garments, scents,
Medicinal powders vast as Meru,
Everything supreme, especially arranged,
I offer to all the Conquerors.

For all those Conquerors I visualize
A vast array of unsurpassed offerings.
By the power of my faith in their excellent deeds,
I prostrate and make offerings to them all.

Or we can make offerings mentally with the short prayer:

May all of space be filled
With offerings from gods and men,
Both set out and imagined,
Like offerings of the All Good One.

CONFESSION

The practice of confession is not just a matter of verbally or mentally admitting to negative actions we have committed. Confession includes all the practices of purification. We definitely need to purify the negative actions that we have committed because they are the main cause of all our suffering and unhappiness.

Even though we may try very hard it is difficult to develop realizations. When we draw close to gaining some experience from our Dharma practice our effort often degenerates and we do not succeed. At times we may feel strong faith in our Spiritual Guide but we can lose this feeling. It is hard to develop faith in Dharma and understand the real meaning of the teachings we receive. When we try to meditate we do not find it easy to concentrate, and when we try to put Dharma into practice in our daily lives we hardly ever maintain a pure practice even for one hour. These difficulties arise because we carry a burden of negativity within our mind, the heavy inheritance of all the non-virtuous actions that we have committed.

In *Guide to the Bodhisattva's Way of Life* Shantideva says:

Who purposely creates the weapons
That harm the beings in the hells?
Who creates the blazing iron ground?
From where do the tempting hallucinations arise?

The Able One says that all such things
Come only from evil minds.

To understand how our own negative actions have caused our present difficulties and unhappiness we need to study and meditate on actions and their effects, the law of karma. This will be explained in detail below. By meditating on karma we shall realize that our bad experiences have been created by our negative mind, and we shall see that it is much more appropriate to develop aversion for the cause than for its effect. We shall easily develop regret for all the negative actions that we have committed and we shall develop the determination to engage in the practice of purification to destroy the negative potentialities that those actions have left within our mind.

If we remember all the negative actions that we have committed we may become discouraged and conclude 'I am a hopeless case. My mind is so full of negativity that I shall never be able to make it pure.' If we start to think like this we need to recall the examples of Angulimala, Tong Den, and Ajatashatru. Inspired by the perverse advice of his bad friends, Angulimala killed nine hundred and ninety-nine people. He then received Dharma teachings and realized his error, but instead of giving up hope he practised purification. As a result he purified all his negative karma and gained a direct realization of emptiness in that very life. The king Ajatashatru killed his father who was a Foe Destroyer and disrobed a nun who was also a Foe Destroyer, but when he heard Buddha expound the *Confession Sutra* he developed strong regret and purified all his negative karma. He gained a direct realization of emptiness and attained the state of a Stream Enterer. The Brahmin Tong Den killed his mother but later purified his mind and became a great disciple of Buddha Shakyamuni.

If it is possible for such heinous crimes to be completely purified, can we doubt that our own non-virtue can be eliminated? At present our mind is like an overcast sky, but if we purify all our negativity and keep the promise to refrain from harmful actions in the future, our mind will become like a clear and cloudless sky.

In *Friendly Letter* Nagarjuna says:

If anyone who has previously been extremely reckless,
Later practises conscientiousness sincerely,
That person will become pure like a stainless moon.

If we do powerful purification every day we can completely purify all our negative karma; if we do middling purification we can reduce our negative karma; and if we do a little purification we can prevent our negative karma from increasing. If we do no purification our negative karma will increase as time goes by and we shall definitely experience its painful results. The degree of purification we attain depends upon the strength of the four opponent powers:

(1) The power of regret
(2) The power of reliance
(3) The power of the opponent force
(4) The power of promise

For our practice of purification to be complete, all four powers must be present.

The power of regret This is the power of our regret for the harmful actions we have committed. We develop regret by remembering all the dangers of our negativity. Indirectly regret destroys both the potentialities of our non-virtuous actions and our wish to repeat such actions in the future. For this reason it is also known as 'the power of destruction'. The stronger our regret, the stronger our restraint. If for example we were to discover that we had swallowed deadly poison we would feel deep regret. How much greater our regret should be for our negative actions, which poison all our future lives!

The power of reliance There are two main objects of our negative actions, the Three Jewels and living beings. Most of our negative actions are committed against other living beings. Motivated by attachment, anger, or ignorance, we kill, steal, lie, and so forth. We have also committed many negative actions against holy beings such as Buddhas, Bodhisattvas, and Spiritual Guides. Driven by delusion we have created heavy negative karma by engaging in actions such as abandoning Dharma, denying the existence of enlightened beings, or showing disrespect towards the Sangha. Therefore, going for refuge by relying upon the Three Jewels, and generating compassion or bodhichitta by relying upon all living beings as our object, are powerful methods for purifying the negative actions that we have committed against them. This is what is meant by the power of reliance.

The power of the opponent force This is the power of any virtuous action we perform as an opponent to whatever non-virtuous action we wish to purify. The opponent can be any virtuous action performed with sincere regret for our negativity. For example, we can make prostrations, recite mantras, recite the names of Buddhas, read the scriptures, meditate on emptiness, make offerings, or practise giving. This remedial action is the actual means of directly destroying non-virtuous potentialities.

The power of promise This is the power of promising to refrain from negative actions. When we make a promise we need to know for how long we are able to keep it. We can avoid some negative actions for the rest of our life and others for only a short while. When it comes to those we cannot avoid completely, we can promise to avoid them for a short time and then gradually extend the duration as our capacity increases. Eventually we shall be able to promise to refrain for the rest of our life. Even those whose livelihood depends upon negative actions such as killing animals can practise like this.

REJOICING

Whenever we rejoice in the virtues and accomplishments of those whose attainments are higher than our own we increase our merit abundantly. Such an action endows us with merit half as great as the merit of those in whom we rejoice, and it increases our own potentiality to gain the same attainments.

Buddha Shakyamuni said that we should practise rejoicing in the virtues of five kinds of person: Buddhas, Bodhisattvas, Solitary Realizers, Hearers, and ordinary beings. It is helpful to read the life stories of Spiritual Guides, Yogis, and Buddhas. By contemplating the Buddhas' qualities of body, speech, and mind and the virtuous actions they performed before and after their attainment of enlightenment, and by considering how many beings they have benefited, we shall develop appreciation and rejoice in their attainments, thinking 'How wonderful it will be if I become a Buddha.' By contemplating how Bodhisattvas develop bodhichitta and successively attain the five Mahayana paths and ten grounds we shall appreciate and rejoice in their deeds and develop the thought 'How wonderful it will be if I become a Bodhisattva.' By contemplating how Solitary Realizers attain a realization of emptiness and attain a middling enlightenment, and how Hearers attain a realization of emptiness and attain liberation, we shall rejoice in their practice of the three higher trainings and increase our own potentiality to gain the same realizations. If we also rejoice in those who, like ourself, have not yet entered a spiritual path but who are practising sincerely, we shall eliminate our jealousy and accumulate great merit. We should rejoice whenever others practise giving, moral discipline, or any other virtue, and whenever they put effort into studying and meditating on Dharma.

There was once a king called King Prasenajit who invited Buddha Shakyamuni and his disciples to lunch. A beggar called Tepa stood at the king's gate and rejoiced in the king's generosity, thinking 'How fortunate King Prasenajit is!' When he had finished his meal Buddha dedicated the merit of the beggar for the sake of all beings. King Prasenajit asked, 'I am the one who has provided this food, so why have you dedicated that beggar's merit and not mine?' Buddha replied 'Today that beggar has performed a more virtuous action and gained more merit.' Buddha knew that the king's motivation for giving him a meal was mixed with worldly concerns whereas the beggar's act of rejoicing was entirely pure.

Our practice of rejoicing will be especially powerful if we can rejoice in the virtues of people whom we dislike or who dislike us. If we can rejoice equally in the virtuous actions, happiness, and prosperity of all beings, we shall overcome jealousy and hatred, and we shall easily attain the realizations of compassion and love.

If we also rejoice in our own virtuous actions we shall increase their power and overcome depression and discouragement. We sometimes make ourself depressed by dwelling on the thought 'I have been practising for a long time but I do not seem to have achieved anything.' By indulging in such thoughts we can become so discouraged that we feel like abandoning our practice. At times like this we should meditate on our own virtue. There is no doubt that we have practised virtue in the past because we now have a precious human life with all the necessary freedoms and endowments and we have the opportunity to learn and practise Dharma. This good fortune comes only as a result of practising moral discipline, giving, patience, and stainless prayer.

Just as our virtue of the past is the cause of our present good fortune, so our virtuous actions of this life will bring future good fortune. Therefore it is entirely appropriate to rejoice in them. We can recall how many times we have listened to Dharma or read Dharma books, how many times we have practised meditation, or how many virtuous actions we have performed. If we remember these and appreciate them without pride we shall be able to rejoice purely and thus greatly increase our virtue. Rejoicing in this way protects us from the great danger of abandoning Dharma. If we give up Dharma through discouragement we create the cause to go for many lifetimes without making contact with Dharma and to dislike Dharma whenever we meet it again.

The practice of rejoicing does not require great exertion. Gungtang Tenpai Drolma said:

If you want to practise great virtue even while you are relaxing you should practise rejoicing.

By cultivating this habit of mind we accumulate a vast amount of merit. Je Tsongkhapa said:

It is taught by Buddha that rejoicing is the supreme virtue.

BESEECHING THE BUDDHAS AND SPIRITUAL GUIDES NOT TO PASS AWAY

Although the actual body of Buddha, the Truth Body, never passes away, the bodies that Buddha emanates to guide living beings do pass away. If there are no emanations of Buddha teaching spiritual practices in a particular world, that world is called a 'barbaric land'. In such a place it is impossible to hear even one word of Dharma. Therefore we should entreat the emanations of Buddha to abide in this world for a long time to bring benefit to all living beings. Beseeching the Buddhas and Spiritual Guides in this way creates great merit.

REQUESTING THE BUDDHAS AND SPIRITUAL GUIDES
TO TURN THE WHEEL OF DHARMA

Forty-nine days after Buddha Shakyamuni attained enlightenment the gods Brahma and Indra requested him to give teachings, saying:

O Buddha, Treasure of Compassion, living beings are like blind men in constant danger of falling. There is no Protector other than you in this world. Therefore, please arise from meditative equipoise and turn the Wheel of holy Dharma.

Buddha accepted this request and began to teach. As a result countless beings have attained liberation and full enlightenment and countless beings have the opportunity to practise Dharma. The kind requests of Brahma and Indra made it possible for us to find Dharma even in these degenerate times. In the same way, if we make requests to the holy beings, asking them to turn the Wheel of Dharma, we shall accumulate merit and create the cause to receive Dharma in this and future lives. Indirectly, we shall help all other living beings.

DEDICATION

Dedication has six aspects: what we dedicate, the purpose of dedicating, the goal to which we dedicate, for whose benefit we dedicate, the manner of dedicating, and the nature of dedication.

We dedicate our virtuous actions of body, speech, and mind. The purpose of dedicating these actions is to prevent them from being destroyed or depleted and to ensure that we experience their good results. If we do not dedicate our virtue it can be destroyed by negative actions such as anger or holding wrong views. The final goal towards which we dedicate our virtuous actions is the goal of full enlightenment. We dedicate for the benefit of all living beings, thinking 'Through the power of my virtuous deeds may I attain enlightenment for the sake of all.' If we have realized emptiness, the manner of making our dedication is by recollecting that the three – the person making the dedication, the actions that are dedicated, and the dedication itself – all lack inherent existence. If we have not realized emptiness, the manner of making our dedication is by considering that these three – dedicator, dedicated, and dedication – all lack inherent existence. In the *Perfection of Wisdom Sutras* Buddha says that our manner of dedicating should unite method and wisdom. This practice is very profound because through this dedication both our merit and wisdom increase and we progress along spiritual paths. Dedication is by nature a virtuous mental factor; it is the virtuous intention that functions both to prevent accumulated virtue from degenerating and to cause its increase.

Whatever our wish may be, if we dedicate all our virtue to that end, our virtue will carry us to our goal. Our virtuous actions are said to be like a horse and our dedication like the reins. When we dedicate we are like a skilful rider who, by using the reins, can direct his horse wherever he wants to go. The Kadampa Teachers taught that whenever we perform virtuous actions there are two important things to remember: to begin with a virtuous motivation and to conclude with dedication.

OFFERING THE MANDALA

The word 'mandala' in this context means 'universe'. When we offer a mandala to the holy beings we are offering everything – the whole universe with all its objects and all the beings who inhabit it. Since the merit we create when we make an offering accords with the nature of the offering, we mentally transform the whole universe into a Pure Land and imagine that all its inhabitants are pure beings and that all its objects are precious substances. We then imagine that we are offering this pure universe in our hands.

A child once filled a bowl with dust and offered it to Buddha Kashyapa, imagining that the dust was gold. As a result of this pure offering the child was reborn as the wealthy King Ashoka. Likewise, if we offer the world as a

Pure Land filled with exquisite objects and precious symbols we shall experience a result in accordance with the pure nature of our offering. If we wish for spiritual attainments we should offer a mandala every day.

REQUESTING THE FIELD FOR ACCUMULATING MERIT IN GENERAL AND THE LAMRIM LINEAGE GURUS IN PARTICULAR TO BESTOW THEIR BLESSINGS

Now we request blessings to attain three great purposes:

(1) To stop wrong thoughts and attitudes from arising in our minds
(2) To cultivate correct thoughts and attitudes
(3) To eliminate outer and inner obstacles to our Dharma practice

If we can perfectly accomplish these three aims we shall attain enlightenment in this life. Although there are countless wrong thoughts and attitudes, there are sixteen in particular that we should know and strive to abandon because they directly prevent realizations of the stages of the path. They are:

(1) Disliking or having disrespect for our Spiritual Guide
(2) Not wishing to take the essence of our precious human life
(3) Not remembering death
(4) Being attached to the pleasures and happiness of this life alone
(5) Not fearing rebirth in the lower realms
(6) Not wishing to go for refuge to the Three Jewels
(7) Not having faith or conviction in the laws of karma
(8) Seeking to accumulate non-virtuous actions and not virtuous actions
(9) Regarding samsara as having the nature of happiness
(10) Wishing to increase delusions and contaminated actions

(11) Being uninterested in attaining liberation
(12) Not wanting to practise the three higher trainings, which are the causes of liberation
(13) Forsaking mother living beings
(14) Self-cherishing
(15) Self-grasping
(16) Disliking the practice of Secret Mantra

Corresponding to these there are sixteen correct thoughts and attitudes that we need to cultivate:

(1) Relying faithfully upon and having respect for our Spiritual Guide
(2) Wishing to take the essence of our precious human life
(3) Remembering death
(4) Not being attached to the pleasures and happiness of this life
(5) Fearing rebirth in the lower realms
(6) Wishing to go for refuge to the Three Jewels
(7) Having faith and conviction in the laws of karma
(8) Seeking to accumulate virtuous actions and not non-virtuous actions
(9) Regarding samsara as having the nature of suffering
(10) Wishing to abandon delusions and contaminated actions, which are the causes of samsaric rebirth
(11) Being determined to attain liberation
(12) Wanting to practise the three higher trainings
(13) Cherishing all mother living beings
(14) Forsaking self-cherishing
(15) Realizing selflessness
(16) Liking the practice of Secret Mantra

In addition to these sixteen correct thoughts and attitudes there are many other virtuous states of mind that we need to cultivate and for which we need to request blessings. For example, when we train our mind in the stages of the vast path of Sutra we cultivate special minds of great love, great compassion, and bodhichitta; and based on these the determination to practise the six perfections of giving, moral discipline, patience, effort, mental stabilization, and wisdom.

The realizations of the stages of the vast path of Secret Mantra – namely, the realizations of the generation stage practice of bringing the intermediate state into the path of the Enjoyment Body and the completion stage realization of the actual illusory body – are the essence of the stages of the vast path for which we need to request blessings. The resultant vajra body that is attained when we attain Buddhahood is the quintessence of all the stages of the vast path of Sutra and Tantra.

The realizations of the stages of the profound path of Secret Mantra – namely, the realizations of the generation stage practice of bringing death into the path of the Truth Body and the completion stage realizations of example clear light and meaning clear light – are the essence of the stages of the profound path for which we need to request blessings. The resultant Truth Body, or Dharmakaya, is the quintessence of all the stages of the profound path of Sutra and Tantra.

To remove all the wrong thoughts and attitudes mentioned above, and to cultivate all these virtuous states of mind in their place, we request the blessings of the Field for Accumulating Merit with the following prayer:

Please pour down your inspiring blessings upon myself and all my mothers, so that we may quickly stop all perverse minds, from disrespect for our kind Teacher to the most subtle dual appearance.

Please pour down your inspiring blessings, so that we may quickly generate pure minds, from respect for our kind Teacher to the supreme mind of Union.

Please pour down your inspiring blessings to pacify all outer and inner obstructions.

When we have made these requests we imagine that the blessings of all the holy beings descend from their hearts in the form of lights and nectars. These enter our body and mind, purifying our negative karma and obstructions, and increasing our merit, good qualities, life span, and realizations. These blessings greatly increase our potentiality to gain the realization of the meditation we are about to do.

We then make requests to the Lamrim lineage Gurus, beginning with our principal Spiritual Guide, reciting the prayer three times:

> **So now my most kind root Guru,**
> **Please sit on the lotus and moon on my crown**
> **And grant me out of your great kindness,**
> **Your body, speech, and mind's attainments.**

Our Spiritual Guide emanates another form in the same aspect which comes to the crown of our head facing the Field for Accumulating Merit. With folded hands he then helps us to make our requests to the other lineage Gurus. We can recite the long prayer by Je Tsongkhapa called *Opening the Door to the Supreme Path* or recite the brief prayer beginning:

> **I make requests to you, Buddha Shakyamuni,**
> **Whose body comes from countless virtues,**
> **Whose speech fulfils the hopes of mortals,**
> **Whose mind sees clearly all existence.**

and ending:

> **I make requests to you, my kind precious Teacher,**
> **Who care for those with uncontrolled minds**
> **Untamed by all the previous Buddhas,**
> **As if they were fortunate disciples.**

After this we make a special request to gain the realization of whatever meditation we are about to do. Since in this instance we are about to meditate on how to rely upon our Spiritual Guide, we request in the following way:

> *I and all my kind mothers continue to take rebirth without freedom or control because we have not yet relied wholeheartedly upon our Spiritual Guide. Please bless us to gain this realization.*

We make this special request three times and then imagine light radiating from the heart of Guru Buddha Shakyamuni to the outermost limits of the Field for Accumulating Merit. From the furthest boundary all the holy beings dissolve into light and gradually gather into the five central groups of Gurus. These in turn dissolve into light and gather into Guru Buddha Shakyamuni who comes to the crown of our head and instantly transforms our principal Spiritual Guide, who is at our crown, into the same aspect as Buddha Shakyamuni. Then we generate strong faith in Guru Buddha Shakyamuni, regarding him as in essence one with all the objects of refuge including our main Spiritual Guide. We offer again the practice of the seven limbs, reciting the short prayer of the seven limbs, after which we offer a mandala. Then we request:

O Guru Buddha,
In nature the wisdom Dharmakaya,
Synthesis of all Spiritual Guides,
Please bestow your inspiration.

O Guru Buddha,
In nature the Sambhogakaya,
Synthesis of all Buddha Jewels,
Please bestow your inspiration.

O Guru Buddha,
In nature the compassion Dharmakaya,
Synthesis of all Dharma Jewels,
Please bestow your inspiration.

O Guru Buddha,
In nature the Supreme Emanation,
Synthesis of all Sangha Jewels,
Please bestow your inspiration.

We repeat our request for blessings and make heartfelt requests to attain the realization of the meditation that we are about to do, recognizing how necessary it is to gain this realization if we are to attain liberation and enlightenment. At this point we can also recite the *Prayer of the Stages of the Path* included within the prayers for the six preparatory practices in *Essence of Good Fortune*.

In response to our requests Guru Buddha Shakyamuni radiates light which enters our body and mind, purifying our non-virtue and eliminating obstructions. In particular, it purifies obstacles to our gaining the realizations that we have requested. Our body is transformed into the nature of light and our mind develops a very strong potentiality to attain these realizations.

Now we have completed all six preparatory practices and we are ready to do our actual Lamrim meditation. Throughout the meditation we should remain aware of our Spiritual Guide, in the aspect of Buddha Shakyamuni, at the crown of our head. Whenever we experience difficulty in our meditation – whether it be distraction, laziness, or any kind of unpleasant feeling about the meditation – we can pause, offer a mandala, and request inspiration from Guru Buddha Shakyamuni, 'Please help me to eliminate this hindrance and apply myself well to the meditation.' Then we can again visualize the light and nectar descending from Guru Buddha Shakyamuni to our heart, eliminating our obstacles and blessing our mind with good energy to continue our meditation. If we practise like this, combining meditation with requests to receive inspiration and blessings, we shall definitely gain realizations. Geshe Dag Powa said:

If we combine with our meditation the practices of purifying negativity, accumulating merit, and making requests for inspiration to our Spiritual Guides and Yidams, there is no doubt that our mind will change. Since our present state of mind is impermanent, if we practise in this way repeatedly, although we may think we have no hope of gaining profound realizations, we shall gain them quickly.

The essence of the six preparatory practices is contained in the prayers called *Essence of Good Fortune* and in a shorter practice called *Prayers for Meditation*, both of which can be found in Appendix II. The sequence of prayers explained above differs slightly from the sequence in *Essence of Good Fortune,* which presents a complete but less extensive system of practice. The prayers should be recited with each session of meditation. Our actual Lamrim meditation is done at the conclusion of the *Prayer of the Stages of the Path* or at the appropriate point within the prayer.

What is Meditation?

Before presenting the actual meditation, there now follows a general explanation of the nature and purpose of meditation. To meditate is to familiarize our mind constantly and thoroughly with a virtuous object. Meditation has many functions: it overcomes inner problems such as those created by anger, jealousy, attachment, and ignorance; it controls our mind and brings inner peace; it enables us to cultivate virtuous intentions that lead us to perform good actions; and it eliminates non-virtuous intentions that lead us to perform harmful actions. By practising meditation we gain experience of the many levels of spiritual realization and progress to higher and higher levels of spiritual attainment until we accomplish the highest of all, the state of Buddhahood.

To practise meditation we first need to learn Dharma by listening to and reading correct instructions. We then need to contemplate the meaning of what we have heard and read. We contemplate Dharma to understand its meaning clearly and to gain conviction, testing it to see if it is logical and coherent, whether it makes sense in terms of our own experience, and whether its purpose is worthwhile. Once we have gained a firm understanding of the meaning of Dharma and have confidence in its reliability we are ready to practise meditation.

There are two types of meditation, analytical meditation and placement meditation. In analytical meditation we engage in a purposeful process of investigation, or thought, about an object; analyzing its various aspects and examining it from various points of view. We use our imagination, mindfulness, and powers of reasoning until through the power of our investigation a special thought or feeling arises in our mind and our state of mind changes. As we shall see, there are different types of object. Some, such as impermanence or emptiness, are objects apprehended by the mind. Others, such as love, compassion, renunciation, or the determination to rely purely upon our Spiritual Guide, are actual states of mind. We engage in analytical meditation until the specific object that we seek appears clearly to our mind or until the particular state of mind that we wish to generate arises.

For example, when we meditate on how to rely upon our Spiritual Guide we consider the various benefits of committing ourself with faith, the dangers of losing our commitment and trust, and the different ways in which we can practise faithful reliance in thought and in deed. Through the power of this analytical meditation we develop a strong determination to rely wholeheartedly upon our Spiritual Guide. When this determination arises clearly and definitely in our mind we have found our object of placement meditation.

In placement meditation we concentrate on a virtuous object single-pointedly, without allowing distractions to disturb our concentration. The object of placement meditation can be any virtuous object, or special thought or feeling, that is generated in our mind through the power of analytical meditation. With placement meditation we hold this virtuous object, thought, or feeling until it begins to fade, then we renew our analytical meditation to make the object clear or definite again. Just as when we make a fire with bellows there comes a time when the fire is strong enough for us to put down the bellows and let it blaze, so there comes a time when we stop analytical meditation and let placement meditation take over. Then, in the same way as a fire gradually loses its intensity so that we have to apply the bellows again, the object of our placement meditation will gradually fade so that we have to apply analytical meditation once again.

Je Tsongkhapa said that meditators should combine these two types of meditation because good analytical meditation brings good placement meditation, and good placement meditation brings good analytical meditation. We need to combine these two types of meditation even when the object of placement meditation is not hard to find or generate in the mind. For example, if we want to do placement meditation on our breath we first have to investigate it in order to identify our object clearly. When our investigation makes the object appear clearly to our mind we stabilize this appearance by doing placement meditation. Objects such as emptiness or bodhichitta are harder to find and so we need to do more analytical meditation; but the process of alternating between analytical and placement meditation is the same.

Analytical meditation makes the object appear clearly or definitely to our mind and placement meditation makes our mind more and more closely acquainted with the object so that eventually the mind and its object mix. For instance, if we do analytical meditation on the sufferings of all living beings, compassion will arise clearly in our mind. When this happens we do placement meditation to make our mind more and more familiar with compassion. Eventually, our mind will mix with compassion. This does not mean that henceforth compassion is the only object of our mind, but that compassion has become inseparable from our mind and so, in all that we think and all that we do, our mind is never without compassion.

In the beginning our placement meditation is very weak and we are hardly able to hold onto our object for more than a moment. Whenever we lose our object we have to keep returning to analytical meditation until the object becomes clear again, and then we renew our effort to stabilize the object. We have to repeat this process over and over again. The way to increase our powers of concentration is explained in detail below.

Since most of the problems we experience when we are new to meditation come from overstraining at placement meditation, it is important to be moderate and avoid becoming tense from exerting too much pressure. The effort we apply should be relaxed and steady, and whenever we become tired we should rest.

The practice of meditation is very extensive. It is not just a matter of sitting cross-legged and doing formal sessions. Even if our placement meditation is weak we can still be practising analytical meditation at any time. For instance, if we now pause to consider more deeply some of the points we have read, we may find that our contemplation leads us naturally into analytical meditation while we are sitting in our armchair. In a similar way, we can engage in analytical meditation while we are walking about, travelling, or doing simple manual work.

What is the goal of meditation? Through analytical meditation we shall perceive our object clearly, then through placement meditation we shall gain deeper levels of experience or realization. The main purpose of all Lamrim meditations is to transform our mind into the path to enlightenment by bringing about the deepest levels of realization. The sign that we have gained perfect realization of any object is that none of our subsequent actions are incompatible with it and that all of them become more meaningful. For example, when we have gained a perfect realization of compassion we are never again capable of willingly inflicting harm upon any other living being and all our subsequent actions are influenced by compassion.

In the instructions that follow, outlines and guidance are given for the analytical meditations, and the objects of placement meditation are indicated. The instructions are in the spirit of guidelines. We should use our own wisdom and be flexible in the way we apply the advice that is given. Whenever a line of thought is indicated for our analytical meditation we should first consider where that line of thought is intended to take us. Then thoughts, feelings, and recollections of our own will naturally spring to mind to take us in the same direction. In a disciplined way we use our own thoughts and experiences to strengthen our meditation while remaining careful to avoid engaging in thoughts and recollections that are irrelevant.

Since the purpose of Lamrim meditation is to gain personal experience of all the stages of the path to enlightenment, many different kinds of reasoning or lines of thought are presented, as well as scriptural references and examples for our consideration. The reasonings are not given merely to establish proofs. In fact, many of the points that we meditate on do not need to be proved because they are self-evident. For example, we meditate on the point 'The time of death is uncertain', but we do not need to prove this logically because everyone knows that the time of death is uncertain. Nevertheless, it is one thing to know that something is true on the level of information and it is quite another thing to have personal experience of its truth. Everyone knows that the time of death is uncertain but how many people live their lives in such a way that they never act or think with the assumption 'I shall not die today'? Most of us spend most of our time thinking and acting as if we were not going to die. Consequently, when death strikes we react with shock, distress, or anger, as if something unheard of and unnatural were taking place.

Very often our habitual ways of thinking and our unexamined assumptions contradict the knowledge that we possess. Lamrim meditations resolve such contradictions. Since our habitual ways of thinking and behaving are deeply rooted we need to use many different methods to dislodge them. Reasoning according to strict syllogistic logic is one way. There are also many other ways of reasoning and many different lines of thought that we can use to induce realizations that will change our mind and bring our behaviour under control. Lamrim presents a many-sided challenge to all our mistaken habits of mind.

It is much more important to gain the actual experiences of Lamrim than just to learn the various points. Although knowledge of the instructions is a necessary prerequisite for gaining experience, if we do not persevere in putting the instructions into practice our knowledge will be worthless. If we have knowledge without experience it will be difficult for us to control our mind, and when we teach others they will find it difficult to gain realizations.

Realizations are not easy to attain. We have to listen to or read the instructions many times. If necessary, we should listen to or read them one hundred times or more, and engage in the meditations over and over again. It is not time to stop until we have gained perfect realizations of every stage of the path to enlightenment. If we find that we are reluctant to receive the instructions once we have listened to them or read them just a few times, this indicates that we have not yet experienced Dharma.

The meditations are presented in sequence because one realization naturally leads to the next. However, we can practise the whole cycle repeatedly rather than stay with one meditation until we gain a perfect realization, because whatever experience we have at each stage deepens in dependence upon our practice of the other stages.

Relying upon a Spiritual Guide

THE ACTUAL MEDITATION

The first meditation on the stages of the path is the meditation on relying upon our Spiritual Guide. This has two parts:

1 The qualifications of a Mahayana Spiritual Guide and a Mahayana disciple
2 The actual meditation on relying upon our Spiritual Guide

THE QUALIFICATIONS OF A MAHAYANA SPIRITUAL GUIDE AND A MAHAYANA DISCIPLE

Reliance upon a Spiritual Guide is called the 'root of the path' because all other spiritual realizations of Sutra and Tantra depend upon it. The many branches and fruits of our Dharma practice are sustained and nourished by the root of reliance upon our Spiritual Guide. Just as in our ordinary education we need to rely upon the help of well-qualified teachers to guide us from the level of nursery school to the completion of college or university training, so in the spiritual training that leads to full enlightenment we need to rely upon a well-qualified Spiritual Guide.

Such a deep root cannot be planted hastily. We need to become acquainted with someone who has all the qualifications of a Spiritual Guide, and gradually gain confidence through their teaching and example so that we can rely completely upon their guidance. Our relationship with our Spiritual Guide is the very source of all spiritual attainments, therefore we must be sure that he or she possesses all the necessary qualifications. It is not sufficient that he is famous

95

for his knowledge of Buddhism or that he is an attractive or charismatic personality. Even if he is an unusually kind and sympathetic person, this alone is not a sufficient basis for our devoting ourself to him completely.

A fully qualified Mahayana Spiritual Guide is someone who possesses ten special qualities. According to *Ornament for Mahayana Sutras* these are:

(1) A mind that is controlled by the practice of moral discipline.
(2) A mind that has become peaceful and undistracted through the practice of concentration.
(3) Reduced self-grasping through the practice of wisdom.
(4) Greater knowledge than the disciple.
(5) Delight in teaching Dharma.
(6) A wealth of scriptural knowledge.
(7) A deep and stable realization of emptiness.
(8) Great skill in explaining Dharma.
(9) Compassion and love for his disciples.
(10) Enthusiasm for teaching Dharma, being free from discouragement or laziness.

If we are not so fortunate as to know someone who has all these qualities we can rely upon a Spiritual Guide who at least practises moral discipline, concentration, and wisdom, who has compassion and love for his or her disciples, and who has gained a realization of emptiness.

To become a perfect Mahayana disciple we need to develop the following qualifications:

(1) A mind that is balanced, free from strong attachment to worldly enjoyments and strong aversion.
(2) The wisdom to discriminate pure Dharma teachings that will bring real benefit from teachings that are false. Without this wisdom a disciple is easily confused and led astray when listening to or reading mistaken teachings.
(3) A strong wish to practise Dharma.

(4) Great faith and respect for his or her Spiritual Guide and for Dharma.

(5) The ability to listen to or read Dharma without laziness or distraction.

It is said that when a fully qualified Mahayana disciple relies completely upon a fully qualified Mahayana Spiritual Guide the attainment of enlightenment is easy.

THE ACTUAL MEDITATION ON RELYING UPON OUR SPIRITUAL GUIDE

The purpose of this meditation is to overcome any non-virtuous attitudes we may have towards our Spiritual Guide, such as feelings of dislike or thoughts of disrespect, and to cultivate the virtuous attitudes of faith and respect. When we succeed in cultivating these virtuous states of mind we continue to meditate to become more and more familiar with them, until they remain in our mind at all times.

The meditation has four parts:

1 The benefits of relying completely upon our Spiritual Guide
2 The dangers of breaking our commitment to our Spiritual Guide
3 How to rely upon our Spiritual Guide by developing faith and respect
4 How to rely upon our Spiritual Guide by engaging in actions of service and devotion

THE BENEFITS OF RELYING COMPLETELY UPON OUR SPIRITUAL GUIDE

To generate a strong determination to rely purely upon our Spiritual Guide we contemplate eight main benefits:

1 We progress towards enlightenment
2 We delight all the Buddhas
3 We are not harmed by demons and other evil influences
4 We easily overcome our faults and delusions

5 Our experiences and realizations of spiritual grounds and paths greatly increase
6 We never lack spiritual friends in all our future lives
7 We do not take rebirth in the lower realms
8 All our wishes, temporary and ultimate, are easily fulfilled

WE PROGRESS TOWARDS ENLIGHTENMENT

We meditate:

If I rely completely upon my Spiritual Guide he or she will reveal what I have to practise to attain full enlightenment. By putting his advice into practice and receiving the merit and inspiration that come from dedicating myself completely to my Spiritual Guide I shall accomplish my goal swiftly, in this very lifetime. Therefore I must rely purely upon my Spiritual Guide.

We can also meditate on the following quotation from the Tantras:

If we make offerings to even the tiniest hair pore of our Spiritual Guide we shall receive greater merit than by making offerings to all the Buddhas and Bodhisattvas in the ten directions.

Sakya Pandita said that if we practise the six perfections, such as giving and so forth, for a thousand aeons, we can accumulate a great amount of merit; but if we rely completely upon our Spiritual Guide we can accumulate the same amount of merit in just one moment. Since the collection of merit is the main cause of a Buddha's Form Body, the more quickly we accumulate merit, the more quickly we progress towards attaining a Buddha's Form Body. Conversely, the more we develop delusions, the more quickly we accumulate non-virtue which takes us swiftly towards the lower realms.

In *One Hundred Verses for the Tingri People* Phadampa Sangye says that if we rely upon our Spiritual Guide he can lead us wherever we wish to go and so we should repay his kindness by offering faith and respect. If we wish to attain enlightenment our Spiritual Guide will lead us there, if we wish to gain the realization of the first spiritual ground he will lead us there, if we wish to attain liberation he will lead us there, and if we wish to be reborn in a Pure Land or a heavenly god realm he will lead us there. He will lead us to whatever virtuous destination we desire.

We can also meditate on examples, such as the story of the Bodhisattva Sadaprarudita mentioned in the *Perfection of Wisdom Sutra in Eight Thousand Lines*. Sadaprarudita could not make progress towards enlightenment even though he had many visions of Buddhas and received teachings from them directly. He asked the Buddhas 'With which Spiritual Guide do I have a good karmic connection?' and they directed him to Dharmodgata. To learn from this Teacher, Sadaprarudita had to exert great effort, and he even had to cut and sell his own flesh to obtain substances to offer. His whole-hearted devotion was completely worthwhile because it was only by relying upon Dharmodgata that he could make swift progress to enlightenment.

Since we do not have the opportunity at present to meet actual Buddhas and receive instructions from them directly, we need to commit ourself to a Spiritual Guide with whom we can cultivate, right now, a relationship that is beneficial in terms of our spiritual development. We may find that we can easily and naturally develop a beneficial relationship with a particular Teacher as a result of our having performed virtuous actions towards that person in the past.

WE DELIGHT ALL THE BUDDHAS

In *Scriptures Received from the Mouth of Manjushri* Vajradhara says:

> When disciples make offerings to their Spiritual Guides,
> I myself and all the other Buddhas enter into the body
> of the Spiritual Guide and accept the offering.

We meditate:

All the Buddhas, including Buddha Vajradhara, have entered the body of my Spiritual Guide. Therefore, if I please my Spiritual Guide, I please all the Buddhas; if I make prostrations to my Spiritual Guide, I make prostrations to all the Buddhas; and if I accumulate merit through actions I perform towards my Spiritual Guide, the merit I accumulate is the same as the merit I would accumulate if I were to perform these actions towards all the Buddhas. Therefore I must rely purely upon my Spiritual Guide.

WE ARE NOT HARMED BY DEMONS AND OTHER EVIL INFLUENCES

In *Extensive Enjoyment Sutra* Buddha says that anyone who has merit and good fortune will accomplish all their wishes. Such a person will be free from possession or hindrance by demons, evil spirits, and so forth, and will be able to attain enlightenment swiftly. We meditate:

By relying completely upon my Spiritual Guide I shall become strong in my practice and I shall develop vast and powerful virtuous energy that will protect me against harm from demonic or other evil influences. Therefore I must rely purely upon my Spiritual Guide.

WE EASILY OVERCOME OUR FAULTS AND DELUSIONS

We meditate:

If I rely upon my Spiritual Guide, through his kindness he will show me how to abandon faults and delusions and so I shall be able to avoid harmful actions and their results.

We can remember the example of Milarepa who, by relying wholeheartedly upon his Spiritual Guide Marpa, abandoned all evil actions and attained full enlightenment very quickly, even though he had committed murder and many other extremely destructive actions.

OUR EXPERIENCES AND REALIZATIONS OF SPIRITUAL GROUNDS AND PATHS GREATLY INCREASE

The main obstacles to our gaining realizations are our negative actions and their imprints. By relying upon our Spiritual Guide we can purify these and gain realizations quickly and easily.

We can remember the example of Dromtonpa, who served Atisha so well that he had no time for meditation. Another disciple of Atisha's, Amai Jangchub, meditated all the time. When Atisha let Dromtonpa and Amai Jangchub compete together to see who had the higher realizations, it was Dromtonpa who won the competition. He had gained higher realizations by completely devoting himself to Atisha and performing pure acts of service.

In a similar way, Geshe Jayulwa devoted himself to his Spiritual Guide, Geshe Chengawa, and had no time for meditation. One day, while he was cleaning Geshe Chengawa's room, Geshe Jayulwa went outside to empty the rubbish bin. As he was coming back inside his mind naturally developed single-pointed concentration on emptiness and, without having to exert extra effort or engage in meditation, he gained a realization of emptiness. This came as a result of his complete dedication to his Spiritual Guide.

WE NEVER LACK SPIRITUAL FRIENDS IN ALL OUR FUTURE LIVES

We can meditate on the advice of Je Phabongkhapa:

Although our Spiritual Guide may at present appear to be ordinary, if we do not assent to this ordinary appearance but practise regarding him or her as a Buddha, we shall create the cause to have actual Buddhas such as Manjushri or Maitreya as our Spiritual Guides in the future. Having actual Buddhas as our Teachers is an effect similar to the cause.

WE DO NOT TAKE REBIRTH IN THE LOWER REALMS

We meditate:

If I rely completely upon my Spiritual Guide I shall purify all the negative karma that causes rebirth in the three lower realms. If I maintain strong faith and respect, then even if my Spiritual Guide rebukes me or strikes me these actions will purify my negative karma.

We can remember the example of the Kadampa Teacher, Lha Tripa, who followed his Spiritual Guide, Geshe Tolungpa, with great devotion, although whenever Geshe Tolungpa met Lha Tripa he would reprimand him. Lha Tripa's own disciples began to take exception to this and eventually one of them declared in front of Lha Tripa that Geshe Tolungpa was not a good Spiritual Guide because he was constantly critical of his disciple. Lha Tripa replied 'You should not say so. Every time my Spiritual Guide criticizes me I receive the blessing of Heruka.' Drogon Tsangpa Gyarepa said:

Whenever my Spiritual Guide beats me, to me this is an empowerment. Whenever my Spiritual Guide rebukes me, to me this is a wrathful mantra. These will remove all my obstacles.

ALL OUR WISHES, TEMPORARY AND ULTIMATE, ARE EASILY FULFILLED

Je Tsongkhapa said that the venerable Spiritual Guide is the foundation of all good qualities. We meditate:

If I rely upon my Spiritual Guide all my temporary wishes, such as the wish to enjoy human happiness, and all my ultimate wishes, such as the wish to attain liberation and full enlightenment for the sake of others, will be fulfilled without difficulty.

When we are meditating on these eight benefits of sincere reliance we are doing the analytical meditation that causes us to develop a strong determination to rely wholeheartedly upon our Spiritual Guide. This determination is a virtuous and unmistaken mind. When it arises clearly, we take it as our object of placement meditation and concentrate upon it, holding it without distraction so that we become more and more familiar with it. By closely acquainting ourself in this way with such a virtuous determination, we reduce non-virtuous attitudes such as distrust or disrespect for our Spiritual Guide and our mind becomes more and more pure.

THE DANGERS OF BREAKING OUR COMMITMENT TO OUR SPIRITUAL GUIDE

If we break our commitment to our Spiritual Guide we shall wander further and further away from enlightenment. If we accept someone as our Spiritual Guide, and then become critical or angry and decide to abandon him or her, we shall bring upon ourself many severe consequences. There are eight main ones:

1 Since our Spiritual Guide is an emanation of all the Buddhas, if we forsake or show contempt for him or her, this action will have the same effect as forsaking or showing contempt for all the Buddhas.

2 Every moment of anger that arises in our mind towards our Spiritual Guide destroys all the good karma that we can create in one aeon and causes us to take rebirth in hell for one aeon.

3 Even though we may practise Secret Mantra for aeons, if we have forsaken our Spiritual Guide it will be impossible to gain realizations.

4 With a critical or angry mind towards our Spiritual Guide our practice of Secret Mantra will become the cause of rebirth in hell.

5 It will be impossible to gain new realizations, and the realizations that we have already gained will degenerate.

6 We shall be afflicted with misfortunes such as disease, fear, and possession by evil spirits.

7 We shall take rebirth in the lower realms repeatedly.

8 In many future lives we shall not meet well-qualified Spiritual Guides and we shall be without Dharma, and whenever we do meet Spiritual Guides we shall continue to lack faith and respect for them.

By meditating on these dangers we shall develop a strong determination never to break our commitment to our Spiritual Guide or to become distrustful or disrespectful towards him or her. When this determination arises clearly in our mind we do placement meditation.

HOW TO RELY UPON OUR SPIRITUAL GUIDE BY DEVELOPING FAITH AND RESPECT

This has two parts:

1 How to develop faith that our Spiritual Guide is a Buddha, which is the root of all attainments
2 How to develop respect for our Spiritual Guide by remembering his or her kindness

HOW TO DEVELOP FAITH THAT OUR SPIRITUAL GUIDE IS A BUDDHA, WHICH IS THE ROOT OF ALL ATTAINMENTS

In general, faith is said to be a 'root' because all good qualities and realizations depend upon it and are nourished by it. In particular, our ability to rely completely upon our Spiritual Guide depends upon our having faith based on conviction that our Spiritual Guide is a Buddha.

In *Lamp of the Jewel Sutra* Buddha says:

Faith precedes all virtuous activities, like a mother.
It protects and increases all beneficial qualities.

In his Lamrim, Gyalwa Ensapa says that all experiences of realization, great and small, depend upon faith. Since faith is the root of all attainments it should be our main practice.

While Atisha was in Tibet a man once approached him asking for Dharma instructions. Atisha remained silent and so the man, thinking that he had not been heard, repeated his request very loudly. Atisha then replied 'I have good hearing, but you need to have faith.'

If a disciple has strong faith, then even if the Spiritual Guide makes some mistake the disciple may still receive benefits. Once in India there was a famine in which many people died. One old woman went to see her Spiritual Guide and said 'Please show me a way of saving my life.' Her Spiritual Guide advised her to eat stones. The woman asked 'But how can I make stones edible?' Her Spiritual Guide replied 'If you recite the mantra of the Goddess Tsunda you will be able to cook the stones.' He taught her the mantra, but he made a slight mistake. He taught OM BALE BULE BUNDE SÖHA, instead of OM TZALE TZULE TZUNDE SÖHA. However, the old woman placed great faith in this mantra and, reciting it with concentration, she cooked stones and ate them.

This old woman's son was a monk and he began to worry about his mother, and so he went home to see her. He was astonished to find her plump and well. He said 'Mother, how is it that you are so healthy when even young people are dying of starvation?' His mother explained that she had been eating stones. Her son asked 'How have you been able to cook stones?', and she told him the mantra that she had been given to recite. Her son quickly spotted the mistake and declared 'Your mantra is wrong! The mantra of the Goddess Tsunda is OM TZALE TZULE TZUNDE SÖHA.' When she heard this the old woman was plunged into doubt. She tried reciting both the mantras but now neither of them would work because her faith was destroyed.

Faith is essential. If we have understanding alone without faith we easily take Dharma on a merely intellectual level. If we do not have faith, even if we master Buddhist logic and become capable of skilful analysis our mind will remain untamed because we shall not be putting Dharma into practice. Without faith we shall not develop spiritual realizations and we shall easily increase our intellectual pride. Therefore, faith is to be cherished as extremely precious. Just as all places are pervaded by space, so all virtuous states of mind are pervaded by faith.

What is faith? Faith is a naturally virtuous mind that functions mainly to oppose the perception of faults in its observed object. There are two types of virtue, natural virtue and virtue by motivation. Natural virtue is a mind that is virtuous through its own power, without depending upon a specific motivation to make it virtuous.

There are three types of faith: believing faith, admiring faith, and wishing faith. By engaging in the following meditation, if we develop conviction that our Spiritual Guide is a Buddha, this is an example of the first type of faith, believing faith. With confidence that our Spiritual Guide is a Buddha, if we believe the Dharma that he or she teaches, this is also an example of the first type of faith. Believing faith is the firmest type of faith because it is based on valid reasoning that brings confidence in persons and objects that are virtuous. Such faith is not shaken by doubts or wrong views.

An example of admiring faith is the faith we have when, by recognizing the good qualities of our Spiritual Guide and the good qualities of the Dharma that is taught, we develop admiration for these and our mind becomes very clear and free from disturbing, negative conceptions. This faith is pure-hearted, and it comes when we develop sincere respect and deep admiration for someone or something that we recognize as being worthy or beneficial.

An example of wishing faith is when, on the basis of admiring faith, we develop the aspiration to cultivate within ourself the good qualities we see in our Spiritual Guide or the good qualities explained in the Dharma that is taught.

To gain conviction that our Spiritual Guide is a Buddha we consider:

1 Why it is necessary to regard our Spiritual Guide as a Buddha
2 How it is possible to regard our Spiritual Guide as a Buddha
3 How to develop conviction that our Spiritual Guide is a Buddha

WHY IT IS NECESSARY TO REGARD OUR SPIRITUAL GUIDE
AS A BUDDHA

We meditate:

If I always regard my Spiritual Guide as a Buddha I shall overcome doubts and hesitations and develop the three types of faith very strongly. With faith I shall gain realizations and quickly receive the fruits of my Dharma practice.

Meditating in this way makes us determine, 'I will always regard my Spiritual Guide as a Buddha.'

HOW IT IS POSSIBLE TO REGARD OUR SPIRITUAL GUIDE
AS A BUDDHA

When we have developed the determination always to regard our Spiritual Guide as a Buddha, we may wonder how to do this. We should meditate:

If I do not allow myself to dwell upon any faults that my Spiritual Guide may appear to have, and if I concentrate only upon his good qualities, attention to his good qualities will gradually exclude attention to his faults.

If we practise sincerely in this way, there will come a time when we shall think 'Perhaps my Spiritual Guide is an enlightened being', and then we shall understand how it is possible to regard our Spiritual Guide as a Buddha.

We continue to meditate:

When I gain the path of accumulation of Secret Mantra I shall be able to perceive my Spiritual Guide directly as Buddha's Supreme Emanation Body. I shall see the whole world as a Pure Land and I shall see all the beings who inhabit it as Gods and Goddesses, Heroes and Heroines. Since there will come a time when I shall see all beings in this way, it is certainly appropriate for me to regard my Spiritual Guide as a Buddha.

By meditating in this way we conclude 'When my mind is tamed and pure I shall see my Spiritual Guide as a Buddha, and so there is no doubt that from now on I can regard my Spiritual Guide as an enlightened being.'

HOW TO DEVELOP CONVICTION THAT OUR SPIRITUAL GUIDE IS A BUDDHA

There are four lines of reasoning that lead us to develop conviction that our Spiritual Guide is a Buddha:

1 Buddha Vajradhara said that Spiritual Guides are Buddhas
2 Our Spiritual Guide performs the enlightened actions of a Buddha
3 In these degenerate times Buddhas continue to work for the benefit of all living beings
4 Appearances are deceptive and our own opinions are unreliable

BUDDHA VAJRADHARA SAID THAT SPIRITUAL GUIDES ARE BUDDHAS

A pure Mahayana practitioner has faith in Buddha Vajradhara and in his words as being completely non-deceptive and reliable. Therefore, such a person can develop conviction that his or her Spiritual Guide is a Buddha simply by reasoning 'My Spiritual Guide is a Buddha because Buddha Vajradhara said that all Spiritual Guides are Buddhas.' In *Two Examination Tantra* Buddha Vajradhara prophesies:

> In degenerate times, when the practice of Buddhadharma is in decline, I shall manifest as a Spiritual Guide. You should understand that I am that Spiritual Guide and you should pay due respect . . . . I shall appear as an ordinary being, and I shall come in many forms.

Who are these Spiritual Guides? Who are the ordinary beings that are emanations of Buddha Vajradhara? Surely they must be the Teachers who are doing so much to help us right now.

OUR SPIRITUAL GUIDE PERFORMS THE ENLIGHTENED
ACTIONS OF A BUDDHA

If we consider what are the actions of an enlightened being we must conclude that they could only be the actions that guide others along correct spiritual paths to liberation and full enlightenment. If we consider who is performing such actions now, we shall see that it is our Spiritual Guide.

Since at present we cannot receive guidance directly from Buddha, if we are to take Buddha's teachings and put them into practice we need a Spiritual Guide to act as our interpreter and intermediary. Just as we need a mouth if we are to take food from our plate and digest it, so we need a Spiritual Guide through whom Buddha's enlightened actions are communicated in such a way that we can actually comprehend and learn from them.

Although this line of reasoning is perfect in establishing that our Spiritual Guide performs the enlightened actions of a Buddha, we may still be unable to gain conviction. If so, the fault does not lie in the reasoning but in our own mind. As a result of our own harmful, deluded actions we carry a heavy burden of negativity within our mind, and this weighs down and obscures our intelligence, preventing us from developing believing faith even when we are meditating on perfect reasons. When this happens we can at least acknowledge that the reasoning itself is valid and that our failure to feel convinced is the result of our own negative habits of mind. Then we can try the next line of reasoning.

IN THESE DEGENERATE TIMES BUDDHAS CONTINUE TO
WORK FOR THE BENEFIT OF ALL LIVING BEINGS

Although it may seem to us that there are no longer any Buddhas, if we think about it we shall see that such a thing is impossible because Buddhas have developed bodhichitta, practised the six perfections, and completed the spiritual grounds and paths solely for the purpose of helping others until the end of samsara. Since benefiting others continuously is the very meaning of full enlightenment, it is impossible for Buddhas to cease helping us.

If we consider how the Buddhas are helping us right now, we shall see that they are helping us principally by means of our Spiritual Guide's instructions and example. Buddhas cannot purify us or take away our suffering directly with their own hands, and they cannot help us by revealing themselves in their actual forms because we are incapable of perceiving these. Therefore, the most skilful and effective way they can help us is by means of our Spiritual Guide. Knowing that Buddhas are helping us right now, it follows that they are helping us as our Spiritual Guides.

APPEARANCES ARE DECEPTIVE AND OUR OWN OPINIONS ARE UNRELIABLE

We may object 'Although these ways of reasoning are valid and lead me to conclude that my Spiritual Guide is a Buddha, when I actually meet my Spiritual Guide he does not appear to be a Buddha because I can see faults and a Buddha would not possess any faults.' To change this way of thinking we meditate:

What appears to my mind is indefinite and uncertain. I cannot be sure that something exists just because it appears to my mind, and I cannot be sure that anything really exists in the way that it appears to exist. Things appear differently at different times. While my mind is impure I shall continue to experience hallucinations and mistaken appearances. Only a completely pure mind can perceive things the way they really are.

Depending upon their individual karma, beings perceive objects differently and with different feelings. For example, a human being perceives plain water where a god perceives nectar and a hungry spirit perceives repulsive substances like pus and blood.

Before they purified their minds many of the Mahasiddhas and Yogis saw their Spiritual Guides in low and imperfect forms. Asanga saw his Spiritual Guide, Maitreya, as a dog.

Naropa saw his Spiritual Guide, Tilopa, as a fisherman. Devadatta and Bhikkshu Legpai Karma saw the completely perfect Buddha as a very limited being. Bhikkshu Legpai Karma could see a cubit of light radiating from the body of Buddha Shakyamuni, but he could not perceive Buddha's inner qualities and so he complained 'This Gautama has got only one cubit of light!'

We can consider the following stories. Gyalwa Ensapa once visited a Sakya monastery in Tibet where he recited the *Perfection of Wisdom Sutra in Eight Thousand Lines* in Sanskrit; but since the monks did not know Sanskrit they could not identify what he was reciting. They thought that he was mumbling some kind of spirit language and they concluded 'This is not a human being, it is a Gelugpa ghost!'

A man called Naro Bon Chung went to see Milarepa after Milarepa had attained enlightenment, but this man saw him as very ordinary. He said 'Before I met this man known as Milarepa I heard high praise of him, but when I approached I found that he was nothing special, just an old man lying on the ground.' If mistakes like these could be made even in the golden age, no wonder we make mistakes so often in these degenerate times. In *Essence of Nectar* Yeshe Tsondru says:

> Until I purify this impure mind, even if all the Buddhas were to appear in front of me I would see them all as ordinary. At present it is impossible for me to see their holy bodies with all the special signs and indications.

While our minds are impure we shall perceive only ordinary appearances. To overcome these we need to develop believing faith that our Spiritual Guide is a Buddha.

When we meditate using these four lines of reasoning we are doing the analytical meditation that causes us to develop conviction that our Spiritual Guide is a Buddha. When this conviction arises clearly in our mind we stop analyzing and hold this new feeling as our object of placement meditation so as to become more and more closely acquainted with it.

The sign that we have gained the realization that our Spiritual Guide is a Buddha is that whenever we think of our Spiritual Guide we think of Buddha, and whenever we think of Buddha we think of our Spiritual Guide. We always think of them as one and the same. A mind that has this realization is very pure. Recognizing our Spiritual Guide as a Buddha is a very powerful method for gaining higher realizations, such as the realizations of generation stage and completion stage of Secret Mantra.

HOW TO DEVELOP RESPECT FOR OUR SPIRITUAL GUIDE BY REMEMBERING HIS OR HER KINDNESS

This has two parts:

1 Remembering that our Spiritual Guide is kinder than all the Buddhas
2 Remembering that our Spiritual Guide is kinder even than Buddha Shakyamuni

REMEMBERING THAT OUR SPIRITUAL GUIDE IS KINDER THAN ALL THE BUDDHAS

How can we say that our Spiritual Guide is kinder than all the Buddhas? Suppose we are very poor and someone gives us some money over a period of time so that eventually we are rescued from our poverty and become very rich. Suppose another person then comes and gives us food and other gifts. Which benefactor is the more kind? Surely it is the one who gave to us in our greatest need.

Our Spiritual Guide helps us directly when we are spiritually impoverished and the Buddhas help us directly when we have a wealth of realizations. At present we have little wisdom, concentration, or mindfulness, and we have only a small amount of merit or good fortune. Yet in our spiritual poverty our Teacher heals and nourishes us with Dharma, enabling us to improve our condition by increasing our wisdom, concentration, and mindfulness, and, by reducing our delusions, making our minds more calm and peaceful.

If we accept and assimilate the wealth of Dharma given to us by our Spiritual Guide we shall eventually attain the concentration of the Dharma continuum and be capable of seeing Buddhas directly. At that time, when our mind is rich with realizations, we shall receive instructions directly from the Buddhas. Therefore the Buddhas are like our second benefactors. Our Spiritual Guide, however, is kinder because he or she helps us when we are in the greatest need.

Countless Buddhas have already manifested in this and other worlds. Seventy-five thousand Buddhas gave the Bodhisattva vows to Buddha Shakyamuni in one of his previous lives, but we ourself have never been one of their disciples. Before the time of Buddha Shakyamuni the first three Buddhas of the one thousand Buddhas came and benefited countless living beings by expounding Dharma, but we were not among their disciples. When Buddha Shakyamuni came and taught Dharma, we were not among the many disciples who received his instructions and attained liberation or full enlightenment. After the time of Buddha Shakyamuni, exalted Bodhisattvas such as Manjushri and Maitreya, and great Teachers such as Nagarjuna and Asanga, appeared in this world and guided many beings to liberation and enlightenment, but we were never among those disciples. Highly realized scholars such as Tilopa, Naropa, and Atisha taught Dharma and helped disciples to attain liberation and full enlightenment, but we were not among those who benefited from their advice. The great Kadampa Teachers came, but again we were not among their disciples. Then Je Tsong-khapa and other realized Teachers came, but we were not among those they led to liberation.

If we ask 'Whose disciple am I? Who is now revealing the spiritual path for me?', we shall see that our Spiritual Guide is now showing us the same kindness that Buddhas of the past showed their disciples. Therefore, as far as we ourself are concerned, our present Spiritual Guide is kinder than all the Buddhas.

REMEMBERING THAT OUR SPIRITUAL GUIDE IS KINDER
EVEN THAN BUDDHA SHAKYAMUNI

Generally, Buddha Shakyamuni is kinder than other Buddhas because he is our main object of refuge and the founder of this present doctrine of Dharma. The Buddhadharma we listen to, contemplate, and meditate on originates from him. We have already considered how very kind he is, but our present Spiritual Guide is even kinder to us because at this time we have no opportunity to make a direct connection with Buddha Shakyamuni. Therefore it is only through personal association with our present Spiritual Guide that we can gain spiritual realizations. Atisha said:

Every single realization that we wish to attain depends upon our receiving the inspiration of our Spiritual Guide.

When we practise Secret Mantra we meditate on our Yidam, or personal Deity, as inseparable from our Spiritual Guide so that we can receive his or her blessings and inspiration more quickly, since these are necessary if we are to succeed in our practice. If we meditate on our Yidam alone, without regarding the Yidam as one with our Spiritual Guide, our meditation will lack power. Therefore in Secret Mantra it is said that whenever we visualize any Deity we should visualize the Deity as inseparable from our Spiritual Guide. Gyalwa Go Tsangpa said:

Many meditators meditate on the generation stage of Secret Mantra, but meditating on the Spiritual Guide is the supreme meditation. Many practitioners recite the mantras of their Yidams, but making requests to our Spiritual Guide is the supreme practice.

The most qualified Tantric practitioners keep the practice of Guru yoga as their main practice. The way to practise Guru yoga is to rely sincerely upon our Spiritual Guide.

Indirectly our interest in Dharma is caused by the habits we have built up in previous lives, but the direct cause of our interest is the blessings and inspiration we have received from our Spiritual Guide. We begin to practise Dharma, avoiding non-virtuous actions and practising virtuous actions, only through the blessings and inspiration of our Spiritual Guide. All our prostrations and other virtuous actions of body, our recitations and other virtuous actions of speech, and our meditation and other virtuous actions of mind are caused by the blessings and inspiration of our Spiritual Guide. The opportunity we now have to gain new realizations, and the realizations we have already gained, all arise in dependence upon the blessings and inspiration of our Spiritual Guide.

Sometimes the blessings of a Spiritual Guide are extraordinary, as in the case of Geshe Jayulwa who, without exerting effort in meditation, gained concentration naturally through the power of his Spiritual Guide's blessings. There are many other examples, such as the example of Naropa, who found it exceedingly difficult to receive teachings from his Spiritual Guide, Tilopa. Tilopa just gave him problems, but he did so to help Naropa purify his mind. On one occasion, instead of giving Dharma instructions Tilopa threw a handful of dust into his disciple's face, whereupon Naropa developed single-pointed concentration and remained there, undistracted, for one week. All the problems that Tilopa gave were blessings in disguise.

HOW TO RELY UPON OUR SPIRITUAL GUIDE BY ENGAGING IN ACTIONS OF SERVICE AND DEVOTION

There are four types of action we can offer to our Spiritual Guide once we have developed the correct mental attitudes of faith and respect:

1 Offering actions of bodily or verbal respect such as making prostrations or reciting praises
2 Offering material things
3 Offering service
4 Offering our own practice of Dharma

We can make these offerings at any time, whether or not our Spiritual Guide is actually present. All of them please our Spiritual Guide, but the offering of our own practice of Dharma is the most pleasing. It is the supreme act of devotion.

When we engage in practices such as *Six-session Guru Yoga* we visualize our Spiritual Guide as Buddha Vajradhara. When we practise *Offering to the Spiritual Guide* – making prostrations, offerings, and requests – we visualize our Spiritual Guide as Lama Losang Tubwang Dorjechang. When we engage in the six preparatory practices, called *Jorbai Cho Drug* in Tibetan, for meditation on Lamrim, we visualize our Spiritual Guide as Buddha Shakyamuni. All these practices are ways of relying upon our Spiritual Guide by engaging in actions of devotion.

CONCLUDING THE MEDITATION

At the conclusion of each session of meditation we imagine that Guru Buddha Shakyamuni at our crown reduces in size and gradually descends from our crown to our heart, where he radiates wisdom light which purifies our body and mind. Our body of wisdom light immediately transforms into the aspect of Buddha Shakyamuni and our mind becomes one with his mind. From our heart, light rays radiate and reach all living beings and their environments. All the countless living beings and their environments are purified and their bodies of wisdom light are transformed into the aspect of Buddha Shakyamuni. At our heart, and at the hearts of all the Buddhas surrounding us, is a moon disc supporting a yellow HUM surrounded by the mantra, OM MUNI MUNI MAHA MUNIYE SÖHA. We recite the mantra, imagining that all the Buddhas are reciting it with us.

When we have finished reciting the mantra we complete our session by dedicating our virtue to the full enlightenment of all living beings.

HOW TO TRAIN THE MIND DURING THE MEDITATION BREAK

When we are out of meditation we can read books and receive further instructions on whatever stage of the path that we have been practising in our meditation session. We should never completely forget our object of meditation. Instead we can use the opportunity of the meditation break to recollect and contemplate the points of our meditation, and to talk with our Dharma friends about the instructions we have received and the experiences we are having. Besides maintaining mindfulness of our object of meditation, our main practice during the meditation break is to protect the doors of the sense powers. Usually, when our sense powers (the eye sense power, the ear sense power, the nose sense power, the tongue sense power, and the body sense power) or our mental power come into contact with their respective objects (forms, sounds, smells, tastes, tactile objects, and other phenomena), delusions easily arise in the mind, causing us to engage in harmful actions that bring suffering as their result. When we have eliminated self-grasping, which is the root of all delusions, our sense powers and their objects can come into contact without our generating delusions. Until that time, we can practise protecting the doors of our sense powers.

We can do this in either of two ways. The first is to avoid making contact with the objects of the sense powers. For example, we avoid letting our gaze fall upon beautiful forms, we avoid crossing paths with our enemies, or we avoid listening to pleasing music. This way of practising is difficult for most people. We could practise like this only if we were living, like Milarepa, in a cave. Therefore, most of us have to practise in the second way.

The second way to protect the sense doors is not by preventing contact with the objects of the sense powers but by protecting our mind from becoming influenced by them. We do this as soon as the sense power and its object have made contact. For example, when we see a very beautiful object we immediately move our attention to something else. The reason why we develop desirous attachment for beautiful objects is that as soon as we have made contact with them we let our attention dwell there and we become engrossed. We start to engage in quite an intense process of thought that resembles analytical meditation, familiarizing our mind with every aspect of the object, both manifest and hidden. As a result of our 'analytical meditation' a powerful feeling of desirous attachment arises clearly in our mind and we hold it there until, eventually, we cannot get rid of it! For example, when we meet a handsome man or a beautiful woman we keep thinking about how beautiful they are and we visualize them in detail – their hair, their complexion, their smile, their eyes, their expression, their figure. We remember all their features from the crown of their head to the tips of their toes. On these occasions our powers of visualization are superb. This 'analytical meditation' makes strong desirous attachment arise in our mind, and this makes us seek the object that we have been visualizing. If we fail to make contact again, we feel depressed. Where does this pain of disappointment come from? It comes from our own 'meditation'! Thus, if we want to be free from such suffering, whenever we encounter a beautiful object we should leave it alone and not allow our mind to dwell upon it. Similarly, if someone says unpleasant things to us we should let these things fall upon deaf ears and avoid dwelling upon them. In this way we shall avoid becoming angry. The same kind of practice is to be applied with regard to all other objects of the sense powers.

If we protect the doors of our sense powers during the meditation break, our concentration in the meditation session will be very good. Je Tsongkhapa taught that the meditation break is more important than the meditation session because our meditation session may last for only a few hours every day, but our meditation break is as long as the rest of our life. If we practise well during the meditation break we shall be practising well for most of our life, and we shall greatly improve the concentration that we have in our meditation session.

During our meditation break we can use our Dharma wisdom to transform all our experiences into spiritual practice. If we are able to do this we shall not have to rely upon books alone to keep our mind on Dharma when we are not meditating. For example, when we go shopping we can use our wisdom to see how some things teach impermanence, some things teach the faults of samsara, some things teach compassion, and some things teach patience. If we practise like this, we shall bring home many virtuous states of mind. Otherwise, when we come home from town we shall be carrying a heavy bag full of delusions.

Manjushri

Nagarjuna

Chandrakirti

Our Precious Human Life

HOW TO TAKE THE ESSENCE OF OUR HUMAN LIFE

This section is presented under the following two headings:

1 How to develop the determination to take the essence of our precious human life
2 Training the mind in the actual methods for taking the essence of our precious human life

HOW TO DEVELOP THE DETERMINATION TO TAKE THE ESSENCE OF OUR PRECIOUS HUMAN LIFE

This has three parts:

1 Recognizing that we now possess a precious human life
2 Meditating on the great value of our precious human life
3 Meditating on the great rarity of our precious human life

RECOGNIZING THAT WE NOW POSSESS A PRECIOUS HUMAN LIFE

A precious human life is a life that has eight special freedoms and ten special endowments that make it an ideal opportunity for training the mind in all the stages of the path to enlightenment. Each of the eight special freedoms is freedom from one of eight conditions that either prevent or seriously impede our spiritual practice. If we have a human life with all these eight freedoms we shall find it relatively easy to overcome any other unfavourable conditions that we might experience. The ten special endowments are all necessary conditions for our practice of Dharma.

By meditating on these eight freedoms and ten endowments we shall recognize that we now possess a life that provides the very best opportunity for spiritual development. Such a recognition will naturally bring a feeling of joy and a deep appreciation of our human life with its great potential. By meditating on the value and rarity of our precious human life we shall develop a spontaneous and continuous desire to take full advantage of it. This virtuous wish naturally leads us to correct spiritual paths and holds us back from entering wrong paths. Therefore, developing the wish to take the essence of this precious human life is said to be the key that unlocks the door of Dharma. It is also said to be our best friend because it influences us powerfully to use our life in the best way.

This section has two parts:

1 The eight freedoms
2 The ten endowments

THE EIGHT FREEDOMS

Four of the eight freedoms are freedoms from being born in a form that is not human:

1 Freedom from being born as a hell being
2 Freedom from being born as a hungry spirit
3 Freedom from being born as an animal
4 Freedom from being born as an ordinary god

An explanation of ways to develop conviction, if we do not already have it, that past and future lives exist, and that there are other realms or conditions of existence apart from the human realm, will be given in detail below. For the purposes of this meditation it is enough to have faith, or at least to keep an open mind.

It is impossible to be born as a human being without first creating the cause, just as it is impossible to gather a good harvest without first planting the seeds. Nothing, not even an atom, arises without causes and conditions. What is the cause of being born human? The cause is to be found in our own mental actions. There is no lawgiver who exists outside ourself and decrees 'You shall be human' or 'You shall inhabit hell.' Furthermore, we cannot take a particular form of life merely by preferring it, for who would ever prefer to be born in hell? As explained in the *Condensed Perfection of Wisdom Sutra*, the main cause of a human rebirth is the practice of moral discipline. It cannot be said, therefore, that human beings will always be born again as human beings or that animals will always be born again as animals. The form of life we take depends upon the quality of our own actions.

Although it is difficult to prove by logical reasoning alone the precise relationships between particular actions and their effects, it is quite easy to understand the relationship between actions and their effects in general. The ripened effect of any action is to be born in a state of existence that is similar in nature to the action itself. The ripened effect of any virtuous action is to be born in a fortunate state, such as that of a human being or a god; and the ripened effect of any non-virtuous action is to be reborn in an unfortunate state, such as that of an animal, a hungry spirit, or a hell being.

All the beings who now inhabit the lower realms of existence have at some time in their countless past lives practised moral discipline. As a result they carry within their minds the potentiality to be born human and to practise moral discipline again. Similarly, in this life and in our past lives we have committed countless destructive actions, and so we carry within our mind many potentialities to be born into a life that is not human and to repeat our destructive actions over and over again. Thus we need to meditate in order to appreciate fully the good fortune that we now enjoy and to develop a heartfelt determination to make the most of it while we can.

FREEDOM FROM BEING BORN AS A HELL BEING

We meditate:

The body and environment of a hell being give rise only to intense pain and so it is impossible for such a being to listen to, contemplate, or meditate on Dharma. When I experience even slight physical pain I cannot listen to Dharma, read Dharma books, or sit down to meditate. Yet beings in hell experience much greater torment than I could ever experience as a human being, and they experience pain constantly for almost incalculably long periods of time. How fortunate I am not to have taken rebirth as a hell being.

FREEDOM FROM BEING BORN AS A HUNGRY SPIRIT

We meditate:

Beings who take rebirth as hungry spirits experience constant hunger and thirst. When I am feeling hungry I cannot give much thought to my spiritual practice and I cannot develop much interest in listening to or reading Dharma. Yet hungry spirits experience extreme hunger and thirst all the time and so they never have the freedom or the wish to practise Dharma. How fortunate I am not to have taken rebirth as a hungry spirit.

FREEDOM FROM BEING BORN AS AN ANIMAL

We meditate:

Although some animals, like dogs, are clever at finding food and can be taught to obey our command, it is impossible for them to train their minds in the stages of the path to enlightenment because animals suffer from great confusion and stupidity. Even if we try to encourage them to meditate they are completely incapable of comprehending our advice. Our spiritual instructions are like wind in their ears. How fortunate I am not to have taken rebirth as an animal.

FREEDOM FROM BEING BORN AS AN ORDINARY GOD

We meditate:

Long-life gods experience only two gross minds – one when they realize that they have taken heavenly rebirth and the other when they are about to die. The rest of their life is spent in a state that resembles sleep in which they become like mindless stones, perceiving nothing. Although their lives are long, these gods cannot reap any benefit from them by practising Dharma, and when they die they are born again in one of the lower realms.

Gods of the form realm other than long-life gods also lack the freedom to practise Dharma because they spend their whole life in a state of solitary tranquillity. They never experience suffering as we do, and they never see the sufferings of others, and so they have no way of developing realizations of renunciation, great compassion, or bodhichitta. Some gods, such as the gods of the desire realm, spend their whole life engrossed in distractions and so they never develop an interest in Dharma, and when they die they are thrown into lower realms. Since from the point of view of Dharma, rebirth as an ordinary god is totally meaningless, how fortunate I am not to have taken such a rebirth.

There was once a doctor called Kumara who followed his Spiritual Guide, Shariputra, with great devotion. Even if Kumara was on an elephant, as soon as he saw Shariputra he would immediately dismount and pay homage. When he died he took rebirth as a god of the desire realm. Shariputra knew of this by means of his clairvoyance and he decided to visit his disciple to see if he could continue to instruct him in Dharma. When Shariputra entered the pleasure garden where this god was now playing, his former disciple merely waved at him from a distance and then withdrew into the company of the goddesses who were his playmates. Shariputra did not get the chance even to greet his former disciple, let alone to offer any spiritual advice.

The remaining four freedoms are freedoms from being born as a human being in conditions that either prevent or seriously impede spiritual practice:

5 Freedom from being born and remaining in a country where there is no religion
6 Freedom from being born and remaining in a country where there is no Buddhadharma
7 Freedom from being born and remaining with mental or physical disabilities
8 Freedom from holding wrong views denying Dharma

FREEDOM FROM BEING BORN AND REMAINING IN A COUNTRY WHERE THERE IS NO RELIGION

We meditate:

If I had been born in a savage and uncivilized place or in a country where religion is not tolerated, it would have been impossible for me to meet Dharma and put it into practice. There are many places in the world today where there is no religion or where people can be imprisoned and even tortured if they try to practise their religion; and there are many places where people have no opportunity to meet a Spiritual Guide who can show them how to train their minds. How fortunate I am not to be in such a place.

FREEDOM FROM BEING BORN AND REMAINING IN A COUNTRY WHERE THERE IS NO BUDDHADHARMA

We meditate:

If I had been born in a country where religion is tolerated but where there is no one practising Dharma and no one to teach it to others, it would still have been impossible for me to develop interest in Dharma and to learn how to put it into practice. How fortunate I am not to be in such a place.

FREEDOM FROM BEING BORN AND REMAINING WITH
MENTAL OR PHYSICAL DISABILITIES

We meditate:

If I had been mentally disabled for life I would not have been able to understand and apply Dharma, and if I had been physically disabled for life it would have been much more difficult for me to make contact with the teachings. If I had been blind I would not have been able to read many Dharma books. If I had been deaf I would not have been able to listen to teachings. If I had been physically disabled it would have been difficult for me to visit Dharma centres or temples and to learn how to meditate. How fortunate I am to be free from mental or physical disabilities.

FREEDOM FROM HOLDING WRONG VIEWS DENYING DHARMA

Holding a wrong view is a state of mind that is like a door closed and locked against Dharma. It is a mind that clings stubbornly to a view that denies the existence of any object that it is necessary to understand in order to attain liberation or full enlightenment. An example is a mind clinging to the view that past and future lives do not exist, without having the openness of mind to investigate whether or not this view is correct. A wrong view may be held dogmatically or opinionatedly as a result of incorrect or imperfect reasoning, or it may be held blindly without even a pretence of reasoning. We meditate:

Holding wrong views is the main obstacle to pure Dharma practice because it prevents us from developing faith in Dharma, and faith is the basis for attaining every spiritual realization. How fortunate I am not to be holding wrong views.

THE TEN ENDOWMENTS

The first five endowments are personal endowments:

1 Being born human
2 Being born and remaining in a country where Dharma is flourishing
3 Being born and remaining with complete powers, free from mental and physical disabilities
4 Not having committed any of the five actions of immediate retribution
5 Having faith in the three sets of Buddha's teachings

We can understand the importance of each of the five personal endowments by contemplating the following analogy. Being born human is like possessing a car. Being born and remaining in a country where Dharma is flourishing is like getting the car on the road. Being free from mental or physical disabilities is like having petrol in the car. Being free from still having to experience the results of any of the five actions of immediate retribution is like having a licence to drive. Having faith in Dharma is like having the confidence to drive. Just as when any of these five conditions of successful motoring is absent we cannot arrive at our destination, so when any of the five personal endowments is absent we cannot reach enlightenment, which is the proper destination of this precious human life.

The five actions of immediate retribution referred to in the fourth endowment are the five worst negative actions: killing one's father, killing one's mother, killing a Foe Destroyer, drawing the blood of a Buddha with harmful intention, and causing division within the Sangha or Dharma community. If we commit any of these actions it is very difficult to gain realizations and when we die we go straight to hell. When that hellish life comes to an end we continue to experience the heavy results of our action as mental obstructions to our Dharma practice. There have been a few exceptions, such as King Ajatashatru who killed his father Bimbisara but later felt regret, purified, and in dependence upon the instructions of Buddha became a Stream Enterer. However, in general, if we commit any of these five actions there is no way to attain liberation in this life.

The remaining five endowments are favourable characteristics of the world in which we take our human rebirth:

6 Taking human rebirth in a world where Buddha has appeared
7 Taking human rebirth in a world where Buddha has taught Dharma
8 Taking human rebirth in a world where pure Dharma is still being taught
9 Taking human rebirth in a world where there are people practising pure Dharma
10 Taking human rebirth in a world where there are benefactors and sponsors for Dharma practitioners

If Buddha had not appeared in this world and turned the Wheel of Dharma, and if pure Dharma had not remained in this world, it would have been impossible for us to receive Dharma instructions and put them into practice. If we are to practise purely and correctly we also need the help of a Spiritual Guide and spiritual friends, and we need the support of benefactors and sponsors. Therefore, all of these endowments are necessary if our spiritual practice is to succeed. We should realize how fortunate we are to have been born into such a world.

When we meditate on these eight special freedoms and ten special endowments we are doing the analytical meditation that causes us to develop joy and deep appreciation for our present human life, seeing that it is perfectly endowed with all the conditions necessary for training the mind in the stages of the path to enlightenment. What is the purpose of deliberately generating joy? It is so that we shall take full advantage of our present opportunity. If a person discovers a piece of gold but does not recognize its value he may throw it away; but if he understands how precious it is he will be delighted with his discovery and he will keep the gold safely and use it meaningfully. In the same way, if we understand that our human life is now perfectly endowed we shall take delight in it and use it meaningfully. This precious human life is impermanent. It may be lost tomorrow. No one can predict how long this opportunity will last. Therefore we need to appreciate our life right now.

When our meditation causes us to generate a special feeling of joy we do placement meditation, acquainting ourself with this feeling more and more closely so that we never lose it.

MEDITATING ON THE GREAT VALUE OF OUR PRECIOUS HUMAN LIFE

This has three parts:

1 The great value of our precious human life from the point of view of our temporary goal
2 The great value of our precious human life from the point of view of our ultimate goal
3 The great value of every moment of our precious human life

THE GREAT VALUE OF OUR PRECIOUS HUMAN LIFE FROM THE POINT OF VIEW OF OUR TEMPORARY GOAL

The goal or aspiration of every living being is to experience happiness. There are two kinds of happiness and hence two kinds of goal – temporary and ultimate. Temporary happiness is the happiness that can be experienced by humans and gods; it is the limited happiness that can be experienced while beings remain bound within samsara. Ultimate happiness is the pure, eternal happiness of liberation and full enlightenment.

If we had not been born human we would not have been able to experience all the joys and pleasures of human life. Other beings such as animals cannot enjoy the happiness we enjoy because they do not possess the appropriate bodily basis. Therefore, just to have this human body is very important from the point of view of experiencing human happiness in this lifetime. Moreover, we can use this perfectly endowed human life to create the causes for temporary happiness in future lives. We can create all the causes for many future human rebirths with all the necessary freedoms and endowments and with seven extra advantages that provide the greatest opportunity to experience the pleasures and happiness that human life can offer. These seven attributes of higher lineage are: nobility, great beauty, great resources, great power, great wisdom, good health, and long life. Of these, great wisdom is the most precious because it enables us to discriminate what is to be practised and what is to be abandoned, and thus to follow correct spiritual paths.

Moral discipline and stainless prayer to gain a human rebirth are the main causes of being born human. Having respect for our parents, our Spiritual Guides, the Three Jewels, and other beings is the main cause of gaining nobility. Patience is the main cause of great beauty. Generosity is the main cause of great resources. Offering protection to others is the main cause of great power. Studying and rejoicing in Dharma is the main cause of great wisdom. Healing and looking after those who are ill is the main cause of good health. Saving the lives of others is the main cause of long life. With our precious human life we can create all of these good causes. If we do so we shall be sure to experience the results, just as when we strike a match and put it on a dry haystack we are sure to have a fire. With this precious human life we can create the cause to have whatever kind of human life we wish. We can be a millionaire, or we can be a wise politician, or we can be an ordained person who keeps pure moral discipline.

THE GREAT VALUE OF OUR PRECIOUS HUMAN LIFE FROM THE POINT OF VIEW OF OUR ULTIMATE GOAL

Our ultimate goal is to attain the pure, eternal happiness of liberation and full enlightenment. Now that we possess a precious human life we can practise and complete the three higher trainings that lead to liberation. The human form is said to be like a boat in which we can cross the ocean of samsara and reach the shore of liberation.

As Shantideva says in *Guide to the Bodhisattva's Way of Life*:

By depending upon this boat-like human form,
We can cross the great ocean of suffering.
Since such a vessel will be hard to find again,
This is no time to sleep, you fool!

Furthermore, with this precious human life we can train in all five main causes of full enlightenment: renunciation, bodhichitta, the correct view of emptiness, and the generation and completion stages of Secret Mantra. Since the human body possesses the six elements that are necessary for the practice of Secret Mantra (skin, flesh, bone, channels, winds, and drops), with this human form we can attain all the experiences of Secret Mantra, including the ultimate realization of full enlightenment, in just one lifetime. If we are reborn as a god of the form or formless realms we shall not have such an opportunity. Even the higher Bodhisattvas born in Pure Lands such as Sukhavati do not have such an opportunity.

We meditate:

Since beginningless time without interruption I have taken samsaric rebirths without freedom or control, in sorrow and in fear. Samsara is the most terrifying prison. Now for the first time I have all the conditions I need to break the bonds of my imprisonment. Therefore, I must not waste this precious opportunity to attain liberation and full enlightenment.

THE GREAT VALUE OF EVERY MOMENT OF OUR PRECIOUS HUMAN LIFE

With this human life, each day, each hour, each minute, can be completely worthwhile. Every single moment of our precious human life has great meaning. In just one hour human beings can create the same amount of merit that a god creates in one aeon. If we meditate on love for just five minutes, or if we make just one prostration to our Spiritual Guide regarding him or her as an emanation of all the Buddhas, we shall create immeasurable merit.

In a very short time we can purify all the negative karma that we have created in the past. The potentialities that we have created in our mind by our past negative actions are formless. Since we cannot see them it is easy to forget that they exist, but if our negative karma were to possess form it would fill the entire universe. All this negativity can be quickly consumed if we use this human life to do strong purification, just as a haystack is quickly consumed by a strong fire.

Je Tsongkhapa said:

> If we contemplate the great value of these freedoms and endowments we shall feel strong regret for having wasted our human body and our time.

Someone who is very miserly but who has to spend a lot of money travelling around will develop a strong sense of loss because he or she greatly values every single penny. In the same way, if we were to develop full appreciation for the value of every single moment of our precious human life we would develop powerful regret whenever we squandered a moment. Je Phabongkhapa said:

> Instead of feeling so much regret when we lose our money, we should develop regret when we waste our human life.

Even if we were to lose all our money we could borrow some, make an appeal, or find a way of making more; but if we lose this human life without having put it to good use it will be almost impossible for us to recover our loss.

This body with all the freedoms and endowments is more precious than the legendary wishfulfilling jewel. With a wishfulfilling jewel we could live in an environment made of precious gems, but what happiness could we derive from that? What happiness could there be in having the power to transform all our possessions into gold? During this life such possessions would be a source of anxiety, and at the time of death we would have to leave them all behind. This precious human life is infinitely more valuable than gold. It is the real wishfulfilling jewel, the real philosopher's stone that makes every moment meaningful and enables us to enter correct spiritual paths.

By meditating on the great value of this precious human life we shall come to see it as a very special opportunity that is not to be wasted. We shall make a very strong determination to use it to accomplish both our temporary and ultimate purposes, and we shall feel a great sense of loss if we waste even a single moment. If we think like this we shall definitely take the essence of this precious human life. However, if we do not meditate in this way there is a great danger that we shall let our life slip by without any meaning. As Shantideva said:

> If, having found the freedom and endowment of a
>   human life,
> I do not strive to practise Dharma,
> There can be no greater self-deception,
> There can be no greater folly.

MEDITATING ON THE GREAT RARITY OF OUR PRECIOUS HUMAN LIFE

This has three parts:

1 Recognizing the rarity of our precious human life in terms of its cause
2 Recognizing the rarity of our precious human life by analogy
3 Recognizing the rarity of our precious human life in terms of numbers

RECOGNIZING THE RARITY OF OUR PRECIOUS HUMAN LIFE IN TERMS OF ITS CAUSE

Even if we understand the great value of our precious human life, we may still waste it if we think that it will be easy to be born a human again. In fact, it is very rare to be born a human because it is rare for anyone to practise pure moral discipline, which is the cause for such a rebirth. In *Precious Garland of Advice for the King* Nagarjuna says:

134

From giving comes wealth,
From discipline comes happiness.

Even when we do observe moral discipline purely it is easy
to destroy it by becoming angry or performing other actions
that destroy our virtue. It is extremely rare to find anyone
who observes pure moral discipline without ever losing it.

There was once a Mongolian who sat listening to a Lama
giving these teachings, and when the Lama came to this point
the Mongolian protested, saying 'You think that human
beings are rare only because you have never been to China!
There are millions and millions of people in China.' However
this Mongolian had missed the point – a human life is rare
not because there are so few of them but because we ourself
rarely create the cause to be reborn as a human. Among all
the actions that we have performed since beginningless time,
very few are pure actions that lead to a human rebirth.

Our human life is also very rare in that each of us possesses only one. We can possess many books, many clothes,
many homes – but no one can have more than one human
life. If we lose it, we cannot borrow another one. Moreover,
this single human life that we now possess is diminishing
with every moment.

RECOGNIZING THE RARITY OF OUR PRECIOUS HUMAN LIFE
BY ANALOGY

In one Sutra, Buddha Shakyamuni asks his disciples 'Suppose
there existed a vast and deep ocean the size of this world,
and on its surface there floated a golden yoke, and at the
bottom of the ocean there lived a blind turtle who surfaced
only once in every one hundred years. How often would that
turtle raise its head through the middle of the yoke?' Ananda
answers that, indeed, it would be extremely rare.

We are just like this blind turtle, for although our physical
eyes are not blind, our wisdom eyes are. The vast and deep
ocean is the ocean of samsara. The blind turtle remaining at
the bottom of the ocean is like our remaining in the lower
realms of samsara, to surface into the fortunate realms only

once in every one hundred thousand years. The golden yoke is like Buddhadharma, which does not stay in one place but moves from one country to another. Just as gold is precious and rare, so Buddhadharma is precious and very hard to find. For most of our previous lives we have remained at the bottom of the vast and deep ocean of samsara, the lower realms. Only very occasionally have we been born as a human being, and even with a human life it is extremely rare to meet Buddhadharma.

RECOGNIZING THE RARITY OF OUR PRECIOUS HUMAN LIFE IN TERMS OF NUMBERS

Harmful actions that are the cause of lower rebirth are much easier to commit than virtuous actions, and so those who are born in the lower realms are much more numerous than those who are born as humans or gods. Of all the states of existence, hell has the greatest number. Fewer beings are born as hungry ghosts, and fewer again as animals. Human beings are rarer than beings born in any of the three lower realms, and among human beings very few have a precious human life with all the freedoms and endowments. Among those who have a precious human life very few practise Dharma, and among those who practise Dharma very few practise purely and gain correct understanding and experience. We may sometimes get the impression that there are many pure Dharma practitioners and many people with realizations, but if we check we shall see that such beings are extremely rare. Milarepa once said to the hunter Gonpo Dorje, 'Buddha said that human life is precious but a human life like yours is very common.' Among those who have a human life it is common to find people like this hunter who completely waste their opportunity and use it only to create causes for future misfortune. However, it is difficult to find someone practising Dharma purely.

When we meditate on the great value and rarity of this precious human life we are doing the analytical meditation that causes us to develop a strong determination not to waste a moment of our human life and to make full use of it by putting Dharma into practice. When this determination arises clearly in our mind we hold it as our object of placement meditation so that we become more and more accustomed to it.

Although we now have a precious human life with all the freedoms and endowments, we may still find it difficult to practise Dharma purely because we may lack other freedoms such as the time to devote to study and meditation. It is rare to find anyone who has ideal conditions, but the most serious impediment to our spiritual development is our own failure to generate a strong wish to engage in practice. Je Tsongkhapa said that to develop the wish to take full advantage of this life with all the freedoms and endowments we should meditate on four points:

I need to practise Dharma.
I can practise Dharma.
I must practise Dharma in this life.
I must practise Dharma now.

Before we can develop the wish to practise Dharma we must first recognize the need to practise Dharma. To do this we meditate:

I need to practise Dharma because I want to experience happiness and avoid suffering, and the only perfect method for accomplishing these aims is to practise Dharma. If I do so, I shall eliminate all my own problems and I shall become capable of helping others.

Even though we may understand the need to practise Dharma, we may still think that we are incapable of doing so. To overcome our hesitation and convince ourself that since we have all the necessary conditions we are definitely capable of practising Dharma, we meditate:

I now have a precious human life with all the freedoms and endowments, and I have all the necessary external conditions such as a fully qualified Spiritual Guide. There is no reason why I should be incapable of practising Dharma.

Even though we may understand the need to practise Dharma and may feel capable of doing so, we may still delay, thinking that we shall practise in some future life. To overcome this laziness of procrastination we need to remember that since it will be very difficult for us to gain another precious human life we must practise in this very lifetime.

Even though we may see that we must practise in this very lifetime, we may still feel that our practice can be postponed until our retirement. To overcome our complacency we need to remember that the time of death is most uncertain and so the only time to practise is right now.

In this way we arrive at four strong resolutions:

I will practise Dharma.
I can practise Dharma.
I will practise Dharma in this very lifetime.
I will practise Dharma right now.

These four resolutions are invaluable because they make us generate naturally a spontaneous and continuous wish to take full advantage of our precious human life. This wish is our best Spiritual Guide because it leads us along correct spiritual paths. Without it, no amount of advice or encouragement from others will lead us to practise Dharma.

On one occasion Aryadeva and Ashvaghosa were about to have a debate. Ashvaghosa was standing on the threshold of a room with one foot inside and one foot outside. To test Aryadeva's wisdom he said 'Am I going out or coming in?' Aryadeva replied 'That depends upon your intention. If you want to go out, you will go out. If you want to come in, you will come in.' Ashvaghosa could think of nothing to say to this because what Aryadeva had said was perfectly correct.

If we desire good things we shall perform virtuous actions and if we desire harmful things we shall perform non-virtuous actions. Since our desire is so powerful it is extremely important to abandon non-virtuous desires. If someone uses his mouth to give advice to others but in his heart cherishes the desire to steal someone else's possessions, then eventually, through the force of his desire, he will accomplish his aim. What is it that commits such a person to prison? Nothing but his own non-virtuous desire. He loses his reputation and falls in everyone's esteem, all through his own wish. On the other hand, if there is an ordinary person who is not highly regarded but who has a sincere and continuous wish to gain bodhichitta, then eventually, through the force of his or her desire, this person will attain spiritual grounds and paths and experience the fruits of practice.

The great Tibetan meditator Gungtang Jampelyang once asked 'What is the difference between a wise man and a fool?' The difference lies in their intention. A wise person is someone who has a good intention, not someone who merely possesses knowledge. Devadatta studied as many texts as an elephant can carry on its back, and yet he cherished a perverse desire to harm Buddha and so he took rebirth in hell where all his scholarship was useless. Amongst the most valuable advice we can receive is to develop a good intention and to maintain it at all times. We need to know our own minds and to exchange our harmful desires for ones that are beneficial. Buddha Shakyamuni said that a correct intention is the root of all Dharma realizations.

TRAINING THE MIND IN THE ACTUAL METHODS FOR TAKING THE ESSENCE OF OUR PRECIOUS HUMAN LIFE

From meditating on the great value and rarity of this precious human life we firmly decide to use it meaningfully, to take its essence. To take the essence of this precious human life means to engage in methods that will bring benefit in our future lives and to stop investing all our energy and concern in activities that are aimed at attaining only temporary benefit in this present life. To take the least essence of this precious human life is to protect ourself from the danger of lower rebirth and to ensure that in our next life we obtain a special human rebirth endowed with the seven attributes of higher lineage by gaining all the realizations of the stages of the path of a person of initial scope. To take the intermediate essence of this precious human life is to protect ourself from uncontrolled rebirth and to attain liberation from samsara by gaining all the realizations of the stages of the path of a person of intermediate scope. To take the great essence of this precious human life is to protect ourself from the danger of self-cherishing and to attain full enlightenment for the benefit of all living beings by gaining all the realizations of the stages of the path of a person of great scope.

All the stages of the path that follow are the actual methods for taking the essence of this precious human life. They are explained in three parts:

1 Training the mind in the stages of the path of a person of initial scope
2 Training the mind in the stages of the path of a person of intermediate scope
3 Training the mind in the stages of the path of a person of great scope

What are the stages of the path of a person of initial scope? They are meditation on the great value and rarity of this precious human life, meditation on death and impermanence, meditation on the sufferings of the three lower realms, the pure practice of going for refuge, and the practice of avoiding negative actions and engaging in virtuous actions. By practising these stages of the path we avoid birth in the lower realms and protect ourself from their sufferings.

How does the practice of a small being protect us from the sufferings of the lower realms? If we meditate on the great value and rarity of this precious human life, and on death and impermanence, we shall practise Dharma purely and go for refuge purely. If we go for refuge purely we shall keep the commitment to avoid negative actions and perform only virtuous actions. If we do this we shall avoid creating the cause of rebirth in the lower realms and create only causes of higher rebirth. Therefore, the realizations of a small being protect us from suffering. They are objects of refuge and are to be regarded as Dharma Jewels because they resemble the actual Dharma Jewels of Superior beings.

What are the stages of the path of a person of intermediate scope? They are the practices of generating renunciation in dependence upon meditation on the dangers of samsara and, motivated by renunciation, the practices of the three higher trainings. By gaining the realizations of a middle being we attain liberation and protect ourself from all the fears and sorrows of samsara.

What are the stages of the path of a person of great scope? They are the minds of great compassion and bodhichitta and, motivated by bodhichitta, the practice of the six perfections – in short, all the paths of Bodhisattvas. By gaining the realizations of a great being we attain full enlightenment – the complete abandonment of all faults and the perfect accomplishment of all good qualities – enabling us to offer protection to all other living beings.

In *Lamp for the Path to Enlightenment* Atisha says:

There are three types of being that should be known;
They are small, middle, and supreme.

In this context a 'small' being means a person of initial scope, a 'middle' being means a person of intermediate scope, and a 'supreme' being means a person of great scope. Our scope for spiritual development is determined by our aspiration. As our aspiration becomes more far-reaching, our capacity for spiritual development increases. In terms of their aspiration all living beings are included within the three types, small being, middle being, and great being.

There are two types of small being, ordinary small beings and special small beings. An ordinary small being is someone whose aspiration does not extend beyond the limited goal of finding worldly happiness in this life alone. Such a person sets his or her sights on obtaining the changeable happiness of this life. He therefore seeks the guidance of ordinary specialists such as business administrators, careers advisors, marriage guidance counsellors, and travel agents. If an ordinary small being also practises Lamrim he will not only become much more successful in all his worldly pursuits, but he will also increase his merit, purify negative karma, and gradually extend his aspiration so that it becomes the aspiration of a special small being.

A special small being is someone who has ceased to be interested in obtaining only the happiness of this life, and who aspires to the happiness of higher states of existence in future lives. Although the aspiration of a special small being extends beyond the welfare of this life, it does not reach further than the limited goal of obtaining the worldly happiness of humans and gods in future lives. A special small being can fulfil this wish by gaining all the realizations of the stages of the path of a small being.

A middle being is someone who has ceased to be interested in obtaining changeable worldly happiness either in this present life or in any future life, and who seeks only the perfect happiness of freedom from all kinds of uncontrolled rebirth. Although the aspiration of a middle being extends beyond obtaining merely worldly happiness, it does not reach further than the limited goal of fulfilling only his or her own welfare. A middle being can fulfil this wish by gaining all the realizations of the stages of the path of a middle being.

A great being is someone who has ceased to be interested in fulfilling only his or her own welfare, and who seeks to become fully enlightened so that he or she can help others to find freedom from their suffering and experience the bliss of Buddhahood. A great being can fulfil this wish by gaining all the realizations of the stages of the path of a great being.

Mahayana practitioners begin to develop bodhichitta, the aspiration of a great being, from the very beginning of their spiritual practice. For a long time, though, this motivation is artificial because spontaneous bodhichitta is generated only after gaining all the realizations of the stages of the path that are common to a small being and a middle being, and some of the realizations of the stages of the path of a great being, such as the realization of great compassion. Great compassion, the determination to release and protect all living beings from their suffering, gives rise to genuine bodhichitta, the determination to become enlightened solely for the sake of benefiting others. Great compassion itself is generated only after we have realized renunciation, the determination to free ourself from samsara; for if we do not sincerely wish to be free ourself, how can we develop such a wish for limitless living beings?

It is not easy to realize renunciation because this special virtuous mind arises only when we have given up attachment to this life and its pleasures. Training the mind in the stages of the path of a middle being is the actual method for gaining the realization of renunciation. Training the mind in the stages of the path of a small being is the actual method for overcoming attachment to this life. Without developing a mind of renunciation it is impossible to generate a mind of great compassion. In the beginning we should develop renunciation, and gradually renunciation will cause compassion to arise. As Shantideva said:

> If we do not even dream of becoming free from samsara ourself, how can we have the wish to release others from its miseries?

Meditation on Death

TRAINING THE MIND IN THE STAGES OF THE PATH OF A PERSON OF INITIAL SCOPE

This has two parts:

1 Developing the aspiration to experience the happiness of higher states in future lives
2 The actual methods for gaining the happiness of higher states of existence in future lives

DEVELOPING THE ASPIRATION TO EXPERIENCE THE HAPPINESS OF HIGHER STATES IN FUTURE LIVES

This has two parts:

1 Meditating on death
2 Meditating on the sufferings of the lower realms

MEDITATING ON DEATH

This has three parts:

1 Considering the dangers of forgetting about death
2 Considering the benefits of remaining mindful of death
3 The actual meditation on death

CONSIDERING THE DANGERS OF FORGETTING ABOUT DEATH

The dangers of forgetting about death are:

1 We shall easily forget Dharma
2 Even if we do not forget Dharma we shall not be likely to put it into practice

3 Even if we do not forget Dharma and we put it
  into practice, our practice will not be pure
4 Even if we do not forget Dharma and we put it
  into practice purely, we shall lack persistent effort
  in our practice
5 We shall continue to perform non-virtuous actions
6 We shall die full of regret

WE SHALL EASILY FORGET DHARMA

If we do not remember death we shall not have any wish to
train our mind in Dharma, and so the door of Dharma will
remain closed to us and we shall not experience the good
results of spiritual practice. Even though we may be fortunate enough to receive Dharma instructions, to us they will
mean almost nothing. Forgetting about death we become
completely engrossed in the concerns of this life alone and
we devote all our energy to its welfare. When death comes
we realize, too late, that all our activities have been futile.

If we remember death again and again we shall overcome
the habit of assuming that we are going to live in this world
for ever, and we shall begin to see ourself as a traveller
bound for future lives. Thinking in this way reduces our
anxieties, irritations, and attachment to this life and all its
pleasures, and it restrains us from committing actions solely
for the sake of this one short life.

When a traveller stays a few nights in a luxurious hotel he
does not develop strong attachment to its comforts because
he knows he will soon be moving on. When he has to leave
the hotel he does not feel miserable, because he has never
regarded it as his real home. In the same way, if we cease to
think of this life as our permanent home and begin to regard
ourself as travellers bound for future worlds, we shall be less
attached to this life and we shall naturally develop great
interest in Dharma, for Dharma alone helps us in all our
future lives.

EVEN IF WE DO NOT FORGET DHARMA WE SHALL NOT BE LIKELY TO PUT IT INTO PRACTICE

If we do not remember death, even if we do think about practising Dharma we shall be inclined to put it off, thinking 'I shall practise Dharma properly when I have finished my work' – but our life ends before our work is done. The tasks and activities of worldly life are endless.

If we stop to think we shall see that almost all the time we are assuming 'I shall not die today.' Day after day we have the same thought. Even on the day of their death many people continue to think 'I shall not die today.' This complacency prevents us from being serious about our Dharma practice. When death actually comes and destroys our complacency we feel great regret, and it seems to us that this precious human life has become completely worthless. We are like someone who has visited a treasure island and, knowing that his family is in poverty, nevertheless returns home empty-handed. If we do not use this precious human life for practising Dharma we are even more foolish than this careless voyager, for what could be more foolish than to arrive at death empty-handed?

EVEN IF WE DO NOT FORGET DHARMA AND WE PUT IT INTO PRACTICE, OUR PRACTICE WILL NOT BE PURE

If we have already been practising Dharma for some time but we have not experienced perfect results the reason is that we have not yet developed mindfulness of death. Although we may be practising Dharma, if we do not remember death our practice will not be pure and we shall not be able to gain realizations.

What is pure Dharma practice? It has been explained by Teachers such as Dromtonpa that if we have renounced attachment to the comforts of this life our Dharma practice will be pure. However, if we have not renounced attachment to the comforts of this life, even if we engage in the advanced practices of Secret Mantra our practice will not be pure. To develop detachment to the pleasures of this life we do not need to abandon our wealth and possessions, our friends and family. Simply being poor and alone does not mean that we have no attachment to the good things of this life; many poor and lonely people are strongly attached to this world and its pleasures.

To renounce attachment to the comforts of this life means to be free from eight worldly attitudes:

(1) Being pleased when receiving resources and respect
(2) Being displeased when not receiving resources and respect
(3) Being pleased when experiencing pleasure
(4) Being displeased when not experiencing pleasure
(5) Being pleased when enjoying a good reputation
(6) Being displeased when not enjoying a good reputation
(7) Being pleased when receiving praise
(8) Being displeased when not receiving praise

While we remain attached to resources and respect, pleasure, a good reputation, and praise, our mind is unbalanced and we are inclined to become overexcited when we possess them and dejected when we lose them. We remain unstable, vulnerable, and emotionally dependent upon these things. Most of our energy goes into securing them and guarding against their loss. When we practise Dharma our motivation is strongly influenced by our attachment and so our practice, like all our other activities, is in the interests of this life alone and aimed at obtaining its enjoyments.

To overcome attachment to the welfare of this life we meditate:

It makes no difference whether or not I receive respect, a good reputation, or praise. I do not receive any great benefit from these and when I lose them I am not greatly harmed. Words of blame cannot hurt me. Wealth is easily lost, and the pleasures of this life are transient. I do not need to be so interested in these things or overly concerned about them.

If we can develop equanimity with regard to the concerns of this life we shall overcome many of our daily anxieties and frustrations. We shall find that we have more energy for our Dharma practice and that our practice becomes pure. By comparison with non-religious people, anyone who has developed equanimity with regard to worldly concerns has a high degree of spiritual attainment.

This balanced attitude is something that we need to cultivate because we do not have it naturally from the very beginning of our spiritual training. If we have been practising Dharma for some time but cannot feel any of its benefits, the reason is that we are not yet practising pure Dharma. Therefore, in the beginning, our immediate aspiration should not be to gain the perfect results of Dharma practice. Rather, it should be to practise purely. If we can accomplish this aim the results will come naturally in their own time. At the beginning of our training, if we are ambitious to experience results, this ambition itself will be an obstacle to our pure practice because it will be mixed with attachment and worldly concerns. However, the ambition to practise purely is the well-balanced attitude of a steady practitioner.

The seventh Dalai Lama, who possessed great wealth but was not attached to any of it, said:

> All I feel belong to me are my vajra and bell and my yellow robes. For a while people are calling many other things the possessions of the Dalai Lama, but in reality these things belong to others. I cannot hold onto them and call them mine.

We need to cultivate the same attitude, thinking that the things we call our own are ours to use temporarily until we pass them on to others, just as others have passed them on to us. If we have no use for any of our possessions we can give them away now so that others can benefit from them.

We may worry that if we develop equanimity with regard to gain and loss, pleasure and displeasure, good and bad reputation, and praise and blame, we shall be bound to experience poverty and deprivation in the future. In fact, equanimity causes us to have greater resources and fewer problems, and cannot be a cause of misfortune. No one has died or ever will die of starvation as a result of developing detachment. In his previous lives Buddha Shakyamuni created enough merit to take rebirth as a universal monarch sixty thousand times in succession. Instead of taking these rebirths he dedicated all the merit so that in degenerate times Dharma practitioners would never be without enough to eat. Because of this, up to now in this world no pure Dharma practitioner has ever died of hunger.

EVEN IF WE DO NOT FORGET DHARMA AND WE PUT IT INTO PRACTICE PURELY, WE SHALL LACK PERSISTENT EFFORT IN OUR PRACTICE

If we forget about death then even if we practise pure Dharma we shall not be able to practise continuously. We shall practise one week and then abandon our practice the next week, or we may keep up our efforts for a month or even a few years and then abandon them. The cure for this laziness is to remember death again and again.

Perhaps we shall experience the fruits of our practice in a future life and perhaps we shall experience them very soon. The time of fruition depends upon our accumulation of merit and the effort we apply in this life. Therefore we need to make a strong resolution: 'Whether I experience the fruits of practice quickly or slowly, I shall nevertheless practise continuously in this life and in all future lives until I attain my goal.'

If we want to cook food we need to leave the stove on continuously and not keep turning it on and off. If the heat is continuous, no matter whether it is high or low our food will eventually be cooked. Similarly, if we continuously apply effort, even if it is only a small effort, it is certain that we shall eventually experience the fruits of our practice.

If we remember death again and again we shall not only want to practise Dharma but we shall actually find it hard to stop practising. Our usual mentality will be reversed.

Instead of having so much time for worldly pursuits and so little time for spiritual practice, we shall find we have more and more time for Dharma and less and less time for meaningless activities. We shall become like the great meditator, Geshe Karagpa. Beside the entrance to this Geshe's cave there was a thorn bush that scratched him every time he went in and out. Each time he would think 'I must prune that bush', but his practice was so intense that he never found time to prune it. He lived like this because he was continuously aware of death.

WE SHALL CONTINUE TO PERFORM NON-VIRTUOUS ACTIONS

If we forget about death we shall often act in harmful, deluded ways to promote or protect our own worldly interests, and we may even resort to violence, endangering ourself and others. Such actions create the cause for us to continue experiencing problems in the future, and they compel us to take rebirth in the three lower realms. Once we are born there it is extremely difficult for us to find our way back again to the happier realms of humans and gods.

WE SHALL DIE FULL OF REGRET

If we do not keep death in mind throughout our life, when the time of our death comes we shall suddenly discover that all our wealth and possessions, our friends and our relatives cannot help us. We shall develop fear, anxiety, and regret, but our tears will be too late. We shall be just like the Tibetan man called Mondrol Chodak, who was greatly admired by all who knew him for his many skills and talents. He led a very full life travelling about from place to place and meeting many different people, but when the time of his death suddenly arrived he thought to himself: 'I have done so much, engaged in so many business ventures, so many worldly activities, but not one of these will be of any use to me now. People say that I am very clever, but in fact I am incredibly stupid because I have completely neglected spiritual practice, which is the only thing that can help me at this time. I have wasted my whole life by doing things that are of no real benefit.' He felt strong regret and wept. In this miserable state of mind he passed away.

The Kadampa Teachers say that it is inappropriate to be afraid at the time of death and that the time to fear death is while we are young. Most people do the reverse. While they are young they think 'I shall not die', and they live recklessly without concern for death; but when death comes they feel fear, frustration, anxiety, and despair. If we develop fear of death right now, we shall be able to meet our death without experiencing these disturbing emotions, and we shall use our time meaningfully. We shall avoid harmful actions and engage in virtuous ones, thus creating the cause to take a fortunate rebirth. When death comes we shall feel like a child returning to the home of its parents and we shall pass away gladly. We shall become like Longdol Lama who lived to a great old age. When the time of his death came he was overjoyed. People asked him why he was so happy and he replied 'If I die this morning I shall be born again this evening as a God or Goddess in a Pure Land. My future life will be far superior to this one.' Longdol Lama had prepared carefully for death and chosen a specific place of rebirth. If we practise Dharma purely we can do the same.

CONSIDERING THE BENEFITS OF REMAINING MINDFUL OF DEATH

The benefits of remaining mindful of death are:

1 We engage in Dharma practice sincerely and energetically
2 Our Dharma practice becomes very powerful and very pure
3 It is important at the beginning of our practice
4 It is important throughout our practice
5 It is important in attaining the final goal of our practice
6 We shall have a happy mind at the time of death

WE ENGAGE IN DHARMA PRACTICE SINCERELY
AND ENERGETICALLY

In *Great Beyond Sorrow Sutra* Buddha says:

When many different animals have been in a field and have left their footprints we see that it is the elephant who leaves the deepest footprint. In a similar way, when we have practised many different meditations we shall experience their effects; but it is the meditation on death that makes the deepest impression on our mind.

When Prince Siddhartha was living in his father's palace he once ventured outside and saw a corpse. It made him think 'I am now living in a splendid palace, but one day I shall be just like this rotting corpse and so my luxurious way of life has no real meaning. I must engage in spiritual practice and attain enlightenment.' It was this meditation on death that made Prince Siddhartha abandon attachment to the enjoyments of his princely life and enter into the spiritual practices that led to his enlightenment.

When Milarepa witnessed the death of one of the benefactors of Lama Yungdon he became so disillusioned with samsara that he developed deep regret for all his previous practices of black magic, and from that time forth he practised Dharma purely. He was able to attain enlightenment in that same life by practising Secret Mantra only because his initial meditation on death made such a deep impression on his mind.

OUR DHARMA PRACTICE BECOMES VERY POWERFUL
AND VERY PURE

In the scriptures, meditation on death is said to be a hammer that shatters our delusions. It is a powerful means of eliminating both our delusions and our negative actions of body, speech, and mind. To use a more modern metaphor we could say that meditation on death is a nuclear explosion that destroys our negativities and eliminates our concern for trivialities. It strongly influences all our actions. If we meditate on death in the morning we shall perform all our actions during the day with the welfare of future lives in mind; but if we forget about death in the morning we shall be likely to perform all our actions during the day with concern only for the benefit of this present life.

If we do not meditate on death we shall not be able to develop the wish to practise purely. If we lack this wish, the door of Dharma will remain closed to us; and even if we meet a Spiritual Guide who gives perfect instructions and advice these will mean almost nothing to us. One of the Kadampa Teachers said:

My real meditation on the middle way is the meditation on death and impermanence. All good qualities arise as a result of this meditation and it is this meditation that makes our practice of Dharma pure.

IT IS IMPORTANT AT THE BEGINNING OF OUR PRACTICE

Meditation on death is important at the beginning of our practice because it makes us develop the wish to practise purely and continuously, thereby opening the door to Dharma for us.

IT IS IMPORTANT THROUGHOUT OUR PRACTICE

Meditation on death is important throughout our practice because it keeps us interested in training our mind in all the stages of the path to enlightenment.

IT IS IMPORTANT IN ATTAINING THE FINAL GOAL OF OUR PRACTICE

Meditation on death is important in attaining the final goal of our practice because it ensures that we shall not give up until we have attained our aim of enlightenment for the benefit of others.

It would be wrong to think that meditation on death is only for beginners. Even the most accomplished meditators who practise Secret Mantra need to meditate on death. In the *Vinaya Sutras* monks and nuns are advised to paint or draw a skeleton in their room so that they will be frequently reminded of death. At the entrance to monasteries, nunneries, and temples it is customary to paint the Wheel of Life, which depicts all the different states of existence drawn within the clutches of the Lord of Death, signifying that every being who dwells within samsara must depart through the jaws of death.

WE SHALL HAVE A HAPPY MIND AT THE TIME OF DEATH

This benefit of remaining mindful of death is easy to understand if we contemplate Longdöl Lama's story mentioned above.

THE ACTUAL MEDITATION ON DEATH

This has two parts:

1 Meditating on death using nine ways of reasoning
2 Meditating on death imagining that the time of our death has come

MEDITATING ON DEATH USING NINE WAYS OF REASONING

This has three parts:

1 Using three ways of reasoning to gain conviction that death is certain
2 Using three ways of reasoning to gain conviction that the time of death is uncertain
3 Using three ways of reasoning to gain conviction that at the time of death and after death only our practice of Dharma is of benefit to us

The purpose of meditating on death using these nine ways of reasoning is not to establish that death is certain, that the time of death is uncertain, and that only spiritual practice is of benefit to us at the time of death and after, because these facts are obvious and do not require proof. However, despite the fact that we know these things we usually assume 'I shall not die today.' If we ever have the thought, 'I may die today', it quickly passes. Our habitual assumption is that our life will go on as usual, and we base all our daily actions on this assumption. Therefore we need to meditate on death to turn our superficial knowledge into a deep, inner conviction that transforms our awareness so that we habitually think 'I may die today', and base all our daily actions on that reality. If we gain constant mindfulness of death we shall naturally become very interested in practising Dharma.

When we meditate using these nine ways of reasoning we are doing the analytical meditations that cause us to come to three firm resolutions:

I must practise Dharma.
I must practise Dharma now.
I must practise Dharma purely.

USING THREE WAYS OF REASONING TO GAIN CONVICTION THAT DEATH IS CERTAIN

The three ways of reasoning are:

1 Death will definitely come and nothing can prevent it
2 Our life span cannot be increased and it decreases continuously
3 Death will come regardless of whether or not we have made the time to practise Dharma

DEATH WILL DEFINITELY COME AND NOTHING CAN PREVENT IT

We meditate:

No matter where I am born, whether it be in fortunate or unfortunate states of existence, I shall definitely have to die. Whether I am born in the happiest condition of samsara or in the deepest hell I shall have to experience death. However far and wide I travel I shall never find a place where I can hide from death, even if I voyage far into space or tunnel deeply underground.

Although Buddha's Truth Body is deathless, his Emanation Bodies pass away. When Buddha Shakyamuni was about to pass away, over ten thousand Foe Destroyers, including Shariputra, chose to die because they could not bear the sorrow of having to witness Buddha's death. Then Buddha asked his disciples to make his last throne in Kushinagar, where he gave his last teaching: 'All produced phenomena are impermanent.' To those with pure karma he revealed the signs and indications of his body and then, remaining on his throne, he demonstrated how to die. Whether or not Foe Destroyers and the Emanation Bodies of Buddhas remain in this world depends upon the karma of living beings who live here. When our good karma and merit decrease, Foe Destroyers and the emanations of Buddhas become fewer and fewer.

No one alive at the time of Buddha Shakyamuni remains alive today, and no one alive at the time of Buddha's disciple, Mahakashyapa, remains alive today. Only their names survive. All those who were alive two hundred years ago have passed away, and all who live now will be gone in two hundred years' time. Meditating on these points we should ask ourself 'Could I alone outlive death?'

When our ripening karma to experience this life comes to an end, no one can prevent our death, not even Buddha. Once in ancient times two Indian clans, the Pakyepas and the Shakyapas, were waging war against one another. The king of the Pakyepas resolved to massacre all the Shakyapas, and so some of the Shakyapas took their children to Buddha for protection. Shariputra offered to protect all the children by means of his miracle powers, but with his clairvoyance Buddha could see that Shariputra would not be able to save the children because all the Shakyapas had created the collective karma to die in that war and their karma was now ripening. However, to console the Shakyapas, Buddha let Shariputra take the children. Shariputra put some of them inside Buddha's begging bowl and he hid others in the sun. Nevertheless, on the same day that the Pakyepas killed all the other Shakyapas, the children inside Buddha's begging bowl and in the sun also perished, although there was no one to inflict death upon them.

When the time of our death arrives there is no escape. If it were possible to prevent death by using clairvoyance or miracle powers, those who have possessed such powers would have become immortal; but even clairvoyants die. The most powerful monarchs who have ruled in this world have been helpless before the power of death. The king of beasts, the lion, who can kill an elephant, is immediately destroyed when he encounters the Lord of Death. Even millionaires have no way of avoiding death. They cannot distract death with a bribe and buy time, saying 'If you postpone my death I shall give you wealth beyond your wildest dreams.'

Death is relentless and will not be compromised. In *Sutra Addressed to a King* it is said that death is like the collapse of an immense mountain in all four directions. There is no way to hold back its devastation. In this Sutra, Buddha says:

Ageing is like an immovable mountain.
Decay is like an immovable mountain.
Sickness is like an immovable mountain.
Death is like an immovable mountain.

Ageing progresses surreptitiously and undermines our youth, our strength, and our beauty. Although we are hardly aware of the process, it is already underway and cannot be reversed. Sickness destroys the comfort, power, and strength of our body. If doctors help us to overcome our first illness, others take its place until, eventually, our sickness cannot be removed. In the same Sutra, Buddha says:

We cannot escape from sickness and death by running away from them. We cannot placate them with riches nor use miracle powers to make them vanish. Every single being in this world must suffer ageing, sickness, and death.

OUR LIFE SPAN CANNOT BE INCREASED AND
IT DECREASES CONTINUOUSLY

In *Guide to the Bodhisattva's Way of Life* Shantideva says:

Remaining still neither day nor night,
This life is continuously slipping away
And never increases in duration;
So why should death not come to one such as me?

From the moment of our conception we head inexorably towards death, just like a racehorse galloping towards its finishing post. Even racehorses occasionally relax their pace, but in our race towards death we never stop, not even for a second. While we are sleeping and while we are awake our life slips away. Every vehicle stops and breaks its journey from time to time, but our life span never stops running out. One moment after our birth, part of our life span has perished. We live in the very embrace of death. The seventh Dalai Lama said:

After our birth we have no freedom to remain even
   for a minute.
We head towards the embrace of the Lord of Death
   like an athlete running.
We may think that we are among the living, but our
   life is the very highway of death.

Suppose our doctor were to break the news to us that we are suffering from an incurable disease and that we have only one week left to live. If our friend were then to offer us a fantastic gift such as a diamond, a new car, or a free holiday we would not get very excited about it. Yet in reality this is our very predicament, for we are all suffering from a mortal disease. How foolish it is to become overly interested in the passing pleasures of this brief life!

If we find it difficult to meditate on death we can just listen to a clock ticking and be aware that every tick marks the end of a moment of our life and draws us closer to death. Atisha used to practise this meditation, taking the sound of drops of water as his example. Or we can imagine that the

Lord of Death lives a few miles up the road from our home, and as we listen to the clock ticking we can imagine ourself taking steps in death's direction. In this way we shall become real travellers.

In *Extensive Enjoyment Sutra* Buddha says:

These three worlds are as impermanent as autumn
   clouds.
The birth and death of beings are like the entrance
   and exit of actors on the stage.

Actors frequently change their costumes and their roles, making their entrance in many different disguises. In the same way, living beings take different forms continually and enter new worlds. Sometimes they are human beings, sometimes they are animals, and sometimes they enter hell. The Sutra continues:

The life span of a living being passes like lightning in
   the sky and perishes as quickly as water falling from a
   high mountain.

DEATH WILL COME REGARDLESS OF WHETHER OR NOT WE HAVE MADE THE TIME TO PRACTISE DHARMA

Although life is short, it would not be so bad if we had plenty of time for Dharma practice, but most of our time is taken up with sleeping, working, eating, shopping, talking, and so on, leaving very little time for pure spiritual practice. Our whole time is easily consumed by other pursuits until, suddenly, we die.

We keep thinking that we have plenty of time for Dharma practice, but if we closely examine our way of life we shall see that the days slip by without our getting down to serious practice. If we do not make the time to engage in Dharma purely, we shall look back on our life at the time of death and see that it has been of very little benefit. However, if we meditate on death we shall develop such a sincere wish to practise purely that we shall naturally begin to modify our daily routine so that it includes at least a little time for practice. Eventually we shall find more time for practice than for other things.

If we meditate on death again and again we may feel afraid; but it is not enough just to feel fear. Once we have generated an appropriate fear of dying unprepared we should search for something that will offer real protection. Gungtang Jampelyang said that the paths of future lives are very long and unfamiliar. We have to experience life after life and we cannot be sure where we shall take rebirth – whether we shall have to follow the path to unhappy states of existence or the paths to happier realms. We have no freedom or independence but must go wherever our karma takes us. Therefore we need to find something that will show us a safe way to future lives, something that will direct us along correct paths and away from wrong paths. We must make effort with our body, speech, and mind to put Dharma into practice. The possessions and enjoyments of samsara cannot help us. Only Dharma reveals a flawless path. Since it is the only possession and enjoyment that will help and protect us in the future, we must make effort with our body, speech, and mind to put it into practice. Milarepa said:

There are more fears in future lives than in this one. Have you prepared anything that will help you? If you have not prepared for your future lives, do so now. The only protection against those fears is the practice of holy Dharma.

If we think about our own life we shall see that we have spent many years with no interest in Dharma, and that even now that we have the wish to practise, still, due to laziness, we do not practise purely. Gungtang Jampelyang said:

I spent twenty years not wanting to practise Dharma. I spent the next twenty years thinking that I could practise later on. I spent another twenty years engrossed in other activities and regretting the fact that I had not engaged in Dharma practice. This is the story of my empty human life.

This could be our own autobiography, but if we meditate on death we shall avoid wasting our precious human life and we shall strive to make it meaningful.

By meditating using these three ways of reasoning we shall develop the conviction 'I shall certainly die.' Considering that at the time of death only our spiritual practice will be of any real assistance to us, we make a firm resolution 'I must practise Dharma.' When this new thought arises strongly and clearly in our mind we do placement meditation to make ourself more and more familiar with it, until we never lose it.

USING THREE WAYS OF REASONING TO GAIN CONVICTION THAT THE TIME OF DEATH IS UNCERTAIN

The three ways of reasoning are:

1 The life span of beings living in this world is not fixed
2 There are many more conditions conducive to death than to survival
3 The human body is very fragile

THE LIFE SPAN OF BEINGS LIVING IN THIS WORLD IS NOT FIXED

Sometimes we fool ourself by thinking 'I am young and so I shall not die soon', but we can see how misguided this thought is merely by observing how many young people die before their parents. Sometimes we think 'I am healthy and so I shall not die soon', but we can see that people who are healthy and looking after the sick sometimes die before their patients. People who go to visit their friends in hospital may die sooner in a car crash, for death does not confine itself to those who are aged and unwell. Someone who is alive and well in the morning could be dead by the afternoon, and someone who is well when he falls asleep may die before he wakes up. Some people die while they are eating and some people die in the middle of a conversation. Some people die as soon as they are born.

Death may not give any warning. This enemy can come at any time and often he strikes quickly, when we least expect it. He may come as we are driving to a party, or switching on our television, or as we are thinking to ourself 'I shall not die today' and making plans for our summer holidays or our retirement. The Lord of Death can creep up on us as dark clouds creep across the sky. Sometimes when we go indoors the sky is bright and clear, but when we step outside again the sky is overcast. In the same way, death can quickly cast its shadow across our life.

THERE ARE MANY MORE CONDITIONS CONDUCIVE TO DEATH THAN TO SURVIVAL

Although our death is certain and our life span is indefinite it would not be so bad if the conditions that lead to death were rare; but there are innumerable external and internal conditions that can bring about our death. It is said that there are eighty thousand types of obstacle or spirit that can destroy our vitality. All of these are conditions that could bring about our death. The external environment causes deaths by famine, floods, fires, earthquakes, pollution, and so on. In a similar way, the internal elements of our body cause death when their harmony is lost and one of them develops in excess. When the internal elements are in harmony they are said to be like four snakes of the same species and strength abiding together peacefully; but when they lose their harmony it is like one snake becoming stronger than the others and consuming them, until finally it dies of hunger itself.

Besides these inanimate causes of death, other living beings such as thieves, hostile soldiers, and wild animals can also bring about our death. Even things that we do not consider to be threatening, things that we think of as supporting and protecting our life, such as our house, our car, or our best friend, can turn out to be causes of our death. People are sometimes crushed to death by their own house or they fall to their death from their own staircase, and each day many people are killed in their cars. Some people die on holiday and some people are killed by their own hobbies and entertainments, such as horse riders who are thrown to their death. Even our friends and lovers can become causes of our death, by mistake or by intention. We read in the newspapers how lovers sometimes kill one another and how parents sometimes kill their own children. The very food we eat to nourish and sustain our life can be the cause of death. If we investigate carefully we shall not be able to find any worldly enjoyment that is not a potential cause of death and that is solely a cause of remaining alive. The Protector Nagarjuna said:

> We maintain our life in the midst of thousands of conditions that threaten death. Our life force abides like a candle flame in the breeze. The candle flame of our life is easily extinguished by the winds of death that blow from all directions.

Each person has created the karma to remain in this life for a certain period, but since we cannot remember what karma we have created we cannot know the exact duration of our present life. It is possible for us to die an untimely death before completing our life span because we can exhaust our merit sooner than we exhaust the karma that determines our life span. If this happens we become so ill that doctors cannot help us, or we find that we are unable to obtain food and other necessities to support our life. However, even when we become seriously ill, if our life span has not ended and we still have merit we can find all the conditions necessary for recovery.

In *Pile of Jewels Sutra* nine main conditions of untimely death are mentioned:

(1) Eating without moderation.
(2) Eating unwholesome food.
(3) Eating food before having properly digested our previous meal.
(4) Retaining undigested food in our stomach for a long time without eliminating.
(5) Vomiting digested food.

(6) Not taking the right medicine.

(7) Not having appropriate skills – such as trying to swim or drive a car without knowing how to.

(8) Travelling at the wrong time – such as driving through a red traffic light or jogging at noon at the height of summer in a very hot country.

(9) Indulging in sex without restraint.

Although Secret Mantra teaches methods for prolonging our life span, they work only if we practise them purely with strong faith and good concentration, and if our meditation is very powerful. Thus at present it is very difficult to extend our life span.

THE HUMAN BODY IS VERY FRAGILE

Although there are many causes of death it would not be so bad if our bodies were strong like steel, but they are delicate. It does not take guns and bombs to destroy them; they can be destroyed by a small needle. In *Friendly Letter* Nagarjuna says:

> There are many destroyers of our life force.
> Our human body is like a water bubble.

Just as a water bubble bursts as soon as it is touched, so a single drop of water in the heart or the slightest scratch from a poisonous thorn can cause our death. In the same text Nagarjuna says that at the end of this aeon the entire world system will be consumed by fire and not even its ashes will remain. Since the entire universe will become empty, there is no need to say that this delicate human body will decay most swiftly.

We can contemplate the process of our breathing and how it continues without break between inhalation and exhalation. If it were to stop, we would die. Yet even when we are asleep and have no gross mindfulness our breathing continues although, in many other respects, we resemble a corpse. Nagarjuna said 'This is a most wonderful thing!' When we wake up in the morning we should rejoice, thinking 'How

amazing it is that my breathing has sustained my life throughout sleep. If it had ceased during the night I would now be
dead!'

By meditating using these three ways of reasoning we shall
develop the conviction that the time of our death is most
uncertain and that the thought 'I shall practise Dharma when
I have finished my work' is very foolish. If we do not make
a firm decision to disengage from worldly tasks from time
to time, they will be endless. In the scriptures worldly activities are likened to the ripples on the surface of water – one
is immediately followed by another. They are like a man's
beard that grows again as soon as it is shaved. If we wait for
our worldly activities to cease before we engage in Dharma
we shall never begin our practice. This meditation causes us
to develop the firm resolution 'I must practise Dharma right
now.' When this resolution arises we should do placement
meditation to stabilize it until we never forget it.

USING THREE WAYS OF REASONING TO GAIN CONVICTION THAT AT THE TIME OF DEATH AND AFTER DEATH ONLY OUR PRACTICE OF DHARMA IS OF BENEFIT TO US

The three ways of reasoning are:

1 At the time of death our wealth cannot help us
2 At the time of death our friends and relatives
  cannot help us
3 At the time of death even our own body is of no
  use

AT THE TIME OF DEATH OUR WEALTH CANNOT HELP US

We meditate:

*Even if I were to possess all the wealth in the world, at the
time of my death it would be useless because I would not be
able to take any part of it along with me and it would not
alleviate the slightest bit of my suffering.*

165

There is a saying in Tibetan that when death comes the king who sits on a golden throne and the poor man who goes begging from town to town are both equal. In the Sutra called *Glorious Tree* Buddha says:

Even if you had enough food stocked up to last you one hundred years, when you die you will have to travel to your next life hungry. Even if you had enough clothes to last you one hundred years, when death comes you will still have to travel to your next life naked.

In *Guide to the Bodhisattva's Way of Life* Shantideva says:

I shall have to leave everything and depart alone
But, through failing to understand this,
I have committed many kinds of evil action
With respect to my friends and others.

There was once a man who was labouring very hard to cut a big round stone and make it square. A passer-by asked him 'Why are you working so hard to make this stone square?' The man replied 'I am doing this so that I can leave the stone behind.' We are just like this man because we spend so much time and put so much effort into accumulating wealth only so that we can leave it all behind when we die.

AT THE TIME OF DEATH OUR FRIENDS AND RELATIVES CANNOT HELP US

In *Guide to the Bodhisattva's Way of Life* Shantideva says:

Of what help will my companions be
When I am seized by the messengers of the Lord of Death?
At that time, only merit will protect me,
But upon that I have not relied.

We came into this world alone and we shall depart alone, and there is no one else who can take on the sufferings of our ageing and sickness and share them with us. Our friends and relatives are all equally powerless to help us at the time of our greatest need, the time of our death. Even if everyone in the world were to become our friend, no one would be able to help us at the time of our death. If they were to hold onto our limbs and clutch our head they would still be unable to hold us back from death. The most powerful people in the world have many security guards surrounding them, but no one can offer real security when the Lord of Death arrives. The great Yogi Mitatso once recited this verse to a king:

It does not matter that you are a king with great
 resources.
When it is time for you to pass on to the next life,
 you will have to go alone and in great fear.
You will have to travel without your possessions and
 wealth, without your queen, your children, or your
 servants.

The first Panchen Lama said:

When death comes it parts us from our friends and relatives so that we never meet them again. It completely destroys the chance of a reunion. There is nothing more severe than this Lord of Death.

In this life, even if we are separated from our friends and relatives for a very long time it is still possible to meet them again; but when death intervenes we are finally separated from our friends and relatives, and when we meet them again in future lives we do not recognize them and they do not recognize us.

AT THE TIME OF DEATH EVEN OUR OWN BODY
IS OF NO USE

From the time of our birth we have cherished and protected our body as our most precious possession, wrapping it up when it has been cold, anointing it with soothing cream when it has been grazed, strongly defending it whenever anyone has tried to harm it. We have such compassion for our body that we can hardly bear it to suffer any pain. If it is thirsty we can hardly endure it, and if it becomes weak and ill we feel miserable. Most of the harmful actions we have committed have been done for the sake of our own body. We carefully tend to all its needs – clothing it, feeding it, washing it, enhancing it. If someone insults our body, saying something like 'Your legs are fat' or 'Your face is like a monkey's face', we cannot stand it; but if someone says the same things about our friend's body we do not think it matters and we may even laugh. Yet this body that we cherish so dearly is treacherous. It deceives us most at the time of death, when it completely deserts us, even though we urgently need its help. The first Panchen Lama said:

This body that we have cherished for so long cheats us
at the time when we need it most.

By meditating using these three ways of reasoning we shall recognize that at the time of death, our wealth, our friends and relatives, and our own body will be of no use, and that the only thing that will really come to our aid is our pure practice of Dharma. Thus we shall become determined to practise Dharma without mixing it with the eight worldly concerns. When this resolution arises strongly and clearly in our mind we do placement meditation to make ourself more and more familiar with it until, eventually, we never lose it.

When as a result of practising these nine rounds of meditation on death we make the three resolutions firmly and clearly, we have developed a realization of death. This awareness is very important. If we try to engage in advanced practices without it, we shall naturally develop the eight worldly concerns and our practice of Dharma will be polluted with worldliness, like wholesome food mixed with poison.

If for any reason we are unable to do these meditations we should at least try to remember death many times each day. This recollection will help us to practise Dharma purely, and reduce the anxieties and irritations that come from being exclusively concerned with the welfare of this one short life. To remove delusions from our mind completely we need to realize emptiness. In the meantime this meditation on death is powerful in temporarily overcoming our delusions.

MEDITATING ON DEATH IMAGINING THAT THE TIME OF OUR DEATH HAS COME

What is death? Some people think that death is like a candle flame going out, but our death cannot be like that. When a candle flame is extinguished its continuum ceases and it completely disappears, but when we die we do not disappear. Our death is like a bird flying from its nest; our body is like the nest and our mind is like the bird. When our consciousness leaves this body we continue to experience fear and hallucinations, we suffer and still need protection. If we practise Dharma we create good habits of mind that continue into our next life. Since the continuum of our consciousness carries the mental habits we have cultivated, our Dharma practice and virtuous actions of this life can help us at the time of our death and in all our future lives.

To prepare for our death we need to meditate by imagining that the time of our death has come. This meditation, sometimes called meditation on the aspects of death, has been recommended by many Teachers, such as Je Phabongkhapa. We meditate on four aspects of death:

(1) Death is impending and will definitely come
(2) What causes death
(3) The way in which we die
(4) What happens when we are dying

We begin by contemplating a corpse or a picture of a corpse and think 'I myself shall soon be just like that.' Then we imagine that we are actually dying, and we meditate:

I shall definitely die, whether through sickness or by accident, and I shall probably die in hospital. When I become ill I shall be taken there and at first my doctor may think that he can cure me. Eventually he will give up hope and stop coming to

*see me. When my relatives find out that he has given up hope
they will feel helpless and distressed, but all they will be able
to do is weep. As I begin to die, my body will lose its warmth
and I shall start to find it difficult to breathe. My body will
become weak and shrunken and I shall not be able to hear
sounds properly or see forms clearly. If my friends and relatives are standing around me I shall not recognize them. My
tongue will become short so that I cannot speak coherently.
Gradually my memory will fade, but before it has completely
disappeared I shall realize that I am dying and become deeply
distressed. I shall think desperately 'How wonderful it would
be if I could live longer', and I shall inwardly beg my friends
and relatives to help me, but they will be completely powerless. Slowly, as the four internal elements absorb, I shall
perceive the different appearances and hallucinations. At
times I shall experience fear. My memory will become more
and more subtle until all the appearances of this life have
vanished. This will be the end of everything in this life – the
end of living in my house, the end of meeting my friends, the
end of talking to my family.*

Dying is like falling asleep. When we have died we enter
the intermediate state, or 'bardo' in Tibetan, which is like the
dream state. In the bardo we may experience hallucinations
that cause anxiety and panic. We may feel as if huge mountains are collapsing in upon us, as if we are sinking into
quicksand, as if we are trapped in the midst of a raging fire,
as if we are caught in a storm and swept away by the wind,
or as if we are drowning in a great river. If we are bound for
birth in one of the lower realms we shall perceive nightmar-
ish beings pushing us downwards. When we awake from the
bardo we perceive a new world, just as when we awake from
sleep we perceive a new day.

If we imagine over and over again that we are actually
experiencing the process of death, intermediate state, and
rebirth, our mind will change for the better. If we find it
difficult to use our imagination in this way, we can visit
cemeteries and look at the gravestones, remembering that

underneath each one lies a dead body. We can take one grave as our object of meditation. Suppose the inscription reads 'Here lies Peter. Died 21st May, 2006', we meditate:

The only difference between Peter and me is a small matter of time. In a short while I shall go where Peter has gone, and just as his body now lies here rotting in the ground, so this body of mine will soon be buried and decomposing.

In this way, we can meditate on the aspects of death. Meditations like this are especially helpful for those who find it easy to forget about spiritual practice and who find it hard to consider anything that is not immediately present.

Many other things can remind us of death. Every night on television we can watch people die. Usually we watch only to gather information or to be entertained; but if we are interested in gaining a realization of death and impermanence we can identify with the people we see dying and think 'I shall soon become just like that person.' In the same way, when we see old people on television we can think 'I shall soon become just like that person', and when we see sick people we can think 'I shall become like that.' If we practise in this way our television viewing will become very beneficial. Some things on television teach impermanence, some teach emptiness, some teach compassion, and some teach how samsara is in the nature of suffering. With Dharma wisdom we can find a teaching in everything, and all things increase our faith and our experience of Dharma. Milarepa said that he regarded everything that appeared to his mind as a Dharma book. All things confirmed the truth of Buddha's teachings and increased his spiritual experience.

The Sufferings of the
Lower Realms

MEDITATING ON THE SUFFERINGS OF THE LOWER REALMS

There is no point in meditating on the sufferings of the lower realms if we do not believe that these unfortunate states actually exist and that we ourself can experience them. Those who have pure faith in Buddha's teachings believe that rebirth exists because it was taught by Buddha. If we cannot gain conviction in this way, we need to meditate using further ways of reasoning.

One way is to investigate the opposite point of view held by many people today, and held in the past by a non-Buddhist school called Charavaka. According to this nihilistic view our death is like a candle flame going out. When we die, our body perishes and our mind ceases to exist. According to the Charavakas, death is total extinction with no continuity. They deny rebirth because they cannot distinguish between gross and subtle levels of mind and so they assume that all minds are gross minds that cease at death. It is true that gross minds, such as our ordinary waking consciousnesses, do cease temporarily at the time of death; but nihilists do not discern the most subtle level of mind that remains and continues into the next life. They conclude that all minds are gross minds that cease when we die.

Buddhist schools teach that there are many levels of consciousness: gross levels of consciousness, subtle levels of consciousness, and the very subtle level of consciousness. When we are awake our consciousness is very gross, but as we fall asleep our consciousness becomes more and more subtle until the very subtle mind of clear light arises. After a while, from the clear light of sleep the grosser minds of the dream state start to develop. When these cease, the very gross minds of the waking state manifest again. In a similar way, as we die our gross minds absorb until the most subtle type of mind arises. At the last moment of the process of dying the mind that remains is the very subtle mind that passes to the next life. After the clear light of death has ceased we develop the grosser minds of the bardo, or intermediate state, which is like the dream state; and out of the bardo we develop the mind of our next life.

The gradual absorption of the grosser levels of consciousness and their re-emergence occurs with every cycle of day and night as we fall asleep and re-awaken, and it occurs with every cycle of death and rebirth as we pass out of one life and enter another. If we carefully examine the process of falling asleep and re-awakening we shall understand how the various levels of consciousness absorb into the very subtle mind and then re-emerge, and we shall see that there is no basis for the view that denies rebirth. We shall realize that our mind is like a tourist that stays temporarily in the resort of this life and then moves on to other lives.

Meditating on the sufferings of the lower realms has many purposes, but the main purpose is to develop a very strong desire never to take rebirth in those unfortunate states. This desire is one of the main causes of going for refuge. Through going for refuge we can actually gain protection from the danger of rebirth in the three lower realms. Going for refuge is the foundation of all Buddhist practices.

In *Friendly Letter* Nagarjuna says that every day we should meditate on the sufferings of hell beings, hungry spirits, and animals. By engaging in this meditation we develop the wish 'How wonderful it would be if I did not ever again have to take rebirth in the lower realms. How wonderful it would be if in my future lives I were to take rebirth only as a human being or a god.' Another reason for meditating on the sufferings of the lower realms is to reduce our pride, because we cannot be sure that we shall not be reborn there.

This meditation also increases our compassion. When we meditate on the sufferings of beings who inhabit the three lower realms we naturally feel compassion for them. If we never accustom our minds to compassion by meditating on these very intense forms of suffering, how shall we ever learn to feel compassion for beings who experience more subtle kinds of misery? Unless we make an effort to develop compassion for those who experience the pains of unfortunate states of existence we shall not be able to develop the realization of great compassion encompassing all beings who are caught within samsara. Since great compassion is what motivates a Mahayanist to attain enlightenment for the sake of others, we can appreciate how important it is to engage in this present meditation. The meditation has three parts:

1 The sufferings of hell beings
2 The sufferings of hungry spirits
3 The sufferings of animals

THE SUFFERINGS OF HELL BEINGS

This has two parts:

1 Gaining conviction that hell exists
2 The actual meditation on the sufferings of hell beings

GAINING CONVICTION THAT HELL EXISTS

Although we may have conviction in rebirth we may still have doubts as to whether or not hell exists. Therefore, before meditating on the pains of hell we need to become certain that such pains actually exist, and that we ourself could experience them.

Hell is an unpopular subject in the West. When we hear someone talking about it we feel embarrassed. When someone argues that hell is a mere superstition we feel reassured, and it seems to us that this view accords with common sense. However, since the issue is so important we should not conclude that hell does not exist unless we can base this view on perfectly valid reasoning. It is clearly unreasonable to conclude that hell does not exist merely because it is unpopular. Old age is also an unpopular subject, and if we say to an old man 'You are still young!' he will be delighted and inclined to believe this falsehood. If we say 'How old you are!' he will feel miserable and think of ways of denying this manifest truth. Yet, whether he likes it or not, he is undeniably old.

If we say 'Hell does not exist because I do not like the idea', this reasoning is incorrect because it does not follow that whatever I do not like does not exist. For example, I do not like my enemy, but if I conclude that my enemy does not exist I am liable to be harmed in a surprise attack. From this we can see how foolish it is to say 'I do not care to believe in the existence of hell.' Those who do not believe in hell often regard those who do as very simple-minded. If we check, however, we shall see that it is their own view that is foolish.

We need carefully to investigate the reasoning of those who deny the existence of hell. They may say 'If a place exists it must be possible to discover its location in this world, but if we search for it we cannot find hell in this world.' This reasoning is unsound because it does not follow that if something exists it must exist as an object of human eye consciousness. For example, there are many planets and galaxies that we cannot perceive with our eye consciousness, and yet they do exist and people believe in them. Many people accept that worlds other than their own exist. Buddhists believe in other realms such as the god realm, Christians believe in heaven, and some scientists believe in other universes; but if we search this world with all the elaborate technology at our disposal we shall not perceive these myriad other worlds.

Even in this world many things exist that we cannot see. Some people find it easy to accept the existence of beings who inhabit this world and yet are unseen by us; beings such as ghosts, spirits, and guardian angels. So why should it be so hard to accept the existence of hell beings?

We should ask anyone who believes in the non-existence of hell to present a perfect method for realizing its non-existence. It would be wonderful if they could do this. Unfortunately no such method exists – but there are many correct reasons that establish the existence of hell.

If we attain a realization of the union of the two truths – conventional truth and ultimate truth – it is easy to gain an incontrovertible realization of the existence of hidden objects such as hell. In the meantime we can gain confidence in the correct view by using reasonings that we can readily understand. These reasonings are of two types:

1 Reasoning using external signs
2 Reasoning using internal signs

REASONING USING EXTERNAL SIGNS

Some human beings in this world occasionally experience sufferings that are like the sufferings of hell. For example, victims of torture are sometimes subjected to severe electric shocks for long periods of time, or they are hung up and flogged so that their skin splits open, or they are slowly burnt like meat. Sometimes water is forced into their nostrils or their eyes are gouged out. Elsewhere people are dying slowly of famine and drought, and in places where wars are being fought some people become like the inhabitants of the reviving hells who experience terrible suffering inflicted by weapons. Some people become like beings in the hot hells, who are trapped in the midst of boiling metal and raging fire.

When people experience these sufferings they inhabit what is known as a 'resembling' or 'occasional' hell, so called because their environment temporarily resembles an environment of hell. The existence of resembling hells is a sign indicating the existence of actual hell. Just as an osprey circling above water indicates that there are fish in the water below, and just as a volcanic eruption indicates fire beneath the surface of the earth, so resembling hells in this world indicate the existence of actual hell elsewhere.

REASONING USING INTERNAL SIGNS

This has three parts:

1 Considering the law of karma in general
2 Considering dreams
3 Considering how the world as it appears to us depends upon karma

CONSIDERING THE LAW OF KARMA IN GENERAL

Most people, whether or not they are religious, believe that we should engage in virtuous actions and avoid actions that are harmful. If we understand the general law of karma – that good actions produce good results and bad actions produce bad results – we shall understand how hell exists; for hell is the painful, terrifying world that is experienced as a result of the most destructive kinds of bad action.

CONSIDERING DREAMS

This line of reasoning is very helpful because it is based on our own immediate experience. When we have nightmares we find ourself in very hostile environments, such as places full of fire. We try to escape, but no matter how fast we run we are still surrounded by fire. Dreams like this are not meaningless. They refer to experiences we have had in this life or in past lives, or to experiences we shall have in the future. Dreams that refer to experiences we have had in past lives arise from the karmic imprints that remain in our mind from actions committed in past lives. Dreams that refer to experiences we have had in this life arise from karmic imprints remaining in our mind from actions committed in this life. Dreams that refer to future experiences also arise from our karmic potentialities. A dream that we are in a land full of fire may indicate that in the past we were born in hell, or it may predict a hellish rebirth in the future. Similarly, if we dream that we are flying in the sky, this could indicate that we were born as a bird in one of our previous lives, or it could indicate that in the past we attained tranquil abiding, or it could predict either of these things for the future.

When we are dreaming, the world of our dreams seems as real as our waking world. If we do not wake up from our nightmare we become a hell being. Yet we feel that dreams are false and that the phenomena we perceive while we are awake are truly existent. In both respects we are wrong, for there is not a single phenomenon that is truly existent, and our dream experiences are as real as any of them. As Buddha Shakyamuni said 'All phenomena are like dreams.'

CONSIDERING HOW THE WORLD AS IT APPEARS TO US
DEPENDS UPON KARMA

When we die, the world that we now experience with our sense consciousnesses will become non-existent, and the world that will appear to us when we take rebirth will be entirely new. If we understand this we shall see that the different worlds do not exist inherently. The way in which our world appears to us depends upon our mind. A pure mind experiences a pure world and an impure mind experiences an impure world. Of all impure worlds, hell is the worst. It is the world that appears to the very worst kind of mind. The world of a hungry spirit is less impure, and the world of animals is less impure again. The world that appears to human beings is less impure than the world that appears to animals, and the world that appears to gods is less impure than the world that appears to human beings. A mind that is completely pure will perceive the world as a Buddha Land, the pure environment of a Buddha.

The same object can be perceived differently by different beings. Milarepa saw his Spiritual Guide, Marpa, as Buddha Vajradhara, whereas ordinary people saw him as an ordinary man with long earrings who drank beer, had a wife, ploughed the fields, and engaged in business. When he gave Dharma teachings Marpa even used to ask for money. He once kicked Milarepa and said 'Haven't you bothered to bring offerings for this empowerment?' Milarepa was able to develop faith in Marpa because he saw him as a pure being.

We can see for ourself that sometimes people develop strong attachment towards someone whom everyone else regards as being very ugly. The person who has attachment sees the object of attachment as beautiful, and this appearance is true for them. We cannot say that one appearance of the object is false and the other is true, because for each appearance there is an observer for whom that appearance is true.

We all have many experiences that others cannot verify by means of their own perceptions. For example, if in my dream last night I flew in the sky, the fact that no one else saw me does not prove that I did not experience flying last night. The experience was real for my own mind and therefore the experience exists. If this is so, how can we possibly invalidate the experience of hell? Living beings are extremely diverse and their experiences are as diverse as the minds that create them.

Perhaps at this very moment hell beings are debating whether or not the human world exists. One may be saying 'The human realm does not exist because I cannot see it.' Others may be saying 'If we create enough merit we shall take rebirth in the human realm and see it for ourself.'

By meditating on these points we shall understand the diversity of karmic appearances and we shall become convinced that it is impossible to disprove the existence of hell.

THE ACTUAL MEDITATION ON THE SUFFERINGS
OF HELL BEINGS

Meditation on the sufferings of hell beings has four parts:

1 The sufferings of beings in the great hells
2 The sufferings of beings in the neighbouring hells
3 The sufferings of beings in the cold hells
4 The sufferings of beings in the resembling hells

THE SUFFERINGS OF BEINGS IN THE GREAT HELLS

The great hells, or hot hells, are located many miles beneath our earth. In these hells the whole environment is pervaded by fire. The ground is composed of blazing hot iron, the sky is covered by a raging fire, and all around there are walls of scorching iron. Within this hostile environment there are eight specific hot hells. They are: the Reviving Hell, the Black Line Hell, the Massed Destruction Hell, the Wailing Hell, the Loud Wailing Hell, the Hot Hell, the Intensely Hot Hell, and the Unceasing Torment Hell. The suffering of the beings who inhabit the Black Line Hell is greater than the sufferings of the beings who inhabit the Reviving Hell, the suffering of the beings who inhabit the Massed Destruction Hell is greater still, and so on. The greatest suffering is experienced by those who inhabit the Unceasing Torment Hell.

Rebirth in the Reviving Hell is taken as a result of beings having killed out of hatred or aggression. In this hell they are born amongst horrifying beings who are continuously attacking each other. Due to their heavy negative karma many horrendous weapons spontaneously appear. With these weapons they pierce and lacerate each other's bodies, slashing them into many pieces. As each piece of flesh falls onto the red hot iron ground it experiences excruciating pain. Eventually the beings die, but only to hear terrifying voices commanding them to revive, and without choice they find themselves born again into a reviving hell. In this way they die and are revived many times each day until their negative karma is exhausted.

In the Black Line Hell the beings are seized by merciless torturers who force them to lie down on the hot iron ground. Their bodies are stretched out like sheets of tarpaulin while the torturers brand them with a criss-cross of black lines. They then experience excruciating torment as their bodies are slowly cut along those lines with burning weapons such as axes, knives, and saws.

In the Massed Destruction Hell the beings are crushed between huge iron mountains that resemble the heads of animals they have killed in the past. They are crushed until all the blood in their bodies is squeezed out. Sometimes they are smashed by a rain of enormous rocks falling from the sky until their bodies are reduced to paste. At other times their bodies are rolled flat by red hot rollers or ground to a pulp in huge iron presses. Throughout all of this, every atom of their flesh and blood is permeated by pain.

In the Wailing Hell the beings are driven by fear to search for a safe place. Eventually they find an iron house, but as soon as they enter the doors slam shut and the house bursts into flames. As their bodies are incinerated they howl and wail in agony, but there is no escape from their prison of fire.

In the Loud Wailing Hell the beings experience sufferings similar to those in the Wailing Hell, except that the pain is even more intense. They are born in an ocean of boiling liquid. Grotesque torturers push them to the bottom with razor-sharp spears and smash them with clubs when they resurface.

In the Hot Hell the beings are fried like fish on red-hot metal. Huge skewers are thrust into their bodies and they are beaten to a pulp on the blazing iron ground. Flames issue from every orifice of their bodies.

In the Intensely Hot Hell the beings are impaled on flaming tridents and their bodies are encased in red-hot metal. They are boiled in cauldrons of molten copper until the flesh falls away from their bones. Then their skeletons are laid out on the blazing ground until their flesh grows back and once again they are hurled into the boiling cauldron.

The Unceasing Torment Hell is the most horrific of all the hells. Huge balls of fire rain down upon the inhabitants, burning every tissue of their bodies until they resemble only a mass of raging flames. Only by their agonizing screams can they be recognized as living beings.

If we are born in these hells we have to spend countless aeons experiencing suffering until our karma is exhausted.

THE SUFFERINGS OF BEINGS IN THE NEIGHBOURING HELLS

Surrounding each of the great hells are the neighbouring hells: the Pit of Fiery Ash, the Swamp of Excrement, the Plain of Razors, the Forest of Sword-leaf Trees, the Mountain of Abrasive Trees, and the Acid River. In the first of these, the inhabitants have to walk through a pit of fiery ash. As their legs sink into the red-hot ashes their skin and flesh are burned away, only to grow back again so that they experience the same torment over and over again. In the Swamp of Excrement the beings drown in a filthy quagmire that resembles rotting corpses. Tiny insects burrow into their bodies, right through to the marrow, causing them excruciating pain. In the Plain of Razors the ground is covered with razor-sharp blades. As the inhabitants walk barefoot over this ground, their feet are cut to shreds. In the Forest of

Sword-leaf Trees the beings are dismembered by razor-sharp leaves that fall from the trees. As they lie wounded on the ground, vicious dogs come and tear the flesh from their bodies. In the Mountain of Abrasive Trees the beings are driven by attachment to seek attractive objects at the top of trees. As they climb, their limbs are ripped and shredded by jagged thorns that protrude downwards. When they reach the top, the object they are seeking disappears and reappears on the ground. As they descend, their limbs are once again torn open by the jagged thorns that have now turned upwards. As they struggle to free themselves from the trees, ferocious birds with iron beaks peck out their eyes. In the Acid River the beings are cast into a river of molten lava and carried along by a very strong current. If they try to scramble out of the river, cruel tormentors on the banks push them back in with hooked sticks.

THE SUFFERINGS OF BEINGS IN THE COLD HELLS

Below the hot hells there are the eight cold hells: the Blistering Hell, the Bursting Blister Hell, the 'Achoo' Hell, the Moaning Hell, the Chattering Teeth Hell, the Cracking Like an Upala Hell, the Cracking Like a Lotus Hell, and the Great Cracking Like a Lotus Hell.

In these hells the ground is solid ice surrounded on all sides by huge mountains of ice. It is pitch black and a terrifying blizzard blows continuously. The inhabitants of these hells are naked. Their wretched bodies shrivel up as they hunch, shivering helplessly in the bitter cold. Hideous blisters form on their skin, and as they burst horrible pus seeps out of them. They wail and moan, making the sound 'Achoo', and their teeth chatter uncontrollably. Through contact with the cold their bodies turn blue and crack open like an upala flower. Then they turn red and crack open like a lotus flower. Finally their bodies become so cold that they crack into pieces.

THE SUFFERINGS OF BEINGS IN THE RESEMBLING HELLS

We can meditate on the sufferings of the resembling hells either by using examples that are given in the scriptures or by using examples that we can see for ourself on television or read about in the newspapers. For instance, when an aeroplane crashes and fire breaks out the passengers become like beings in the Wailing Hell, feeling that they are trapped inside a scorching iron house. In winter when people die of exposure their suffering is like the suffering of a cold hell. When people are crushed to death in an earthquake their suffering is like the suffering of the Massed Destruction Hell.

In the scriptures the following example is given. When Buddha Shakyamuni was living in India, a merchant called Million Ear (so called because he wore ear ornaments worth a million gold coins) once arranged with his friends to visit an island. Since he was the first to arrive at their meeting point on the seashore he decided to take a short nap, but when he awoke he found that his friends had departed without him. He tried to make his own way to the island but he got lost and ended up on the wrong island. On this island there was a splendid mansion. When night fell Million Ear could see a man inside being served by four exquisitely beautiful goddesses. All night long this man enjoyed himself with the four goddesses, but when day came the mansion turned into a fiery furnace and the goddesses turned into ferocious dogs savaging the man. When night fell again, the scene changed. The furnace turned back into a splendid mansion and the dogs became goddesses delighting the man.

When Million Ear returned to the mainland he asked Buddha to explain the meaning of what he had seen. Buddha told him that the mansion was a resembling hell, and he said: 'That man was once a butcher. My disciple Katyayana tried to persuade him to take a vow against killing, but the man was afraid that if he took such a vow he would not be able to support himself and his wife. Katyayana skilfully enquired "Could you abandon killing during the night?" and the butcher realized that he could certainly abandon killing while he was asleep, and so he took a vow not to kill after dark. As a result he did not have to take rebirth in one of the actual hells, but he took rebirth in this resembling hell. During the daytime he experiences the pains of hell as a result of his actions of killing during the day, but at night he enjoys great happiness as a result of keeping his vow purely after dark.'

THE SUFFERINGS OF HUNGRY SPIRITS

In general, hungry spirits have greater mental capacity than animals. Some are very powerful, some can see the future, some even have miracle powers and contaminated clairvoyance with which they help or harm human beings, and some can understand Dharma if it is explained to them. However they all have a greater degree of suffering than animals.

The location of hungry spirits varies. They can visit and be seen in the human realm. On one occasion a novice monk whose mother had been dead for many years saw a hungry spirit and was so frightened that he turned and fled, but the hungry spirit called after him 'Please, my son, do not run away.' When he heard these words, the monk stopped and asked 'Who are you?', and the spirit answered 'I gave you birth, my son. I have been a hungry spirit for twenty-five years and in all that time I have not been able to find any food or even a drop to drink.' Then this hungry spirit began to cry. The monk was moved by compassion for his mother and so he requested Buddha, 'Please help my mother for she has been reborn as a hungry spirit.' Although Buddha made prayers, as a result of the harmful actions she had committed in the past, when this hungry spirit died she took another rebirth as a hungry spirit. The only difference was that this time she was wealthy, but since she had been so miserly in the past she was unable to give anything away to others. When her son realized that she had taken rebirth again as a hungry spirit he practised generosity for her sake. He offered a beautiful cloth to Buddha, but his mother stole it and returned it to him. Again the monk offered the cloth to Buddha and again his mother stole it back, thinking that it was wasteful to give the cloth to Buddha. Her mind was so well acquainted with miserliness that she repeated this compulsive theft six times.

Once a Teacher called Buddhajana visited the realm of hungry spirits. He met a female spirit there who said to him 'My husband went to the human world twelve years ago to try to find food, but he has not returned and during that time I and my children have had nothing to eat or drink. If you meet my husband when you are back in the human world, please ask him to come home.' Buddhajana said 'There are many hungry spirits wandering about in the human world. How will I be able to recognize your husband?' The spirit replied 'My husband has only got one eye and his right arm is shorter than his left.' When Buddhajana was back in the human realm he offered special cakes to hungry spirits. Since his concentration was so powerful they were able to come and receive his offerings. One day Buddhajana recognized the husband among those who came, and he said 'Your wife and children have not been able to find food for twelve years. Your wife asks you to return home soon.' The hungry spirit said 'I am very keen to see my family. For twelve years I have been wandering in this human world trying to find food, but all I have been able to find is this.' He opened the palm of his hand and showed the Teacher some dried spit, and said 'I managed to obtain this only through the great kindness of one monk who made a dedication as he was spitting. This is the only fruit that I shall take home from my long search.'

In general there are six kinds of suffering that hungry spirits experience:

1 Intense heat
2 Intense cold
3 Intense hunger
4 Intense thirst
5 Great fatigue
6 Great fear

In addition, they experience three particular kinds of suffering: external hindrances, internal hindrances, and hindrances to obtaining food and drink.

Hungry spirits can see human food from a distance, but when they approach it it disappears and they have to experience the anguish of disappointment. The only way that they can actually obtain human food is by its being especially dedicated for them. While they search for food they experience constant anxiety, fearing that any food or drink they see will be snatched away from them before they can lay hold of it.

Hungry spirits also experience particular sufferings because of their peculiar shape. Their throats are blocked so that even when they obtain food they can swallow it only with great difficulty. Their bodies are huge and ugly, with large, distended bellies and emaciated limbs. Their necks are very thin and their heads are enormous and heavy. When they try to move about, their legs can hardly support their bodies. They live in a desert where it is almost impossible to find water. They resemble human beings who are dying of extreme hunger and thirst.

Hungry spirits wander for years in search of food, and when they find it and swallow it, it becomes like fire in their stomachs and this fire flares out through all their orifices. Some scriptures say that the sparks of fire seen in the desert are the fire of tormented hungry spirits.

THE SUFFERINGS OF ANIMALS

In general there are five kinds of suffering that animals experience:

1 Ignorance and stupidity
2 Heat and cold
3 Hunger and thirst
4 Exploitation by human beings for labour, food, resources, and entertainment
5 Being prey to one another

In addition, they experience particular sufferings according to the environment in which they live. Some animals live close to human beings and others live in very distant places where there are no human beings, such as in the depths of the ocean or in polar regions. In these places it is dark, there is no sunshine, and the animal populations are packed densely together.

There was once a man who killed many animals and offered them to Ishvara. Later, his business became very successful and so when the time of his death came he advised his son to follow his example and make many sacrifices so that he too would enjoy a profitable business. This man then died and took rebirth as a bull, and his son dutifully took the bull and slaughtered it as an offering to Ishvara. The bull then took rebirth as an ox and, obedient to his father's advice, the son took the ox and slaughtered it as another offering to Ishvara. In this way the son butchered his father seven times.

The father of a Bonpo family once took rebirth as a worm inside a patch of cow dung. Milarepa said to the son of the family, 'Your father has been reborn as a worm. If you do not believe me, I will show you.' He then took the boy to the cow dung and told him to look inside. When the worm was discovered, Milarepa blessed it, and it jumped over its son; and then the boy believed what he had been told.

We have to ask ourself 'What would I do if I were reborn as an ox for the slaughter or as a worm inside a patch of cow dung? In such a limited condition it would be extremely difficult for me to find release from lower rebirths.' It is said that it is easier to become enlightened once we have achieved a human form than it is to achieve a human rebirth again once we have fallen into the lower realms.

When we meditate on the sufferings of the lower realms we should imagine that we ourself are actually experiencing these sufferings. We should identify closely with these experiences, remembering that we have had them in the past and that we have created the causes to experience them again in the future. We do the meditations imagining that the time of our own death has come, and that we have taken rebirth in these painful states; and we meditate in detail upon the miseries of our new condition.

By meditating on the sufferings of the lower realms we are doing the analytical meditation that causes us to develop fear of such misfortunes and a sincere wish never to experience them in the future. When this wish arises clearly in our mind we stop our analytical meditation and do placement meditation to become more and more familiar with it.

Going for Refuge

It is common to assume that the happiness of this life is more important than the happiness of future lives, but if we consider carefully we shall see that the happiness of future lives must be more important because this life is brief whereas future lives are many and long. We work so hard and put so much effort into securing happiness for ourself later on in this life, but it makes more sense to work as hard as we can to prepare for future lives. We are certain to experience these, whereas the future of this life is very uncertain. We make plans for our holidays and years of retirement, and yet our future life may come sooner. Our future life is not far away. We do not have to travel great distances or climb high mountains to find it, for only one breath separates us from it. As soon as our breath fails, our future life has begun.

If someone were to ask us 'Which do you think is more worthwhile, immediate happiness that is short-lived, or future happiness that is long-lasting?', we would all choose future, long-lasting happiness. Therefore, if we are wise, we shall understand how important it is to ensure the welfare of our future lives.

We do not like to think about death and sickness and the problems and pains of this life, and we regard these as the greatest dangers. However, Buddha said that losing our moral discipline is much more dangerous than dying, because our death destroys only this present life whereas the actions we commit when we lose our moral discipline endanger all our future lives. In his *Advice* Atisha says:

Vajradhara

Tilopa

Naropa

Since future lives last for a very long time, gather up riches to provide for the future.

Atisha's advice is to practise giving and moral discipline, which are the main causes of gaining higher rebirth. These are the best insurance policies for future happiness. Both the young and the old need to take this advice to heart.

The actual methods for gaining the happiness of higher states of existence are:

1 Going for refuge, the gateway to Buddhadharma
2 Gaining conviction in the law of karma, the root of all good qualities and happiness

GOING FOR REFUGE, THE GATEWAY TO BUDDHADHARMA

Going for refuge is defined as a strong desire to go for refuge to the Three Jewels, arising in dependence upon fear of any of the sufferings of samsara and faith in the Three Jewels. If we just recite a prayer of going for refuge without having this aspiration we are not actually going for refuge.

In *Very White Superior Intention Questions* Je Tsongkhapa put many questions to Tibetan meditators. Later, the first Panchen Lama wrote a text containing answers to these questions. The following is his answer to the question 'What is the actual nature of going for refuge?'

Dreading samsara, I realized that the Three Jewels have complete power to give protection. With fear and faith, if we go for refuge sincerely to the Three Jewels, this is the actual nature of going for refuge. You, Omniscient Tsongkhapa, know this.

There are three ways of going for refuge: the refuge of a small being, the refuge of a middle being, and the refuge of a great being. A small being goes for refuge motivated principally by fear of the sufferings of the lower realms. A middle being goes for refuge motivated principally by fear of any kind of uncontrolled rebirth. A great being goes for refuge motivated principally by great compassion, feeling unable to bear the thought that others must suffer the miseries of samsara. Whereas a middle being fears his or her own future suffering, a great being fears the future suffering of all living beings and desires to release all of them from samsaric rebirth. The refuge of a great being is also known as 'Mahayana refuge'.

Only people who have Dharma wisdom fear lower rebirth or any kind of samsaric rebirth. People who have not developed any level of spiritual aspiration fear death more than rebirth. The Kadampa Teacher Geshe Potowa said:

It is not death that I fear so much as rebirth, for death is in the very nature of our rebirth.

To be born within samsara is to suffer birth, ageing, sickness, and death. We cannot become free from these until we abandon samsara.

Although an ordinary small being is concerned only for the welfare of this life, such a being sometimes develops the wish to find protection from fear and suffering. With this wish, if an ordinary small being goes for refuge to the Buddha Jewel he or she will receive benefit. In eastern Tibet a man was once caught by a tiger, but he went for refuge to Avalokiteshvara and was immediately released from danger. The scriptures give many similar examples of people who have been rescued from danger by going for refuge to Tara. The refuge of an ordinary small being is a type of refuge, but it is not perfect refuge. If we are to go for refuge perfectly we need to be motivated at least by concern for the welfare of future lives.

Each way of going for refuge has two levels: simple and special. A small being goes for simple refuge when, motivated by fear of the sufferings of the lower realms and faith in the Three Jewels, he or she sincerely requests the objects of refuge, 'Please protect me from rebirth in the three lower realms.' This request can either be made inwardly or by reciting a prayer of going for refuge. This is the most common way of going for refuge.

A small being with more wisdom and greater familiarity with Dharma will first develop fear of the sufferings of the lower realms, and will then consider what provides real protection against them. By careful investigation he or she will realize that perfect protection can be found only by gaining all the realizations of the stages of the path of a small being. He or she will become determined, 'With the help of the Buddha Jewel and the Sangha Jewel I must realize the Dharma Jewel of a small being.' This determination is the special way of going for refuge of a small being.

The realizations of the stages of the path of a small being are the Dharma Jewel of a small being. If we gain this Dharma Jewel we shall be held back from rebirth in the lower realms because this Dharma Jewel directly eliminates such future sufferings by removing their causes. Neither the Buddha Jewel nor the Sangha Jewel can take away our suffering directly in the way that someone can remove a thorn from our flesh.

Strictly speaking, Dharma Jewels are possessed only by Superior beings; but it is very beneficial for us to regard all our Dharma experiences, no matter how small, as if they were real Dharma Jewels. In this way, if we value our small spiritual achievements we shall protect and nurture them so that they will eventually grow into the actual Dharma Jewels of a Superior being. However, if we disregard our small achievements we shall easily become discouraged and we shall tend to neglect the practices of purification and accumulating merit. With a disparaging attitude towards our first spiritual experiences there is no way we can develop more profound realizations.

In the *Condensed Perfection of Wisdom Sutra* Buddha says:

Continuous drops of water falling into a pot will make it full. First there is one drop, then two, three, four . . . until the pot is overflowing.

Our Dharma realizations develop in the same way. The Dharma Jewels of Superior beings do not appear all at once but develop gradually. First there is some small experience of moral discipline and other virtues and insights, and these increase until they become real Dharma Jewels. Buddha Shakyamuni said:

I shall prostrate to the new moon and not to the full moon.

The 'new moon' refers to the first realizations that we develop and the 'full moon' refers to the advanced and qualified realizations of Superior beings. Buddha's meaning is that since great realizations arise in dependence upon small ones we should protect and honour our first experiences of Dharma.

By developing Dharma Jewels within our own mind we are protected from future suffering because the function of a Dharma Jewel is to eliminate the cause of suffering. It gives us temporary help and ultimately it leads us to liberation and full enlightenment. For example, if we gain continuous mindfulness of death, this will help us temporarily by reducing our desirous attachment and other delusions, and it will help us ultimately by leading us to meditate on emptiness and attain liberation.

A middle being goes for simple refuge when, motivated by fear of the sufferings of samsara and faith in the Three Jewels, he or she sincerely requests the objects of refuge, 'Please protect me from the miseries of samsaric rebirth.' A middle being with more wisdom and greater familiarity with Dharma will first develop fear of the sufferings of samsara, and will then consider what provides real protection. By careful investigation he or she will realize that perfect protection can be found only by gaining all the realizations of the stages of the path of a middle being. He or she will become determined, 'With the help of the Buddha Jewel and the Sangha Jewel I must realize the Dharma Jewel of a middle being.' This determination is the special way of going for refuge of a middle being.

The realizations of all the stages of the path of a middle being are the Dharma Jewel of a middle being. In particular, the realizations of the three higher trainings directly eliminate the causes of uncontrolled rebirth and provide direct protection against the miseries of samsara.

In a similar way, a great being goes for either simple refuge or special refuge. A great being who goes for special refuge first develops great compassion, wishing to release and protect all living beings from the pains of samsara. He or she then considers how to do this, and realizes that it is only by attaining enlightenment that he or she will be able to offer guidance and protection to others. Therefore, he or she develops the determination to realize the Dharma Jewel of a great being – in particular the ultimate realization of enlightenment. This determination is the special way of going for refuge of a great being. It is known as 'going for resultant refuge'.

The explanation of going for refuge is in seven parts:

1 The causes of going for refuge
2 The objects of refuge
3 The way of going for refuge
4 The measurement of going for refuge perfectly
5 The benefits of going for refuge
6 The commitments of going for refuge
7 How to go for refuge by practising three rounds of meditation

THE CAUSES OF GOING FOR REFUGE

It has already been explained that the causes of going for refuge are fear of suffering and faith in the Three Jewels as perfect sources of protection. Since faith does not arise spontaneously in our mind we need to cultivate it by meditating on the good qualities of the Three Jewels.

THE OBJECTS OF REFUGE

This has two parts:

1 Identifying the objects of refuge
2 Understanding why the Three Jewels are suitable objects of refuge

IDENTIFYING THE OBJECTS OF REFUGE

The objects to which we go for refuge are the Three Jewels:

1 The Buddha Jewel
2 The Dharma Jewel
3 The Sangha Jewel

THE BUDDHA JEWEL

The Three Jewels are explained extensively by Maitreya in *Sublime Continuum of the Great Vehicle*. There the Buddha Jewel is defined as the ultimate source of refuge having eight good qualities, such as non-produced. The eight good qualities are given in one verse:

Non-produced and effortlessly attained,
Not realized by the conditions of others,
Having wisdom, compassion, and power;
Only Buddha possesses the two purposes.

'Non-produced' refers to the qualities of abandonment of a Buddha. Specifically it refers to the true cessations that are the abandonment of the two obstructions – delusion-obstructions and obstructions to omniscience. Since these true cessations are permanent they are called 'non-produced'. Since the two obstructions are the source of all faults, being free from them Buddha is free from all faults.

'Effortlessly attained' means that Buddhas accomplish everything effortlessly because they are free from conceptual thought. They do not need to develop a motivation, thinking 'Now I will do this.' To accomplish anything, beings other than Buddhas first have to develop a motivation and then exert effort. In this world there are many great oceans, lakes, rivers, and other places where water gathers. When the moon shines and the sky is clear the moon's reflection appears effortlessly on the surfaces of all these waters. Just as the moon needs no motivation to appear there, so it is with Buddhas. Whenever we visualize the Buddhas in front of us our mind becomes like water on a clear, moonlit night, and the Buddhas appear in front of us without effort. They do not have to make up their minds to travel there from a far distant place.

'Not realized by the conditions of others' means that Buddhas have special good qualities of body, speech, and mind that cannot be comprehended by other beings. For example, Buddhas can manifest as anything that is needed to help living beings. They can emanate as men, as women, or even as inanimate objects – but how they develop emanations is beyond our understanding. Shantideva said that to those who wish for islands, Buddhas manifest as islands, and to those who wish for boats, Buddhas manifest as boats. Buddhas manifest as clothes, as medicine, or as food for those who need them.

Once Tara manifested as an island called Chandradeva to help a man called Chandragomin. Chandragomin was very handsome and a highly respected scholar. A princess called Tara fell in love with him and so her father ordered him to marry her. At first he accepted, but later he began to feel uneasy because his own personal Deity was Tara and he felt it would be inappropriate to marry a princess by the same name. When he refused to marry the princess, her father became enraged and he commanded his men to throw Chandragomin into the river Ganges. As he was being swept away, Chandragomin went for refuge to Tara and prayed to her. In response, Tara manifested as an island and received him onto her shores. Chandragomin lived there for a long time and built a temple. Today there is quite a big town on the island, but ordinary people see the island as an ordinary place and do not realize that it was manifested by Tara, for such a thing is beyond their comprehension.

The good qualities of a Buddha's speech also cannot be comprehended by others. Je Tsongkhapa said that if all the beings in this world were to gather together at the same time and put questions to Buddha in their own language, with only one word Buddha would be able to answer all their questions in all their different languages.

The volume of a Buddha's speech remains the same at every distance. Buddha Shakyamuni's disciple Maudgalyanaputra once decided to test this quality of his speech. While Buddha was giving a discourse he first listened at his feet and then went a mile away and listened again, and the voice sounded exactly the same. He then went a thousand miles away and listened, and the voice sounded exactly the same. By means of his miracle powers he then went to another universe and listened, and the voice sounded exactly the same. As he returned closer and closer to Buddha the voice was everywhere the same as it had been when he was sitting at Buddha's feet. This wonderful quality of a Buddha's speech is incomprehensible to other beings.

'Wisdom' refers to a quality of a Buddha's mind that directly cognizes all phenomena clearly without confusing them. Without such direct awareness it is difficult really to benefit others effectively. Unlike other beings, Buddhas can directly cognize all objects of knowledge because only Buddhas have eliminated the two obstructions. Although the mind of every being is clear in nature, its clarity is obstructed, like a clear sky overcast by clouds. When these cloud-like obstructions are completely eliminated, our mind directly cognizes all phenomena and we become a Buddha.

It is hard for us to understand another person's state of mind, even that of our best friend or our own child. We cannot see another's intention, whether they wish to harm us or whether they really mean us well. Only Buddhas know the minds of other beings. On one occasion Buddha Shakyamuni was requested to demonstrate his clairvoyance. He consented, and all the people in a large assembly were asked to write their name on a piece of paper, fold it, and put it into a sack. This sack was so heavy that an elephant had to be used to transport it. When Buddha received the names he returned each one to the right person. We ourself would be lucky to be able to do this with only a few names.

'Compassion' refers to a Buddha's great compassion for all living beings without exception. A Buddha's compassion for each living being is like a mother's compassion for her only child.

'Power' refers to a Buddha's perfect ability to free all living beings from suffering.

'Only Buddha possesses the two purposes' means that only Buddhas have accomplished their two purposes of attaining enlightenment themselves and thereby gaining the perfect ability to accomplish their main purpose of bringing benefit to others.

There are two types of Buddha Jewel, conventional and ultimate. A Buddha's Emanation Body (Skt. Nirmanakaya) and Enjoyment Body (Skt. Sambhogakaya) are conventional Buddha Jewels; and a Buddha's Nature Body (Skt. Svabhavikakaya) and Wisdom Truth Body (Skt. Jnanadharmakaya) are ultimate Buddha Jewels.

The Nature Body of a Buddha, sometimes called the 'Entity Body', is the ultimate nature of a Buddha's mind, its lack of inherent existence. The mind and the emptiness of the mind are one nature or entity. Since our present mind is covered by the two obstructions, the emptiness of our present mind is also covered by the two obstructions. If we meditate on the stages of the path to enlightenment and gain all the realizations our mind will become free from the two obstructions and we shall become a Buddha Jewel. Then our mind itself will be the Wisdom Truth Body of a Buddha, and the emptiness of our mind will be the Nature Body of a Buddha. The emptiness of the mind that has become free from the two obstructions is called the 'Nature Body of a Buddha' because it is the ultimate nature of a Buddha's mind. The Nature Body is called a 'Buddha Jewel' because it is completely free from the two obstructions. It is called the 'Truth Body of a Buddha' because it is the emptiness of a Buddha's mind, and an emptiness is an ultimate truth. It is called an 'ultimate Buddha Jewel' because it is an ultimate truth and it is a Buddha Jewel.

The two conventional Buddha Jewels, the Enjoyment Body and the Emanation Body, are the Form Body of a Buddha (Skt. Rupakaya). The two ultimate Buddha Jewels, the Nature Body and the Wisdom Truth Body, are the Truth Body of a Buddha (Skt. Dharmakaya). The Wisdom Truth Body of a Buddha is a Buddha's omniscient mind. A Buddha's omniscient mind is a conventional truth because it is a functioning thing, but it is called an 'ultimate Buddha Jewel' because it is a wisdom consciousness placed single-pointedly on ultimate truth, and it is a Buddha Jewel.

THE DHARMA JEWEL

In *Sublime Continuum of the Great Vehicle* the Dharma Jewel is defined as a perfectly purified truth in the continuum of a Superior being which has any of the eight good qualities, such as inconceivable. The eight good qualities are given in one verse:

Inconceivable, non-dual, non-conceptual,
Pure, clear, side of the antidote,
That which frees from attachment;
The two truths are the definition of Dharma.

The actual Dharma Jewel is the third and the fourth of the four noble truths – true cessations and true paths – which are attained through practising Buddha's teachings. An explanation of these two truths is given later, in the section on the four noble truths. Four of these eight good qualities are qualities of true cessations and four are qualities of true paths.

When, in dependence upon true paths, we abandon any delusion or any imprint of delusion completely, we attain a true cessation. A true cessation cannot be explained by comparing it with something else, saying for example, 'It looks like this' or 'It feels like that.' A true cessation is a non-affirming negative phenomenon, a negative phenomenon that does not affirm any positive phenomenon. It is permanent because it is the emptiness of a mind that has attained complete abandonment of any obstruction through the power of a true path. A true cessation is not merely the final abandonment of any delusion or imprint of delusion – it is the emptiness of a mind that has attained such a cessation.

When we attain true cessations, although we may still experience sickness, old age, and death, these do not cause us suffering. Since true cessations protect us from suffering they are Dharma Jewels and holy objects of refuge. There are many types of true cessation, such as cessations of intellectually-formed delusions and cessations of innate delusions.

When we gain a direct realization of emptiness and attain the released path of the path of seeing we abandon intellectually-formed delusions. Then by continuing to meditate on emptiness we eventually overcome all innate delusions and all the imprints of delusions as well.

Although at present we cannot experience actual true cessations we can still eliminate our delusions temporarily. Temporary cessations are similitudes of true cessations and so they are extremely precious. For example, if we meditate on love and patience to overcome the anger we feel towards someone, we may gain a slight experience of these practices and experience a temporary cessation of anger. This meditation on love and patience resembles a true path leading to a true cessation, and so we should regard the temporary absence of anger that we attain from our practice of love and patience as a true cessation and an actual Dharma Jewel.

The first three qualities of true cessations are mentioned in the first line of Maitreya's verse: 'inconceivable, non-dual, non-conceptual'. 'Inconceivable' means that conceptual minds cannot understand true cessations exactly because true cessations need to be directly experienced in order to be perfectly understood. Since true cessations are experienced mainly through the power of meditation, they cannot be correctly understood by those who gain merely an intellectual understanding of Dharma without putting it into practice. 'Non-dual' (literally 'not two') refers to the absence of one or both of the two obstructions. 'Non-conceptual' means that true cessations are not endowed with conceptuality, because only minds can be endowed with conceptuality and true cessations are not minds.

The first three qualities of true paths are mentioned in the second line of Maitreya's verse: 'pure, clear, side of the antidote'. 'Pure' means that a true path is a mind that is not mixed with delusions. 'Clear' means that a true path is a mind that sees its objects clearly. 'Side of the antidote' means that a true path functions as an antidote to either of the two obstructions; it is like a tool that eliminates all the mental faults and defilements that cause our problems.

The third line of Maitreya's verse mentions explicitly the fourth quality of a true path and implicitly the fourth quality of a true cessation. 'That which frees from attachment' means that true paths are methods by which we gain true cessations which free us completely from delusions such as attachment.

The last line, 'The two truths are the definition of Dharma', refers to the two types of Dharma Jewel, conventional and ultimate. Conventional Dharma Jewels are Buddha's scriptures, and ultimate Dharma Jewels are true cessations and true paths.

If we meditate on these eight good qualities we shall develop a strong wish to have Dharma Jewels within our mind, and we shall be happy to put effort into our practice.

In *Guide to the Bodhisattva's Way of Life* Shantideva says that when we have taken rebirth in the lower realms there is no refuge. This means that when we are reborn in the lower realms we have no freedom to practise Dharma and so we cannot develop Dharma Jewels within our mind. Although Buddhas do visit the lower realms and can from their own side offer perfect protection, unless living beings make an effort themselves to put Dharma into practice, Buddhas cannot help them directly.

The Dharma Jewel is therefore said to be the actual cure for our mental disease. Just as doctors and nurses can help their patients only if the patients themselves actually take the medicines that are prescribed, in the same way we can receive help from the Buddha Jewel and the Sangha Jewel only if we ourself apply inwardly all the instructions and effect our own cure by attaining real Dharma Jewels. By making the effort to develop Dharma Jewels within our mind, we shall eventually become objects of refuge for others.

Drugpa Kunleg once visited a famous temple in Lhasa and when he saw the Buddha statue there he exclaimed:

O Buddha, to begin with you and I were exactly the same,
But later you attained Buddhahood through the force of your effort,
Whereas due to my laziness I remain in samsara;
So now I must prostrate to you.

THE SANGHA JEWEL

In *Sublime Continuum of the Great Vehicle* the Sangha Jewel is defined as a Superior being who has any of the eight good qualities, such as realization and freedom.

A Superior being is someone who has realized emptiness directly and has attained the realization of peace by practising the three higher trainings. Since we cannot see these actual Sangha Jewels we should regard as an actual Sangha Jewel anyone who is keeping the Pratimoksha vows purely, anyone who is keeping the Bodhisattva vows purely, anyone who is keeping the Tantric vows purely, and anyone else who is helping others and showing a good example. If we ourself want to become a Sangha Jewel we need to subdue our uncontrolled minds with the practice of Dharma. If we remain always with a peaceful mind we shall become a good example for others.

In the *Vinaya Sutras* it is said that any group of four or more fully ordained monks or nuns is a Sangha community. In Buddhist countries the Sangha community is honoured and highly valued because lay Buddhists need to receive encouragement and inspiration from seeing with their own eyes the good example the Sangha provides.

The first four qualities of the Sangha Jewel are qualities of realization:

(1) Realization
(2) Realizing ultimate truth
(3) Realizing conventional truth
(4) Realizing the nature of the inner mind

In the fourth realization, 'inner' indicates that mind is a subject and 'nature' refers to the different levels of mind. Therefore, this quality is the realization of the different levels of subject mind.

The remaining four qualities are qualities of freedom:

(5) Freedom from all faults
(6) Freedom from obstructions to liberation
(7) Freedom from obstructions to omniscience
(8) Freedom from obstructions of inferiority

Although it is usually said that there are two types of obstruction, delusion-obstructions and obstructions to omniscience, in some Mahayana texts a third type of obstruction, obstructions of inferiority, is mentioned. An obstruction of inferiority is anything that prevents us from developing and enhancing bodhichitta, such as the self-cherishing mind.

Hinayana practitioners do not gain freedom from obstructions of inferiority, but they can become Sangha Jewels because they can gain some of the eight good qualities of a Sangha Jewel, such as freedom from obstructions to liberation. Even a Hinayanist on the path of accumulation who is not yet an actual Sangha Jewel has many excellent qualities.

From among the thirty-seven realizations conducive to enlightenment he or she has accomplished the first three groups: the four close placements of mindfulness, the four correct abandoners, and the four legs of miracle powers. When a Hinayanist attains the path of preparation he or she has accomplished the next two groups, the five powers and the five forces. When the Hinayanist attains the path of seeing he or she has accomplished the next group, the seven branches of enlightenment. When the Hinayanist attains the path of meditation he or she has accomplished the next group, the eight branches of superior paths. If a Hinayana Sangha Jewel can accomplish such good qualities, what need is there to say how many and how great are the excellences of Mahayana Sangha Jewels? By meditating on the good qualities of the Sangha Jewel we shall develop a strong determination, 'I myself will become a Sangha Jewel.'

Among the many external things that we need, we usually consider jewels to be the most precious and rare. Similarly, among living beings, teachings, and communities, Buddha, Dharma, and Sangha are the most precious and rare. Therefore they are called the 'Buddha Jewel', the 'Dharma Jewel', and the 'Sangha Jewel'; and they are our ultimate objects of refuge.

UNDERSTANDING WHY THE THREE JEWELS ARE SUITABLE OBJECTS OF REFUGE

If we realize why Buddha is a suitable object of refuge we shall easily realize that the Dharma he taught and the Sangha who follow his advice are also suitable objects of refuge. There are four main reasons why Buddha is a perfectly reliable source of guidance and can offer complete protection from suffering:

1 Buddha is free from all fear
2 Buddha is very skilful in liberating living beings
3 Buddha has compassion for all living beings without discrimination
4 Buddha benefits all living beings whether or not they have helped him

BUDDHA IS FREE FROM ALL FEAR

If Buddhas were not free from all kinds of fear they would still be taking rebirths without choice and, not being free themselves, they would not be able to offer help to others. If one person trapped and bound within samsara tries to help someone else gain freedom, it is like one drowning person trying to help another, or like one person who is falling to the ground trying to prevent the fall of another person who is already tumbling down on top of him.

Buddhas are free from fear because they have eliminated the minds of self-grasping and self-cherishing, which are the causes of all fear and harm. If we cannot gain certainty by realizing this correct reason we can study the life story of Buddha Shakyamuni and see how many times he demonstrated complete fearlessness and invulnerability to any kind of harm.

Buddha's jealous cousin, Devadatta, tried many times to murder him, sometimes using poisons and sometimes hurling rocks; but when he threw the rocks it was just like throwing them into empty space. Weapons cannot harm a Buddha any more than they can destroy space.

Once a huge, powerful elephant belonging to King Ajata-shatru became crazy and ran amok. Everyone fled out of the way of this wild animal and no one felt able to subdue it. When the elephant rampaged into the place where Buddha was teaching, panic broke out and all the disciples fled. Even the Foe Destroyers who possessed miracle powers were terrified and flew high into the sky. Buddha alone remained undisturbed. He touched the crown of the elephant's head and its madness was instantly pacified.

On another occasion a man called Shri Samva tried to kill Buddha by throwing him into a deep, fiery pit, and when he saw that Buddha was completely unharmed by the fire he tried to poison him, but Buddha drank the poison as if it were medicine.

BUDDHA IS VERY SKILFUL IN LIBERATING LIVING BEINGS

Even though Buddhas possess countless good qualities, such as perfect fearlessness and great compassion, they would not be able to guide others towards enlightenment and protect them from harm if it were not for their great skill. Without their supremely skilful means they would be just like an armless mother helplessly watching her children drown.

Buddha Shakyamuni demonstrated the skill of the Buddhas by pacifying and directing the violent mind of Angulimala. No one alive at that time was more severely afflicted with anger than Angulimala. Although this madly hostile man had been incited by false teachers to murder nine hundred and ninety-nine people, Buddha was able to tame him and guide him to liberation. Buddha was also able to lead Lam Chung to liberation even though Lam Chung was the most unintelligent person alive at that time and could not memorize even a single verse after making tremendous effort for months. In spite of Lam Chung's great dullness Buddha was able skilfully to lead him to gain realizations and increase his wisdom so that eventually he became an eminent Teacher. With skill Buddha overcame the great pride of the divine musician Pramudita and led him on the spiritual path. He overcame the extreme desirous attachment of Nanda, and the severe disabilities of the aged Shri Datta, leading them both along the path to liberation. It would be impossible to name all the occasions on which Buddha used his skilful means to help people overcome their obstacles and practise the path to liberation and enlightenment.

Everything that Buddha taught is a skilful method for overcoming our mental problems and transforming our minds into spiritual paths. The human world is said to be in the desire realm because we are particularly afflicted with desirous attachment. We all suffer from innate desirous attachment and we find it very hard to remove from our mind attachment to attractive objects of the senses. Even while we are dreaming we never forget desirous attachment but easily become completely oblivious to all the virtuous thoughts and feelings we have been trying to cultivate in our waking hours. Buddha taught special methods for transforming our desirous attachment into the spiritual path, and he revealed how to transform all our ordinary activities into spiritual practices by using methods such as the yoga of sleeping, the yoga of dreaming, the yoga of rising, and the yoga of eating. If we study the complete instructions on Sutra and Tantra we shall be able to appreciate Buddha's unsurpassed skill.

BUDDHA HAS COMPASSION FOR ALL LIVING BEINGS WITHOUT DISCRIMINATION

Once Devadatta became seriously ill. When Buddha's disciples told him that his malevolent cousin was about to die, he said 'I feel no difference between Devadatta and my son Rahula. If what I say is true, may Devadatta recover immediately.' With these words Devadatta instantly recovered. In their compassion Buddhas feel no difference between their most bitter opponents and their own sons; they feel compassionate concern for everyone without any discrimination.

At present we are very biased in our attitudes towards other people. We feel close to our friends and family and we readily offer to help them, but we feel very distant from the people we do not like and we do not think of helping them. If we begin now to develop a more balanced attitude towards our friends and our enemies, we shall be establishing the foundation of equanimity that we need in order to build the impartial mind of great compassion possessed by all the Buddhas.

BUDDHA BENEFITS ALL LIVING BEINGS WHETHER OR NOT THEY HAVE HELPED HIM

In their love for living beings Buddhas benefit all without a thought of whether or not they themselves have received benefit from them. We on the other hand repay the kindness we have received, but we are not unconditionally kind to others.

Nagarjuna said that there is not a single living being who has not received benefit from Buddha. Just by receiving Buddha's blessings even stupid animals can develop peaceful, virtuous states of mind and thus attain higher states of rebirth and enjoy higher happiness. A wild boar was once being chased through a forest by a hunter. Just as it was at the point of collapse, the terrified animal reached a clearing in which stood a stupa, a symbolic representation of Buddha's mind. Overcome by exhaustion, the boar collapsed and died. Although from its own side the boar had no power to cultivate a virtuous mind, as a result of seeing the stupa it received Buddha's blessings, and through the power of these blessings it was able to die peacefully and take rebirth in the god realm.

By meditating on these good qualities we shall develop confidence and faith in Buddha, the Dharma he taught, and the Sangha who are sincerely practising Dharma. When this special feeling of faith in Buddha, Dharma, and Sangha arises definitely in our mind, we do placement meditation to become more and more closely acquainted with it.

THE WAY OF GOING FOR REFUGE

There are four ways of going for refuge:

1 Going for refuge understanding the good qualities of the Three Jewels

2 Going for refuge differentiating the qualities of
  each of the Three Jewels
3 Going for refuge by promising to go for refuge
4 Going for refuge by abandoning going for ultimate
  refuge to other objects

GOING FOR REFUGE UNDERSTANDING THE GOOD QUALITIES
OF THE THREE JEWELS

By understanding and meditating on the good qualities of
the Three Jewels, if we develop confidence and faith in them
and then go for refuge, this is going for refuge understanding the good qualities of the Three Jewels.

GOING FOR REFUGE DIFFERENTIATING THE QUALITIES
OF EACH OF THE THREE JEWELS

The excellences of the Three Jewels can be differentiated in
six ways. Accordingly, there are six ways of going for refuge
differentiating the qualities of the Three Jewels:

1 Going for refuge understanding the different
  natures of the Three Jewels
2 Going for refuge understanding the different
  functions of the Three Jewels
3 Going for refuge differentiating the Three Jewels
  by an analogy
4 Going for refuge distinguishing the time of going
  for refuge
5 Going for refuge understanding the different ways
  in which merit is increased by going for refuge to
  each of the Three Jewels
6 Going for refuge understanding the different ways
  in which the Three Jewels help our practice

GOING FOR REFUGE UNDERSTANDING THE DIFFERENT
NATURES OF THE THREE JEWELS

The nature or defining characteristic of the Buddha Jewel is
to have attained enlightenment. The nature of the Dharma

Jewel is to be the result of Buddha's attainment of enlightenment, because as a result of attaining enlightenment Buddha taught Dharma to help others gain the same experience. The nature of the Sangha Jewel is to have attained realizations by putting Buddha's teachings into practice. If we understand the different natures of the Three Jewels and then with faith we go for refuge, this is going for refuge understanding the different natures of the Three Jewels.

GOING FOR REFUGE UNDERSTANDING THE DIFFERENT FUNCTIONS OF THE THREE JEWELS

The main function of the Buddha Jewel is to reveal the spiritual path to disciples by giving perfect Dharma teachings; the main function of the Dharma Jewel is to protect living beings from fear and suffering; and the main function of the Sangha Jewel is to help others by setting a good example. If we go for refuge knowing this, this is going for refuge understanding the different functions of the Three Jewels.

GOING FOR REFUGE DIFFERENTIATING THE THREE JEWELS BY AN ANALOGY

The Dharma Jewel is like a boat, the Buddha Jewel is like a skilful navigator, and the Sangha Jewel is like the crew. If we see how we need to depend upon all three to cross the ocean of samsara and then with faith we go for refuge, this is going for refuge differentiating the Three Jewels by an analogy.

GOING FOR REFUGE DISTINGUISHING THE TIME OF GOING FOR REFUGE

Remembering the good qualities of the Three Jewels we should go for refuge at all times. Usually we remember to go for refuge only when we are experiencing difficulties, but if we always go for refuge, even when everything is going well, we shall become so close to Buddha that when we experience misfortune we shall receive help easily. If we go for refuge only at times of crisis we may not be able to receive help immediately. For this reason we should always have an image of Buddha close to us, reminding us of our refuge. At all times we need to keep the determination, 'With the help of the Buddha Jewel and the Sangha Jewel I must develop the Dharma Jewel in my mind.'

GOING FOR REFUGE UNDERSTANDING THE DIFFERENT WAYS IN WHICH MERIT IS INCREASED BY GOING FOR REFUGE TO EACH OF THE THREE JEWELS

By going for refuge and making offerings to the Buddha Jewel we increase the merit that causes us to attain the Form Body of a Buddha; by going for refuge and making offerings to the Dharma Jewel we increase the merit that causes us to attain the Truth Body of a Buddha; and by going for refuge and making offerings to the Sangha Jewel we increase the merit that causes us to become a Sangha Jewel.

GOING FOR REFUGE UNDERSTANDING THE DIFFERENT WAYS IN WHICH THE THREE JEWELS HELP OUR PRACTICE

If we realize that the Dharma Jewel is the actual cure for our mental sickness, that the Buddha Jewel is the spiritual doctor who prescribes the cure, and that the Sangha Jewel is the spiritual nurse who assists the doctor, and then with faith we go for refuge, this is going for refuge understanding the different ways in which the Three Jewels help our practice.

GOING FOR REFUGE BY PROMISING TO GO FOR REFUGE

We are going for refuge by promising to go for refuge if we regard the Buddha Jewel as our Spiritual Guide, the Dharma Jewel as our actual refuge, and the Sangha Jewel as our spiritual friends, and then make a promise in front of the visualized assembly of Buddhas:

From now on I will go for refuge to Buddha, my Spiritual Guide. I will go for refuge to Dharma, my actual refuge. I will go for refuge to Sangha, my spiritual friends.

GOING FOR REFUGE BY ABANDONING GOING FOR ULTIMATE REFUGE TO OTHER OBJECTS

If we recognize that worldly gods are not suitable objects of refuge and then make the promise, 'I will not go for ultimate refuge to objects other than the Three Jewels', this is going for refuge by abandoning going for refuge to other objects. If we go for refuge to teachers whose instructions contradict those of Buddha we shall be led onto wrong paths; and if we go for refuge to worldly gods, although we may receive some short-term benefits we shall be diverted from perfect paths leading to liberation and enlightenment. However, when we abandon going for refuge to other objects we should not do so out of sectarianism. Our motivation should be simply to keep our refuge vows purely and avoid the harm we would inflict upon ourself by breaking our commitments. If we have perfect faith in Buddha there is no reason why we should ever need to go for refuge to other objects.

Some people with pure faith can make the promise: 'I will go for refuge only to the Three Jewels.' This promise is very beneficial but it will be stronger and more stable if it is based on faith gained through logical conviction. The famous Buddhist scholar Todzun Drubche was formerly a non-Buddhist, and highly trained in non-Buddhist scriptures. He went with his brother to Mount Kailash, which was regarded by non-Buddhists as the palace of Ishvara. When he arrived there Todzun Drubche discovered that even Ishvara was going for refuge to Buddha and so he developed faith in Buddha and trained in Buddhist scriptures. He later composed a text called *Praising Buddha as a Teacher Far Superior to Any Other*, in which he wrote:

> O Buddha, I go for refuge to you, abandoning all other teachers. What is my reason? It is that you alone are completely free from all faults and endowed with all good qualities . . . . The more I compare non-Buddhist and Buddhist teachings, the stronger my faith in you grows.

Todzun Drubche was able to develop strong faith in Buddha based on logical conviction because he realized that Buddha has abandoned all faults and perfected every good quality. From his experience of non-Buddhist teachings he could understand clearly the superiority and profundity of Buddha's teachings. He realized that some non-Buddhist teachings posit a permanent, partless, independent self, and that any teaching supporting this view supports self-grasping ignorance, which gives rise to all the actions that cause samsaric rebirth.

In *Praise to Dependent Relationship* Je Tsongkhapa says of Buddha:

Realizing the way things exist, you taught it well.
Learning and practising what you taught
We abandon all faults
Because you have shown how to cut their root.

Anyone who diligently relies for a long time
Upon teachings that contradict your own
Invites many faults
Because those teachings nourish self-grasping.

O Wise is the scholar who understands
The difference between these two.
How could he fail to develop faith in you
From the depths of his heart?

THE MEASUREMENT OF GOING FOR REFUGE PERFECTLY

To go for refuge perfectly we need to do three things. First, by contemplating the sufferings and dangers of samsara we need to have developed a heartfelt fear of them, either on our own behalf alone or on behalf of all living beings. Second, by contemplating the good qualities of the Three Jewels we need to have developed confidence and faith in them as completely reliable sources of guidance, and we need to have seen that sincerely going for refuge to them is a perfect safeguard against future suffering. Third, having cultivated the two causes – fear of suffering and faith in the Three Jewels – we need to go for refuge. When these three conditions have come together our refuge is perfect.

THE BENEFITS OF GOING FOR REFUGE

If we go for refuge purely and sincerely we experience eight special benefits:

1 We become a pure Buddhist
2 We establish the foundation for taking all other vows
3 We purify the negative karma that we have accumulated in the past
4 We daily accumulate a vast amount of merit
5 We are held back from falling into the lower realms
6 We are protected from harm inflicted by humans and non-humans
7 We fulfil all our temporary and ultimate wishes
8 We quickly attain the full enlightenment of Buddhahood

WE BECOME A PURE BUDDHIST

If we wish to gain liberation from all suffering and attain the ultimate happiness of full enlightenment we definitely need to become a pure Buddhist. This is because it is only by following the guidance of Buddha and taking the advice he gave that we shall be able to experience the complete path to liberation and full enlightenment.

WE ESTABLISH THE FOUNDATION FOR TAKING ALL OTHER VOWS

All vows, from the lay person's Pratimoksha vows to the Tantric vows, depend upon our going for refuge. If we take vows and keep them purely, all our realizations of concentration and other spiritual paths will develop easily. We do not need to inflict upon ourself great physical austerities as taught in other traditions. On the basis of going for refuge we can develop constant mindfulness by keeping our vowed restraints purely. Our practice of pure moral discipline will bring great benefits and make even our sleep a virtuous action that creates the cause for future happiness. Thus the

practice of going for refuge is said to be like the ground and
all other spiritual practices are said to be like the plants that
grow from it.

WE PURIFY THE NEGATIVE KARMA THAT WE HAVE ACCUMULATED IN THE PAST

There was once a god called Sumati Samudra who lived in
the Land of the Thirty-three Heavens. When this god began
to experience the signs that he was going to die he saw that
he was about to be reborn as a pig. By contrast with the style
of life he was enjoying in the god realm it was obvious that
the life of a pig is in the nature of suffering. Observing the
filthiness of the pig's life Sumati Samudra felt as if he would
die of disgust, and so he went to seek help from Indra, his
object of refuge. Indra said 'It is not in my power to hold you
back from lower rebirth, but do not give up hope. I shall find
a way.' Indra then descended to Earth and approached
Buddha saying 'A god called Sumati Samudra is about to die
and take lower rebirth. He seeks protection from such misery.' Buddha gave instructions on refuge, which Indra passed
on to Sumati Samudra. The god practised going for refuge
purely and sincerely for seven god realm days. When he
finally passed away Indra looked to see where he had taken
rebirth. Gods are able to see some worlds that exist below
their own realms, but Indra could not see Sumati Samudra
anywhere. Buddha then said 'He has taken rebirth in Tushita
Pure Land, which exists above the Land of the Thirty-three
Heavens.' By practising refuge purely Sumati Samudra purified all the negative karma that would have thrown him into
rebirth as a pig and he created the cause to take rebirth in
Tushita.

WE DAILY ACCUMULATE A VAST AMOUNT OF MERIT

It has already been explained that even if we do not have a
good motivation, whenever we behold the images of the
Three Jewels or visualize them we create a great amount of
merit. What need is there to say how much more merit we

shall accumulate if we go for refuge purely from the depths of our heart with a good motivation?

WE ARE HELD BACK FROM FALLING INTO THE LOWER REALMS

Since going for refuge purifies negative karma, it removes the cause of our taking rebirth in the three lower realms. If we practise the simple way of going for refuge of a small being we shall be held back from the pains of lower rebirth. If we practise the special way of going for refuge of a small being we shall cultivate inwardly the Dharma Jewel of a small being, which will be our stable and constant safeguard against lower rebirth. Similarly, if we go for the refuge of a middle being we shall be prevented from taking rebirth anywhere within samsara, and if we go for the refuge of a great being we shall be prevented from abandoning Mahayana paths for Hinayana paths.

WE ARE PROTECTED FROM HARM INFLICTED BY HUMANS AND NON-HUMANS

To receive protection from harm inflicted by humans and non-humans our practice of going for refuge must be regular and consistent. As mentioned before, if we go for refuge only when we are faced with problems we shall not receive immediate assistance. The fears that our practice of going for refuge averts are the fears that we are not yet experiencing. Those that are already upon us cannot be taken away because they are the effects of karma that is already ripening. We can prevent our bad karma from ripening by going for refuge, but once we are already beginning to suffer the bad effects of our negative actions there is nothing to be done but to accept and endure them. However, if we go for refuge sincerely and continuously we shall destroy the effects of harmful actions that have not yet begun to ripen as harsh and painful experiences.

WE FULFIL ALL OUR TEMPORARY AND ULTIMATE WISHES

Everyone who has faith in Buddha and who goes for refuge purely and sincerely fulfils all their wishes, both temporary and ultimate. We cannot gain certainty about this by using logical reasoning alone, but pure Dharma practitioners realize it is true from their own experience.

WE QUICKLY ATTAIN THE FULL ENLIGHTENMENT OF BUDDHAHOOD

If we establish a strong foundation for our spiritual practice by going for refuge purely and sincerely, we shall easily attain the realizations of all the stages of the path to enlightenment.

THE COMMITMENTS OF GOING FOR REFUGE

This has two parts:

1 The special commitments
2 The general commitments

THE SPECIAL COMMITMENTS

There are six special commitments. In relation to each of the Three Jewels we are committed to make one abandonment and one acknowledgement:

1 One abandonment and one acknowledgement with regard to the Buddha Jewel
2 One abandonment and one acknowledgement with regard to the Dharma Jewel
3 One abandonment and one acknowledgement with regard to the Sangha Jewel

ONE ABANDONMENT AND ONE ACKNOWLEDGEMENT WITH REGARD TO THE BUDDHA JEWEL

By going for refuge to the Buddha Jewel we are committed to abandon going for ultimate refuge to teachers who contradict Buddha's view, or to worldly gods. This does not mean that we cannot receive help from others, but that we do not rely upon others as providing ultimate protection from suffering.

By going for refuge to the Buddha Jewel our other special commitment is to acknowledge any image of Buddha as an actual Buddha. It is said that whenever we see a statue of Buddha made of materials such as iron, wood, or bronze we should not regard the rarity of the material or the quality of the craftsmanship, but we should see it as an actual Buddha, and pay homage by making offerings and prostrations and going for refuge. If we practise like this, our merit will increase abundantly.

ONE ABANDONMENT AND ONE ACKNOWLEDGEMENT
WITH REGARD TO THE DHARMA JEWEL

By going for refuge to the Dharma Jewel we are committed to abandon harming others. Instead of treating others badly we try, with the best motivation, to help and benefit them. We first need to concentrate on reducing harmful thoughts towards those who are close to us, such as our friends and family. When we have developed a good heart towards these people we can gradually extend the scope of our consideration to include more and more people until it includes all beings. If we can abandon harmful thoughts and cultivate beneficial intentions we shall easily develop the realizations of great love and great compassion. In this way, from the very beginning of our practice of going for refuge we begin to increase compassion, which is the very essence of Buddhadharma.

By going for refuge to the Dharma Jewel we are committed to acknowledge any Dharma scripture as an actual Dharma Jewel. We need to respect every letter of the scriptures and every letter of explanation of Buddha's teaching. Therefore we must treat Dharma books with great care and avoid walking over them or putting them in inappropriate places where they might be damaged or abused. For example, we do not balance them on top of a waste paper basket or use them to support our coffee mug, and we always avoid sitting on them or playing with them. Each time we neglect or spoil our Dharma books we create the cause to become more ignorant because these actions are similar to the action of abandoning Dharma. Once Geshe Sharawa saw some people playing carelessly with their Dharma books and he said to them, 'You should not do that. You are already ignorant enough without making yourself even more stupid!'

The Dharma Jewel is the source of all health and happiness. Since we cannot see Dharma Jewels with our eyes, we need to honour Dharma texts as actual Dharma Jewels, realizing that actual Dharma Jewels arise only in dependence upon our learning, contemplating, and meditating on the scriptures, and putting their advice into effect in our daily life.

ONE ABANDONMENT AND ONE ACKNOWLEDGEMENT
WITH REGARD TO THE SANGHA JEWEL

By going for refuge to the Sangha Jewel we are committed to abandon being influenced by people who reject Buddha's teaching. This does not mean that we should abandon the people themselves but that we should not let their views influence our mind. Without abandoning love and consideration for others we need to be vigilant and make sure that we are not being led astray by their bad habits and unsound advice.

By going for refuge to the Sangha Jewel we are committed to acknowledge anyone who wears the robes of an ordained person as an actual Sangha Jewel. Even if ordained Sangha are poor we still need to pay respect because they are keeping moral discipline, and this is something very rare and precious.

THE GENERAL COMMITMENTS

There are six general commitments:

1 To go for refuge to the Three Jewels again and again, remembering their good qualities and the differences between them

2 To offer the first portion of whatever we eat and drink to the Three Jewels, remembering their kindness

3 With compassion, always to encourage others to go for refuge

4 Remembering the benefits of going for refuge, to go for refuge at least three times during the day and three times during the night

5 To perform every action with complete trust in the Three Jewels

6 Never to forsake the Three Jewels even at the cost of our life, or as a joke

TO GO FOR REFUGE TO THE THREE JEWELS AGAIN AND AGAIN, REMEMBERING THEIR GOOD QUALITIES AND THE DIFFERENCES BETWEEN THEM

This has already been explained.

TO OFFER THE FIRST PORTION OF WHATEVER WE EAT AND DRINK TO THE THREE JEWELS, REMEMBERING THEIR KINDNESS

Since we need to eat and drink several times each day, if we always offer the first portion to the Three Jewels, remembering their kindness, we shall greatly increase our merit. We can do this with the following prayer:

I make this offering to you Buddha Shakyamuni,
Whose mind is the synthesis of all Buddha Jewels,
Whose speech is the synthesis of all Dharma Jewels,
Whose body is the synthesis of all Sangha Jewels.
O Blessed One, please accept this and bless my mind.
OM AH HUM   (3x)

We may sometimes doubt 'Is Buddha so kind? I never see him and I do not have direct communication with him.' Although we may sometimes have this doubt, in fact all our happiness comes as a result of Buddha's kindness. All Buddha's actions are pervaded by compassion and concern for others, and it is these actions that enable us to perform the virtuous deeds that are the causes of our happiness.

Since we do not yet understand the law of karma it often seems to us that our happiness is created by external conditions and by other people such as our parents and our friends. Similarly, it seems that all our problems are also created by others. In general, every functioning thing has two types of cause: the main cause, or substantial cause, and secondary causes, or contributory causes. Since happiness is a state of mind, its main cause must also be a state of mind. Other things such as our friends, our wealth, our job, or our holidays can act only as contributory causes of happiness. We know this by observation. It is evident that some people have successfully assembled many contributory causes of happiness such as great wealth and resources and beautiful partners, and yet they experience misery and discontent because they do not possess the state of mind that is the substantial cause of happiness. Since happiness is a state of mind we can see how misleading it is to place all our expectations of bliss and contentment on transient possessions.

If we compare some western countries with some countries in the Third World we can see that from the point of view of material progress those western countries are more advanced. If material prosperity were the principal cause of human happiness, westerners would be many times happier than the inhabitants of the Third World, but in fact there is far more mental distress and neurosis amongst westerners and a much higher rate of suicide. This indicates that real happiness depends mainly upon our state of mind. Buddha taught how to examine our mind and see which states produce misery and confusion and which states produce health and happiness. He taught how to overcome the compulsively non-virtuous minds that confine us to states of discontent and misery, and how to cultivate the virtuous minds that liberate us from pain and lead us to the bliss of full enlightenment. By learning Buddhadharma we shall discern the real cause of happiness and we shall appreciate and never forget Buddha's great kindness.

If we are now able to learn Dharma and meet Spiritual Guides it is only through Buddha's kindness. Our own human body is a correct sign proving his kindness. It is by virtue of Buddha's blessings and instructions that we were able to create the cause to take rebirth in a human form with all the freedoms and endowments necessary for spiritual practice. We can now apply the methods that lead to full enlightenment and gain realizations only because Buddha was kind enough to turn the Wheel of Dharma and show his example in this world. Even the small wisdom that we possess to discriminate what is beneficial and what is harmful, and to identify Buddha's teaching as worthwhile, comes as a result of Buddha's kindness.

Since Buddhas attain enlightenment for the sake of all living beings and not just to benefit Buddhists, they also manifest as teachers of other religions and give instructions in accordance with the needs and inclinations of different practitioners. Buddhas can help non-Buddhists to avoid rebirth in the three lower realms because other religious traditions present methods for abandoning harmful actions and cultivating virtue. Buddhas can also help those who are not religious because they can manifest in any form that brings benefit to living beings.

WITH COMPASSION, ALWAYS TO ENCOURAGE OTHERS TO GO FOR REFUGE

If we know someone who is interested in Dharma but who does not go for refuge we cannot help them by immediately urging them to go for refuge because they first need to develop for themselves the causes of going for refuge: fear of suffering and faith in the Three Jewels. We can help them best by gently encouraging them to develop these causes. We can talk to them about impermanence, how the conditions of this life change and how our body will grow old and decay; and we can talk about the sufferings of old age and sickness, drawing attention to them when we see examples in other people or on the television. We can talk about death, how its time is so uncertain and how we shall have to part from our friends and possessions. We can talk about what will happen after death, encouraging the other person to think about it and develop conviction in rebirth. We can talk about how most living beings experience lives of gross misfortune. With care and concern, if we introduce these thoughts into our conversations the other person will begin to lose his complacency and, when he starts to feel uncomfortable, he will naturally become interested to find out what can be done. At this point we can help him to realize that an enlightened being does exist and has revealed the way for every living being to attain the same state. Then we can talk about the practice of going for refuge and the good qualities of the Three Jewels.

If we help someone else tactfully in this way, without being arrogant or impatient, we shall bring them real benefit. It is never certain that the material gifts we give to others actually help them. Sometimes they even cause other people to increase their delusions. The perfect way to help others is by leading them along spiritual paths. If we cannot teach extensively we can at least give proper advice to those who are unhappy and help them to solve their problems by means of Dharma.

REMEMBERING THE BENEFITS OF GOING FOR REFUGE, TO GO FOR REFUGE AT LEAST THREE TIMES DURING THE DAY AND THREE TIMES DURING THE NIGHT.

We must go for refuge at least once every four hours and try never to forget our refuge. If we develop this constant mindfulness we shall gain realizations very quickly. Remembering the benefits of going for refuge prompts us to maintain our mindfulness at all times. In this respect we aim to become like a businessman who never forgets his projects even when he is relaxing.

TO PERFORM EVERY ACTION WITH COMPLETE TRUST IN THE THREE JEWELS

To ensure the success of whatever virtuous actions we engage in we should rely upon the Three Jewels. There is no need to seek the inspiration and blessing of worldly gods; but by sincerely making offerings and requests we should try to receive the blessings of Buddha, Dharma, and Sangha.

NEVER TO FORSAKE THE THREE JEWELS EVEN AT THE COST OF OUR LIFE, OR AS A JOKE

The main reason that we should never abandon the Three Jewels is because going for refuge is the foundation of all Dharma realizations.

Once a Buddhist was taken captive and his enemy said to him 'Give up your refuge in Buddha or I will kill you.' This Buddhist refused to forsake his refuge and so he was killed; but when clairvoyants looked they saw that he had been immediately reborn as a god.

The special and general commitments of going for refuge are given to help us to gain the realizations of the stages of the path. They are skilful methods for training our mind and therefore we should not regard them as if they were punishments or unnecessary constraints.

HOW TO GO FOR REFUGE BY PRACTISING THREE ROUNDS OF MEDITATION

To practise going for refuge in three rounds of meditation we first sit comfortably and visualize the objects of refuge in the space in front of us. During the first round of meditation we mainly emphasize recollection of the different sufferings of the three lower realms. When we have deeply considered these we remind ourself that if we do not attain liberation in this lifetime we shall almost certainly take lower rebirth because we have committed many non-virtuous actions that are the causes of such miserable rebirths.

Now we begin the second round of meditation, during which we imagine that the time of our death has come and that we have lost our opportunity to attain liberation or create Dharma Jewels in our mind, and so we are definitely bound for lower rebirth. Then we imagine vividly that we have actually taken lower rebirth as, say, a pig. We visualize ourself as a pig, establishing the visualization by doing detailed analytical meditation, thinking:

Now I am a pig. My face is like this. My body is like this. My tail is like this. I am surrounded by other pigs. They look like this and this.

We visualize our pig family and how we all live in our pigsty eating filthy scraps and smelling of excrement. When we have visualized ourself, our companions, and our abode, we imagine that the farmer arrives to take us away. We have to leave our family behind and we are packed tightly into a lorry with lots of other pigs squealing and grunting. We are taken down the motorway at great speed. We then imagine our bewilderment as we enter the slaughterhouse and the moment of horror when it dawns upon us that we are about to be killed. We imagine that our life is violently torn from us. Our body is decapitated and immediately slit open, gutted, and then sliced into pieces. We then think how some pieces are thrown away, some are given to dogs, and some are minced into sausages or made into chops and packaged in cellophane, then frozen and sold in the supermarket. We imagine how our best pieces are taken home and fried, and how human beings eat them.

In one text it says that if we have not realized renunciation it is more beneficial to practise generation stage as an animal, hell being, or hungry spirit than to practise generation stage as a Deity. If we practise self-generation as a being of one of the lower realms we shall develop renunciation rapidly.

During the third round of meditation we mainly emphasize recollection of the good qualities of the Three Jewels, remembering that the Three Jewels alone have the power to protect us from all the sufferings of the lower realms. We remind ourself that the Dharma Jewel is our actual refuge and that the attainment of this actual refuge depends upon relying upon Buddha and Sangha. In this way we develop strong faith in the Three Jewels.

When we have completed these three rounds of meditation and have generated the causes of going for refuge very powerfully in our mind, we recite the prayer of going for refuge as many times as we can, or we collect refuge prayers in the way that has been explained in the instructions for the preparatory practices.

The practice of going for refuge is very extensive because it includes all the practices of the stages of the path to enlightenment. To practise the special way of going for refuge of a small being means to put effort into gaining all the realizations of the stages of the path of a small being. To practise the special way of going for refuge of a middle being means to put effort into gaining all the realizations of the stages of the path of a middle being. To practise the special way of going for refuge of a great being means to put effort into gaining all the realizations of the stages of the path of a great being.

When Atisha first arrived in Tibet he taught mainly refuge and so the Tibetans named him 'The Refuge Lama'. Atisha was delighted with this title because he thought 'Now I really can benefit the Tibetans because their practice of going for refuge will be the foundation for their attainment of all other spiritual realizations.'

Karma

GAINING CONVICTION IN THE LAW OF KARMA, THE ROOT
OF ALL GOOD QUALITIES AND HAPPINESS

The law of karma is a special instance of the law of cause
and effect, according to which all our actions of body, speech,
and mind are causes and all our experiences are their effects.
The law of karma explains why each individual has a unique
mental disposition, a unique physical appearance, and unique
experiences. These are the various effects of the countless
actions that each individual has performed in the past. We
cannot find any two people who have created exactly the
same history of actions throughout their past lives and so
we cannot find two people with identical states of mind,
identical experiences, and identical physical appearances.
Each person has a different individual karma. Some people
enjoy good health while others are constantly ill. Some
people are very beautiful while others are very ugly. Some
people have a happy disposition that is easily pleased while
others have a sour disposition and are rarely delighted by
anything. Some people easily understand the meaning of
Dharma instructions while others find the instructions difficult and obscure.

Karma refers mainly to action, and specifically to the mental intention that initiates any action. In general it refers to
any of the three components: actions, their effects, and the
potentialities that actions leave in the mind from the moment
of their completion to the time when they ripen and their
results are experienced. There are three types of action:
mental actions, bodily actions, and verbal actions. A mental
action is a complete train of thought and not just the mental

intention that initiates a train of thought. Bodily actions and verbal actions are also initiated by mental intentions, and are accompanied by mental actions. When an action is complete it creates a potentiality within our mind. The potentiality ripens when the conditions are right, as a seed ripens in the spring when it receives the right amount of heat and moisture. Whether a potentiality is virtuous or non-virtuous, whether it ripens as happiness or suffering, depends upon the action.

If we understand the law of karma we shall understand how we can control our future experiences by abandoning harmful actions that are the causes of misery and by practising virtuous actions that are the causes of happiness. Meditating on the law of karma is like looking into a mirror that shows us what to abandon and what to practise. It reveals the causes of our present experiences and the prospect for our future lives if we do not gain mastery over our habitual negativities. Even if we understand the law of karma intellectually, we still need to meditate on it again and again to develop deep conviction. When we have conviction we shall naturally dread our own negativity and make a strong resolution to practise moral discipline. Without real conviction we shall not generate enough energy to train our mind and so we shall continue compulsively to perform the harmful actions that cause rebirth in states of misery.

Without practising moral discipline, even if we go for refuge sincerely we shall not find perfect protection from rebirth in the three lower realms because we shall be breaking our refuge commitment. To go for refuge without practising moral discipline is to be like a prisoner who, by relying upon someone else's influence, manages to regain his freedom, but then continues to perform his old crimes so that it is only a matter of time before he is caught and thrown into prison again.

Practising moral discipline with strong conviction in the law of karma is the Dharma Jewel of a small being and the basis for developing all other Dharma Jewels. It offers complete protection from lower rebirths and directs us towards all the other realizations of the stages of the path. Without it, even if we become an accomplished Buddhist scholar our position in life will be very precarious.

Atisha's Spiritual Guide Avadhutipa said:

> Until we have eliminated self-grasping, our main practice should be the practice of moral discipline . . . . There are many famous scholars who have been reborn in hell.

Just as the law of this country does not make exceptions for intellectuals, so the law of karma does not exclude people on account of their learning. Devadatta, for example, was a great scholar who memorized as many texts as an elephant can carry on its back. Intellectually he understood the meaning of all of them, but because he had never experienced inwardly a deep, heartfelt conviction in the law of karma he continued to commit obsessively negative actions, and as a result he was reborn in the seventh hot hell.

In the scriptures the example is given of one practitioner of *Yamantaka Tantra* who had some attainments such as the ability to use wrathful mantras, but since he had no real conviction in the law of karma and lacked the realization of compassion he used the mantras to kill people. As a result he was reborn as a hungry spirit. Since his negative karma ripened in that way, even the powerful Yamantaka could not help him.

The explanation of the law of karma has four parts:

1 The general characteristics of karma
2 Particular types of action and their effects
3 The eight attributes of a fully endowed human life
4 How to practise moral discipline having gained conviction in the law of karma

THE GENERAL CHARACTERISTICS OF KARMA

There are four general characteristics of karma:

1 The results of actions are definite
2 The results of actions increase

3 If an action is not performed its result cannot be experienced
4 An action is never wasted

THE RESULTS OF ACTIONS ARE DEFINITE

In the *Vinaya Sutras* Buddha says:

For every action we perform we experience a similar result.

Just as when a gardener sows a pea seed it is definite that peas and not barley will grow, and when he sows nothing it is definite that nothing will grow, so when we perform positive actions it is definite that we shall experience happy results, when we perform negative actions it is definite that we shall experience unhappy results, and when we perform neutral actions it is definite that we shall experience neutral results.

In *Wheel of Sharp Weapons* Dharmarakshita says that if we now experience any mental disturbance it is because in the past we disturbed the minds of others; and that the main cause of any painful physical illness that we experience is a similar harmful action that we have performed in the past, such as injuring others by beating, shooting, intentionally administering wrong medicines, or serving poisonous food. If this main cause is absent it is impossible to experience the suffering of physical illness. Foe Destroyers, for example, can eat poisonous food without experiencing any pain because they have ceased the harmful actions and potentialities that are the main causes of such suffering.

In the same way, the main causes of the sufferings of hunger and thirst are actions such as selfishly stealing the food and drink of others. Dharmarakshita said that if we experience oppression this is the result of looking down on, beating, or demanding work from people of inferior position, or it is the result of having an attitude of contempt instead of love for others, despising them instead of showing them loving-kindness. The main causes of the sufferings of poverty are wrongs committed against others, such as deliberately preventing them from obtaining necessities or destroying their possessions. The main causes of the sufferings of being separated from friends and family are actions such as seducing other people's partners or purposefully alienating their friends and the people who work for them. The main causes of the sufferings of not having a good relationship with our Spiritual Guides are actions such as abandoning their advice, intentionally disturbing their peace of mind, or being dishonest and hypocritical towards them.

Usually we assume that bad experiences like these arise only in dependence upon the conditions of this present life. Since we cannot account for most of them in these terms, we often feel that our experiences are undeserved and inexplicable and that there is no justice in the world. In fact, most of our experiences in this life are caused by actions we committed in past lives.

In the scriptures the story is told of a man called Nyempa Sangden who was so ugly that people felt upset to look at him, but whose voice was so melodious that when people heard it they longed to be close to him. Buddha alone can see the exact relationship between actions and their effects and he explained about Nyempa Sangden: 'There was once a king who hired many men to build a large stupa. After a while one of the builders became tired and depressed and began to feel hostile towards the king's project. He muttered to himself "What is the point of building such a huge stupa?" However, when the stupa was complete and had been consecrated, the builder felt regret that he had been so angry, and made the offering of a beautiful bell for the stupa. The builder's hostility caused the man's ugliness and his offering of the bell caused his divine voice.'

We need to understand how the quality of our present actions determines the quality of our future experiences. Without knowing this we ignorantly create all the wrong causes. Wishing for happiness we create the cause of suffering and we destroy the very means of fulfilling our wish. In *Guide to the Bodhisattva's Way of Life* Shantideva says:

Although living beings wish to be free from
   suffering,
They run straight towards the causes of suffering;
And although they wish for happiness,
Out of ignorance they destroy it like a foe.

By meditating strongly on this point we shall develop the
determination: 'I will abandon non-virtuous actions because
suffering is their result and I will engage in virtuous actions
because happiness is their result.' We then take this determination as our object of placement meditation.

THE RESULTS OF ACTIONS INCREASE

Even very small non-virtuous actions bear large fruits of
suffering and very small virtuous actions bear large fruits of
happiness. In this way great suffering or great happiness can
grow from small actions – our actions are like small seeds
such as tiny acorns that produce huge oak trees. Although
we may create a very small non-virtuous action, as long as
we fail to purify it, its power to produce suffering increases
day by day.

In the scriptures the example is given of a nun called
Upala who before her ordination experienced extraordinary
misfortune. Of the two children she had by her first husband,
one was drowned and the other was savaged and eaten by
a jackal. Her husband was killed by a poisonous snake. After
losing her family Upala returned to her parents' home, but
soon after she arrived there the house caught fire and burnt
to the ground. She then married a non-Buddhist and had a
child by him, but this man was an alcoholic and one night
he got so drunk that he killed his child and forced his wife
to eat its flesh. Upala fled from this wild man and escaped
into another country, where she was taken captive by thieves
and forced to marry their chief. A few years later her husband
was caught and, according to the custom in that country,
both he and his wife were buried alive. However the thieves
desired the woman and so they dug her up again and forced
her to live with them. Having experienced all these terrible

miseries and misfortunes Upala developed a very strong wish to find freedom from every kind of suffering existence and so she sought Buddha and told him her story. Buddha explained to her that in her previous life she had been one of the wives of a king and that she had been very jealous of the other wives. Her jealousy alone was enough to cause the extravagant sufferings of her present life.

By meditating on this point we shall develop a strong determination to avoid even the slightest non-virtue and to nurture even the smallest good thoughts and good deeds. When this determination arises definitely in our mind we do placement meditation to make it constant and stable. If we can keep our determination all the time without ever forgetting it, our actions of body, speech, and mind will become so pure that there will be no basis for suffering and we shall develop realizations quickly.

IF AN ACTION IS NOT PERFORMED ITS RESULT CANNOT BE EXPERIENCED

In a war when soldiers fight one another some are killed and others survive. The survivors are not saved because they are braver than the others but because they did not create the cause to die at that time.

In the scriptures the example is given of a queen called Ngo Sangma who followed a Buddhist Teacher and gained the realization of a Never Returner. She gathered a following of five hundred female disciples who all developed miracle powers. One day the building in which they were assembled caught fire. The queen and all of her disciples immediately flew into the sky to escape from the flames, but the queen understood that they had all created the collective karma to die in the fire on that day. Since this karma was already ripening it was unavoidable. The queen said to the others, 'The only way we can now purify our non-virtuous actions is by experiencing their effect.' All the women then flew back into the fire like moths leaping into a candle flame.

The women had a poor maidservant called Gurchog who had no miracle powers and had to make her escape by running through the sewers. She had neither spiritual realizations nor time to practise Dharma, yet since she was the only one who had not created the cause to die in that fire, she alone escaped.

We can find many other such examples in the daily newspapers. When a terrorist plants a bomb in a large building some people are killed while others escape in spite of being at the centre of the blast. When there is an aeroplane crash or a volcanic eruption some people are killed and others escape, although their survival seems like a miracle. In many accidents the survivors themselves are astonished by their escape and feel it is strange that others died who were so close to them when the disaster occurred.

By meditating on this point we shall develop the strong determination: 'I will practise purification and engage only in virtuous actions.'

AN ACTION IS NEVER WASTED

Buddha said:

The actions of living beings are never wasted even though hundreds of aeons may pass before their effects are experienced.

Actions cannot simply vanish and we cannot give them away to someone else and thus avoid our responsibility. Although the momentary mental intentions that initiated our past actions have ceased, the potentialities they have created in our mind do not cease until they have ripened. The only way to destroy negative potentialities before they ripen as suffering is to do purification with the four opponent powers. However, it is easier to destroy our positive potentialities, for if we fail to dedicate our virtuous actions they can be made completely powerless by just one moment of anger. Our mind is like a treasure-trove and our virtuous actions are like the jewels. If we do not safeguard them by making dedication, whenever we become angry it is as if we had put a thief among our treasures.

If one thousand years pass between the time when we commit an action and the time when we experience its effect, during all of that time the potentialities of our action are carried within our mind. For example, if we commit the action of killing and all the causes for us to experience the effect of that action do not come together for one hundred lifetimes, still the potentialities of our action of killing remain within our mind throughout all of those lives. At the end of our ninety-ninth lifetime, when we are about to die, we may develop strong attachment to warmth, and this attachment will activate our negative potentiality, thus providing the right conditions for us to experience the ripened effect of our non-virtuous action. The attachment we have at the time of death is like water and the negative potentialities left in our mind by our action of killing are like a seed sown in a field. When the water-like delusion of attachment nourishes our seed-like potentiality it ripens as an extremely painful rebirth in one of the hot hells.

We can consider the example of Shri Datta who committed many extremely negative actions such as offering poisonous food to Buddha. When he grew old, Shri Datta became interested in Dharma and requested Buddha to give him ordination. It is said that anyone who receives ordination must have at least some virtuous potentiality that is a cause of liberation. Clairvoyant disciples of Buddha examined Shri Datta but they could not find a single such virtuous potentiality and so they declared 'This Shri Datta is not fit to be ordained because he does not have even the slightest virtuous potentiality that is a cause of liberation.' However these disciples could not see the subtle potentialities that are seen only by enlightened beings. When Buddha looked he saw a tiny potentiality for virtue within Shri Datta's dark mind. He told his disciples, 'Many aeons ago Shri Datta was a fly who once unknowingly happened to make a circumambulation of a stupa. Since this action was by nature virtuous it has left a trace of goodness in Shri Datta's mind and so he is capable of attaining liberation.' Buddha then granted the ordination and as a result Shri Datta's positive potentialities increased and he actually attained liberation in that lifetime.

In *Guide to the Middle Way* Chandrakirti says that moral discipline is the only cause of happy rebirths and liberation for Bodhisattvas, Solitary Realizers, Hearers, and ordinary beings. To practise moral discipline means to abandon negative actions having understood their dangers. Although there are some negative actions that we cannot abandon immediately due to our strong negative habits of mind, there are some that we can definitely discontinue right now. We need to train our mind gently and steadily, first dealing with the non-virtuous actions we can abandon easily, and then gradually building up the determination, courage, and skill we need to eliminate even our most stubborn bad habits. As long as we have the sincere wish to overcome all of our non-virtuous actions and potentialities, they will naturally become weaker and weaker and we shall find it easier and easier to perform virtuous actions. We do not need to worry, because a continuous and sincere determination is sufficient to undermine the strength of all our non-virtuous tendencies.

We have to be skilful and practise within our capabilities. Some people are able to abandon negative actions as soon as they understand the teachings on karma, while others have a correct understanding and yet continue for a long time to engage in compulsive negativities. If we try to force ourself to overcome all our bad habits at once we shall become anxious and then depressed. We are bound to experience failure and discouragement if our resolutions are too ambitious. Such discouragement is very dangerous because it easily persuades us to abandon Dharma. Since there is no way we can succeed in our spiritual practice while our mind is tense and unhappy, we should always practise in moderation, allowing our mind to remain joyful and relaxed. Then our meditation will work, our mind will become clearer, and our memory will improve. Whenever we become aware of our non-virtuous actions and negative states of mind, instead of becoming depressed and angry, feeling overwhelmed and disappointed every time they arise, we should respond wisely and creatively by making confession and practising purification.

PARTICULAR TYPES OF ACTION AND THEIR EFFECTS

This has four parts:

1 Non-virtuous actions and their effects
2 Virtuous actions and their effects
3 Factors in the power of any action
4 Throwing actions and completing actions

NON-VIRTUOUS ACTIONS AND THEIR EFFECTS

This has three parts:

1 The ten non-virtuous actions and factors in their completion
2 Factors in the severity of non-virtuous actions
3 The effects of non-virtuous actions

THE TEN NON-VIRTUOUS ACTIONS AND FACTORS IN THEIR COMPLETION

Non-virtuous actions are paths that lead to the lower realms. We first need to identify them and understand how they lead to misery and confusion. With this understanding we shall naturally strive to refrain from them. Non-virtuous actions are countless, but most of them are included within the ten:

1 Killing
2 Stealing
3 Sexual misconduct
4 Lying
5 Divisive speech
6 Hurtful speech
7 Idle chatter
8 Covetousness
9 Malice
10 Holding wrong views

The first three are bodily actions, the next four are primarily verbal actions, although they include some bodily actions, and the last three are mental actions.

We experience the full result of an action only when the action is complete, and it is complete only when all four factors are present: the object, the intention, the preparation, and the completion.

KILLING

The object of killing is any other being from the smallest insect to a Buddha. For there to be a full intention to commit any negative action three factors must be present: correct discrimination, determination, and delusion. In the case of killing, correct discrimination is a correct identification of the person we intend to kill. For example, if we want to kill John but we kill Peter, thinking that Peter is John, we have not completed either the action of killing John or the action of killing Peter, although our action is still harmful and will incur some negative result. The factor of determination is our determination to kill the person we have correctly ident-ified. If we kill someone accidentally without having any wish to inflict harm, our action is not complete. When we commit the action our mind must also be influenced by delusion. It is possible that someone may kill without being influenced by any delusion, as when someone kills out of compassion to save the lives of others. To do this a person must have great wisdom and courage to take upon themself whatever negative results the action brings. Usually when someone kills, the action is motivated by one of the root delusions: anger, desirous attachment, or ignorance. A thief may kill out of attachment, believing that his victim is going to prevent his theft. A soldier may kill out of hatred for his enemy, or out of ignorance, thinking that at a time of war killing is not a negative action. Some people happily kill animals, fish, birds, and so forth in the mistaken belief that it is not a non-virtuous action. In some religions it is even taught that some acts of killing are virtuous, such as the killing of animals for sacrifice.

The third factor, preparation, refers to our preparing the means to engage in the action. We may engage in the action directly or we may employ someone else to commit the deed for us. For example, we may kill by administering poison to our victim, or by hiring someone else to shoot him. The action of killing is complete when the victim dies before we do. At that time, provided all the other factors are present, we have created the cause to experience the full negative result of our action.

It is mistaken to think that the consequences of our non-virtuous actions can be avoided by employing someone else to commit them. In fact, if we use someone else as our agent the total effect of our action will be twice as severe because two people will have to suffer the bad results. In addition, we shall have to experience the consequences of exploiting someone else for our own selfish purposes without having concern for their future welfare.

We tend to think that people who have power over others are very fortunate. In reality, however, their position is very dangerous because it is extremely difficult for such a person to avoid performing tremendously destructive actions. For example, if a ruler orders an army to engage in battle, and in the battle one thousand enemy soldiers are killed, each soldier will experience the negative result of however many people he killed; but the ruler will incur the negative result of killing one thousand human beings. People in power can commit immensely destructive actions in the amount of time it takes to write their signature or press a button. The Protector Nagarjuna used to pray never to become a politician in any of his future lives because he knew that if he were to gain any worldly authority and power he would have to take personal responsibility for all the actions he commanded others to perform.

When a group of people agree to perform any action, and that action is completed, each person individually incurs the result of the action. There may be only one object of the action but there are as many actions as there are participants. The same applies even if the group appoints only one person actually to perform the deed. However, if we order or appoint someone else to perform an action and then we change our mind before the action is complete, we do not incur the full result.

STEALING

The object of stealing is anything that someone else regards as their own. This includes other living beings such as another person's child or animal. If we take something that no one claims to possess, such as an object found in a rubbish bin, the action of stealing is not complete.

We must correctly identify the object of stealing. If we want to steal our enemy's possessions but we steal someone else's possessions, thinking that they belong to our enemy, our action of stealing from either person is not complete. We must also be determined to steal, and we must be influenced by delusion. Usually theft is committed out of desirous attachment but sometimes people steal out of hatred, wishing to cause grief to their enemy, and sometimes people steal out of ignorance, thinking that there is nothing wrong with stealing or that it is justified. For example, people may avoid repaying loans or paying taxes, fines, or fees, believing that the system that requires these payments is unjust, or they may steal from their employer thinking that it is all right because he or she does not pay them enough.

There are many methods of stealing. We may engage in the action secretly or openly. We may use devious methods such as bribery, blackmail, or emotional manipulation of the person whose possessions we want. The action of stealing is complete when we think to ourself 'This object is now mine.' When we borrow something from someone else we may grow fond of it and lose our intention to return it. If we eventually start to think of the object as our own, then, provided the other factors are present, we have completed the action of stealing. As long as we still hesitate to call something our own, our action is not complete. For example, if we get on a train without purchasing a ticket we may remain unsure throughout our journey whether or not we shall have to pay, but when we have arrived at our destination and successfully dodged all the ticket collectors we shall feel that we have gained possession of a free train journey. When we develop this triumphant thought our action of stealing is complete.

SEXUAL MISCONDUCT

If we have taken vows of celibacy the object of sexual misconduct is any other person. If we are not celibate and we have a partner, the object of sexual misconduct is anyone else. If we are not celibate and we do not have a partner, the object of sexual misconduct is any of the following: anyone else's partner (husband, wife, boyfriend, or girlfriend); our own parent; a child; anyone with a vow of celibacy; pregnant women; animals; or anyone who does not consent.

We must correctly identify the object of sexual misconduct. For example, if we are not celibate and we do not have a partner, and we have sexual intercourse with someone believing that they do not have a partner when in fact they are married, our action is not complete. We must also be determined to commit sexual misconduct, and we must be influenced by delusion. Usually sexual misconduct is committed out of desirous attachment, but sometimes it is committed out of hatred, as when soldiers rape the wives and daughters of their enemies. Sometimes people commit sexual misconduct out of ignorance, not realizing that there is anything wrong with it or thinking that it is healthy or exalted, as when someone has sexual relationships with other people's partners believing that free love is a path to liberation.

There are many ways to engage in the action of sexual misconduct. The action is complete when sexual bliss is experienced by means of the union of the two sex organs.

LYING

There are many objects of lying but most are included within the eight: what is seen, what is heard, what is experienced, what is known; and what is not seen, what is not heard, what is not experienced, and what is not known. Some instances of lying are not verbal actions. For example, a person may lie by making physical gestures, by writing, or even by remaining silent.

For the action of lying to be complete we must correctly identify the object. If we mistake the object, saying, for instance

'My offering bowls are made of gold', when we mean to say 'My offering bowls are made of brass', the action is not complete. We must also be determined to lie, and we must be influenced by delusion. In the case of lying, any of the root delusions may be involved. There are many ways of engaging in a lie, but the action is complete only when the person to whom the lie is directed has understood our meaning and believes what we have said or indicated. If the other person does not understand us, our action is not complete. For example, if we whisper a lie into the ear of our dog there is no way he will believe us and so we cannot incur the full negative result.

DIVISIVE SPEECH

The object of divisive speech is two or more people who have a relationship with one another. If their relationship is good our divisive speech causes it to deteriorate or destroys it completely, and if their relationship is bad our divisive speech makes it worse. We must correctly identify the object, and we must be determined to damage a relationship between people by using divisive speech. Our mind must be influenced by delusion. Again, any of the three root delusions may be involved.

There are two types of divisive speech: that which is true but harmful to utter, and that which is false, such as slander or propaganda. Divisive speech does not have to be a verbal action. We can destroy harmony and good will among people by using means other than speech, such as by writing or by silence. There are many ways of engaging in divisive speech, but the action is complete only when as a result of our action a good relationship is damaged or a bad relationship is made worse.

HURTFUL SPEECH

The object of hurtful speech is any person who can be hurt by what we say. If we get angry with the weather and abuse it, our action of hurtful speech is not complete because the weather cannot be wounded by our words. We must correctly identify the object. If we mistake the object – for example, if we want to insult Peter but we insult John, thinking he is Peter – our action is not complete. We must also be determined to speak hurtfully, and we must be influenced by delusion. Usually when we speak hurtfully we do so in anger, and there is always some degree of anger involved in this action; but we may also utter hurtful words out of desirous attachment. For instance, we may tell someone that they are fat in the hope that they will feel miserable enough to leave their chocolate cake for us! Sometimes we may speak hurtfully out of ignorance, not considering that others could be hurt by what we say. We may even be deliberately offensive in the belief that it benefits others to receive harsh words.

There are many ways of engaging in hurtful speech, such as by sarcasm. With sarcasm we can speak gently, with a smile on our face, and yet shoot words like arrows into someone else's mind. The purpose of hurtful speech is to inflict such pain upon others. As an arrow pierces the body of our enemy, hurtful speech pierces another person's sensibility. Hurtful speech is not necessarily a verbal action; we can inflict this pain without using words. For example, we can humiliate or mock someone with a gesture. Whenever we are with other people we must guard our speech and consider whether or not our words will hurt them. We check inwardly 'Could these words be disturbing? Could they create unhappiness?' Atisha said that when we are on our own we should be especially watchful of our mind, and when we are with others we should be especially watchful of our speech.

The action of hurtful speech is complete when the person to whom our action is directed understands our words, believes that they have been uttered in earnest, and is disturbed. If this person does not understand our words, thinks that we are joking, or remains untroubled by what we say, the action is not complete.

IDLE CHATTER

The object of idle chatter is any object that is meaningless. Again, we must correctly identify the object, we must be determined to engage in the action, and we must be influenced by delusion.

There are many ways of engaging in idle chatter. For example, we can just utter everything that comes into our head. We can talk without purpose or without any sense of responsibility. Any talking that is mindless or of no real benefit is idle chatter. This action can be non-verbal. For example, if we spend a lot of time reading frivolous books full of romance and fantasy, this is a type of idle chatter. Although this action is not by nature a severely non-virtuous action, if we indulge in it frequently it will fill our life with trivialities and become a serious obstacle to our Dharma practice. The action of idle chatter is complete when others have heard our words.

COVETOUSNESS

The object of the mental action of covetousness is anything that belongs to someone else. It can be a material possession, a job, a high position, or someone else's partner. We must correctly identify the object, we must be determined to possess it, and we must be influenced by delusion. Most often when we experience covetousness our mind is disturbed by desirous attachment. We engage in the action by repeatedly considering how to obtain the object, and we complete the action when we choose a particular method and decide to apply it to procure the object for ourself.

Our determination to get the object, our repeated consideration of the best method to use, and our decision definitely to get the object by our chosen method together constitute the train of thought that is the mental action of covetousness. Provided all the factors are present the action is complete, regardless of whether or not we actually put our decision into effect.

MALICE

The object of malice is any other person. We must correctly identify the person, we must be determined to express our malice towards them, and we must be influenced by one of the root delusions. We engage in malice by repeatedly considering how to harm someone else, and we complete the action when we choose our method and decide to put it into effect.

Our determination to express our ill will, our repeated consideration of the best method to use, and our decision definitely to inflict harm by our chosen method together constitute the train of thought that is the mental action of malice. Provided all the necessary factors are present, the action is complete, and we shall incur the full result of our malice whether or not we actually express our malice with a bodily or verbal action.

HOLDING WRONG VIEWS

To attain liberation and enlightenment there are certain objects that we need to know, such as the existence of past and future lives, the law of karma, the four noble truths, and the Three Jewels. To commit the negative action of holding wrong views we must be determined to deny the existence of such an object, thinking, for example, 'I have not seen my future lives and so I will assert that there are no future lives.' We must also correctly identify which object it is that we are denying, and our mind must be influenced by delusion.

We engage in holding wrong views by repeatedly considering how to deny the object's existence. There are many methods for doing this, such as by repudiating the object dogmatically, by using incorrect ways of reasoning, or by developing faith in someone who teaches wrong views. We complete the action when we choose our method and decide to rely upon it in order to hold onto our wrong view tightly. At this point we have closed our mind, and we have created the cause to experience the full negative result of our action.

FACTORS IN THE SEVERITY OF NON-VIRTUOUS ACTIONS

The degree of suffering we experience as a result of any negative action depends upon the power of the action, and its power is determined by six factors:

1 The nature of the action
2 The intention
3 The method
4 The object
5 How often the action is committed
6 The application or non-application of an opponent

THE NATURE OF THE ACTION

Some non-virtuous actions are by nature more non-virtuous than others. The degree of severity of any non-virtuous action corresponds to the degree of harm the action inflicts upon others. Among the three non-virtuous bodily actions and the four non-virtuous verbal actions, killing is by nature the most destructive, and then, in decreasing order, stealing, sexual misconduct, lying, divisive speech, hurtful speech, and idle chatter. Among the non-virtuous mental actions, covetousness is the least severe, malice is more severe, and holding wrong views is the most severe.

THE INTENTION

The degree of negativity of any action depends upon the power of the delusion that is involved. For example, to kill in a violent rage is more negative than to kill with mild anger. To chatter meaninglessly in order to prevent someone else from doing something worthwhile is more negative than to chatter meaninglessly because we are at a party and everyone else is doing the same.

THE METHOD

The severity of a non-virtuous action also depends upon the degree of harm our chosen method inflicts upon others. For example, killing an animal swiftly is less destructive than killing sadistically, applying slow and painful torture, or reducing our victim to a state of terror by chasing it for miles across fields with a pack of ferocious hounds.

THE OBJECT

Any non-virtuous action is more powerful if our object is an object of refuge or someone who has been especially kind to us, such as our mother or father.

HOW OFTEN THE ACTION IS COMMITTED

The more often we perform a non-virtuous action the more powerful it becomes. For example, idle chatter is not by nature a very severe negative action, but if we indulge in it compulsively and repeatedly at every available opportunity it becomes much more non-virtuous and brings much heavier results.

THE APPLICATION OR NON-APPLICATION OF AN OPPONENT

The power of our non-virtuous actions is lessened when we perform virtuous actions as well, but if we perform only non-virtuous actions they will have a more severe effect.

Since the severity of a non-virtuous action depends upon all six factors, an example of the most severe type of evil deed would be for someone to kill their mother in a fit of blind rage by using a poison that inflicts slow and agonizing death, and for the killer to be someone who commits such sadistic murders compulsively without ever regretting them or having the slightest good impulse. The mildest type of evil deed would be for a Dharma practitioner who usually keeps pure moral discipline and habitually practises virtues such as patience and generosity, occasionally, and without being influenced by strong delusion, to engage in some senseless talk at a party.

THE EFFECTS OF NON-VIRTUOUS ACTIONS

A non-virtuous action has three types of effect:

1 The ripened effect
2 The effects similar to the cause
3 The environmental effect

THE RIPENED EFFECT

The ripened effect of a negative action is rebirth in one of the three lower realms. The most severe negative actions ripen as rebirth in the hell realm, less severe actions as rebirth in the hungry ghost realm, and the least severe negative actions as rebirth in the animal realm.

THE EFFECTS SIMILAR TO THE CAUSE

There are two types of effect that are similar to the cause:

1 Tendencies similar to the cause
2 Experiences similar to the cause

Even when our positive potentialities eventually ripen as a human rebirth we shall experience these two types of effect as further repercussions of our non-virtuous action. We experience effects that are tendencies similar to the cause by continuing to have a strong compulsion to repeat similar non-virtuous actions. This effect makes it extremely difficult for us to avoid creating the cause for many future rebirths in the lower realms. For example, the tendency similar to the action of killing is to have a strong drive to destroy living beings. When some people see a spider in their room they automatically respond by crushing it to death, and some children cannot resist tormenting or torturing animals. These are tendencies that resemble destructive actions committed in the past. Similarly, the tendency resembling the action of sexual misconduct is to feel strongly attracted to other people's partners.

The effects that are experiences similar to the ten non-virtuous actions are as follows. The experience similar to killing is that our life is short and full of sickness and disease. By killing we cut short the life of someone else and so we ourself experience a short life and our vitality is damaged by ill health. If we are experiencing such things in this life we can identify them as the results of our own actions. The experience similar to stealing is that we lack wealth and possessions, and when we do manage to gather some resources together they are stolen from us or people borrow them and fail to return them. The experience similar to sexual misconduct is that we are quickly separated from our friends and family, our partners abandon us for someone else, the people who work for us soon resign, and we experience loneliness. We can see that some people who are old and ugly have many friends and a devoted partner, while others who are young and beautiful cannot find a loyal partner or make friendships that last.

The experience similar to lying is that no one trusts what we say and people do not listen to our advice; the experience similar to divisive speech is that we find it hard to develop harmonious relationships with others; and the experience similar to hurtful speech is that others say unpleasant things to us and speak badly about us. Whenever someone hurts us by speaking offensively or sarcastically we can recognize this as the result of our own previous harsh words. The experience similar to idle chatter is that people do not take seriously what we say. They regard us as foolish and do not pay attention to our comments and opinions.

The experience similar to covetousness is that our desires are not fulfilled and we fail to obtain what we want; the experience similar to malice is that we are constantly prone to fear and we panic in dangerous situations; and the experience similar to holding wrong views is that we have great confusion and find it difficult to develop wisdom. Moreover, when we listen to or read Dharma teachings we are full of doubt. If we now find it hard to remove misconceptions and attain realizations, this is the result of our clinging to wrong views in the past.

THE ENVIRONMENTAL EFFECT

The third effect of a negative action is that if we take another human rebirth, for example, our environment and the things that surround us are hostile, dangerous, or uncomfortable. The environmental effect of killing is that the place in which we live is poor, and it is hard to find food and other necessities; the environmental effect of stealing is that the place in which we live is barren, and plants and crops will not flourish there; and the environmental effect of sexual misconduct is that the place in which we live is unclean and breeds disease.

The environmental effect of lying is that we live in a place where people cheat and deceive us, and where there is no one we can trust; and the environmental effect of divisive speech is that the place in which we live is rugged and mountainous, and there is little transport so people have to carry heavy loads. Since divisive speech makes smooth and harmonious relationships between people difficult and painful, we have to inhabit a hard and inhospitable environment where communications are difficult to establish. The environmental effect of hurtful speech is that we have to live in a place where there is dense undergrowth, or plants that sting and tear our flesh, causing us discomfort whenever we move about; and the environmental effect of idle chatter is that we live in a place where fruit and crops do not grow properly, or at the right time, and so they are wasted.

The environmental effect of covetousness is that we have to live in a place where material resources are easily destroyed or lost, or where our bodily strength and beauty quickly degenerate; the environmental effect of malice is that we are reborn in a place that is ravaged by war and disease, or where there is continuous conflict; and the environmental effect of holding wrong views is that we are reborn in a place that lacks water and where resources are quickly exhausted. It is a place where nothing precious exists – no works of art, no valuable treasures, no scriptures, no Spiritual Guides.

If we do not purify our negative karma by applying the four opponent powers we shall have to experience all these different types of effect. It is said that if someone knows these effects and yet continues to commit non-virtuous actions, they are like someone with perfect eyesight who walks straight off the edge of a cliff!

VIRTUOUS ACTIONS AND THEIR EFFECTS

This has three parts:

1 The ten virtuous actions and factors in their completion
2 Factors in the beneficial power of virtuous actions
3 The effects of virtuous actions

THE TEN VIRTUOUS ACTIONS AND FACTORS IN THEIR COMPLETION

The ten virtuous actions are:

1 Abandoning killing
2 Abandoning stealing
3 Abandoning sexual misconduct
4 Abandoning lying
5 Abandoning divisive speech
6 Abandoning hurtful speech
7 Abandoning idle chatter
8 Abandoning covetousness
9 Abandoning malice
10 Abandoning holding wrong views

Virtuous actions are paths that lead to the temporary happiness of higher rebirths and to the ultimate happiness of liberation and full enlightenment. Just as there are ten non-virtuous actions, so there are ten principal virtuous actions. Each of the ten principal virtuous actions is a restraint from one of the ten non-virtuous actions, based on a clear recognition of its dangers.

To refrain deliberately from non-virtuous actions, having understood their dangers, is the practice of moral discipline.

Since wisdom realizing the effects of negative actions and a firm decision to practise restraint are both necessary in order to practise moral discipline, it cannot be said that we are performing virtuous actions just by not engaging in any negativity. Babies do not perform non-virtuous actions such as stealing, and yet they are not practising moral discipline because they do not understand the dangers of non-virtuous actions and they have not come to a firm decision to abandon them.

The same four factors that complete a non-virtuous action must all be present for virtuous actions to be complete. In the case of virtuous actions, however, the factor of intention does not include the third component, delusion. By taking the first of the ten virtuous actions, abandoning killing, as our example, all the others can be understood.

The object of abandoning killing is any other living being or group of people. Some people are able to take all living beings as their object, and make a firm decision never to kill any of them, but others have to begin by taking a more limited object. For example, fishermen can take all living beings who are not fish as their object, and then take fish as their object for short periods of time, such as during the night and on Sundays, keeping the intention to increase these periods of time whenever they can. We must correctly identify the object, and we must be determined to abandon killing, understanding its dangers. We engage in the action by repeatedly considering what it means to abandon killing, and we complete the action when we choose our method and make a firm decision to abandon killing by putting our method into practice. Once we have made this decision, as long as we remain mindful of it our practice of moral discipline is pure. If the thought to kill arises in our mind and we act upon it, our moral discipline is broken. Our decision to refrain from killing is like a vow, but it does not have to be taken in front of our Spiritual Guide or in front of the visualized objects of refuge.

Non-Buddhists can practise the moral discipline of restraint from the ten non-virtuous actions because they can understand the harmful effects of such actions and make a firm decision to practise restraint. If for any reason we are unable to study, meditate, or recite prayers, we can still practise the moral discipline of abandoning non-virtuous actions, and this, even on its own, is a great and vast spiritual practice.

FACTORS IN THE BENEFICIAL POWER OF VIRTUOUS ACTIONS

These can be understood from the section on the factors in the severity of non-virtuous actions. For instance, abandoning killing is more beneficial than abandoning stealing, and so on. The extent to which an action is virtuous also depends upon the power of the virtuous intention that is involved. The degree of benefit that results from our chosen method also affects the power of our virtuous action, as does the object. The more often we perform a virtuous action the more powerful it becomes, and the power of our virtuous action is strengthened if we do not later develop regret but instead rejoice in our action.

THE EFFECTS OF VIRTUOUS ACTIONS

A virtuous action also has the three kinds of effect: the ripened effect, the effects similar to the cause, and the environmental effect. The ripened effect of a very powerful virtuous action is rebirth as a god of the form or formless realms; the ripened effect of a less powerful virtuous action is rebirth as a god of the desire realm; and the ripened effect of the least powerful virtuous action is rebirth as a human being.

Effects that are tendencies similar to virtuous actions are strong tendencies or impulses to perform the same kinds of virtuous action in our future human rebirths. This makes it easy for us to create the causes for many happy rebirths. Effects that are experiences similar to virtuous actions are that in future human rebirths we shall experience the same kinds of benefit our virtuous actions allowed others to experience. For example, the experience similar to the action of abandoning killing is that we enjoy a long life and good health; the experience similar to the action of abandoning stealing is that we effortlessly accumulate wealth and possessions; and the experience similar to the action of abandoning sexual misconduct is that we have stable friendships and a happy family life.

We can tell what attitudes we have had in the past and what actions we have engaged in simply by observing our present states of mind and our experiences. If we now have a strong interest in Dharma this indicates that we have practised Dharma in the past. Some people can realize renunciation, bodhichitta, and the correct view of emptiness without doing much meditation because they have familiarized themselves with these meditations in past lives. Although we forget our experiences of past lives, the potentialities of our past actions remain within our minds and it is easy for us to resume our old habits.

The environmental effects of virtuous actions are opposite to the environmental effects of non-virtuous actions. For example, the environmental effect of abandoning killing is that when we take, say, a human rebirth, the place where we live is abundant in all the necessities for long life and good health. The food is plentiful and nourishing and the medicines are effective.

An environmental effect is not a quality of external conditions but a quality of the mind that experiences them. The same external conditions can be experienced as different environmental effects for different minds. For example, in a place where most people find the food good and nourishing, there are some people who experience nausea and indigestion when they eat it. A doctor can give the same medicine to two people, and one is cured by it while the other becomes more sick. This inequality is not in the medicine but results from the different actions these two people performed in the past. Although many of our troubles and sufferings seem to be caused by external circumstances they are actually the environmental effects of our own bad actions.

When Milarepa was meditating in seclusion he survived on nettles. For him these were good and nourishing and they kept his body healthy and strong. It was not that the nettles were good in themselves, but Milarepa enjoyed them as the environmental effect of his own virtue.

FACTORS IN THE POWER OF ANY ACTION

There are four factors that determine the power of an action, whether it be virtuous or non-virtuous:

1 The person who is the object of the action
2 The vows taken
3 The object that is instrumental in the action
4 The motivation

THE PERSON WHO IS THE OBJECT OF THE ACTION

Actions are more powerful when they are performed towards those who have been especially kind and helpful towards us, such as our parents, our Spiritual Guides, Buddhas, and Bodhisattvas.

THE VOWS TAKEN

If we take vows all our actions become more powerful. If we take novice vows our actions are more powerful than if we take only lay vows; if we take vows of full ordination our actions are more powerful than if we take only novice vows; if we take the Bodhisattva vows our actions are more powerful than if we take only the Pratimoksha vows; and if we take the Tantric vows our actions are more powerful than if we take only the Bodhisattva vows. Vows are the basis for accumulating a great amount of merit. If we take a vow and keep it purely, then even when we are asleep we are practising moral discipline. In *Guide to the Bodhisattva's Way of Life* Shantideva says that when someone takes Bodhisattva vows:

> From that time forth, for him there will arise –
> Even if he is asleep or apparently unconcerned –
> Vast and powerful merit, equal to space,
> That flows without interruption.

THE OBJECT THAT IS INSTRUMENTAL IN THE ACTION

To take the action of giving as our example, the action is more powerful if we give something that is useful or helpful to the other person. If we give a starving child food, this is more powerful than if we give the child a toy. If we give a monk a pair of shoes, this is more powerful than if we give him shampoo. In general, if we give anyone Dharma instructions this is more powerful than giving any material gift because material gifts last only for a short time whereas the gift of Dharma lasts forever.

THE MOTIVATION

Actions are more powerful if we perform them with a strong motivation. For example, if we give something with a strong wish to benefit someone else, this is more powerful than if we give something away because we have no use for it ourself. If we give with the motivation of renunciation, this is more powerful than giving with a simple wish to help; and if we give with the motivation of bodhichitta our action will be even more powerful. If with bodhichitta we give money to one person, we receive the merit of having given money to every single living being. The merit of such an action is immeasurable, whereas if we give money with the thought of benefiting only one person we receive the merit of benefiting only one person. Therefore, when we engage in virtuous actions it is wise to do so with the best motivation. If we are motivated by faith, all our virtuous actions become very powerful.

An example of the most powerful type of virtuous action is to go for refuge on a day when we have taken the eight Mahayana precepts. This action is powerful with respect to the object because our object is the Three Jewels; it is powerful with respect to the vows we have taken because we are keeping the Mahayana precepts; it is powerful with respect to the object that is instrumental in our action because what we are offering is our practice of Dharma; and it is powerful with respect to our motivation because our motivation is bodhichitta.

THROWING ACTIONS AND COMPLETING ACTIONS

There are two types of contaminated action: throwing actions and completing actions. A throwing action is so called because it is the main cause of a samsaric rebirth and so it is said to 'throw' us into samsara. Virtuous throwing actions throw us into the fortunate worlds of humans and gods, and non-virtuous throwing actions throw us into the unfortunate worlds of hell beings, hungry spirits, and animals.

Most of the virtuous actions of ordinary beings are causes of samsaric rebirth because they are tainted by self-grasping. For example, when we make a strong decision, 'I will refrain from non-virtuous actions', we grasp this 'I' as an inherently existent I. Although our intention in performing any virtuous action is not deluded, our mind is still mixed with the delusion of self-grasping. This delusion is continuously present in the mind of an ordinary being.

Nevertheless, there are some virtuous actions of ordinary beings that are not causes of samsaric rebirth. For example, if we visualize Buddha and make offerings, make prostrations, or go for refuge, these actions cannot be throwing actions, even if we perform them without a good motivation. These actions can only be causes of liberation by virtue of the special power of the object, the Three Jewels.

A completing action is an action that is the main cause of an experience we have once we have taken a particular rebirth. All human beings are thrown into the human world by virtuous throwing actions, but the experiences they have as human beings vary considerably depending upon their different completing actions. Some experience a life of suffering whereas others experience a life of ease. Similarly, animals have all been thrown into the animal world by non-virtuous throwing actions, but their experiences as animals vary considerably depending upon their different completing actions. Some of them, such as domestic pets, experience a luxurious animal life, receiving more care and attention than some human beings. Hell beings and hungry spirits have only non-virtuous throwing actions and only non-virtuous completing actions, for they experience nothing but suffering during their lives.

One throwing action may throw us into many future lives. In the scriptures the example is given of a man who became angry with a fully ordained monk and told him he looked like a frog. As a result, this unfortunate man was reborn as a frog five hundred times. However, just one rebirth is sometimes sufficient to exhaust the power of our throwing action.

Some actions ripen in the same life in which they are performed, some ripen in the next life, and some ripen in lives after that. If we practise moral discipline in this life we may experience the effects later on in this life. If parents are good to their children their actions may ripen in their old age when the children return their kindness. If children are good to their parents their actions may ripen when they have become adults and have helpful children of their own.

THE EIGHT ATTRIBUTES OF A FULLY ENDOWED HUMAN LIFE

If we wish to create the cause to gain a human rebirth in the future we should also strive to create the causes for a human rebirth that is highly qualified in terms of its usefulness for Dharma practice. A human rebirth alone will not necessarily afford ideal conditions for spiritual practice because there are many kinds of unfortunate human rebirth which are almost as limited as an animal rebirth. If we create the causes for a highly qualified human rebirth, even if we do not accomplish our ultimate aim of liberation or full enlightenment in this life we shall at least ensure that we have the best opportunity to do so in the future.

A highly qualified human existence is one that has the eight attributes of a fully endowed human life: long life, beauty, high status, wealth and resources, persuasive speech, power and influence, freedom and independence, a strong mind and a strong body. These are explained in three parts:

1 Their advantages
2 Their functions
3 Their causes

THEIR ADVANTAGES

The greatest advantage of these eight attributes is that they endow our human life with the very best opportunity to attain liberation and enlightenment in one lifetime.

THEIR FUNCTIONS

Long life enables us to fulfil our desires and complete our Dharma practice. Beauty makes it easier for us to attract disciples when we give Dharma instructions, and it helps them to develop faith in us. High status makes people trust us, obey us, and follow our advice; people more readily assume that we are honest and they are more inclined to listen carefully and consider what we say. Wealth and resources enable us to give generously, and this makes people feel pleasantly disposed towards us, so we have more influence over them. This attribute is especially helpful as a means of encouraging worldly people to take an interest in Dharma. For example, we can invite them to our home and when they are relaxed and comfortable we can gently introduce Dharma into our conversation, or we can give them books or tapes, or pay for them to visit a Dharma Centre. It is said that if we want to help others by giving Dharma instructions two things are necessary: wisdom gained through experience and wealth. If a wealthy person has Dharma wisdom their motivation will be good and they will use their wealth well to bring benefit to others.

Persuasive speech makes others trust what we say and take our words to heart. Power and influence make others comply with our wishes and put our instructions into practice. Freedom and independence mean that we do not experience so many interferences to our practice. A strong body enables us easily to perform virtuous actions of body; it allows us to exert ourself as Milarepa did when his Spiritual Guide told him to make a building nine stories high. We shall also be free from physical hindrances such as illness. A strong mind enables us to understand Dharma quickly. We are able to eliminate doubts and hesitations, and we develop wisdom and concentration, making our mind even more powerful. We more easily attain clairvoyance, miracle powers, and other realizations.

If we gain a human rebirth with all these special attributes but fail to make good use of them by developing our own Dharma practice and helping others to practise Dharma, we shall not receive any of the benefits of having taken such a fortunate rebirth. There are many people who have these eight attributes but who do not put them into the service of Dharma. Therefore, while trying to create the cause for such a rebirth in the future we should also pray sincerely that when we gain such a wonderful opportunity we shall use it for the sake of Dharma. If we practise in this way we shall definitely attain liberation or full enlightenment in our next life.

THEIR CAUSES

Milarepa once said to a farmer:

You are farmers of this life,
But I am a farmer of future lives.
If you examine carefully you will see
Who receives more benefit.

If we sow good seeds in our field-like consciousness we can be sure that they will ripen. As Dharmakirti said:

If all the causes and conditions are assembled, nothing can prevent the effect from arising.

The seeds that we need to sow now are the causes of a human rebirth with the eight attributes. Causes of long life are to avoid harming others and to actively dispel dangers that threaten their lives. Whenever we can we must save the lives of living beings. Further causes of long life are to help those who are held captive, to give medicines to those who are sick, and, with a good heart, to nurse others.

Causes of beauty are to overcome anger and intolerance with patient acceptance, to offer light before images of Buddha, to make statues or paintings of Buddha, to make stupas, to repair old images or statues of Buddha or enhance them by offering fine garments or adding gold to their faces, and to give clothes to other human beings. By such actions we make others more attractive and thus create the cause to become more beautiful ourself. Whenever we see a beautiful person we can recognize their beauty as the result of their own graceful actions.

The main cause of high status is to overcome pride. It is easy to develop pride. As soon as we acquire some new piece of knowledge, some new skill, or some new article of clothing that enhances our physical appearance, we develop pride. Our pride grows just like our shadow. As a child grows up his or her shadow becomes bigger and bigger. In the same way, as our knowledge accumulates, our pride increases. In this way pride prevents our spiritual progress and makes us less capable of gaining realizations, even though our knowledge of Dharma may increase. Pride undermines our studies and makes them useless. Another cause of high status is to respect all beings, not only our parents, our Teachers, or our elders and superiors. We should never look down on anyone or treat them with contempt. We should regard even an earthworm as a worthy object of respect and consideration.

The main cause of wealth and resources is to practise giving by making offerings to the Three Jewels and giving wealth and resources to other beings. The main cause of persuasive speech is to be mindful of what we say and to abandon the four non-virtuous actions of speech. The main cause of power and influence is to practise prostration and to respect others, especially those who are powerful and influential over us, such as our parents and Teachers. The main cause of freedom and independence is to eliminate the problems and dangers that threaten others and to help them gain their own freedom and independence. The cause of a strong body is to help those who are physically weak to regain their strength by giving them nourishment and medicine, and to avoid exploiting others physically. For example, we should not make animals carry heavy burdens for us or confine them to an unhealthy, artificial environment.

Causes of a strong mind are to help others overcome their mental problems and depression and to help them become happy, to increase others' wisdom and concentration, to engage in moral discipline, to develop our own concentration, and to develop our own wisdom by listening to or reading extensive Dharma instructions.

A further cause of attaining any or all of these eight attributes is to make pure and sincere prayers to attain them for the benefit of all living beings.

HOW TO PRACTISE MORAL DISCIPLINE HAVING GAINED CONVICTION IN THE LAW OF KARMA

To practise moral discipline we need to meditate again and again on the law of karma, remembering the instructions and dwelling especially on the points we find most helpful. When we are not meditating we can read books that explain karma. When by contemplating and meditating we develop conviction and become determined to abandon non-virtuous actions we try to put this determination into effect in our lives. If we practise like this, our non-virtuous potentialities will be purified and our mind will become like a sky free from clouds, where the sun can shine without obstructions.

At this stage we can gain only a general understanding of karma. We cannot prove by reasoning exactly how each individual action produces its own effect. Only Buddhas can see these relationships exactly. Therefore, to practise moral discipline perfectly we need to have faith in Buddha. If we understand the nature of Buddha we shall realize that it is impossible for a Buddha to teach anything that is false. It is said that Buddhas have no motivation to utter falsehoods because they have nothing to gain from them. In *King of Concentration Sutra* it says:

The moon and the stars may fall to the earth, the earth with all its mountains and dwelling places may disappear, and space itself may disappear, but it is impossible for Buddha to tell a lie.

There is nothing that Buddhas could gain from deceiving anyone because they have accomplished everything they need to accomplish for themselves and their only wish is to be of benefit to others. Therefore, all that they teach is completely reliable and can be accepted on faith whenever the weakness of our own reasoning and experience lets us down.

PART TWO

The Intermediate Scope

Atisha

Dromtonpa

Geshe Potowa

Developing the Wish to Attain Liberation

TRAINING THE MIND IN THE STAGES OF THE PATH OF A PERSON OF INTERMEDIATE SCOPE

If we practise all the stages of the path of a small being and gain realizations, we shall be protected from the sufferings of the lower realms and we shall be sure of gaining rebirth in the more fortunate states of humans and gods. Is this the highest goal we can attain? Surely not. Even humans and gods are bound to experience many miseries. These more fortunate states of existence do not bring pure and lasting happiness, and they do not safeguard us against taking lower rebirth again in the future. As long as we remain in samsara it is almost impossible for us to avoid committing non-virtuous actions that are causes of lower rebirth. Since there is no real security to be found anywhere in samsara, we must aim to become completely free from any kind of uncontrolled rebirth. In *Guide to the Bodhisattva's Way of Life* Shantideva says:

> From time to time, they take a fortunate rebirth
> And briefly enjoy some temporary happiness,
> But soon they die and fall into the lower realms,
> Where they experience unbearable suffering for a
>   very long time.

By gaining the realizations of the stages of the path of a small being we become like a prisoner who has been given a week's reprieve to visit his friends and family. The prisoner will naturally enjoy his brief holiday, but his happiness will not be perfect because he will remain aware that he must shortly return to prison. Similarly, we ourself cannot enjoy perfect happiness until we have become completely free from uncontrolled rebirth within the prison of samsara. The pleasures of human beings and gods are like the tainted enjoyments of a prisoner when he is released for only one week. Therefore we need to develop a strong determination to become completely free from samsara. When we have this determination spontaneously and continuously we have developed the realization of renunciation.

The instructions for training the mind in the stages of the path of a middle being are in three parts:

1 Developing the wish to attain liberation
2 A preliminary explanation for establishing the path that leads to liberation
3 How to practise the path that leads to liberation

DEVELOPING THE WISH TO ATTAIN LIBERATION

The principal method for attaining liberation is the practice of the three higher trainings: training in higher moral discipline, training in higher concentration, and training in higher wisdom. Within these practices are included all the paths of the Hinayana and all the paths of the Mahayana. If we practise the three higher trainings with the motivation of renunciation alone we shall attain liberation, and if we practise them with the motivation of bodhichitta we shall attain enlightenment.

To help us to develop a strong wish to attain liberation Buddha taught two methods – meditation on the four noble truths and meditation on the twelve dependent-related links. By meditating on these we correctly identify samsara and liberation, become determined to abandon samsara and attain liberation, become convinced that we are capable of doing so, and develop conviction in the path that leads to liberation.

When we meditate on the first noble truth, true sufferings, we are meditating on the faults of samsara. This meditation mainly causes us to develop renunciation because it reveals the nature of samsara. Since renunciation is a firm decision to become free from samsara it arises in our mind only when we have realized what samsara is and what are its faults.

When we first hear the word 'renunciation' it is easy to mistake the object that is forsaken by this mind. For instance, we may think that someone who has renunciation forsakes all material possessions and all human relationships, or we may think that someone who does not eat meat or who has taken a vow of celibacy has realized renunciation. In fact, the object that is forsaken by the mind of renunciation is samsara, and samsara does not exist outside ourself. Therefore we cannot become liberated merely by abandoning our possessions, changing our lifestyle, or becoming a nun or a monk.

If our possessions, environment, and enjoyments are not samsara, if our friends and relatives are not samsara, and if our worldly activities and jobs are not samsara, what is samsara? Samsara is uninterrupted rebirth without freedom or control. There is not a single living being in samsara who has been free to choose his or her present form of life or who enjoys freedom and control over his or her experiences in this life. We did not choose the country where we were born or the parents we have, and we cannot choose when we shall die. We did not choose to be rich or poor. It may seem that there are many people who enjoy freedom, but in fact those people are bound to experience suffering just like everyone else. They become sick without choice, they die without choice, and they take rebirth without choice. They do not experience real peace and pure happiness.

If someone were to ask us 'Are you free to eat dinner tonight?' we would say that we are free. Actually we have no freedom because we cannot say for sure that we shall not die before the evening. We cannot be certain that we shall not become ill and incapable of eating anything. Since we have no control over the conditions of our existence we do not have freedom to choose what we shall experience in this life.

If we send a helium balloon up into the sky when there is a lot of wind, the balloon will go wherever it is blown. The balloon itself cannot determine its own direction. We are just like this balloon, blown by the winds of our karma in the direction of our next life. Our lives follow one another in uninterrupted succession, like the spokes of a wheel rapidly spinning. Immediately after death comes birth, and birth soon transforms into death.

Samsara is in the nature of suffering as fire is in the nature of burning. If we do not want to get burnt we must be afraid to touch fire. If we want to avoid suffering we must be afraid of being reborn without choice. Being born as a god and being born in hell are the same in so far as both conditions are unfree and the basis for suffering. If we are wise we shall want to find release from all samsaric conditions, both high and low. Geshe Potowa said:

It is not sickness and death I fear so much as samsaric rebirth.

And in *Treatise of Four Hundred Verses* Aryadeva says:

Those who are wise develop equal fear of high rebirth and rebirth in hell. If we cut the continuum of uncontrolled rebirth we attain liberation, and eliminate the basis for all our suffering.

Considering this we should realize that for as long as we remain in samsara we shall have no freedom and we shall be bound to experience continuous suffering. In this way we should develop a strong wish to attain liberation from samsara. How to develop the wish to attain liberation is now explained under the following two headings:

1 Introduction to the four noble truths
2 Meditating on true sufferings

The Four Noble Truths

The four noble truths are:

1 True sufferings
2 True origins
3 True cessations
4 True paths

They are called 'noble truths' because they are seen to be true by Superior beings, or Noble Ones. For example, the environments, enjoyments, and bodies of samsara are seen by Superior beings to be the nature of suffering, and it is true that they are the nature of suffering – therefore they are called 'true sufferings'.

In *Sutra of the First Wheel of Dharma* Buddha says:

You should know sufferings.
You should abandon origins.
You should attain cessations.
You should meditate on paths.

Through knowing true sufferings we should develop a strong wish to eliminate them; to eliminate them we must strive to abandon their main cause, true origins; and to abandon true origins we must attain true cessations by meditating on true paths.

TRUE SUFFERINGS

There are two types of true suffering: internal true sufferings and external true sufferings. Internal true sufferings are those that are within the continuum of the body and mind of any being within samsara, such as our present body and mind. External true sufferings are those that are not within the continuum of the body and mind of a sentient being, such as the various environments and enjoyments of beings within samsara. Although they are not all sufferings in the sense of being painful experiences, they are called true sufferings because they are all the nature of suffering. In *Compendium of Abhidharma* Asanga says:

> What are true sufferings? You should know that they are the rebirths of sentient beings and the places in which they are born.

Our uncontrolled rebirths in samsara, our impure environments such as the world in which we live, our contaminated aggregates such as our present body and mind, and all our worldly pleasures and pains are true sufferings. All of these are the effects of contaminated throwing actions. Since it is not easy for us to know that all these are true sufferings, Buddha said 'You should know sufferings.'

There are two types of contaminated throwing action: non-virtuous throwing actions and virtuous throwing actions. Non-virtuous throwing actions have three types of effect: the ripened effect, the effects similar to the cause, and the environmental effect. The ripened effects of non-virtuous throwing actions are the aggregates of hell beings, hungry ghosts, and animals. The effects similar to the cause of non-virtuous throwing actions are the painful feelings of hell beings, hungry ghosts, and animals. The environmental effects of non-virtuous throwing actions are the environments experienced by hell beings, hungry spirits, and animals. All these effects of non-virtuous throwing actions are true sufferings.

Virtuous throwing actions also have three types of effect: the ripened effect, the effects similar to the cause, and the environmental effect. The ripened effects of virtuous throwing actions are the contaminated aggregates of humans, demigods, and gods. The effects similar to the cause of virtuous throwing actions are the different types of contaminated happiness of humans, demi-gods, and gods. The environmental effects of virtuous throwing actions are the abodes of humans, demi-gods, and gods. All these effects of virtuous throwing actions are also true sufferings.

TRUE ORIGINS

All powerful delusions and all throwing actions whether virtuous or non-virtuous that are motivated by strong delusions – their main causes – are true origins. The explanation of throwing actions has already been given and the explanation of delusions will be given below.

TRUE CESSATIONS

By practising the stages of the path of a small being we can attain the cessation of the suffering of hell beings, hungry ghosts, and animals; by practising the stages of the path of a middle being we can attain the cessation of the suffering of humans, demi-gods, and gods; and by practising the stages of the path of a great being we can attain the cessation of all obstructions and faults. By practising patience we can attain the cessation of the suffering of anger; by rejoicing we can attain the cessation of the suffering of jealousy; by meditating on impermanence we can attain the cessation of the suffering of attachment; and by practising purification we can attain the cessation of negative karma. We can attain such cessations before we realize the ultimate nature of phenomena directly and thus become a Superior being; but these are not actual true cessations. Although these cessations provide the foundation for attaining true cessations, only Superior beings attain actual true cessations.

A true cessation is the ultimate nature of a mind that has attained the final cessation of any delusion or fault through the power of a true path. How can we attain this? Let us take an example. When a Mahayana practitioner develops spontaneous bodhichitta he or she enters the Mahayana path of accumulation and becomes a Bodhisattva. At this stage the

Bodhisattva has an intellectual understanding of emptiness but has not yet realized emptiness directly. With the motivation of bodhichitta he or she then meditates on emptiness single-pointedly. Through the power of this meditation the Bodhisattva's mental stabilization becomes stronger and its object, emptiness, is perceived more and more clearly. When he or she attains tranquil abiding meditating on emptiness, the concentration is so firm that a subtle wisdom consciousness can examine the object, emptiness, without disturbing the concentration. Just as a fish can swim in a still pond without disturbing the calm surface of the water, so the subtle wisdom consciousness can examine the object without disturbing the stillness of the mind. When this wisdom induces a special suppleness, the Bodhisattva has attained superior seeing observing emptiness and entered the Mahayana path of preparation.

At this stage he has not yet gained a direct realization of emptiness although his wisdom is very powerful and he has a clear appearance of emptiness. While meditating the Bodhisattva even feels as if his mind has become mixed with emptiness but, in fact, while his mind is placed single-pointedly on emptiness, conventional phenomena still appear to it. In other words, he or she still has dualistic appearance. For example, if the Bodhisattva is meditating on the emptiness of his body, his mind of concentration still perceives a generic image of the emptiness of the body. The appearance of a generic image must be eliminated, and this can be done only by realizing emptiness directly. On the Mahayana path of preparation the Bodhisattva meditates on emptiness to abandon all traces of dualistic appearance and to gain a direct realization. By repeated meditation the object becomes clearer and clearer and the Bodhisattva's mind becomes closer and closer to it until, finally, the generic image disappears altogether and his or her mind completely mixes with emptiness as water mixes with water. At this point the Bodhisattva attains a completely non-conceptual, or direct, realization of emptiness, and becomes a Superior Bodhisattva on the Mahayana path of seeing.

When a Superior Bodhisattva arises from meditative equipoise on emptiness he or she no longer develops any intellectually-formed delusions. These would not arise in his mind even if he tried to cultivate them. The emptiness of the mind free from intellectually-formed delusions is the first true cessation.

At this stage innate delusions are yet to be abandoned. Although the Bodhisattva abandons intellectually-formed delusions on the path of seeing, he or she does not begin to abandon innate delusions until the path of meditation. By repeated meditation on emptiness on the path of meditation the different levels of innate delusion are gradually abandoned. When the Bodhisattva attains the true cessation that is the emptiness of the mind free from all innate delusions, he or she attains the eighth ground. The Bodhisattva continues to meditate on emptiness and gradually abandons the imprints of delusions – the obstructions to omniscience. When all these have been completely abandoned he or she attains full enlightenment and enters the Mahayana Path of No More Learning.

From this brief explanation we can see that there are many kinds of true cessation. If we attain even the least of these we shall become free from many faults and sufferings. Therefore, true cessations are actual Dharma Jewels and holy objects of refuge.

TRUE PATHS

As mentioned before, the practices of the stages of the path of a small, a middle, and a great being cause us to gain a cessation of all faults; but all these practices are not necessarily true paths. A true path is any spiritual path of a Superior being that is a method for attaining any true cessation. Without first attaining true paths there is no way to attain true cessations. Just as there are many kinds of true cessation, so there are many kinds of true path, because each true cessation has a true path that leads to it.

Buddha taught true sufferings as the first of the four noble truths because first we need to meditate on them to realize that samsara has the nature of suffering and to develop a firm decision to find release from it. Once we have generated this determination it is easy to exert effort in applying the actual methods for attaining liberation. A prisoner who has no wish to become free will languish in his prison without ever putting effort into applying the means for his escape. Similarly, if we lack the sincere wish to be released from this prison of samsara we shall not generate the effort needed to attain liberation.

At present we do not clearly distinguish between objects to be abandoned and objects to be attained. According to Dharma the main object to be abandoned is samsara. To abandon samsara we need to abandon true sufferings and true origins and to attain true cessations and true paths. All objects to be abandoned are included within true sufferings and true origins, and all objects to be attained are included within true cessations and true paths. True origins are the causes of true sufferings, and true paths are the methods for attaining true cessations.

In *Commentary to Valid Cognition* Dharmakirti says:

Those who sincerely wish to attain liberation do not need a Teacher who is clairvoyant and can see how many insects live underneath the ground or how many atoms are assembled there; nor do they need a Teacher who can see far into the distance, for even vultures can do that. What they need is a Teacher who knows what are the objects to be abandoned, what are the objects to be accomplished, and what are the methods for abandoning and accomplishing them. If those who desire liberation follow a Teacher who reveals such correct spiritual paths, they will accomplish their aim. Without such a Teacher, liberation is impossible.

Meditation on True Sufferings

The purpose of meditating on true sufferings is to realize that the whole of samsara is the nature of suffering and thereby to generate a strong wish to attain liberation. By doing this meditation we develop renunciation with respect to our own suffering, and compassion with respect to the suffering of all other living beings.

Because there are many different types of suffering in samsara, this meditation is quite elaborate. We begin by considering the sufferings of samsara in general, and then we consider the particular sufferings of each state of samsaric rebirth. Finally we meditate on the three types of suffering. You may wonder why it is necessary to do such extensive meditation on suffering. The reason is because at present we have very strong attachment to samsara, and due to this we have no desire to attain liberation even though there is no prospect of happiness in samsara. To overcome this attachment it is necessary to see clearly how every aspect of samsara is the nature of suffering.

Since our attachment to samsara is so strong we must attack it from many sides. If people have a common enemy they go into battle brandishing many different kinds of weapon and they employ many methods for overcoming their enemy. In a similar way, when we meditate on true sufferings we attack our enemy of attachment to samsara from every side and with many methods. If we use only one method our attack will not be so strong and our determination to abandon our attachment will not be so firm; but if we undermine our enemy from all sides and attack it with many critical thoughts we shall be able to destroy it completely.

This meditation is now presented in three parts:

1 The general sufferings of samsara
2 The particular sufferings of each state of samsaric rebirth
3 The three types of suffering

THE GENERAL SUFFERINGS OF SAMSARA

There are many sufferings that are experienced in common by all beings in samsara. These include:

1 Uncertainty
2 Having no satisfaction
3 Having to leave our body over and over again
4 Having to take rebirth over and over again
5 Having to lose status over and over again
6 Having no companionship

UNCERTAINTY

In samsara no condition is certain. Our experiences and our relationships quickly change. High rebirth soon turns into low rebirth, friends turn into enemies, and enemies turn into friends. The seventh Dalai Lama said:

High status soon turns into servitude.
Beauty quickly changes, like a flower in autumn.
Wealth is soon lost, as if merely lent.
Life quickly perishes, like lightning in the sky.

We may think that high status brings security, but if we check we shall see that high status is extremely unstable. Those in high positions have greater responsibilities, bringing with them more anxieties and experiences of mental pain due to criticism by others and even threats to their life. For example, when a country is invaded or when there is a revolution all those who enjoy high status are the first to be killed or imprisoned. In a democracy politicians easily lose their popularity and good reputation.

Our beauty is fragile. Even when we are young our physical appearance varies greatly depending on our state of mind.

In the morning we may get out of bed feeling wonderful and looking radiant. Within just one hour things may start to go wrong and we begin to look downcast. Our face soon becomes dull and lifeless and our body loses its vitality. Our beauty is as changeable as our mind.

Our physical health is never stable. In one day we can be well in the morning but sick by the evening. We feel comfortable for a short while but we soon experience discomfort and try to seek relief. Within each day our physical well-being fluctuates many times. Our mental health is changeable as well. In one minute we can go from laughter to tears. We cannot maintain a constantly happy mind.

Our wealth and possessions are easily lost. Even if we manage to keep them for most of our life, in the end we have to forsake them because we cannot take our savings with us to spend in our next life. Our wealth and possessions are just like things that we have borrowed from someone else and must soon return.

Good fortune and prosperity are uncertain. If our work or our business is going well we may consider ourself to be safe and sound, but all it needs is a change in our environment or a change of government and all our good prospects could suddenly be ruined.

Friendships are unstable. When we first make friends it feels as if we are going to be friends for ever, but our feelings change and sometimes our good feelings turn into bitter hostility. It takes only a few words to destroy trust and open communication between friends. The smallest event or the slightest thought can transform our feelings of friendliness into feelings of jealousy or resentment. For those whose minds are still bound by delusions, friendships are unreliable and uncertain. In *Guide to the Bodhisattva's Way of Life* Shantideva says:

> One moment they are friends,
> The next moment they become enemies;
> And even while they are enjoying themselves, they
>   become angry –
> How unreliable worldly beings are!

In *Friendly Letter* Nagarjuna says that in samsara sometimes our father is reborn as our son, our mother is reborn as our wife, our enemy is reborn as our friend, and our relatives are reborn as our enemies – there is no certainty.

There was once a couple who lived in a house together with their son and his wife. Behind the house was a small lake. The father was very fond of fishing and every day he would catch fish and bring them home for the family to eat. One day a stranger fell in love with the son's wife and committed adultery with her. When the son found out, he killed him. Since the murdered man was so attached to the wife, he was reborn as her child. Shortly afterwards the old mother died, and since she was so attached to the house and the family she was reborn as their pet dog. Later the old father died, and since he was so fond of fishing he took rebirth as one of the fish in the lake. The son then went fishing and caught that fish. He took it home and his wife fried it. The dog smelt the fish and came to get the bones. As the son ate the fish that was his father, he cradled the child who was his enemy, and kicked away the dog that was his mother. With his clairvoyance Shariputra beheld this scene and declared 'Samsara makes me laugh!'

Since our relationships are so changeable there is no reason to become overly attached to our friends and relatives or to develop hostility towards our enemies. All of these relationships will alter – it is just a matter of time.

While Shri Datta, a follower of Buddha, was a layman called Pelgye he once took a walk along the seashore and came across the skeleton of a huge whale. As soon as he saw it he experienced a strange feeling of familiarity. Buddha's disciple Maudgalyanaputra understood what he was feeling and said to him 'Don't you remember this whale? You are gazing at your own skeleton.' Pelgye asked him 'What could I have done to deserve such a monstrous form?' Maudgalyanaputra replied 'In one of your past lives you were a king. One day, while you were engrossed in a game, one of your ministers came and asked you whether or not a certain criminal who had just been taken prisoner should be put to death.

Not wishing to give your attention to the matter you just said "Yes, yes, kill him." When the game was over you remembered the interruption and asked the minister whether the prisoner was dead. When the minister replied that the man had been put to death according to orders, you developed strong regret. As a result of your recklessness on that occasion you took rebirth as this whale and you had to go for a long time without finding food. When you were about to die of starvation some sailors sailed so close to you that they almost sailed straight into your mouth. Just in time they realized what was happening and they took refuge in Buddha. As soon as you heard their prayers you died and your body was washed up here on the beach, but you took rebirth as a human being due to hearing their prayers of going for refuge.'

Small actions caused Shri Datta to go in three lifetimes from being a king to being a whale to being a man. From his example we can see how extremely variable are the conditions of our existence while we remain subject to rebirth without control. If we do not attain liberation in this life, again and again we shall have to endure the uncertainty of our rebirth.

HAVING NO SATISFACTION

Most of the problems we experience come from our seeking satisfaction in the pleasures of samsara when no real satisfaction can be derived from them. For instance, if we seek satisfaction from drinking alcohol we shall keep drinking and drinking without ever finding what we seek. Similarly, if we try to find contentment by smoking or taking drugs we shall never find the satisfaction we desire.

If we continue to seek satisfaction in such limited pleasures without realizing that these things can never give us what we want, we shall create many compulsive bad habits and cause problems for ourself and others. We may destroy our health, hurt and deceive other people, and even break the law and find ourself in prison. We shall create unhappy relationships with other people and influence others to act in ways that are harmful to their health and peace of mind.

All the difficulties we have in our relationships with others come because we do not know how to be content. When marriages break up it is because people cannot completely satisfy one another. If we have very strong desirous attachment we shall never be content with another person because no one will ever be able to give us all we desire. Sometimes people are torn apart by their desirous attachment. It prevents them from leaving their partner, and it prevents them from feeling happy with that relationship alone.

If we consider why nations go to war we shall find that the basic reason is very simple. Human beings cannot be content with their own wealth and resources but must appropriate more and more. Millions of people have died in warfare as a result of humankind's collective discontent.

Even people who appear to have everything do not have satisfaction. In fact, the wealthiest people are often the most dissatisfied. As their wealth increases, so does their discontent. It is extremely rare to find anyone who can say with complete sincerity 'I do not need anything. I am completely content.'

We who take rebirth in samsara are like moths who are not satisfied merely to behold the beauty of a candle flame but must leap into it. We are like flies who cannot be content with merely the smell of food but must land on it only to be caught and killed. All the lethal situations we find ourself in are created by our own dissatisfaction.

In *Friendly Letter* Nagarjuna says:

Always be content. If you practise contentment, even though you have no wealth, you are rich.

Without contentment we are spiritually impoverished even if we possess a great amount of wealth. A poor person who is satisfied with what he or she has and who has no strong craving to amass wealth is inwardly a rich person. Such a person has less misery, fewer problems, and greater peace of mind.

In India a poor man called Telwa once found a very precious jewel. He thought to himself 'I do not need this jewel.' He was satisfied with what he received each day. He pondered to himself 'Who has the greatest need for this jewel?' He thought about all the other poor people he knew but they were like him and did not feel strong desire for extra wealth. Then he realized 'I must give this jewel to the king because he is the most needy person.' When he presented the jewel to the king, the king was astounded and asked 'Why are you practising such generosity towards me?' Telwa explained 'I realize that you are the most poverty-stricken man around. You have so many possessions, but inwardly you are poor because you lack the satisfaction you desire. You have a strong craving to possess more things. Therefore, I am offering this jewel to you.'

If we remain in samsara we shall have to experience dissatisfaction and discontent in all our future lives.

HAVING TO LEAVE OUR BODY OVER AND OVER AGAIN

Throughout all our lives we have taken countless different bodies, and have had to depart from each one. Each time we have had to experience the pains of death. In *Essence of Nectar* Yeshe Tsondru says:

> If the flesh and bones of all the bodies we have taken in the past still remained, they would form a mountain as large as Mount Meru. If the blood and liquids of all our past bodies still remained, their volume would be greater than the entire ocean.

We have been reborn as high gods such as Brahma and Indra, and we have had enjoyments much greater than the ones we experience now. We have inhabited palaces of gold and precious gems, and we have tasted the nectar of gods. We have enjoyed divine companionship on beds of silk and brocade. Many times we have taken rebirth as a universal monarch with a great retinue and many precious possessions. But now we eat ordinary food, and when someone gives us a job we feel overjoyed, even though we have become just like their servant. By comparison with the possessions we enjoyed in the past, what we own now is insignificant. Repeatedly we have had to lose our glory and magnificence. All the beautiful possessions and delightful experiences of our past lives have vanished like figments of our imagination.

Unless we attain freedom from samsara we must endlessly experience the sufferings of having to leave our body over and over again without choice.

HAVING TO TAKE REBIRTH OVER AND OVER AGAIN

The continuum of our very subtle mind has no beginning and we have taken rebirth countless times. If the whole substance of this planet were formed into tiny beads, and if we were to cast each bead individually into space, saying 'This is the mother of my past life', we would not have enough beads to account for all our past mothers.

Since we have taken repeated rebirth in samsara we have had to endure all the pains of birth over and over again, and we have had to endure all the sufferings of the various states of existence we have entered.

In *Relieving the Sorrow* Ashvagosha says that we have taken rebirth in hell countless times, and the henchmen have poured boiling water down our throats. If all this water were gathered together it would form a huge ocean. Similarly, we have taken rebirth countless times as scavenger animals or insects such as dung beetles and dung flies. If we were to collect together all the excrement that has nourished our bodies it would form a mountain as high as Mount Meru. If just a small amount of excrement now touches our skin we furiously scrub it off, feeling that we cannot bear it; but countless times in the past we lived on excrement. We have been born countless times as insects and worms, and we have eaten more earth than the Earth itself. We have been born countless times as scorpions and mated with other scorpions, although now we are filled with revulsion when we see one. Countless times in the past we have experienced the sorrow of parting from our friends and possessions. If all the tears we have shed were gathered together they would form a huge ocean. Countless times in the past we have fought with our enemy and our head has been cut off. If we were to collect all our heads they would make a pile bigger than the planet. Just as countless times in the past we have had to experience all this, so too must we endure it in all our future lives. To avoid this we need to attain liberation within this one lifetime.

HAVING TO LOSE STATUS OVER AND OVER AGAIN

In the *Vinaya Sutras* Buddha says:

> The end of collection is dispersion.
> The end of rising is falling.
> The end of meeting is parting.
> The end of birth is death.

Whatever possessions we have accumulated during our life will be lost either before death or at the time of death. Whoever gains a good reputation or high social status will eventually experience a decline because the highest positions in samsara are like the top of a wheel; once we have reached the top, all we can do is descend. In the scriptures it says that a person who has the ambition to gain high social status is just like a tree climber. The first part of the ascent is safe and easy because the trunk is thick. The middle part of the climb is also safe because the branches are still quite dense; but the higher the person climbs the more perilous it becomes because the branches become fewer and fewer and more and more slender. Eventually the climber is bound to fall because the topmost twigs are too fragile to support his or her weight. In his *Advice* Gungtang Rinpoche says:

> If we climb the tree of ambition and reach the most slender branches at the top, we are bound to fall. It is far safer to remain in the middle.

There was once a Tibetan prime minister called Sangye Gyatso who ruled the whole of Tibet. During his life he enjoyed a high reputation as a scholar, but he was killed by a king called Lhasang who impaled his head on a bridge near Lhasa for fifteen days. The crows came and pecked at the flesh and the people could not bear to look at it. His wife and children were left to go begging. In a very short time this man fell from the most honoured to the most despised position. He had to die suddenly and violently, without respect, while poorer people could die gently and peacefully in their own homes attended by their families and treated with dignity. Such experiences do not belong only to the past, for there are many similar examples in the world today.

Whenever we meet someone it is certain that we shall have to part from them. In this life we experience many temporary separations from our friends and relatives; but eventually we have to experience the final separation of death. Everything that comes together ends in separation, and every birth ends in death. Geshe Sangpuwa said:

> In samsara we change constantly from low states to high ones, and from high states to low ones again. This situation fills me with pity.

Contemplating all this we should understand the wretchedness of samsara and strive to be free from such suffering in the future by attaining liberation in our own lifetime.

HAVING NO COMPANIONSHIP

In *Guide to the Bodhisattva's Way of Life* Shantideva says:

> At birth I was born alone
> And at death I shall have to die alone.
> Since I cannot share these sufferings with others,
> What use are friends who prevent me from practising virtue?

From time without beginning we have had to suffer the pains of every rebirth on our own, and throughout our lives we have had to experience the pains of illness, ageing, and death without any companion to share the burden of our suffering. No matter how much we may want to share the sufferings of our friends we cannot actually take them upon ourself. Every person has to endure his or her own suffering. Even the most gregarious people who have plenty of friends and who never seem to be alone have to depart from this life and take rebirth on their own.

Just as leaves in autumn that have fallen from the tree can never return to their branches, so when we die we cannot be reunited with our friends of this life. In our next life there are no familiar faces. Our mother is different, our father is different, and all our friends and relatives are different. When we meet again the people who were once our friends we cannot recognize them because their appearance is completely transformed. All the appearances of our next life are new and strange. Fearing the misery of having to endure these experiences in future lives, we should be encouraged to seek liberation now.

If we meditate on these six general sufferings of samsara we shall develop a strong determination to find release from samsaric rebirths. We shall think to ourself:

I must be mindful and apply the methods for attaining liber-
ation. If I do not apply these methods right now, when shall
I ever again find the opportunity to attain liberation? Once
I have taken lower rebirth again it will be impossible for me
to develop even the thought of becoming free from samsara.

When this determination arises clearly and definitely in our mind we do placement meditation to become more and more familiar with it.

THE PARTICULAR SUFFERINGS OF EACH STATE OF SAMSARIC REBIRTH

This has two parts:

1 The sufferings of the lower realms
2 The sufferings of the higher realms

The first part has already been explained.

THE SUFFERINGS OF THE HIGHER REALMS

This has three parts:

1 The sufferings of human beings
2 The sufferings of demi-gods
3 The sufferings of gods

THE SUFFERINGS OF HUMAN BEINGS

The main sufferings of human beings can be divided into seven:

1 Birth
2 Ageing
3 Sickness
4 Death
5 Having to part with what we like
6 Having to encounter what we do not like
7 Failing to satisfy our desires

BIRTH

We may wonder why it is necessary to meditate in detail upon all the painful experiences that we have had in the past. The purpose is to avoid having to go through all those experiences again in the future. While we remain in samsara these sufferings never end. We have to experience them over and over again every time we take rebirth.

We have already considered how wonderful it is to be born human, but our human life is of real value only when we use it to practise Dharma. In itself it is a true suffering and has no precious qualities. To realize that our human life has the nature of suffering we need to remember the pains of birth. Although we cannot remember our experiences while we were in our mother's womb or during our very early childhood, the pains of human life began from the time of our conception. Everyone can observe that a new-born baby experiences anguish and pain. The first thing a baby does when it is born is scream. Rarely has a baby ever been born in complete serenity, with a peaceful, smiling expression on its face.

Meditating on the sufferings of birth has five parts:

1 The extreme pains experienced in the womb and during birth
2 The unceasing pains we experience after birth
3 Birth is the basis for all the sufferings of life
4 Birth is the foundation for all delusions
5 Birth changes into death

THE EXTREME PAINS EXPERIENCED IN THE WOMB AND DURING BIRTH

When our consciousness first enters the union of our father's sperm and our mother's ovum our body is a very hot, watery substance like white yoghurt tinted red. In the first moments after conception we have no gross feelings, but as soon as these develop we begin to experience manifest pain. Our body gradually becomes harder and harder, and as our limbs grow it feels as if our body is being stretched out on a rack. Inside our mother's womb it is hot and dark. Our home for nine months is this small, tightly compressed space full of unclean substances. It is like being squashed inside a small water tank full of filthy liquid with the lid tightly shut so that no air or light can come through.

While we are in our mother's womb we experience much pain and fear all on our own. We are extremely sensitive to everything our mother does. When she walks quickly it feels as if we are falling from a high mountain and we are terrified. If she has sexual intercourse it feels as if we are being crushed and suffocated between two huge weights and we panic. If our mother makes just a small jump it feels as if we are being dashed against the ground from a great height. If she drinks anything hot it feels like boiling water scalding our skin, and if she drinks anything cold it feels like an icy-cold shower in midwinter.

When we are emerging from our mother's womb it feels as if we are being forced through a narrow crevice between two hard rocks, and when we are newly born our body is so delicate that any kind of contact is painful. Even if someone holds us very tenderly, their hands feel like thorn bushes piercing our flesh, and the most delicate fabrics feel rough and abrasive. By comparison with the softness and smoothness of our mother's womb, every tactile sensation is harsh and painful. If someone picks us up it feels as if we are being swung over a huge precipice, and we feel frightened and insecure. We have forgotten all that we knew in our past life; we bring only pain and confusion from our mother's womb. Whatever we hear is as meaningless as the sound of wind, and we cannot comprehend anything we perceive. In the first few weeks we are like someone who is blind, deaf, and dumb, and suffering from profound amnesia. When we are hungry we cannot say 'I need food', and when we are in pain we cannot say 'This is hurting me.' The only signs we can make are hot tears and furious gestures. Our mother often has no idea what pains and discomforts we are experiencing. We are completely helpless and have to be taught everything – how to eat, how to sit, how to walk, how to talk.

THE UNCEASING PAINS WE EXPERIENCE AFTER BIRTH

Although we are most vulnerable in the first few weeks of our life, our pains do not cease as we grow up. We continue to experience various kinds of suffering throughout our life.

BIRTH IS THE BASIS FOR ALL THE SUFFERINGS OF LIFE

Just as when we light a fire in a large house the heat from the fire pervades the whole house, and all the heat in the house comes from the fire, so when we are born in samsara suffering pervades our whole life, and all the miseries we experience arise because we were born. Our birth has the nature of suffering and it is the basis for all the sufferings of this life.

BIRTH IS THE FOUNDATION FOR ALL DELUSIONS

Since we have been born as a human we cherish our human body and mind and cling onto them as our own. In dependence upon our human aggregates we develop self-grasping, which is the root of all delusions. Our human rebirth is like a field and our delusions are like poisonous plants that grow in it. If the field did not exist, such poisonous plants would have no place to take root and flourish.

BIRTH CHANGES INTO DEATH

The pains of birth and the pains of this human life eventually turn into the pains of death. Death arises in dependence upon birth. Our birth and our death are one continuum.

AGEING

As we grow old we experience five main deprivations:

1 Loss of beauty and health
2 Loss of physical strength and vitality
3 Loss of power in our sense and mental faculties
4 Loss of enjoyments
5 Loss of life span

LOSS OF BEAUTY AND HEALTH

In *Extensive Enjoyment Sutra* Buddha says that ageing steals our beauty, our health, our good figure, our fine complexion, our vitality, and our comfort. Ageing turns us into objects of contempt. It brings many unwanted pains, and takes us swiftly to our death.

As we grow old we lose all the beauty of our youth, and our strong, healthy body becomes weak and burdened with illness. Our once firm and well-proportioned figure becomes bent and disfigured, and our muscles and flesh shrink so that our limbs become like thin sticks and our bones poke out. Our hair loses its colour and shine, and our complexion loses its lustre. Our face becomes wrinkled and our features grow distorted.

LOSS OF PHYSICAL STRENGTH AND VITALITY

Milarepa said:

How do old people get up? They get up as if they were heaving a stake out of the ground. How do old people walk about? Once they are on their feet they have to walk gingerly, like bird-catchers. How do old people sit down? They crash down like heavy luggage whose harness has snapped.

In a poem, Gungtang Rinpoche wrote:

Old peoples' hair becomes white,
But not because they have washed it clean.
It is a sign they will soon encounter the Lord of
    Death.

They have wrinkles on their forehead,
But not because they have too much flesh.
It is a warning from the Lord of Death: 'You are
    about to die.'

Their teeth fall out,
But not to make room for new ones.
It is a sign they will soon be unable to eat human
    food.

Their faces are ugly and unpleasant,
But not because they are wearing masks.
It is a sign they have lost the mask of youth.

Their heads shake to and fro,
But not because they are in disagreement.
It is the Lord of Death striking their heads with the
    stick he holds in his right hand.

They walk bent and gazing at the ground,
But not because they are searching for lost needles.
It is a sign they are searching for lost beauty,
    possessions, and memories.

They get up from the ground using all four limbs,
But not because they are imitating animals.
It is a sign their legs are too weak to support their
    bodies.

They sit down as if they had suddenly fallen,
But not because they are angry.
It is a sign their body has lost its strength.

They sway their bodies as they walk,
But not because they think they are important.
It is a sign their legs cannot carry their bodies.

Their hands shake,
But not because they are itching to steal.
It is a sign the Lord of Death's itchy fingers are
    stealing their possessions.

They eat very little,
But not because they are miserly.
It is a sign they cannot digest their food.

They wheeze frequently,
But not because they are whispering mantras to the
    sick.
It is a sign their breathing will soon disappear.

When we are young we can travel around the whole world, but when we are old we can hardly make it to our own front gate. We become too weak to engage in many worldly activities, and our spiritual activities are often curtailed. For example, we cannot make many prostrations or go on long pilgrimages. We cannot attend teachings that are given in places that are hard to reach or uncomfortable to inhabit. We cannot help others in ways that require physical strength and good health. Deprivations such as these often make old people very sad.

LOSS OF POWER IN OUR SENSE AND MENTAL FACULTIES

When we grow old we become like someone who is blind and deaf. We cannot see clearly, and we need stronger and stronger glasses until we can no longer read. We cannot hear clearly, and so it becomes more and more difficult to listen to music or to the television, or to hear what others are saying. Our memory fades. All activities, worldly and spiritual, become more difficult. If we practise meditation it becomes harder for us to gain realizations because our memory and concentration are too weak. We cannot apply ourself to study. Thus, if we have not learnt and practised Dharma in our youth, the only thing to do when we grow old is to develop regret and wait for the Lord of Death to come.

LOSS OF ENJOYMENTS

When we are old we cannot derive the same enjoyment from the things we used to enjoy, such as food, drink, and sex. We are too weak to play games and we are often too exhausted even for entertainments.

LOSS OF LIFE SPAN

As our life span runs out we cannot join young people in their activities. When they travel about we have to stay behind. No one wants to take us with them when we are old, and no one wants to visit us. Even our own grandchildren do not want to stay with us for very long. Old people often think to themselves, 'How wonderful it would be if young people would stay with me. We could go out for walks and I could show them things'; but young people do not want to be included in their plans. As their life draws to an end, old people experience the sorrow of abandonment and loneliness. They have many special griefs.

SICKNESS

In *Extensive Enjoyment Sutra* Buddha says that just as the wind and snow of winter take away the glory of green meadows, trees, forests, and herbs, so sickness takes away the youthful splendour of our body, destroying its strength and the power of our senses.

When we are sick we experience five main sorrows:

1 Loss of power and control over the functions of our body
2 Increasing unhappiness
3 Loss of enjoyments
4 Having to experience what we do not want to experience
5 Knowing that our sickness is incurable and that our life is coming to an end

LOSS OF POWER AND CONTROL OVER THE FUNCTIONS OF OUR BODY

If we are usually fit and well, when we become sick we are suddenly unable to engage in all our normal physical activities. Even a champion boxer who is usually able to knock out all his opponents becomes completely helpless when sickness strikes.

When we fall ill we are like a bird that has been soaring in the sky and is suddenly shot down. When a bird is shot, it falls straight to the ground like a lump of lead, and all its glory and power are immediately destroyed. In a similar way, when we become ill we have to experience sudden incapacity. If we are seriously ill we may become completely dependent upon others and lose even the ability to control our bodily functions. This transformation is hard to bear, especially for those who pride themselves on their independence and physical well-being.

INCREASING UNHAPPINESS

When we are ill we cannot do our usual work or complete all the tasks we have set ourself, and so we feel frustrated. We easily become impatient with our illness and depressed about all the things we cannot do. To add to our unhappiness, we have to endure all the pains the illness brings.

LOSS OF ENJOYMENTS

When we are sick we cannot enjoy the things that usually give us pleasure, such as sport, dancing, drinking, or eating rich foods. We cannot enjoy the company of our friends. All these limitations make us feel even more miserable.

HAVING TO EXPERIENCE WHAT WE DO NOT WANT
TO EXPERIENCE

When we are sick, not only do we have to experience all the unwanted pains of the illness itself, but we also have to experience all sorts of other unwished for things. For example, we have to take whatever cure is prescribed, whether it be a foul-tasting medicine, a series of injections, a major operation, or abstinence from something we like very much. If we are to have an operation we have to go to hospital and accept all the conditions there. We may have to eat food we do not like and stay in bed all day long with nothing to do, and we may feel anxiety about the operation. Our doctor may not explain to us exactly what the problem is and whether or not he or she expects us to survive.

KNOWING THAT OUR SICKNESS IS INCURABLE AND
THAT OUR LIFE IS COMING TO AN END

If we learn that our sickness is incurable, and we have not used our life to practise Dharma, we shall suffer anxiety, fear, and regret. We may become depressed and give up hope, or we may become angry with our illness, feeling that it is an enemy that has maliciously deprived us of all our joy.

DEATH

When we die we experience five main griefs:

1 Departing from our possessions
2 Departing from our friends
3 Departing from those who live and work with us
4 Departing from our body
5 Experiencing mental and physical pain

DEPARTING FROM OUR POSSESSIONS

If during our life we have worked hard to acquire possessions, and if we have become very attached to them, we shall experience great suffering at the time of death, thinking 'Now I have to leave all my precious possessions behind.' Even now we find it difficult to lend one of our most treasured possessions to someone else, let alone to give it away. No wonder we become so miserable when we realize that in the hands of death we must abandon everything.

DEPARTING FROM OUR FRIENDS

When we die we have to part from even our closest friends. We have to leave our partner, even though we may have been together for years and never spent a day apart. If we are very attached to our friends we shall experience great misery at the time of death, but all we shall be able to do is hold their hands. We shall not be able to halt the process of death, even if they plead with us not to die. Usually when we are very attached to someone we feel jealous if they leave us on our own and spend time with someone else, but when we die we shall have to leave our friends with others forever.

DEPARTING FROM THOSE WHO LIVE AND WORK WITH US

When we die we shall have to leave our Spiritual Guides, our family, and all the people who have helped us in this life.

DEPARTING FROM OUR BODY

When we die, this body that we have cherished and cared for in so many ways will have to be left behind. It will become mindless like a stone, and will be buried in the ground or cremated.

EXPERIENCING MENTAL AND PHYSICAL PAIN

If we have not practised Dharma and cultivated virtuous actions, at the time of death we shall experience fear and distress, as well as physical pain.

When we meditate on the sufferings of death we can recall the signs of death and how we have to experience these without choice. When our consciousness departs from our body, all the potentialities we have accumulated in our mind by performing virtuous and non-virtuous actions will go with it. Other than these we cannot take anything else out of this world. All other things deceive us. Death ends all our activities – our conversation, our eating, our meeting with friends, our sleep. Everything draws to a close on the day of our death, and we must leave all things behind, even the rings on our fingers.

In Tibet, beggars used to carry a stick to defend themselves against dogs. To understand the complete deprivation of death Tibetans remember that at the time of death beggars have to leave even this old stick, the most meagre of human possessions. All over the world we can see that names carved on stone are the only possessions of the dead.

We can contemplate the example of Prince Siddhartha who could have possessed every worldly thing he desired. His father's kingdom had great resources and it was hoped that Siddhartha would become the future king. His parents arranged for him to have all kinds of pleasure and they gave him many beautiful consorts, but one day Prince Siddhartha ventured outside the pleasure palace and there he saw, in turn, a sick person, an old person, a corpse, and a monk. When he had seen and contemplated these things Prince Siddhartha developed a strong interest in Dharma, and he left the palace to meditate in the forest. His father tried to dissuade him but Prince Siddhartha said: 'If you can guarantee that I shall not experience the sufferings of sickness, old age, death, and rebirth, I shall stay in the palace and become the king after you. Do you have a perfect method that will protect me from these dangers? Please, if you have one, teach me what it is and I shall come home happily. However, if you do not possess such a method there is nothing in my worldly life that can offer real protection from these four rivers of suffering. Not even my mother can protect me from these miseries. Only Dharma provides protection; therefore,

I must practise Dharma.' Since his father could not offer Prince Siddhartha a method for gaining perfect freedom, the prince stayed in the forest and, by practising Dharma, he became enlightened and revealed how all living beings can attain the same state.

HAVING TO PART WITH WHAT WE LIKE

Before the final separation at the time of death we often have to experience temporary separation from the people and things we like. We may have to leave our country where all our friends and relatives live, or we may have to leave the job we like. We may lose our reputation. Many times in this life we have to experience the misery of departing from the people we like, or forsaking and losing the things we find pleasant and attractive; but when we die we have to part forever from all the companions and enjoyments of this life.

HAVING TO ENCOUNTER WHAT WE DO NOT LIKE

We often have to meet and live with people whom we do not like, or encounter situations that we find unpleasant. Sometimes we may find ourself in a very dangerous situation such as in a fire or a flood, or we may be caught in a situation where there is violence such as in a riot or a battle. Our lives are full of less extreme situations that we find annoying. Sometimes we are prevented from doing the things we want to do. On a sunny day we may set off for the beach, but find ourself stuck in a traffic jam. Sometimes we experience interference from spirits who disturb our meditation and other spiritual practices. There are countless conditions that frustrate our plans and prevent us from doing what we want. It is as if we are living in a thorn bush – whenever we try to move we are wounded by circumstances. People and things are like thorns piercing our flesh and no situation ever feels entirely comfortable. The more desires and plans we have, the more frustrations we experience. The more we want certain situations, the more we find ourself stuck in situations we do not want. Every desire seems to invite its own obstacle. Undesired situations befall us without our looking for them. In fact, the only things that come effortlessly are the things we do not want, and only the wishes we do not have are the ones that are easily fulfilled. No one wants to die, but death comes effortlessly. No one wants to be sick, but sickness comes effortlessly. If we take rebirth without freedom or control we have an impure body and we inhabit an impure environment, and so undesirable things pour in upon us. In samsara this kind of experience is entirely natural.

FAILING TO SATISFY OUR DESIRES

We have countless desires, but no matter how much effort we make we never feel that we have satisfied them. Even when we get what we want we do not get it in the way we want. We possess the object but we do not derive satisfaction from possessing it. For example, we may dream of becoming wealthy, but if we actually become wealthy our life is not the way we imagined it would be, and we do not feel that we have fulfilled our desire. This is because our desires do not decrease as our wealth increases. The more wealth we have, the more we desire. The wealth we seek is unfindable because we seek an amount that will satiate our desires, and no amount of wealth can do that. To make things worse, in obtaining the object of our desire we create new occasions for discontent. With every object we desire come other objects we do not want. For example, with wealth come taxes, insecurity, and complicated financial affairs. These unwished for accessories prevent us from ever feeling that we have really got what we want. Similarly, we may dream of having a holiday in the South Seas, and we may actually go on holiday in the South Seas, but the experience is never quite what we expect and with our holiday come other things such as sunburn and great expense.

If we check we shall see that our desires are inordinate. They want all the best things in samsara – the best job, the best partner, the best reputation, the best house, the best car, the best holiday. Anything that is not the best leaves us with a feeling of disappointment. It leaves us still searching for but not finding what we want. However nothing imperma- nent can give us the complete and perfect satisfaction we desire. Better things are always being produced. Everywhere new advertisements announce that the very best thing has just arrived on the market, but a few days later another best thing arrives and it is better than the best thing of a few days ago. There is no end of new things to captivate our desires.

Children at school can never satisfy their own or their parents' ambitions. Even if they come top of their class they feel they cannot be content unless they do the same again the following year. If they go on to be successful in their jobs their ambitions will be as strong as ever. There is no point at which they can rest with the feeling that they are com- pletely satisfied with what they have done.

We may think that at least people who lead a simple life in the country must be content, but if we check we shall find that even farmers search for but do not find what they want. Their lives are full of problems and anxieties, and they do not enjoy real peace and satisfaction. Their livelihoods depend upon many uncertain factors outside their control, such as the weather. Farmers have no more freedom from discontent than businessmen who live and work in the city. Business- men look smart and efficient as they set off to work each morning carrying their briefcases; but although they look so smooth on the outside, in their hearts they carry many dis- satisfactions. They are still searching for but not finding what they want.

If we reflect on this situation we may decide that we can find what we are searching for by abandoning all our pos- sessions. However if we check we shall see that even poor people are looking for but not finding what they seek. Poor people cannot find the necessities of life. Again, we cannot avoid this suffering by frequently changing our situation. We may think that if we keep getting a new partner or a new job, or keep travelling about, we shall eventually find what we want; but even if we were to travel to every place on the globe, and have a new lover in every place, we would still be seeking another place and another lover. In samsara there is no real fulfilment of our desires. The seventh Dalai Lama said:

> Whoever I behold, of high position or low, ordained or lay, male or female, they differ only in appearance, dress, behaviour, and status. In essence they are all equal. They all experience problems in their lives.

Whenever we have a problem it is easy to think that our problem is caused by our particular circumstances, and that if we were to change our circumstances our problem would disappear. We blame other people, our friends, our food, our government, our times, the weather, society, history, and so forth. However, external circumstances such as these are not the main causes of our problems. All our problems are mainly caused by our own past actions, and once their effects are ripening there is no way we can avoid them. Therefore, instead of trying to run away from our problems by constructing new situations in life, we need to recognize these painful experiences as the consequences of our own harmful actions and develop a heartfelt wish to abandon their causes. In other words, the most constructive response to our problems is to develop sincere renunciation, recognizing that the sufferings we create for ourself are in the very nature of our samsara.

If we meditate on these seven types of suffering we shall come to the conclusion:

> *I have experienced these sufferings over and over again in the past and, if I do not attain liberation, I shall have to experience them over and over again in the future. Therefore I must escape from samsara.*

When this determination arises clearly and definitely in our mind we do placement meditation.

THE SUFFERINGS OF DEMI-GODS

Demi-gods are similar to gods but their bodies, possessions, and environments are inferior. Although their status in samsara is higher than that of human beings, they do not experience pure happiness. In *Friendly Letter* Nagarjuna says that it is the nature of demi-gods always to be jealous of the gods' glory, and because of this they have great mental suffering; and although they have intelligence they have karmic obstructions that prevent them from beholding the truth.

Since they have very strong karmic obstructions demi-gods cannot realize the ultimate nature of reality. Thus, although there are Superior beings among humans and gods, there are no Superior beings among demi-gods. Most of the problems human beings experience come about because of their desirous attachment, but for demi-gods the main mental affliction is jealousy. Their jealousy is like a thorn piercing their minds, causing them to experience both mental and physical suffering for long periods of time. Demi-gods cannot bear to see or know about the good qualities of gods and they engage in perpetual battle with them; but they are always the losers. They spend most of their lives fighting, and when the battle is lost the gods cut off their heads and limbs. Therefore there is no peace in the realms of demi-gods.

THE SUFFERINGS OF GODS

We may think that it would be wonderful to be a god, but gods do not enjoy real happiness. Gods of the desire realm have to defend themselves in battle against the demi-gods and many of them are killed. Some gods have more merit than others and when one god meets another who is more meritorious the less fortunate god feels overwhelmingly depressed. Stronger gods also often seize the partners of weaker ones. The lives of gods are full of conflict and they always experience dissatisfaction. Even if they experience enjoyment, still their desires grow stronger.

Gods of the desire realm have more mental suffering than human beings. For human beings, the sufferings of ageing last for a long time whereas the sufferings of death are brief. For gods of the desire realm it is the other way around. For a short time after they take rebirth in the god realm they can remember where they lived in their previous life, and just before they die they can see where they will take rebirth. For this reason they are sometimes called 'beings of three occasions', indicating that they perceive conditions of the past, present, and future. The knowledge that gods have of their next rebirth brings anguish at the time of death because most of them fall into lower rebirths. All the good things that can be enjoyed in samsara are the results of good actions. By enjoying them we use up our good potentialities. Since the gods enjoy such an abundance of good things they greatly deplete their accumulation of merit, and while they are in the god realms they do not replenish their merit because they cannot muster the motivation to engage in virtuous actions. They have such abundant enjoyments, such beautiful dwellings, such lovely girlfriends and boyfriends, such marvellous distractions, that they never have the incentive to practise Dharma.

When they are about to die, gods experience ten specific signs: their magnificent bearing and fine complexion begins to degenerate; they begin to feel uncomfortable on their usual seat or couch; the flower garlands they wear begin to fade and wilt; their garments begin to smell, whereas normally they have no odour; they begin to perspire; usually their bodies are radiant with light, but when their death approaches their light grows dim; when they bathe, their bodies become wet, whereas normally their bodies never retain moisture; their clothing and ornaments make unpleasant sounds; they begin to blink, whereas normally their eyes remain wide-open; usually gods are attracted to many different objects, but at the time of their death their attention is attracted to only one object, such as a particular friend or place.

When gods experience these signs of death they feel fear, just as we do when we think we are about to fall from a great height. Gods can see that they are about to plunge into the lower realms. To make it worse, a dying god receives no sympathy. Other gods treat him or her as an outcast. The most they will do is offer flowers in his direction from a great distance. The life span of a god is much greater than the life span of a human being, and the sufferings of their death last for about three hundred human years, and sometimes for one thousand human years. Therefore it is said that it is more fortunate to be an elderly human being who can recite one mantra such as OM MANI PÄME HUM than it is to be a youthful god.

Gods of the form and formless realms do not experience sufferings like those experienced by the gods of the desire realm. They do not experience the signs of death, they do not have to engage in battle, and they do not experience dissatisfaction or any kind of painful feeling. All the same, they do experience pervasive suffering and they do lack freedom. Eventually, just like the gods of the desire realm they too have to take rebirth in the lower realms. Therefore there is no pure and lasting happiness even among the gods of the form and formless realms, whose state of existence is the most fortunate of all states within samsara.

THE THREE TYPES OF SUFFERING

True sufferings can be divided into external and internal true sufferings. External true sufferings are those that are not within the continuum of the body and mind of a sentient being – for example, the various environments and enjoyments of beings within samsara. Internal true sufferings are those that are within the continuum of the body and mind of any being within samsara – for example, our present body and mind. Internal true sufferings are samsara. They can be divided into three:

1 The suffering of manifest pain
2 Changing suffering
3 Pervasive suffering

THE SUFFERING OF MANIFEST PAIN

The suffering of manifest pain is any unpleasant bodily or mental feeling. This kind of suffering is easily recognized by everyone, but the other two kinds of suffering are more difficult to identify.

CHANGING SUFFERING

For samsaric beings every experience of happiness or pleasure that arises from samsara's enjoyments is changing suffering. These experiences are contaminated and have the nature of suffering. We need to meditate repeatedly on this point because it is not obvious to us that our worldly pleasures are changing suffering.

We can gain a better understanding by considering the following analogy. If we have a very painful illness and our doctor prescribes painkillers we take these and for a while we stop feeling the pain. At that time we actually experience a feeling that is merely the reduction of pain, but because the strong painful feeling has gone we feel happy and experience pleasure. This pleasant feeling is changing suffering.

To understand this clearly we should consider the explanation given by Aryadeva in *Treatise of Four Hundred Verses*:

> Although it can be seen that the increase of happiness
> is destroyed [by its cause], it can never be seen that the
> increase of suffering is destroyed [by its cause].

If we increase the cause of our worldly happiness, our happiness will change into suffering, but if we increase the cause of suffering, our suffering will never change into happiness. For example, if we enjoy eating food our pleasure may increase as we eat the first few mouthfuls, but if we continue to eat more and more our pleasure will turn into pain. If the pleasure we get from eating food were real happiness, eating food would be a real cause of happiness – but eating food cannot be a real cause of happiness because it causes us to feel sick, and a real cause of happiness can never be a cause of suffering. The good feeling we get from eating is no other than the feeling of diminished hunger. In a short time it changes again into the manifest suffering of hunger. If we eat more and more, eating itself, which is the cause of our initial pleasure, destroys the pleasure of eating and causes us to experience pain. If we continue to eat, we can eat and eat, but eating will never destroy the pain of eating.

Similarly, if we sit in the same position for a long time and then stand up it will seem that standing is a cause of happiness, but if we remain standing for a few hours we shall begin to feel that standing is unbearable. If we then sit down, sitting will seem like a cause of happiness. Neither standing nor sitting are real causes of happiness because both of them are causes of changing suffering.

The same goes for all our worldly pleasures. For example, we may feel that real happiness is to be found in the bliss of sexual orgasm, but if this were so then we would experience more and more bliss the more we engaged in sexual intercourse. In fact, if we overindulge in sex we eventually lose our lust and begin to feel ill. Therefore sexual orgasm cannot be a cause of real bliss. It is a cause of changing suffering.

PERVASIVE SUFFERING

Buddha said:

The childish do not realize that pervasive suffering is like a hair in the palm of the hand.

'The childish' are ordinary beings who do not understand what they cannot see with their own eyes or experience directly. Just as the bodies of children are frail and lacking in power, so the minds of ordinary beings are weak and unable to make clear discriminations. If a hair is placed on the palm of the hand of a blind person he will not realize that the hair is on his palm because he cannot see or feel it. Ordinary beings are just like this blind person, for although pervasive suffering pervades our mind and body we cannot realize it directly because for us it is a hidden object.

Pervasive suffering is so called because it covers or pervades all the three realms from the lowest of the desire realm, the Unceasing Torment Hell, to the highest formless realm, peak of samsara; and it is the basis from which all true sufferings, external and internal, arise. An example of pervasive suffering is our present contaminated aggregates. These five aggregates are the basis upon which we impute I, which is the basis of our self-grasping. Self-grasping and all other delusions and the sufferings they cause arise from these five aggregates. The appropriated aggregates of a samsaric being have the nature of suffering and are said to be 'contaminated' for three reasons: because they are produced by contaminated causes, delusions; because they depend upon delusions; and because they are the basis for developing delusions. Our appropriated aggregates are called 'aggregates' because they are composed of many parts. Our body is an aggregate of many parts, such as limbs, and our mind is an aggregate of many parts, such as mental factors and past and present moments. The appropriated aggregates are said to be 'appropriated' because they have developed or been appropriated in dependence upon deluded causes. They are also known as 'deluded aggregates' because they are the basis for developing delusions, just as a herb is known as a medicinal herb when it is the basis for making medicine.

The appropriated aggregates are like the roots of a tree. From these roots grows the trunk of our self-grasping apprehending I and mine. From this trunk the branches of other delusions develop, and from these come the stems of actions and the fruit of great suffering. Just as a tree, its trunk, branches, stems, and fruit have basically the same substantial nature, so the appropriated aggregates, delusions, and contaminated actions all have the nature of suffering. All the sufferings of the hell realms arise from the appropriated aggregates of the hell beings who experience them; all the sufferings of hungry spirits arise from the appropriated aggregates of the beings who experience them; all the sufferings of animals arise from the appropriated aggregates of the beings who experience them; all the sufferings of human beings arise from the appropriated aggregates of the beings who experience them; and all the sufferings of demi-gods and gods arise from their appropriated aggregates. Therefore, if we want freedom from the various sufferings of samsara we need to develop the determination to abandon all appropriated aggregates. Our appropriated aggregates are like a huge bundle of thorns that we are carrying on our bare back. As long as we carry this burden, suffering is inevitable. With each step we take, a thorn pierces our flesh.

Usually when we think about our own body and mind we develop self-cherishing, but if we meditate repeatedly upon pervasive suffering we shall realize that all contaminated or appropriated aggregates have the nature of suffering. Then we shall develop renunciation – the wish to abandon contaminated aggregates, the basis for all suffering.

By engaging in each analytical meditation on the general and particular sufferings of samsara we generate a strong determination to cut the continuum of samsaric rebirth, thinking 'I must abandon appropriated aggregates.' When this thought of renunciation – a mind determined to attain liberation – arises clearly, we should practise placement meditation so that we never lose it.

Delusions and Actions, Death and Rebirth

Actual liberation, or nirvana, is a final cessation of samsaric rebirth that has been attained by meditating on true paths. This is our main object of attainment. To attain it we need to abandon all delusions and contaminated actions which are the source of samsaric rebirths. Since it is very important to understand that delusions and actions are the main cause of samsaric rebirth, and to understand the process of samsaric rebirth, these will now be explained.

IDENTIFYING THE DELUSIONS

This has two parts:

1 Definition of delusion
2 The six root delusions

DEFINITION OF DELUSION

The definition of delusion is a mental factor that arises from inappropriate attention and functions to make the mind unpeaceful and uncontrolled.

THE SIX ROOT DELUSIONS

Although delusions are countless, there are six root delusions, and all other delusions are branches of these six. The six root delusions are:

1 Desirous attachment
2 Anger
3 Deluded pride
4 Ignorance
5 Deluded doubt
6 Deluded view

These delusions act as the basis for all error and conflict and for the contaminated actions that throw us into states of samsaric rebirth.

It is easy to see from our own experience how gross anger and desirous attachment disturb our mind and make us lose control. For example, when we are relaxing and our mind has become calm, if we hear someone making a loud noise outside our room and we become angry, our anger immediately destroys our peace of mind and may even make us leave our seat and take action against the offender. Or, again, if we are quietly reading, studying, or writing, and someone for whom we have strong desirous attachment walks into the room, we immediately become agitated and self-conscious, and it is difficult to concentrate or to do anything naturally.

We can learn to identify the delusions by observing our own mind and noticing which states make us unquiet and uncontrolled. When our mind is not affected by strong delusions we are at ease and our mind is clear. By watching our own minds we shall learn to discriminate between non-virtuous, disturbing states, and virtuous states that bring peace. In this way we shall develop wisdom and gain realizations.

DESIROUS ATTACHMENT

Desirous attachment is a mental factor that observes its contaminated object, feels it to be attractive, exaggerates its attractions, considers it desirable, develops desire to possess it, and feels as if it has become absorbed into the object.

Desirous attachment develops as follows. First we perceive or remember a contaminated object and feel it to be attractive, then we focus our attention on its good qualities and exaggerate them. With an exaggerated sense of the attractiveness of the object we then hold it to be desirable and develop desire for it. Finally our desire attaches us to the object so that it feels as if we have become glued to it or absorbed into it. Only when all these stages are completed has desirous attachment occurred.

The stages of focusing on an object's good qualities, exaggerating them, and considering the object to be desirable are called 'inappropriate attention'. Inappropriate attention induces desire, and desire attaches us to the object. Therefore, if we do not want to develop desirous attachment we need to intervene at the early stages of its evolution and prevent inappropriate attention.

Desirous attachment is like oil that has soaked into fabric whereas other delusions are like dust that has settled on the surface. Just as it is much harder to remove oil from fabric than it is to remove dust, so it is much harder to remove the mind from an object of desirous attachment than it is to remove the mind from the object of any other delusion. This is because the mind of desirous attachment is absorbed into its object more deeply and more closely. If we become angry with someone who has abused us we can quickly separate our mind from the object of our anger, especially if the same person later flatters us or apologizes. We can even smile and laugh with someone who not long ago filled us with hatred. It is comparatively easy to pacify our anger, but desirous attachment is not so easy to overcome. It is as if the object of desirous attachment sticks to our mind even when the delusion is not very strong.

There are three types of desirous attachment: that which is experienced by beings in the desire realm; that which is experienced by beings in the form realm; and that which is experienced by beings in the formless realm. We who inhabit the desire realm experience the most gross type of desirous attachment. The rope of desirous attachment tightly binds our mind to the prison of samsara and so it is hard for us to develop a sincere wish to become free.

When we have removed all the delusions of the desire realm we experience the delusions of the form realm, and when we have removed all of these we experience the delusions of the formless realm. By comparison with the gross desirous attachment of the desire realm, the desirous attachment of the form realm is very subtle.

We can remove the delusions of the desire realm temporarily by meditating on mundane paths. To do this we first need to attain tranquil abiding, and then the absorption of close preparation of the first mental stabilization. When we do this meditation we concentrate on seeing the desire realm as very unclean and faulty and the form realm as very peaceful. To overcome the delusions of the desire realm permanently we need to develop supramundane paths, which arise in dependence upon a direct realization of emptiness.

Not all desires are desirous attachment. It is important to distinguish between virtuous and non-virtuous desires. Virtuous and compassionate desires are not delusions because they do not destroy our peace of mind. For example, a sincere wish to attain enlightenment for the benefit of others is a desire, but it is not desirous attachment because such a wish cannot confuse and disturb our mind and it cannot harm ourself and others.

ANGER

Anger is a mental factor that observes an animate or inanimate object, feels it to be unattractive, exaggerates its bad qualities, considers it to be undesirable, becomes antagonistic, and develops the wish to harm the object.

The stages of focusing on an object's bad qualities, exaggerating them, and considering the object to be unpleasant are inappropriate attention. In dependence upon such inappropriate attention we become antagonistic and develop the wish to harm the object. When all these stages are completed we have generated anger.

There are three types of anger according to its degree: big, middling, and small; and there are nine types according to person and time, as follows:

(1) Anger towards someone or something that harmed us in the past. For example, if we remember how someone hurt us in the past we may dwell on this and develop an exaggerated idea of the injury inflicted and the harmfulness of the person who inflicted it. We shall then feel antagonistic and want to take revenge on that person. Recollection of events that took place hundreds of years ago can cause hostility between people and make modern nations engage in fierce warfare.

(2) Anger towards someone or something that is harming us now.

(3) Anger towards someone or something that might harm us in the future. We frequently develop anger on the basis of an uncertainty. For example, if we are competing with someone for a job and we think that they will get the job, we may develop anger in anticipation of our loss. Individuals competing against one another have this kind of anger; and nations, observing events that may happen in the future, fight or build up hostile machinery against one another on the basis of this suspicion. Even when there is only a very remote chance that we

might be harmed, we can develop very strong anger on the basis of this possibility.

(4) Anger towards someone or something that harmed our friends or relatives in the past.

(5) Anger towards someone or something that is harming our friends or relatives now.

(6) Anger towards someone or something that might harm our friends or relatives in the future.

(7) Anger towards someone or something that helped our enemy in the past.

(8) Anger towards someone or something that is helping our enemy now.

(9) Anger towards someone or something that might help our enemy in the future.

Anger is experienced only in the desire realm. It is like a fire that consumes the merit we have accumulated from performing virtuous actions. Thus, in *Guide to the Bodhisattva's Way of Life* Shantideva says that there is no evil greater than anger.

Anger harms everyone. It harms the person who experiences it and it harms the people it is directed against. Although everyone wants to have stable and lasting friendships, these are hard to achieve because anger destroys our relationships. People who enjoy one another's company at night sometimes feel like killing each other the next day. Most broken marriages result from anger.

To prevent anger developing, as soon as we notice its early stages – such as inappropriate attention or slight feelings of hostility – we need to sever contact with the object and quench the first sparks of anger by meditation, reminding ourself of all the harm anger brings to ourself and others. Once anger has flared up in our mind it is difficult to control. It becomes like a forest fire raging in whichever direction the wind blows. Therefore by watching our own mind we must learn to identify anger in its early stages and avert it before it explodes.

DELUDED PRIDE

Deluded pride is a mental factor that feels arrogant for slight reasons. If we are beautiful or handsome, if we have knowledge and understanding, if we are rich, if we have a good reputation, if we are good at sport, or if we are skilful with words, we can use any of these as a pretext for thinking that we are someone special, and develop pride.

When we have pride it feels as if we are standing on top of a high mountain looking down at everyone else inhabiting the valleys far below. If we listen to or read Dharma instructions with such an attitude of self-importance we shall not derive much benefit. Just as rain that falls onto the peak of a high mountain does not stay there but quickly descends and gathers in the valley below, so the Dharma that we hear when we are inflated with pride will not remain within our mind.

With pride we cannot develop good qualities and realizations. We are easily made unhappy because no one else shares the same exalted view that we have of ourself and so they fail to show us the kind of respect and consideration we feel due to us. We easily feel slighted or abused. Our pride makes us extremely vulnerable and highly susceptible to injury. With the opposite attitude of humility we are not inclined to feel neglected or misused and we are in a position to accept spiritual advice and learn from the instructions. Being receptive to guidance, our good qualities and realizations increase abundantly.

There are seven types of deluded pride: pride over inferiors, pride over equals, pride over superiors, pride in identity, pretentious pride, emulating pride, and wrong pride.

Pride over inferiors is the pride we have when we observe someone who is inferior to us in some respect and think 'I am better than that person.' Pride over equals is the pride we have when we observe someone who is equal to us in some respect and think 'I am better than that person.' Pride over superiors is the pride we have when we observe someone who is superior to us in some respect and think 'I am better than that person.' This pride is also known as 'pride beyond pride' because its object is usually someone who also has pride.

Pride in identity is the pride we have when we identify with something such as a role, an idea, a job, or a country, thinking that because of our identity we are better than others. For example, we may develop pride, thinking 'I am a Buddhist', 'I am a Christian', 'I am a teacher', or 'I am very intelligent.' Almost everyone has this kind of pride. Even beggars can have it, thinking 'I am a clever beggar.' We can develop this pride by identifying with whatever makes us different from others and thinking that this quality makes us noteworthy. In a group of people one person may develop pride, thinking 'I am American', while another develops pride, thinking 'I am British.' Pride in identity is not just a matter of recognizing a fact about ourself – it is an inflated feeling of self-importance that arises when we grasp on to a particular identity.

Pretentious pride is the pride we have when we have an inflated idea of our attainments, thinking that we have gained certain good qualities or realizations that we have not gained. For example, we may sometimes be subject to hallucinations, and when we experience these we may think that we have developed clairvoyance because we perceive special objects. Or we may sometimes achieve a calm mind for a short time and think that we have attained tranquil abiding. Or, again, we may gain some new understanding of a simple subject and think that we have gained great wisdom.

We have developed emulating pride when we observe someone much more highly accomplished or holding a much higher position than ourself, and think 'I am almost as accomplished as that person', or, 'I have a lot in common with that person.' For example, we have emulating pride if we have no spiritual attainments but we imitate Yogis and Yoginis, thinking to ourself 'I am similar to these highly realized practitioners.'

Wrong pride is pride we take in something that we have done badly or incorrectly, believing that what we have done is excellent and praiseworthy. For example, if we give a Dharma discourse full of false information and incorrect advice and we think to ourself 'That was an excellent teaching', we have developed wrong pride. Again, if we give someone disastrous advice and then think 'How wise I am', this is wrong pride.

IGNORANCE

There are two definitions of ignorance: a general definition given by Asanga and Vasubandhu, and a specific definition given by Dharmakirti and Chandrakirti. There is no contradiction between these two systems because the first gives a broad definition of ignorance in general, and the second gives a definition of a specific type of ignorance – the ignorance that is the root of samsara.

According to the first system, in *Compendium of Abhidharma* Asanga defines ignorance as:

> A mental factor that is confused about the nature of an object and that functions to induce wrong awareness, doubt, and other delusions.

According to this definition, ignorance is a lack of knowing or understanding. An example is the confusion we experience when we are reading a book and cannot understand its meaning. This ignorance is like a darkness in our mind, preventing us from clearly understanding our object. According to this system, the ignorance not understanding selflessness – the ultimate nature of persons and other phenomena – induces self-grasping, or true-grasping, which is the root of all other delusions and all samsaric rebirths. This ignorance not understanding selflessness acts as the basis for, but is distinct from, self-grasping, which is a wrong awareness grasping its object as inherently existent.

According to the tradition of Dharmakirti and Chandrakirti a mind that does not know or realize its object is not necessarily ignorance. They say that only self-grasping is ignorance. As selflessness is the main object to be understood in order to abandon self-grasping, the root cause of samsara, these scholars say that only a mental factor that holds the opposite of that held by the wisdom realizing selflessness is an instance of ignorance.

In *Praise to Dependent Relationship* Je Tsongkhapa says:

Whatever faults there are in this world
Their root is ignorance.

The reason why we continue to follow samsaric paths is that because of our ignorance we do not know the nature of objects clearly and perfectly. Two types of ignorance can be distinguished: ignorance of ultimate truths, the ultimate nature of objects; and ignorance of conventional truths, the conventional nature of objects. The ultimate nature of all objects is emptiness. Buddha taught conventional truths to lead us to an understanding of ultimate truths. Since the method for realizing ultimate truths is to examine conventional truths, when we study emptiness it is necessary to study conventional truths. These are presented differently by each of the four Buddhist philosophical schools. By studying each presentation we are gradually led to an understanding of the correct and perfect view presented by the supreme system, the Madhyamika-Prasangika school. In this way we understand correct spiritual paths that lead to liberation, and we eliminate both ignorance of conventional truths and ignorance of ultimate truths.

Buddha taught the view presented by the Chittamatra school specifically to help us to overcome desirous attachment by realizing that the objects we perceive are in the nature of our own mind and do not exist separate from it. According to this system, objects that appear to exist externally are manifested by the mind. These objects are only mental appearances arisen from their seeds carried by the consciousness-basis-of-all. These seeds ripen as objects appearing to the mind. Although the objects and the minds that perceive them arise simultaneously, we have mistaken appearances of the objects as existing external to our mind, and we grasp them as existing in this way. Since we grasp at the objects as existing externally we develop desirous attachment for those that seem attractive. By understanding conventional and ultimate truths as they are presented by the Chittamatra school we reduce our desirous attachment and come closer to realizing the correct view of emptiness presented by the Madhyamika-Prasangika school.

In general, there are two main types of ignorance: ignorance of karma and ignorance of emptiness. Ignorance of karma functions principally to make us continue taking lower rebirths. As long as we remain confused about actions and their effects we continue to engage in non-virtuous actions that are the causes of lower rebirth. Ignorance of emptiness functions principally to keep us bound within samsara. Even if we understand karma, we continue to create the causes for samsaric rebirths until we have realized emptiness directly.

DELUDED DOUBT

Doubt is a mental factor that engages its object two-pointedly or wavers in hesitation between two alternative viewpoints. Not all doubt is deluded doubt. Deluded doubt is a specific type of doubt where the object is anything that it is important to realize in order to attain liberation, such as karma or true sufferings, and where the hesitation is in favour of the incorrect view denying the existence of such an object. Deluded doubt is a doubt that interferes with attaining liberation. The doubts we have about objects that are not important to know in order to attain liberation are not deluded. For example, if someone comes in the door and we wonder 'Is this John?', our doubt is not one of the root delusions.

It is important to distinguish between deluded doubts and doubts that are the beginning of wisdom. The former are to be abandoned but the latter are necessary if we are to gain realizations. When we first listen to or read Dharma we have many doubts because Dharma contradicts our wrong views and incorrect assumptions and makes us undecided about them. This kind of indecision is a sign that we are beginning to develop wisdom, because it is the starting-point for becoming certain of correct views. If we receive Dharma teachings without ever developing this kind of doubt, there is no way to gain conviction in the teachings. For example, when we first hear teachings on emptiness we may begin to doubt 'I think that objects exist externally, but do they really exist like that?', or, 'Objects seem to be substantial, but are they really insubstantial, like dreams?' Without such doubts at the beginning, it is impossible to realize emptiness later. These doubts are doubts tending towards the truth. They take us in the right direction and actually help us to increase our understanding and clarity of mind.

By contrast, deluded doubts destroy our faith in what is virtuous and worthwhile and make us undecided about objects that are trustworthy and beneficial. They destroy the lucidity and joy that we experience when we generate admiring faith. They undermine our virtuous aspirations, and make our previously peaceful mind unsettled and uneasy. If we listen to or read correct Dharma instructions and think to ourself, 'Those teachings are probably wrong', or, 'That instruction is probably useless', these are deluded doubts. If we receive correct explanations of emptiness and develop a slight understanding, and then someone comes along and argues very cleverly against the correct view and we start to think 'The reasonings I heard before are probably wrong', this is deluded doubt. Again, if we receive from our Spiritual Guide perfect instructions for meditation but someone else, with the air of a great meditator, tells us 'That method is inferior. I know much better ways of meditating', we may doubt our Spiritual Guide and the instructions he or she has given. Such doubt can arise when we are about to perform a virtuous action or when we have embarked upon some altruistic deed. It makes us think that we have been mis-guided and so it destroys our good intention.

Deluded doubt is very dangerous because it quickly halts our spiritual practice and throws us into confusion. It can arise when our faith and effort degenerate, or when we meet someone or read something that contradicts Dharma. Deluded doubt can also arise as a result of inappropriate, excessive, or untimely analysis. There are times when it is appropriate and beneficial to apply analytical investigation, such as when we are studying subtle topics like subtle impermanence or emptiness; and there are times when it is beneficial to refrain from analysis, such as when we have gained an adequate understanding of certain gross conventional truths. Over-analysis or untimely analysis induces excessive doubts, which interfere with our practice.

It is especially important to avoid deluded doubt when we are practising Secret Mantra because success in Tantric practices depends upon our having perfectly pure faith. If we develop deluded doubts about our practice of Secret Mantra we shall not gain much benefit, even if we practise for aeons. Therefore, in Secret Mantra even blind faith is better than overanalysis because blind faith can induce strong virtuous determinations whereas overanalysis brings doubt and confusion.

DELUDED VIEW

The first five root delusions are called delusions that are non-views. The sixth root delusion, deluded view, is of five types:

1 View of the transitory collection
2 Extreme view
3 Holding false views as supreme
4 Holding wrong moral disciplines and conduct as supreme
5 Wrong view

VIEW OF THE TRANSITORY COLLECTION

The view of the transitory collection is a deluded view that observes one's own I and conceives it to exist inherently.

If someone abuses us we cling tightly to our I. The I we conceive at such times is unrelated to our body and mind. The mind clinging to such an independent I is the view of the transitory collection. It observes the I and conceives it to exist inherently without depending upon anything else. When we develop the view of the transitory collection we may not be aware that we are clinging to an inherently exist-ent I. We might not be able to express it in this way but we are, in fact, conceiving an I that does not depend upon any-thing else. We are observing our I and holding it to be true. Suppose someone is called 'Peter'. When Peter thinks 'I am Peter', the Peter that appears vividly to his mind is con-ceived as inherently existent and not dependent upon any-thing else such as the limbs of his body.

To identify this I in our own case we can consider what is the I reading this book. When we are reading we do not think 'My body is reading this book', or 'My mind is reading this book.' We think 'I am reading this book', and the I we con-ceive is different from, or unrelated to, our body and mind. The mind that clings to an independent I reading this book is the view of the transitory collection. Its conceived object does not exist.

When we first receive teachings on emptiness and begin to consider how the conceived object of the view of the transitory collection does not exist, we may find it difficult to establish the I that does exist. It is good if this happens because we do need to lose the independent I that we nor-mally cherish. The reason why we cannot at first establish the I that exists is that we have not yet understood subtle conventional truths and so it seems to us that emptiness negates our I altogether. For the time being it is all right to focus on the manifest I that we perceive normally and think that it does not exist at all. This is because this way of thinking helps us to doubt the existence of the conceived object of the view of the transitory collection, and this doubt will lead us to develop the wisdom realizing emptiness.

The I that does not exist is the conceived object of the view of the transitory collection, and the I that does exist is its observed object. The observed object is the I imputed in dependence upon the collection of the five aggregates. The view of the transitory collection observes the merely impu-ted I, but conceives it to exist inherently.

The transitory collection is the five aggregates, the basis of imputation of the merely imputed I; and that I is the observed object of the view of the transitory collection. The merely imputed I is transitory in nature because it is impermanent, and it is the nature of a collection because it exists in dependence upon the collection of the five aggregates.

There are two types of view of the transitory collection: the view of the transitory collection conceiving I and the view of the transitory collection conceiving mine. The second develops in dependence upon the first. When we have the view of the transitory collection conceiving mine, principally we are conceiving our I to exist inherently, while at the same time we are clinging to something as belonging to this inherently existent I and thinking 'This is mine.' From these two views of the transitory collection all other delusions arise. In *Guide to the Middle Way* Chandrakirti says that first we grasp our I as existing inherently, and then we become attached to what is mine, thinking 'This is my possession', or 'This is my friend.' Then out of attachment we engage in actions that are causes of samsaric rebirth.

EXTREME VIEW

Extreme view is a deluded view that observes the I that is the conceived object of the view of the transitory collection and grasps it either as permanent or as completely ceasing at the time of death. Extreme view stabilizes and strengthens the view of the transitory collection.

HOLDING FALSE VIEWS AS SUPREME

If we hold any false view such as the view of the transitory collection, extreme view, wrong view, or any other negative view, and we regard our false view as exalted and superior to other views, this is holding false views as supreme. This delusion exaggerates and strengthens our false views, and makes it more difficult for us to abandon them and adopt correct views.

HOLDING WRONG MORAL DISCIPLINES AND CONDUCT
AS SUPREME

Correct moral discipline prevents us from engaging in non-virtuous actions and helps us to engage in virtuous actions, thereby preventing rebirth in the lower realms of samsara. Nevertheless, there are some people holding wrong views who believe that we can prevent rebirth in the lower realms or even attain liberation from samsara by practising wrong moral discipline and conduct. They view such inappropriate practices as supreme. For example, there was once a religious master who with clairvoyance saw that in his previous life he had been a dog, but since he did not have wisdom realizing karma he concluded that a dog's life is the cause of human rebirth. Therefore he taught all his disciples to practise the moral discipline of simulating a dog's way of life. He told them to keep the commitments of going around on all fours and sleeping outside in a kennel, and he told them that if they practised this 'moral discipline' purely and behaved exactly like a dog they would be sure to gain a human rebirth in their next life. A mind holding such moral discipline as supreme is an example of holding wrong moral disciplines and conduct as supreme.

According to some religious teachers, if we practise the moral discipline of inflicting extreme deprivations, hardships, and pains upon our body we shall purify our mind and attain liberation. Other religious systems require disciples to take from their teacher the commitment of performing animal sacrifice – holding this to be a supreme method for attaining liberation. Some non-religious people hold wrong conduct as supreme when for example they practise sexual misconduct or take drugs in the belief that these are paths to perfect freedom and bliss.

WRONG VIEW

A wrong view is a mind that observes any object that it is important to realize in order to attain liberation or enlightenment, such as karma or emptiness, and denies its existence.

It has been explained that we engage in the non-virtuous mental action of holding a wrong view by repeatedly considering how such an important object does not exist, and we complete the action by coming to a firm decision that the object does not exist, grasping our denial with conviction.

If we hold a wrong view we cannot meditate on correct paths or practise pure Dharma. Even though we may not actually have wrong views, if we still carry within our mind the potentialities for them, these potentialities will obstruct our spiritual practice. For example, if someone explains clearly and logically about rebirth but we cannot develop conviction, our difficulty is created by our potentialities for wrong view. These are obstacles to generating faith and they hinder our understanding of the instructions and advice we receive.

The main cause of wrong views is ignorance, the cause of all delusions. In *Treatise of Four Hundred Verses* Aryadeva says:

> Just as the body sense power pervades the entire body,
> So ignorance pervades all delusions.

Our body sense power functions wherever we experience bodily sensations. In a similar way, ignorance is present wherever there are delusions.

It has been explained that, in general, ignorance or unknowing is very extensive, but that the main ignorance is self-grasping. Although every living being, including the tiniest insect, conceives a self and grasps it at all times, even during sleep, it is difficult to recognize self-grasping when we look for it. In fact, when we can recognize self-grasping clearly we are already very close to realizing selflessness. The main self-grasping to investigate is our grasping at our own self, the view of the transitory collection.

There are two types of self-grasping, innate and intellectually-formed. Not all beings possess intellectually-formed self-grasping because it is a mind that arises in dependence upon incorrect reasoning and not all beings are capable of analytical investigation. Intellectually-formed self-grasping is acquired mainly by those who adhere to philosophical views. For example, if someone called Tom is not content merely to use his name 'Tom' but begins to speculate: 'What is Tom? Is my body Tom? Is my mind Tom?', he may eventually come to the conclusion that Tom is independent of his body and mind, and he may feel satisfied that he has identified Tom. If he develops such conviction as a result of incorrect reasoning or incomplete analysis, that self-grasping is intellectually-formed.

Innate self-grasping is common to all living beings. This is the self-grasping that is the root of samsara, the root of all faults and suffering, and the source of all delusions.

THE STAGES BY WHICH DELUSIONS DEVELOP

In general there are two types of self-grasping: self-grasping of phenomena and self-grasping of persons. When we observe our five aggregates they appear to exist inherently, and so we grasp at them as existing in that way. This is an instance of self-grasping of phenomena. It is our ignorance of the real or ultimate nature of phenomena that causes us to grasp at self of persons. In dependence upon self-grasping of phenomena we conceive, or imagine, an I and grasp it as inherently existent. This is an instance of self-grasping of persons. In dependence upon it we discriminate between self and others, conceiving the two to be inherently different. Then we generate self-cherishing. With self-cherishing, whenever we behold what is attractive we develop desirous attachment; whenever we behold what is unattractive we develop aversion or anger; and whenever we behold what is neither attractive nor unattractive we develop ignorance. From these three delusions all other delusions arise.

In *Commentary to Valid Cognition* Dharmakirti says:

> If we have [grasping at] self we shall have [grasping at] others. From discriminating self and others we shall develop desirous attachment and hatred. Out of desirous attachment and hatred we shall engage in nonvirtuous actions. Through this, all faults and sufferings arise.

This means that if we grasp at our own self as inherently existent we shall grasp at the self of others as inherently existent.
From grasping at self and others in this way we shall conceive self and others to be inherently different. From this
discrimination we shall develop self-cherishing – cherishing
ourself over and above all others. With self-cherishing we
shall develop desirous attachment, hatred, and all other delusions. These delusions will compel us to engage in actions
that are causes of taking appropriated aggregates. From taking
appropriated aggregates all the sufferings of samsara arise.

Once we destroy self-grasping ignorance we shall destroy
all our delusions because this ignorance is the root of all
delusions. Just as there are some medicines that are regarded
as universal remedies for all diseases, so there is one remedy
for all our delusions. This panacea is the wisdom realizing
selflessness.

In *Sutra on the Ten Grounds* Buddha says:

Whatever faults exist in this world all arise from self-
grasping. If we are free from this conception of self,
there are no faults.

THE CAUSES OF DELUSIONS

There are six causes of delusions:

1 The seed
2 The object
3 Distraction and being influenced by others
4 Bad habits
5 Familiarity
6 Inappropriate attention

In *Treasury of Abhidharma* Vasubandhu explains that whenever the first, the second, and the sixth causes are assembled,
delusion necessarily arises. If the seed of delusion, also
known as the 'non-abandoned source of delusion', the object,
and inappropriate attention are assembled together, it is
definite that delusions will develop.

Although we cannot finally abandon delusions until we abandon self-grasping by gaining a direct realization of emptiness, we can overcome our delusions temporarily by learning to identify and prevent their causes. If we train our mind in this way, we shall be able to overcome our delusions for longer and longer periods of time; and if we combine this practice with training in meditation on emptiness we shall eventually gain a direct realization and gradually our delusions will be completely extinguished, like the flame of a candle.

Some non-Buddhists doubt the existence of liberation. They say 'Where is this liberation that Buddhists talk about? We cannot see any examples of liberation.' Doubts such as these are dispelled by our own experience. If we train in reducing and overcoming the causes of delusions we shall understand that although our delusions may at present be very strong, they are not permanent because they can be reduced by applying opponents. If delusions are not permanent and opponents exist it is definite that delusions can be removed once and for all. Even if we do not make any effort to remove the causes of our delusions, we can see from our own experience that delusions are impermanent because they lessen in time. For example, when we are angry we cannot sustain the same degree of anger for very long.

The wisdom realizing emptiness is the general antidote to all delusions, and each delusion has its own specific opponents. For example, the meditation on unattractiveness is an opponent to desirous attachment, the meditations on love and compassion are opponents to anger and hatred, the practice of giving overcomes miserliness, the practice of rejoicing overcomes jealousy, and the meditation on dependent relationship overcomes ignorance. If we are not accustomed to meditating we cannot overcome delusions immediately. However, by practising the opponents we shall lessen our delusions and gain certainty from our own experience that it is possible to become completely free from all delusions and attain liberation.

Dharmakirti said that our contaminated aggregates are not permanent because opponents can destroy their causes.

By applying the opponents we can overcome all the causes of the contaminated aggregates. If we abandon their causes we attain a true cessation, and when we attain this true cessation samsara ceases for us and we experience liberation.

THE SEED

The seed of delusion is the potentiality to develop delusion. This is created in our mind by delusions we have developed in the past, and it is the substantial cause from which delusions arise. While we have the seed of delusion, whenever we come into contact with an object we naturally develop delusions. If we have abandoned the seeds of all delusions, as Foe Destroyers have done, we shall not develop delusions when we come into contact with objects. Foe Destroyers cannot develop delusions even if they try because they have destroyed the substantial cause of delusions.

THE OBJECT

The object of delusion is any object we are observing when we develop a delusion. It need not be perceived directly, but if it is, rather than just remembered, the delusion will develop more strongly. Objects of desirous attachment are objects that appear attractive, and objects of aversion are objects that appear unattractive. It is virtually impossible for us to avoid all objects of delusion. Even if we were to live in an isolated cave there would be some parts of the cave that would appear more attractive than other parts, and some kinds of weather that would seem more pleasant than others. We would soon find ourself preferring this sort of birdsong to that sort of birdsong, and we would still have the memories of other objects of delusion. It is sometimes helpful to move to a place where objects of delusion are fewer; for example, if we live and work in the city it is sometimes beneficial to spend some time in a quiet place in the country. However, if we spend a long time there we shall soon find almost as many objects of delusion as there are in the city. Since we are so accustomed to finding plenty of objects of delusion wherever we go, our main practice with regard to objects of delusion is to practise restraining the doors of the sense powers, as already explained.

DISTRACTION AND BEING INFLUENCED BY OTHERS

If we associate closely with friends who have no interest in spiritual development and who habitually engage in harmful actions, we ourself easily develop the same bad habits and lose our enthusiasm and respect for spiritual practice. Our friendships have a powerful influence over us. Since we tend to imitate our friends, we need to associate with friends who admire spiritual training and who apply themselves to it with joy. Daily contact with our spiritual friends is very important because we do not often have the opportunity to spend a lot of time with our Spiritual Guide. If we come under the influence of our spiritual friends we shall develop the same good qualities and virtuous aspirations, and we shall be inspired by their example to put effort into our study and practice of Dharma.

BAD HABITS

If we develop bad habits of speech, or habits of watching films or reading books that disturb our mind, these will make our delusions stronger. For example, if we often chatter idly about sex, talk senselessly to someone we find attractive, or spend hours reading pornography or romantic fiction, we shall arouse and increase our desirous attachment. Similarly, if we engage frequently in arguments with people we do not like, talk often with others about people who have offended us, or spend hours reading horror stories or war novels that make us admire acts of violence and bloodshed, we shall arouse and encourage our own destructive impulses.

FAMILIARITY

If we are very familiar with delusions they will arise naturally and spontaneously in our mind. For example, if we have become accustomed to expressing our anger openly without control it will be very easy for us to lose our temper. Although we all have some familiarity with every delusion, our degree of familiarity with each one differs. Some people are very familiar with desirous attachment and so it arises in their mind at the slightest suggestion and they experience strong compulsions to obtain the objects they desire. Others are so used to jealousy that as soon as they hear a word of praise for someone else they feel depressed. To reduce our familiarity with delusions we mainly need to apply conscientiousness and mindfulness.

INAPPROPRIATE ATTENTION

Inappropriate attention is a mind that focuses on the qualities of a contaminated object and exaggerates them. It is what actually generates delusions. For example, if we remember how someone harmed us in the past and we dwell on this, exaggerating the harm that was done, inappropriate attention will cause hatred to arise strongly in our mind. If we dwell on the good qualities of an object and exaggerate them, inappropriate attention will cause desirous attachment to arise strongly in our mind. Again, if we hear correct instructions but we begin to question them in inappropriate ways, thinking, for instance, 'My Spiritual Guide has been teaching about liberation, but where are all these liberated beings? I cannot see them', we shall develop deluded doubt towards our Teacher and the instructions he or she has given. This deluded doubt is generated by inappropriate attention probing the instructions pointlessly.

There was once a Tibetan Geshe called Geshe Ben Gungyal who used to spend all his time in his room, doing no meditation in the traditional posture, and reciting no prayers. His unorthodoxy attracted attention, and others asked him, 'You do not recite prayers and you do not meditate in the usual way, so what do you do all day long in your room?' Geshe Ben Gungyal replied 'I have only one task – I am thrusting the spear of the opponents into the head of my delusions.

When a delusion raises its ugly head I increase my alertness and with effort I plunge the spear straight into it. Then it leaves me in peace and I am happy. That is what I do all day long in my room.'

The 'spear of the opponents' refers to meditation on emptiness and all the other meditations that are specific opponents to delusions. This practice of applying opponents is very extensive. If we neglect it and spend all our time reciting prayers while allowing all sorts of delusion to develop in our mind and remain there, our meditations will be very feeble. The early Kadampas used to say that those who wish to lead a virtuous life need to do only two things: harm their delusions as much as possible and benefit others as much as possible. There should never be a time when we do not know what to practise, because we must wage continuous warfare against our delusions, not confining this battle to our meditation sessions. If we have an understanding of emptiness we can attack our delusions by recollecting emptiness. For example, if we are getting angry we can reflect that our anger, the object of our anger, and we ourself all lack inherent existence and are merely imputed by conception. In this way our anger will disappear, just as our fear vanishes as soon as we realize that the object of our fear does not exist. If we get frightened, thinking that we have seen a poisonous snake, our fear will disappear if someone picks up the snake and ties a knot in it, demonstrating that it is only a piece of rope. In the same way, recollection of emptiness swiftly dispels our delusions.

If we have not gained an understanding of emptiness and if we do not have experience of the meditations that are specific opponents to our delusions, whenever we become aware that we are developing inappropriate attention we can eliminate it temporarily by doing breathing meditation. Inappropriate attention is conceptual thought, and breathing meditation temporarily removes all negative conceptual thoughts from our mind, making it calm like water that has become pure and still. Atisha says in *Lamp for the Path to Enlightenment*:

Moreover the Blessed One has said
'The great ignorance of conceptualization causes us to
   fall into the ocean of samsara.
[A mind] of non-conceptual concentration
Is free from conception and as clear as space.'

THE DANGERS OF DELUSIONS

In *Ornament for Mahayana Sutras* Maitreya says that delusions
harm us and they harm other living beings. They destroy our
moral discipline and they cause our inner good qualities to
decrease. They cause the good qualities of honour and reputation to cease. Delusions are objects blamed by the Buddhas
and Bodhisattvas. They are objects towards which Protectors
show wrathful aspects. Delusions cause us to experience
abuse, mental torment, and anxieties. They cause our previous
attainments to decrease and they prevent us from gaining
new realizations. They cause us to take rebirth in the lower
realms.

In *Guide to the Bodhisattva's Way of Life* Shantideva says:

If all living beings, including the gods and demi-gods,
Were to rise up against me as one enemy,
They could not lead me to the fires of the deepest hell
And throw me in;

But this powerful enemy of the delusions
In an instant can cast me into that fiery place
Where even the ashes of Mount Meru
Would be consumed without a trace.

Delusions are our real enemies. Once we have controlled
these inner enemies, all our external enemies are naturally
pacified. Even if all other living beings were to become our
enemies they would not be able to hurt us very much. The
very worst they could do would be to destroy our present
life; they could never harm our future lives. However, our
real enemies, the delusions, can harm us in this life and in
all our future lives as well. If we love and respect our external enemies they may eventually lose their hostility and

return our friendship and respect; but if we love and respect our delusions they will just grow worse. Whereas our external enemies give us plenty of warning, making warlike sounds and fierce gestures, our inner enemies attack us slyly from within. From time without beginning they have been lurking in the depths of our heart inflicting harm upon us.

Furthermore, if we check we shall see that even when external enemies harm us it is really our own delusions that are to blame. Shantideva says:

> . . . those who harm me
> Are provoked into doing so by my own karma.

When someone develops the intention to harm us, what makes that person have such a destructive thought? If we consider we shall see that we ourself are responsible for the harm we receive because we are the present object of that person's harmful thought, and our own past actions created the cause for that person to harm us in this life. What drove us to commit harmful actions in the past? Our own delusions. Thus the main cause of all our sufferings is the delusions that abide within our own mind. Our external enemies are the mere instruments of harm and they would be completely powerless to cause us pain if it were not for our own bad actions.

HOW ACTIONS ARE CREATED IN DEPENDENCE UPON DELUSIONS

In dependence upon delusions we create non-meritorious actions and meritorious actions. Non-meritorious actions are non-virtuous actions, and their fully ripened effect is rebirth in the lower realms. Meritorious actions are virtuous actions. They are of two types: fluctuating and unfluctuating. Fluctuating meritorious actions are virtuous throwing actions whose fully ripened effect is rebirth in the higher realms of humans, demi-gods, and desire realm gods. All non-meritorious and fluctuating meritorious actions of body and speech are created mainly through the power of a mental action or intention that moves the mind to its object. For example, when we think of engaging in a negative action such as killing, it is the mental factor intention that directs our mind to the object and encourages us to engage in the action. Without first creating a mental action there is no way to create a verbal or bodily action.

Unfluctuating meritorious actions are virtuous throwing actions whose virtuous fully ripened effect is rebirth as a god of the form or formless realm. Unfluctuating meritorious actions are created mainly through the power of tranquil abiding. They are so called because once we have created them it is definite that we shall take rebirth in the upper realms. For example, once we have entered the bardo, or intermediate state, of the form realm it is definite that we shall be reborn in the form realm. By contrast, if we complete a virtuous action that is the cause of human rebirth it is not definite that we shall take a human rebirth. This is because once we have entered the bardo of a human being we can still die from that state and enter the bardo of a god of the desire realm.

All three types of action are created in dependence upon delusion because all of them are created by a mind that has self-grasping ignorance. Therefore all three types of action are causes of taking rebirth within samsara.

THE WAY WE DIE AND TAKE REBIRTH

This has three parts:

1 The way we die
2 The way we enter the intermediate state
3 The way we take rebirth

THE WAY WE DIE

This has five parts:

1 The signs of death
2 The causes of death
3 The conditions of death
4 The minds of death
5 The sign that dying has ended

THE SIGNS OF DEATH

The signs of death are of two kinds: distant and close. The distant signs can be experienced even when we are not suffering from any particular illness. They are experienced between six and three months before we die. Distant signs of death are of three kinds: bodily, mental, and dream signs. They do not necessarily indicate that we shall soon die, but when they persist this means that death is probably imminent. If we know what these distant signs of death are, we shall know when we are experiencing them, and so we shall be warned to make preparations that will benefit our future life. We shall know that it is time to make sure that we are engaging in pure Dharma practice and to apply any methods we have learnt for extending our life span, such as the practices of Amitayus and White Tara; or any methods we have learnt for transferring our consciousness at death.

Some of the distant bodily signs of death are the following: while we are passing urine or excrement we continuously hiccup; we can no longer hear the buzzing sound of our inner ear when we block our ears; when we apply pressure against our fingernails and then release the pressure the blood does not quickly return; during sexual intercourse we constantly hiccup; during sexual intercourse, if we are a woman we release white drops instead of red and if we are a man we release red drops instead of white; for no reason we cannot taste things; for no reason we cannot smell things; our exhaled breath is cold – when we blow on our hand it feels cold instead of warm; our tongue shrinks and feels rolled or swollen, and when we poke it out we can no longer see its tip; in the dark when we press the top of our eyeball with our finger so that the eyeball protrudes a little we can no longer see colourful shapes and patterns; we hallucinate a sun at night; when we sit in the sun in the morning we can no longer see in our shadow streams of energy flowing from the crown of our head; saliva no longer forms in our mouth; the end of our nose becomes pinched; black marks appear on our teeth; our eyeballs sink further into the hollows of our eyes.

Distant mental signs of death include: a change in our usual temperament – for example, we become aggressive when we are usually kind and gentle, or we become gentle when we are usually aggressive and ill-tempered; for no reason we dislike the place where we live, our friends, and other objects of attachment; we feel sad for no reason; our wisdom and intelligence become less clear and less powerful.

Distant dream signs include repeated dreams that we are falling from a high mountain, that we are naked, or that we are travelling south on our own across a desert.

The close signs of death will be explained later.

THE CAUSES OF DEATH

There are three principal causes of death: the ending of the karmically determined life span, exhaustion of merit, and loss of power of the life force. As a result of having kept moral discipline in a previous life and having engaged in other virtuous actions such as saving others' lives, we have now obtained a human rebirth with the average life span of, say, seventy years. Although we have created the cause for a life of this length, it is possible to die earlier or to live longer. Severe negative actions done in this life can shorten our life span, while virtuous actions such as refraining from killing, and caring for the sick, can lengthen it. Some people die due to lack of merit even though their life span has not ended. They are unable to find the necessities to sustain life, such as food or the right medicine. The few remaining years of their life span are then 'carried over' into a future human rebirth, which will probably be short and characterized by misfortune. Other people rich in merit can find excellent conditions and thereby manage to live a few years longer than their karmically determined life span.

The third cause of death is loss of power of the life force. The life force is the power of our life-supporting wind. This wind, which abides at our heart, functions to maintain the connection between our mind and body. When its strength diminishes, the connection is broken and we die. Illness, spirits, accidents, or a negative and unhealthy life style can all weaken our life force.

If our life span, merit, and life force are all exhausted we shall definitely die, but if one or two of these causes of life remain it is possible to renew the others. For example, if our life span and life force are still intact but our merit has run out, we can create more merit by performing virtuous actions. If our life force is damaged, then provided we have merit or life span we can restore it by engaging in practices such as vase breathing at our heart. This is one of the best methods to increase the power of our life-supporting wind. To do this we gather the winds from the upper and lower parts of our body at our heart, imagining that they dissolve into our life-supporting wind. Then we hold our winds and mind at the heart, remaining concentrated there for as long as we can.

Our life force is our most precious possession and so we need to stabilize and increase it. Once it is destroyed, it cannot be restored. If we lose any other possession our loss can be restored, but when our life span finishes we cannot borrow any more time to complete the tasks of this life. Therefore, if we are wasting our vitality in meaningless pursuits we should feel this as the greatest loss. If our life is short or we squander it we cannot complete our spiritual practice.

THE CONDITIONS OF DEATH

The conditions of death are countless. Some people die of physical illness and others are killed in accidents or natural disasters. Some people are killed by their enemies and others kill themselves. Some people die of starvation, while others die of the food they eat. Although food is one of the most enjoyable things in life, eating unhealthy food is a condition for diseases and degenerative illnesses such as cancer. As explained before, anything can become a condition of our death, even the things we consider life-sustaining.

THE MINDS OF DEATH

The minds we have when we are dying are of two types, gross and subtle. Whereas the gross minds of death can be virtuous, non-virtuous, or neutral, for ordinary beings the subtle minds of death are only neutral. When we are dying, if our last gross mind is virtuous it will cause the good potentialities carried in our mind to ripen as a virtuous mental action that will lead us directly to higher rebirth as a human or a god. A virtuous mind at death is like water – it nourishes the virtuous potentialities that remain like dry seeds within our field-like consciousness. In a field, if two kinds of seed are sown, barley seeds and wheat seeds, but only the wheat seeds are watered, these will be certain to ripen first. In a similar way, while we still carry both virtuous and non-virtuous potentialities within our mind, a virtuous mind at the time of death will ensure that our virtuous potentialities are the ones that will ripen. This holds even if we have led a very immoral life and committed many non-virtuous actions. However, we do not thereby escape the effects of all our non-virtuous deeds. If we take a human rebirth our human life may be afflicted with great suffering or our life span may be short. If we do not purify our negative karma we shall eventually experience the fully ripened effect of our actions by taking rebirth in the lower realms.

Sometimes people who have no interest in spiritual practice and who lead careless, immoral lives enjoy better conditions and greater worldly success than people who are practising Dharma. Observing this, we may sometimes feel discouraged and think 'What is the point of practising Dharma! Other people are not even trying to lead good lives but good things just fall into their laps, whereas although I practise diligently I seem to experience only hardships for all my pains.' If we start to think like this it is because we are viewing only the present situation and we have not fully understood how actions and their effects follow in succession. If we are now experiencing difficulties, these are the effects of our past actions. They are not the effects of our present spiritual practice, for the effects of our present spiritual practice will be happiness in the future. In the same way, the good fortune of people who are not interested in spiritual practice is the effect of merit they created in the past and is not a result of their present life style. Whatever harmful actions they commit in this life will bring hardships in the future.

When we die, if our last gross mind is non-virtuous it will cause the bad potentialities we carry in our mind to ripen as a non-virtuous mental action, and this will lead us directly to a lower rebirth. From this we can see how important it is to develop a happy and virtuous state of mind at the time of death. We can also see how to be of great benefit to others when they are dying by encouraging them to develop a positive mind and creating for them conditions that will help them to generate good thoughts. In this way we can bring measureless benefit to our friends and relatives, even if they have no interest in Dharma. One of the greatest acts of kindness that we can show towards someone else is to help them to die peacefully and joyfully, for if they attain a happy rebirth in this way they will have attained the same result as someone who has successfully practised transference of consciousness.

When the gross minds of death have ceased and the mind becomes the subtle mind of death, there are no gross feelings – pleasant, painful, or neutral – and no gross discriminations. Since for ordinary beings the subtle minds of death are neutral, these are powerless to induce virtuous minds.

THE SIGN THAT DYING HAS ENDED

When we have experienced the distant signs of death, the close signs of death will occur. First the earth element of the body dissolves. The external sign of this dissolution is that the body becomes thin; and the internal sign is a mirage-like appearance to the mind. Next the water element dissolves. The external sign is that the mouth and tongue become very dry, and the liquids of the body, such as urine, blood, and sperm, decrease; and the internal sign is a smoke-like appearance.

Next the fire element dissolves. The external sign is reduced warmth of the body and coldness in the area around the navel, the centre of the body's heat; and the internal sign is a sparkling-fireflies-like appearance. Next the wind element dissolves. The external sign is reduced power of movement due to the decreasing power of the winds that flow through the channels of the body and cause us to generate gross minds; and the internal sign is a candle-flame-like appearance. The mind perceiving this appearance is the last of the gross minds of death.

The first subtle mind of death is the mind perceiving a white appearance. When this appearance ceases, the mind has become more subtle and perceives a red appearance. This mind again becomes more subtle and transforms into the mind of black near-attainment, to which only black appears. At this stage it is as if the dying person has no mindfulness. Since there is no physical movement, no heartbeat, and no movement in the channels, some people think that this is the end of dying; but in fact the consciousness has not yet left the body. The mind of black near-attainment transforms into the most subtle mind perceiving the clear light of death, a clear bright appearance like the light of dawn. This is the sign that the most subtle mind that resides within the indestructible drop at the heart has manifested and all other minds have ceased to manifest. Then the indestructible drop opens and the white and red drops separate, releasing the consciousness, which immediately departs from the body. The white drop descends through the central channel to emerge through the tip of the sex organ, and the red drop ascends through the central channel to emerge through the nostrils. When this happens it is the sign that the consciousness has left the body and the process of dying has ended.

THE WAY WE ENTER THE INTERMEDIATE STATE

The intermediate state is so called because it is the state between death and the next rebirth. This section will be explained under the following three headings:

1 How to gain conviction that the bardo exists by
   considering the analogy of the dream state
2 The attributes of the body of a bardo being
3 What appears to a bardo being

HOW TO GAIN CONVICTION THAT THE BARDO EXISTS BY CONSIDERING THE ANALOGY OF THE DREAM STATE

The existence of the bardo can be proved by scriptural citation, by experience, and by logical reasoning; but the easiest way for ordinary beings to gain conviction is by considering the analogy of the dream state, which closely resembles the bardo. Both the dream body and the bardo body arise in dependence upon subtle energy winds. Both lack flesh, bones, blood, and inner organs, but both have complete sense powers. Just as the dream body develops from the clear light of sleep, so the bardo body develops from the clear light of death; and just as the dream body is known only to the dreamer, so the bardo being is seen only by other bardo beings and not by ordinary beings who do not have eye clairvoyance. The location of the dream body quickly moves and changes, and acquaintances made in our dream are fleeting. Similarly, the location of the bardo being easily shifts and changes, and acquaintances made in the bardo are short-lived.

As we fall asleep the gross winds gather into our heart and we experience the same signs as the close internal signs of death, from the mirage-like appearance to the clear light. Yogis and some meditators who have developed their mindfulness can remain aware of these signs as they fall asleep, but for most people these signs are not clearly perceived because we lack mindfulness during sleep. After the clear light of sleep we do not immediately wake up but we enter the dream state and develop a dream body. In a similar way, as we die, the gross winds gather into our heart and we perceive the internal signs of death. From the clear light of death we do not immediately reawaken into a new life but we enter the bardo and develop a dream-like bardo body.

THE ATTRIBUTES OF THE BODY OF A BARDO BEING

The body of a bardo being has five attributes: (1) the shape is the same as the shape of the bardo being's next rebirth; (2) it has complete sense powers; (3) its eye sense power can perceive very distant things and can see through any kind of material obstruction; (4) it is not obstructed by any material object and so the bardo being can walk straight through walls, mountains, and so forth; and (5) the eye sense power can perceive other bardo beings.

When people perceive the ghost of someone who has died, this is not the bardo being because the bardo being takes a new form similar to its next rebirth and, as already mentioned, it can be seen only by other bardo beings and those who have eye clairvoyance. Thus, a bardo being cannot communicate with the friends and relatives of its last life. Sometimes spirits appear in the form of a dead person and the people who see them think that they are beholding the person who has died.

WHAT APPEARS TO A BARDO BEING

In the bardo, beings experience many hallucinations. Those who have led a very non-virtuous life feel as if they are falling headlong downwards from darkness to darkness. From the darkness arise dreadful hallucinations which cause the bardo being great fear and misery. Bardo beings experience four terrifying sounds: (1) due to the changed appearance to the mind of the earth element they hear a sound like the thunderous collapse of a huge, rocky mountain, and they become frightened and feel as if they are being crushed beneath a falling mass; (2) due to the changed appearance to the mind of the water element they hear a sound like the huge waves of an ocean, and they become frightened and feel as if they are being carried away by the tide; (3) due to the changed appearance to the mind of the fire element they hear a sound like a fire raging in all four directions, and they become frightened and feel as if they are trapped in the midst of a fire; and (4) due to the changed appearance to the mind of the wind element they hear a sound like a violent storm, and they become frightened and feel as if they are being swept away in a whirlwind. Bardo beings who are about to take rebirth in hell see hideous beings who appear as torturers. Just to behold them brings unbearable fear and suffering. The bardo beings are terrorized by these torturers and they hear them urging one another on, saying 'Lash that person.' Hearing these words, the bardo beings panic and feel as if they are being seized and carried away by these violent executioners.

Those who have led a virtuous life experience joy in the bardo. They feel as if they are ascending from joy to joy and everything appears pervaded by moonlight. Those who are going to take human rebirth feel as if they are floating forwards, and those who are going to take rebirth as gods feel as if they are floating upwards in space.

Someone who has led a virtuous life will die peacefully and gently and will not experience disturbing hallucinations, but someone who has led a non-virtuous life will experience fearful hallucinations at the time of death and in the bardo. There was once a Tibetan aristocrat who was the manager of the prayer festival, and every year he stole tea that had been offered to the monks. Tibetan tea comes in small, hard blocks before it is broken up to make the brew. When the aristocrat was about to die, he hallucinated hundreds and hundreds of blocks of tea crushing him to death.

Geshe Chekhawa mainly practised bodhichitta and the meditation on taking and giving. He used to pray, 'How wonderful it would be if I were to take rebirth in hell to help all the beings who are tortured there.' One day his breathing stopped and his assistant thought that he was dying, but after a few hours Geshe Chekhawa awoke and said 'My wish will never be fulfilled, for I have perceived the signs that I shall take rebirth in a Pure Land.' Geshe Chekhawa received this vision as a result of his virtuous actions and meditation, and was bound to take rebirth in a Pure Land because his compassionate wish to take rebirth in hell was so great.

THE WAY WE TAKE REBIRTH

This has three parts:

1 The causes and conditions of taking rebirth
2 How we take rebirth
3 The nature of rebirth

THE CAUSES AND CONDITIONS OF TAKING REBIRTH

The main causes of taking rebirth are our own actions, our accumulated throwing karma. The secondary, or co-operative, causes of rebirth – the conditions of rebirth – are of two kinds, distant and close. The distant condition is the karma of our parents to have us as their child. The close conditions are the conditions such as our parents having sexual intercourse, and the sperm and ovum joining in our mother's womb. All these causes and conditions must come together for there to be rebirth.

HOW WE TAKE REBIRTH

If the bardo being is to take a human rebirth it circles closer and closer to the place of rebirth like a fly circling around meat. It comes closer to the home of its new parents, to the room, to the bed. When the bardo being sees its new parents copulating it develops a strong desire to join in. If it is to be female it tries to embrace the father, and if it is to be male it tries to embrace the mother; but its desire is frustrated and so it dies in anger. As it dies, the bardo being experiences all the signs of death very rapidly; and when the clear light of death ceases, its consciousness enters the union of the sperm and ovum inside the mother's womb. It enters by passing through the mouth of the father, descending to the sex organ, and then emerging through the sex organ into the mother's womb. The first moment after conception only black appears to the mind of the new human being, and then all the remaining signs of dying are experienced in reverse order as the consciousness becomes more and more gross. At first, the body in the mother's womb is liquid, like yoghurt. It gradually hardens, and after a few weeks it resembles a fish. A few weeks later it resembles a turtle, and then a lion. Eventually, the body resembles a human being. After nine months and ten days the baby is born.

THE NATURE OF REBIRTH

As previously explained, uncontrolled rebirth has the nature of suffering and is the basis from which all the sufferings of the three realms arise.

The Twelve
Dependent-related Links

AN EXPLANATION OF THE TWELVE
DEPENDENT-RELATED LINKS

This has four parts:

1 A general explanation of dependent-related
   phenomena
2 The twelve dependent-related links
3 An explanation of the diagram of the Wheel of Life
4 The actual meditation on the twelve
   dependent-related links

A GENERAL EXPLANATION OF DEPENDENT-RELATED
PHENOMENA

A dependent-related phenomenon is a phenomenon that
exists in dependence upon its parts. Since all phenomena
have parts, and since all phenomena exist in dependence
upon their parts, all phenomena are dependent-related phenomena. In *Fundamental Wisdom of the Middle Way* Nagarjuna
says:

Because there is no phenomenon
That is not a dependent arising,
There is no phenomenon that is not empty.

'Dependent arising' sometimes means arising in dependence
upon causes and conditions, but here Nagarjuna uses the term
to refer to dependent-related phenomena. The definition of
dependent related is existing (or established) in dependence
upon its parts. Produced, or impermanent, phenomena exist
in dependence upon their causes and conditions, and unproduced, or permanent, phenomena exist in dependence upon

their parts (such as their aspects, divisions, and directions). Since all phenomena are either produced or unproduced, it follows that every phenomenon is dependent-related.

There are three levels of dependent relationship: gross, subtle, and very subtle. Every functioning thing that we perceive directly is gross dependent-related. For example, a rose arising from its causes is gross dependent-related. However, the rose existing in dependence upon its parts is subtle dependent-related, and the rose existing as a mere imputation by thought is very subtle dependent-related. One single rose arises from its causes, exists in dependence upon its parts, and exists as a mere imputation by conceptual thought. There are not three different roses but one rose existing in three different ways. Because there are three different ways of understanding the way in which the rose exists, there are three kinds of dependent-related rose – gross, subtle, and very subtle. All functioning things exist in these three ways.

To take another example, the dependent relationship between a pot and its cause is a gross dependent relationship because it is easily understood. The dependent relationship between a pot and its parts is a subtle dependent relationship because it is more difficult to understand than a gross dependent relationship. The dependent relationship between a pot and the conceptual thought conceiving pot is a very subtle dependent relationship because it is the most difficult to understand. We can understand very subtle dependent relationship only after we have realized lack of inherent existence.

In *Essence of Good Explanation* Je Tsongkhapa says that among wisdoms the wisdom realizing dependent relationship is supreme, among Teachers the Teacher of dependent relationship is supreme, and among praises the praise of dependent relationship is supreme. In *Treatise of Four Hundred Verses* Aryadeva says:

If we see dependent relationship,
No ignorance will arise.
Therefore, with a great deal of effort,
We should try to realize dependent relationship.

THE TWELVE DEPENDENT-RELATED LINKS

Understanding gross dependent-related phenomena helps us to understand subtle dependent-related phenomena, and understanding subtle dependent-related phenomena helps us to understand very subtle dependent-related phenomena. Since the twelve dependent-related links are principally related as cause and effect, they are presented as examples of gross dependent-related phenomena. By studying, contemplating, and meditating on them we shall understand more easily subtle and very subtle dependent-related phenomena.

The twelve dependent-related links are called 'links' because they interrelate without any break, like a circular chain of twelve links that binds us within samsara. They are sometimes called 'limbs' because samsara is like a body that has twelve interdependent parts. Again, samsara is likened to a wheel and the twelve dependent-related phenomena are likened to the spokes that revolve unceasingly, taking us from one rebirth to another. If we understand these twelve dependent-related links we shall understand what binds us within samsara and we shall see clearly what has to be done to attain liberation. The twelve are:

1 Dependent-related ignorance
2 Dependent-related compositional actions
3 Dependent-related consciousness
4 Dependent-related name and form
5 Dependent-related six sources
6 Dependent-related contact
7 Dependent-related feeling
8 Dependent-related craving
9 Dependent-related grasping
10 Dependent-related existence
11 Dependent-related birth
12 Dependent-related ageing and death

DEPENDENT-RELATED IGNORANCE

Dependent-related ignorance is a desire realm ignorance that grasps persons and phenomena to be inherently existent and that induces the development of throwing karma. Here 'persons' refers to all beings including oneself, and 'phenomena' refers to all phenomena other than persons. All objects of knowledge are therefore included within these two categories. Accordingly, there are two types of dependent-related ignorance: that which apprehends persons to be inherently existent and that which apprehends phenomena other than persons to be inherently existent. The former is of two types: ignorance apprehending oneself to be inherently existent, the view of the transitory collection, and ignorance apprehending other persons to be inherently existent. This ignorance directly contradicts the wisdom realizing selflessness. It is a delusion but it is neither virtuous nor non-virtuous.

When a blind person gazes at the view from the top of a high mountain it appears to him or her as though darkness covers everything. In a similar way, when we observe persons and other phenomena our confusion with regard to their ultimate nature is like a darkness that prevents us from realizing their emptiness. Ignorance of the real or ultimate nature of persons and phenomena makes us grasp them as inherently, or truly, existent. This true-grasping is dependent-related ignorance. It is a wrong awareness. In dependence upon it we develop inappropriate attention and all the different kinds of delusion.

When we can clearly identify this first link, dependent-related ignorance, we are approaching a realization of selflessness. This is because in identifying what kind of object is conceived by self-grasping ignorance and how it is held by that mind we are identifying the object negated by the wisdom realizing selflessness. The wisdom directly realizing emptiness eliminates dependent-related ignorance, the first dependent-related link, the root of samsara.

To identify in our own experience this ignorance and its conceived object we need to engage in repeated contemplation and meditation. If our mind is agile and alert we can use many different methods. For example, while we are meditating we can deliberately arouse strong self-grasping by imagining that we are in great danger. We can imagine that the floor of our meditation room is caving in, that a fire has broken out in the room, or that a bomb is falling on our house. If we powerfully imagine a situation like this, we shall develop fear and a strong sense of I. When this sense of I has arisen in our mind we have a great opportunity to identify our dependent-related ignorance grasping at I and, if we analyze skilfully, we shall also be able to identify the conceived object of this ignorance.

Not all types of ignorance are dependent-related ignorance. For example, gods of the form and formless realms and Superior beings who are not Foe Destroyers have ignorance that is not dependent-related ignorance. Even Bodhisattvas from the first through to the seventh spiritual grounds have some ignorance, but their ignorance is not dependent-related ignorance because it cannot produce a throwing action that is the cause of samsaric rebirth.

DEPENDENT-RELATED COMPOSITIONAL ACTIONS

Compositional actions are throwing actions that are rooted in ignorance and cause us to take rebirth in samsara. They are of two types: virtuous and non-virtuous. Every day we create countless compositional actions. They are so called because they throw us into samsara by bringing together, or composing, all the causes for a samsaric rebirth; rather as a potter makes pots by bringing together all the different materials that are needed.

Not all actions are compositional actions. For example, some Superior beings and gods of the form and formless realms engage in contaminated actions but their actions do not throw them into samsara. However, they do carry within their minds the potentialities of past throwing actions and so they can still take rebirth again in other realms of samsara.

DEPENDENT-RELATED CONSCIOUSNESS

As soon as any compositional action is complete it leaves a potentiality within our consciousness. The consciousness that receives and carries the potentialities of compositional actions is dependent-related consciousness. The function of this link is to hold the potentiality of a compositional action until it ripens as an effect. Not every consciousness is dependent-related consciousness. The consciousness before it receives the potentiality or imprint of a compositional action is like paper, and the potentiality is like a seal that is placed on the paper-like consciousness by the stamp of a compositional action. Only the mind that receives this potentiality is dependent-related consciousness.

DEPENDENT-RELATED NAME AND FORM

Dependent-related name and form refers only to the aggregates of a person immediately at the moment of conception. Dependent-related form is the form aggregate, and dependent-related name refers to the remaining four aggregates: feeling, discrimination, compositional factors, and consciousness. Dependent-related name is so called because it refers to the aggregates that are the basis for imputing or naming a person. For beings who possess form, the form aggregate is also included within the basis for imputing a person, but it is named separately because beings in the formless realms do not have a form aggregate and so their names are imputed upon the basis of only the other four aggregates.

For a human being, at the moment of conception all five aggregates are present even though they are not yet fully developed. The fertilized ovum is the form aggregate, and the consciousness that enters it has the five all-accompanying mental factors: feeling, discrimination, intention, contact, and attention, which constitute the remaining three aggregates. At this stage these mental factors are subtle and neutral.

DEPENDENT-RELATED SIX SOURCES

Dependent-related six sources refers to the five sense powers – the eye, the ear, the nose, the tongue, and the body sense powers – and the mental power, before the six consciousnesses have begun to function. At the moment of conception the body sense power and the mental power are present, but the remaining four sense powers develop gradually as the form aggregate evolves in the womb. When all six powers are generated they are called 'dependent-related six sources' because they are the sources of the six consciousnesses, although at this stage the six consciousnesses are not yet awakened. Thus, the six sources are said to be like empty rooms in a house waiting to be occupied by the six consciousnesses.

DEPENDENT-RELATED CONTACT

In dependence upon the complete evolution of the sense organs of the foetus, the six powers are developed; and when these meet their objects, the six consciousnesses are generated. When the power, the object, and the consciousness all come together, the foetus knows the object as pleasant, unpleasant, or neutral. The mental factor that knows its object as pleasant, unpleasant, or neutral is dependent-related contact.

DEPENDENT-RELATED FEELING

Dependent-related feeling is a mental factor that arises in dependence upon dependent-related contact. Whereas dependent-related contact knows its object as pleasant, unpleasant, or neutral, dependent-related feeling actually experiences the object as pleasant, unpleasant, or neutral.

DEPENDENT-RELATED CRAVING

In general, craving is a mind of attachment that develops in dependence upon feeling. If we experience pleasant feelings we crave never to be separated from them; if we experience unpleasant feelings we crave freedom from them; and if we experience neutral feelings we crave their continuity without degeneration. Dependent-related craving is a specific type of craving that arises at the time of death. When ordinary beings die they develop craving not to be separated from their body, their environment, or their enjoyments and possessions; and they crave freedom from the unpleasant feelings and experiences of death. These types of attachment experienced at the time of death are dependent-related craving.

DEPENDENT-RELATED GRASPING

In general, grasping is an intensified form of craving. The initial moments of attachment are craving, and the increase of attachment is grasping. Grasping is the mind that wants to take or seize a pleasant object right now, or wants to reject or eliminate an unpleasant object right now. Dependent-related grasping is a specific type of grasping that arises at the time of death. Together, dependent-related craving and dependent-related grasping activate the potentialities created in the mind by compositional actions; that is, they activate the karma that throws us into our next samsaric rebirth.

DEPENDENT-RELATED EXISTENCE

Dependent-related existence is a mental action or intention that has the power immediately to produce the next rebirth. It is a cause named after its effect, the next samsaric existence. Whereas dependent-related compositional action is the distant cause of samsaric rebirth, dependent-related existence is the close cause. It is not definite that a compositional action will ripen since it is possible to purify a non-virtuous action or destroy the potentiality of a virtuous action, but it is definite that dependent-related existence will produce its result.

Dependent-related existence can be either virtuous or non-virtuous, even though it is always induced by the delusions of craving and grasping. For example, if after generating grasping, a dying person performs a virtuous mental action such as going for refuge to Buddha, this will ensure that virtuous potentialities are activated. When this happens it is definite that the dying person will take rebirth in the higher realms. By contrast, if a dying person develops grasping and this induces a non-virtuous mental action such as a harmful thought or a wrong view, this will ensure that non-virtuous potentialities are activated. When this happens it is definite that the dying person will take rebirth in the lower realms.

DEPENDENT-RELATED BIRTH

The first moment of any samsaric rebirth, when the consciousness has entered the new form, the moment of conception, is dependent-related birth. Dependent-related birth and dependent-related name and form occur simultaneously.

DEPENDENT-RELATED AGEING AND DEATH

Dependent-related ageing begins in the second moment after birth and continues until the moment of death. Ageing is the momentary transformation of our physical condition. It is not confined to those who have lived for many years. Dependent-related death is the final cessation of the relationship between the mind and the body, and occurs at the precise moment when the consciousness leaves the body.

Six of the twelve dependent-related links – ignorance, compositional actions, consciousness, craving, grasping, and existence – are causes; and the remainder are effects. The first three links are called 'distant' or 'projecting' causes, and are not certain to bring their effects. The eighth, ninth, and tenth links are called 'close' or 'establishing' causes, and are certain to bring their effects. The four links – name and form, six sources, contact, and feeling – are 'projected' effects; and the last two links – birth and ageing and death – are 'achieved' or 'established' effects.

The first link, ignorance, is like a seed; and the second link, compositional actions, is like sowing the seed in a field. The third link, consciousness, is like the field; and the eighth and ninth links, craving and grasping, are like the water and manure that nourish the seed. The tenth link, existence, is like the seed at the time when it has received full nourishment and is ready to sprout; and the links of birth and name and form are like the sprouting of the seed. The links of six sources, contact, and feeling are like the stages of growth of the crop, ageing is like the ripening of the crop, and death is like the reaping.

Buddha taught the twelve dependent-related links in the order explained and not in the order of six causes and six effects because the order as it is given shows how one round of twelve links may take two, three, or more lifetimes to complete.

How is one round of twelve dependent-related links completed in two lifetimes? Suppose we create a virtuous throwing action in this lifetime. When the action has left a potentiality within our mind, the first three links are complete. If when we die we develop craving and grasping and a virtuous mind, such as going for refuge with the wish to gain a human rebirth in our next life, this virtuous mind will act as the existence link and thus ensure that our virtuous potentiality is activated. At this point the six causes are complete. After death, when our consciousness has entered our new mother's womb, we shall develop the dependent-related name and form of a human being. This and dependent-related birth occur simultaneously. The second moment after dependent-related birth, dependent-related ageing begins, and gradually dependent-related six sources, contact, and feeling develop. Finally, dependent-related death is experienced, completing one round of twelve dependent-related links within two lifetimes.

How is one round of twelve dependent-related links completed in three or more lifetimes? Suppose we create a virtuous action in this lifetime, leaving a virtuous potentiality within our mind. If at the time of death, in dependence upon craving and grasping, we develop a non-virtuous state of mind such as hatred towards our relatives, this will activate non-virtuous potentialities carried within our mind and prevent the virtuous ones from ripening at that time. In this case, dependent-related existence will be non-virtuous and we shall be thrown into rebirth in the lower realms as, say, a dog. After death we shall develop the dependent-related birth and dependent-related name and form of a dog, and then the links of ageing, six sources, contact, and feeling will develop. When our dog's life is about to end, in dependence upon craving and grasping we may develop a virtuous state of mind and thus activate the virtuous potentiality for higher rebirth that we have been carrying within our mind. In this case, the three distant causes for higher rebirth were created in the previous life when we were a human being, and the three close causes are created in the present life as a dog. After death we shall develop the dependent-related birth and dependent-related name and form of a human being. Then the links of ageing, six sources, contact, and feeling will be completed within three lifetimes when the human being dies. The process is the same even if many lifetimes intervene between the life in which the three distant causes are created and the life in which the three close causes are created.

In *Essence of Dependent Relationship* Nagarjuna says:

From three develop two;
From two develop seven;
From seven develop three.

This means that from three delusions, ignorance, craving, and grasping, two actions develop, compositional actions and existence. From these two actions seven fruits of suffering develop: consciousness, name and form, six sources, contact, feeling, birth, and ageing and death. From these seven, again, the three delusions develop. In this way the chain interlocks and samsara is established in perpetual motion.

The Wheel of Life

AN EXPLANATION OF THE DIAGRAM OF THE WHEEL OF LIFE

This has three parts:

1 The benefits of contemplating and meditating
  on the diagram
2 The origin of the diagram
3 The symbolism of the diagram

THE BENEFITS OF CONTEMPLATING AND MEDITATING
ON THE DIAGRAM

With Dharma wisdom, if we contemplate and meditate on
the meaning of the diagram of the Wheel of Life we can gain
many experiences and realizations of the stages of the path.
We can develop the realizations of the stages of the path of
a small being – such as the realization of the great rarity and
value of this precious human life, the realization of death
and impermanence, the realization of the sufferings of the
lower realms, and the realization of going for refuge. We can
develop the realizations of the stages of the path of a middle
being – such as the realizations of the four noble truths and
the twelve dependent-related links, the realization of renunciation, and the realizations of the three higher trainings. We
can also develop the realizations of the stages of the path of
a great being – such as great compassion, great love, bodhichitta, tranquil abiding, and superior seeing.

Even if we contemplate deeply the most sublime paintings
and works of art we cannot gain benefits that compare with
the benefits of contemplating and meditating on the diagram
of the Wheel of Life because this diagram reveals the complete path to liberation and full enlightenment. Other works

Make effort to destroy it.
Enter into Buddhadharma.
Eliminate the Lord of Death
As an elephant destroys a grass hut.

The Wheel of Life

of art may hold our attention for some time, and they may make the artist famous and the art dealers rich, but they cannot communicate so vast and profound a meaning to those who behold and meditate upon them.

THE ORIGIN OF THE DIAGRAM

The origin of the diagram of the Wheel of Life is explained in *Extensive Enjoyment Sutra* and in other Sutras. According to these a king called Bimbisara once received a marvellous gift from a friend. This friend lived in an irreligious country and he was so wealthy that the king could not think of anything to give in return. He asked Buddha 'My friend already possesses so many things. What is the best gift I can offer him?' Buddha knew that this friend was ready to receive Dharma and so he explained to the king how to draw the diagram of the Wheel of Life in all its detail. He then said to the king 'Give this diagram to your friend and he will definitely be satisfied.' As soon as King Bimbisara's friend beheld the diagram he developed a special feeling, even though he had never received any Dharma instructions. When he read a verse that Buddha had written at the bottom of the diagram he immediately understood the meaning of the Wheel of Life. He developed the realization of renunciation and gained a direct realization of emptiness. Then he began to teach his people, and when they studied and meditated on the twelve dependent-related links they also gained the realization of subtle dependent-related phenomena and a direct realization of emptiness. In this way they entered the spiritual paths of Superior beings.

King Bimbisara's friend was able to gain a direct realization of emptiness in dependence upon three things: the ripening of good karmic potentialities, receiving the inspiration of Buddha, and beholding the diagram of the Wheel of Life.

THE SYMBOLISM OF THE DIAGRAM

The diagram of the Wheel of Life represents all the environments of samsara and all the beings who inhabit them. It reveals the nature of samsara and the paths that take us and keep us bound there.

At the centre of the diagram are three animals: a pig, a pigeon, and a snake. In the *Vinaya Sutras* it is stated that the bird at the centre is a pigeon, but these days many diagrams have other birds in its place. There are two ways of drawing these animals. One way is to draw them in a circle with the pigeon coming out of the mouth of the pig, and the snake coming out of the mouth of the pigeon and joining the pig at its tail. The more authentic way is to draw both the pigeon and the snake coming out of the mouth of the pig.

These three animals represent the three mental poisons – the pig represents ignorance, the pigeon represents desirous attachment, and the snake represents hatred. The symbolism is appropriate because pigs do suffer from great ignorance, pigeons do suffer from strong desirous attachment, and snakes do suffer from strong hatred. The pigeon and snake coming out of the mouth of the pig indicate that desirous attachment and hatred develop from ignorance. The way of drawing these three animals according to the first system also has meaning because showing them in a circle indicates that they are mutually dependent.

The innermost circle is surrounded by another circle that is half white and half black, indicating that after death there are two paths: the white, virtuous path that leads to the higher rebirths of humans and gods, and the black, non-virtuous path that leads to the lower realms. On the white side of the circle three bardo beings are drawn in the aspect of their next rebirth. One is a human, one is a demi-god, and one is a god. These bardo beings are upright and ascending to the top of the Wheel. On the black side of the circle another three bardo beings are drawn upside-down and falling. One is an animal, one is a hungry spirit, and one is a hell being.

This half-white, half-black circle is surrounded by another circle divided into six compartments representing the six realms of hell beings, hungry spirits, animals, humans, demi-gods, and gods. In some diagrams gods and demi-gods are represented together. There are infinite world systems inhabited by living beings, but all of them are contained within the six realms.

Around this circle is a rim with twelve divisions. Inside each section is a drawing representing one of the twelve links:

(1) Ignorance is represented by an old, blind woman.

(2) Compositional actions is represented by a potter making pots, some good and some bad.

(3) Consciousness is represented by a monkey scampering restlessly up and down a tree, indicating how our consciousness moves restlessly up and down the tree of samsara.

(4) Name and form is represented by a man rowing a boat, indicating that just as we need a boat to travel across the ocean, so we need the boat-like aggregates to take rebirth in ocean-like samsara.

(5) Six sources is represented by an empty house with five windows, indicating that just as a house stands empty before its owners move in, so, when the embryo has just developed, the six sources are like rooms in an empty house waiting to be occupied by the six consciousnesses. (The five windows in the diagram represent the five sense powers but the mental power is also implied).

(6) Contact is represented by a man and a woman embracing.

(7) Feeling is represented by a man shot in the eye with an arrow.

(8) Craving is represented by a man drinking beer.

(9) Grasping is represented by a monkey grabbing fruit.

(10) Existence is represented by a pregnant woman about to give birth.

(11) Birth is represented by a baby being born.

(12) Ageing and death is represented by a man carrying a corpse on his back.

The entire Wheel of Life is drawn within the clutches of Yama, the Lord of Death, reminding us of impermanence and showing that there is not a single being in this Wheel of Life who is outside the control of death. Yama holds the Wheel in his mouth and embraces it with his claws, indicating that all living beings repeatedly go through the jaws of death. The Lord of Death is the greatest obstacle to our liberation. He holds up a mirror called the 'mirror of action' in which all the actions of living beings, virtuous and non-virtuous, are clearly reflected.

The Wheel of Life represents true sufferings and true origins, revealing how true sufferings arise in dependence upon true origins. Outside the Wheel of Life Buddha stands pointing to a moon. Buddha standing outside the Wheel of Life shows that Buddhas are outside samsara because they have become liberated by abandoning samsaric paths and attaining true paths. The moon represents true cessations. By pointing at the moon Buddha is saying 'I have travelled along liberated paths and attained the city of liberation.'

At the bottom of the diagram is the verse written by Buddha:

Make effort to destroy it.
Enter into Buddhadharma.
Eliminate the Lord of Death
As an elephant destroys a grass hut.

The first line urges us to make an effort to abandon samsara and the second line tells us how to do it. The third and fourth lines teach that by practising the three higher trainings we can eliminate the sufferings of birth, ageing, and death completely, as an elephant demolishes a grass hut.

THE ACTUAL MEDITATION ON THE TWELVE DEPENDENT-RELATED LINKS

There are four ways of meditating on the twelve links:

1 Meditation in serial order on the dependent relationship of the side of delusion

2 Meditation in reverse order on the dependent
   relationship of the side of delusion
3 Meditation in serial order on the dependent
   relationship of the perfectly purified side
4 Meditation in reverse order on the dependent
   relationship of the perfectly purified side

The first two ways of meditating are said to be 'of the side
of delusion' because they reveal the step-by-step development of samsara from its root cause, ignorance. The second
two ways of meditating are said to be 'of the perfectly purified side' because they reveal the cessation of the twelve
dependent-related links and the attainment of liberation.

If we meditate on each link separately, considering how
each one causes the next – how dependent-related ignorance
causes dependent-related compositional actions and so forth
up to dependent-related ageing and death – we are doing
the meditation in serial order on the dependent relationship
of the side of delusion. This meditation reveals how, over
and over again, true sufferings arise from true origins. If we
first meditate on the sufferings of this life such as sickness,
ageing, and death, and then we meditate on each link in
reverse order, considering how all the sufferings of this life,
implied in the link of dependent-related ageing and death,
come from dependent-related birth, and how dependent-
related birth comes from dependent-related existence and so
forth back to dependent-related ignorance, we are doing the
meditation in reverse order on the dependent relationship of
the side of delusion. This meditation makes us develop a
strong determination to eliminate ignorance by contemplating and meditating on emptiness.

If we first meditate on the cessation of dependent-related
ignorance and how it is the method that brings about the
cessation of dependent-related compositional actions, and if
we continue to meditate in this way on the cessation of each
link and how it comes about in dependence upon the cessation of its previous link, we are doing the meditation in
serial order on the dependent relationship of the perfectly

purified side. If we first meditate on the cessation of the sufferings of this life, that is, on the cessation of dependent-related ageing and death, and how this cessation comes about by means of the cessation of dependent-related birth and so forth back to the cessation of dependent-related ignorance, we are doing the meditation in reverse order on the dependent relationship of the perfectly purified side.

If we practise these four ways of meditating on the twelve links, continually and without distraction, this becomes a powerful method to increase our wisdom and our concentration.

The Path to Liberation

This is explained in two parts:

1 The bodily basis we need to attain liberation
2 The paths we need to follow to attain liberation

THE BODILY BASIS WE NEED TO ATTAIN LIBERATION

It has been explained that the human form provides the best bodily basis for attaining liberation. Beings who are born in the lower realms have no opportunity to practise Dharma and so it is impossible for them to attain liberation. It is difficult for gods to attain spiritual realizations because some of them have many strong distractions and some of them lack the necessary conditions for gaining realizations. By contrast, with a human body it is comparatively easy to develop the realizations of renunciation, bodhichitta, emptiness, and so forth.

Nevertheless, just to have a human body is not sufficient to attain liberation because we also need to exert effort. As Geshe Potowa said, we have taken many samsaric rebirths but we have never attained liberation naturally without exerting effort. This has never happened to us or to anyone else in the past, and it will never happen in the future, because it is impossible to attain liberation without making an effort. Therefore, the time for engaging in spiritual practice and engaging in the methods for destroying samsara is right now, while we have this human body. Once we have lost the opportunity this life affords we shall have lost our chance to gain pure peace.

THE PATHS WE NEED TO FOLLOW TO ATTAIN LIBERATION

This has three parts:

1 The three higher trainings
2 Why we need to practise the three higher trainings to attain liberation
3 How to practise the three higher trainings

THE THREE HIGHER TRAININGS

The three higher trainings are the means by which we escape from samsara and attain liberation. They are:

1 Training in higher moral discipline
2 Training in higher concentration
3 Training in higher wisdom

TRAINING IN HIGHER MORAL DISCIPLINE

With the motivation of renunciation, when we practise any moral discipline – from the moral discipline of abandoning killing to the moral discipline of keeping all three sets of vows, the Pratimoksha, Bodhisattva, and Tantric vows – we are practising higher moral discipline. Without the motivation of renunciation any practice of moral discipline is a cause of higher rebirth in samsara, but it is not a cause of liberation.

In *Friendly Letter* Nagarjuna says:

Always practise superior moral discipline,
Superior concentration, and superior wisdom.
These three perfectly include
All the two hundred and fifty-three trainings.

Fully ordained monks take two hundred and fifty-three vows, and all of them are contained within the practice of higher moral discipline because they are taken with the motivation of renunciation. The same applies to the Bodhisattva and Tantric vows. If we take the Pratimoksha vows before developing renunciation our vows are not actual but provisional Pratimoksha vows. If we subsequently listen to, contemplate, and meditate on the stages of the path we shall develop the realization of renunciation. When this happens our provisional Pratimoksha vows are transformed into real Pratimoksha vows. Geshe Potowa used to say 'Dromtonpa is my ordaining Abbot.' Since Dromtonpa was a layman he could not actually be an ordaining Abbot. Geshe Potowa was implying that it was due to Dromtonpa's guidance that he developed the realization of renunciation and thus transformed his provisional monk's vows into real ones.

Through this we can understand clearly how important it is for those who have received the Pratimoksha, Bodhisattva, and Tantric vows to practise Lamrim. If we neglect the practice of Lamrim it is almost impossible these days for us to keep our vows purely without breaking them.

TRAINING IN HIGHER CONCENTRATION

With the motivation of renunciation any practice of concentration is a practice of higher concentration, even if we do just one round of breathing meditation. If we do not have renunciation, even if we are able to concentrate on a very elaborate visualization this is not a practice of higher concentration. An exception is where our object of meditation is a Buddha or a Deity recognized as one with Buddha. If these are our objects of concentration and we meditate with great faith, then even without having the motivation of pure renunciation we are practising higher concentration and creating the cause to attain liberation. If we concentrate on any other object without the motivation of renunciation we do not create the cause for liberation, but provided our object is virtuous we do create the cause for higher rebirth within samsara.

TRAINING IN HIGHER WISDOM

With the motivation of renunciation, whenever we meditate on ultimate truths we are practising higher wisdom.

Anyone who practises these three higher trainings is said to be 'maintaining Buddhadharma by means of realization'. There are two ways of maintaining Buddhadharma: maintaining Buddhadharma by means of scripture and maintaining

Buddhadharma by means of realization. We maintain the first when we listen to, read, and study Dharma, and we maintain the second when we actually put the instructions into practice and gain realizations.

WHY WE NEED TO PRACTISE THE THREE HIGHER TRAININGS TO ATTAIN LIBERATION

Each of the three higher trainings is a cause of liberation, but to attain liberation we need to practise all three completely. By taking the twelve dependent-related links as our object of concentration and meditating on them we shall realize that self-grasping ignorance is the real enemy of those who seek liberation, and we shall develop a strong determination to abandon it. By taking the four noble truths as our object of concentration we shall develop a strong wish to be released from samsara and all its associated sufferings. Therefore, taking either the twelve links or the four noble truths as our object of concentration causes us to develop strong renunciation. With renunciation, if we take emptiness as our object of concentration we shall develop a special wisdom called 'superior seeing'. Only this wisdom can directly eliminate the self-grasping ignorance that is the root of samsara.

To develop superior seeing we first need to have attained tranquil abiding, and to attain tranquil abiding we need to practise pure moral discipline, which is the supreme method for gaining pure concentration. Thus, attaining liberation depends upon the experience of higher wisdom; the experience of higher wisdom depends upon the experience of higher concentration; the experience of higher concentration depends upon the experience of higher moral discipline; and the experience of higher moral discipline depends upon the realization of renunciation that arises as a result of meditating on the twelve dependent-related links or the four noble truths.

In Vasubandhu's *Treasury of Abhidharma* self-grasping ignorance is sometimes called a 'seed' and sometimes a 'root'. It is called a 'seed' because all sufferings arise from it as crops grow from seeds, and it is called a 'root' because all the fears, frustrations, and sufferings of samsara grow from it as fruits and flowers grow from the root of a tree. We cannot abandon self-grasping ignorance unless we meditate on emptiness because other meditations, such as meditations on love, compassion, and bodhichitta, do not directly eliminate ignorance. Dharmakirti said:

[Meditations on] love and so forth do not oppose ignorance;
Therefore, they cannot destroy ignorance completely.

It is only a direct realization of emptiness that actually frees us from samsara. When we realize emptiness intellectually, by means of a generic image, our realization is not clear and we need to continue to meditate on emptiness to attain a direct realization. This is not easy because we lack pure concentration. Without training in concentration our mind is easily distracted and we cannot keep it placed on our object of meditation. When we become free from the turbulence of distractions our mind becomes clear and still and we can observe our object of meditation clearly. If at night we try to read a book by flickering candlelight we shall find it hard to make out the words on the page. Similarly, without strong concentration our mind is like a candle flame flickering in the breeze, and if we try to meditate on an object by the light of unstable concentration we shall not be able to observe our object clearly.

To attain perfect concentration we must overcome all forms of distraction. These are of two types: outer distractions and inner distractions. Outer distractions develop when we come into contact with external objects that cause delusions to arise in our mind. Inner distractions are more subtle. They develop in meditation when we remember objects of attachment and so forth. Subtle memories which recall objects of attachment, subtle conceptual thoughts, mental sinking, and mental excitement are all inner distractions. We first need to pacify the gross, outer distractions before we can eliminate the subtle, inner distractions. When our concentration becomes stable our mind is like a motionless candle flame clearly illuminating its object. Then conceptual thoughts are pacified, our mind becomes lucid, and we can clearly observe subtle objects such as emptiness.

It is concentration that reduces and finally eliminates the distance between the mind and its object, causing the mind and its object to mix. When our concentration placed on emptiness improves and our mind mixes with emptiness, this concentration can eliminate self-grasping and all other delusions and enables us to attain the perfect peace of liberation. Therefore, the wisdom realizing emptiness is said to be like an axe. However, although it is sharp, it will not cut the tree of ignorance unless it is driven into the wood with the firm hand of concentration. In *Condensed Exposition of the Stages of the Path* Je Tsongkhapa says:

> No matter how much it investigates, a wisdom separate from the path of tranquil abiding will never destroy the delusions.

Just as we need the pure concentration of tranquil abiding to develop superior seeing, so we need pure moral discipline to develop this concentration because it is pure moral discipline that overcomes distractions and other obstacles to tranquil abiding. The practice of moral discipline accomplishes two tasks: it pacifies outer distractions and it strengthens mindfulness which overcomes inner distractions. Moral discipline prevents us from indulging in negative actions and it directs the mind to correct spiritual paths. To practise pure moral discipline we need to apply mindfulness and alertness. Without these we easily forget the commitments we have taken and all the good resolutions we have made.

Moral discipline is like a field, concentration is like the plants that grow in it, and wisdom is like the harvest. Moral discipline makes our body and speech pure and free from faults, whereas concentration and wisdom make our mind completely pure and free from faults. Thus all three are necessary to attain liberation.

HOW TO PRACTISE THE THREE HIGHER TRAININGS

This has three parts:

1 How to practise higher moral discipline
2 How to practise higher concentration
3 How to practise higher wisdom

HOW TO PRACTISE HIGHER MORAL DISCIPLINE

The best way to keep moral discipline purely is to contemplate again and again its benefits, and to rely at all times upon mindfulness and alertness. In *Friendly Letter* Nagarjuna says:

Just as the earth supports all life,
So moral discipline is the foundation for all good
    qualities.

In *King of Concentration Sutra* Buddha says:

When Buddhadharma is degenerating it is more meritorious to keep moral discipline for one day than to make offerings to thousands and thousands of Buddhas for many aeons during fortunate times.

At a time when Buddhadharma is degenerating it is especially hard to find anyone who practises moral discipline, and even among those who do it is difficult to find anyone who can keep moral discipline purely because at such a time inner obstacles and delusions are very strong.

There are four main causes of the degeneration of pure moral discipline: (1) not knowing the nature and function of moral discipline, how to practise it, what objects are to be abandoned, and so on; (2) lack of respect; (3) strong and plentiful delusions; and (4) non-conscientiousness.

Usually when we commit negative actions we do so out of ignorance, not knowing what is to be abandoned by moral discipline. Some people engage in these actions happily because they do not realize their faults. Even those who have taken upon themselves the moral disciplines of the Pratimoksha, Bodhisattva, and Tantric vows soon break them if they do not know what are the objects to be abandoned by these disciplines. Therefore, if we are to keep moral discipline purely we need to know all the objects to be abandoned, and we need to contemplate again and again the harmful consequences of breaking our commitments and vows.

If we lack respect for Buddha and his teachings we shall commit non-virtuous actions and we shall not put effort into our practice of moral discipline; but if we trust and respect Buddha, the Dharma he taught, and the spiritual community that is putting Dharma into practice, we shall develop strong conviction in the law of actions and their effects and we shall naturally exert ourself to keep moral discipline. Therefore, to practise pure moral discipline we need to develop faith in and respect for Buddha, Dharma, and Sangha.

When we commit non-virtuous actions and do not keep our commitments purely it is often because our delusions are so powerful and overwhelming. Therefore, to practise pure moral discipline we need to make an effort to diminish powerful delusions, first working to reduce the strongest ones by applying the appropriate methods.

If we are not conscientious we shall just let our mind do what it wants. We shall lead a reckless life and easily break our vowed rules of moral conduct. Without conscientiousness our mind is like a crazy, wild elephant. To practise conscientiousness means, principally, to cultivate mindfulness and alertness. Mindfulness prevents us from forgetting our moral discipline. For example, if we take a vow in the morning to refrain from a particular kind of action, mindfulness keeps, as it were, a mental eye on this vow throughout the day, making sure that we do not forget it. Alertness checks from time to time to make sure that our conduct is in accordance with our vow and to make sure that our mindfulness remains strong.

In addition to mindfulness and alertness we also need to cultivate a sense of shame and consideration for others. Sense of shame is a mental factor that restrains us from committing non-virtuous actions or breaking a vow by making us check our actions against the moral discipline we have adopted. For example it makes us think 'It would be inappropriate for me to engage in this action because I am a Buddhist', or 'I cannot do that because I am ordained.'

Consideration is a mental factor that holds us back from non-virtues by making us consider the effect our actions have on others. For example, we may think 'If I do this it will give the Buddhist community a bad name', or 'If I do this it will make people lose faith in Sangha', or 'If I do this my Spiritual Guide will be ashamed of me.' Restraining ourself in this way is a practice of consideration.

All four – mindfulness, alertness, sense of shame, and consideration – help us to maintain conscientiousness and keep pure moral discipline; but principally we need to rely upon mindfulness.

HOW TO PRACTISE HIGHER CONCENTRATION

There are seventeen different concentrations from the point of view of the three realms: the nine concentrations of the desire realm, the four concentrations of the form realm, and the four concentrations of the formless realm.

The nine concentrations of the desire realm are: placing the mind, continual placement, replacement, close placement, controlling, pacifying, completely pacifying, single-pointedness, and placement in equipoise. These nine include all the concentrations experienced before attaining tranquil abiding. Any experience of concentration we have before attaining actual placing the mind is included within the first concentration.

After we have attained tranquil abiding our concentrations are concentrations of the form or formless realms. The four concentrations of the form realm are: the first mental stabilization of the form realm, the second mental stabilization of the form realm, and so forth. The concentrations of the formless realm are: the absorption of infinite space, the absorption of infinite consciousness, the absorption of nothingness, and the absorption of peak of samsara. In general, these seventeen concentrations are mundane paths. They are named in ascending order, from lowest to highest. Only when we gain the highest concentration of the three realms – the absorption of peak of samsara – do we attain uncontaminated clairvoyance and miracle powers.

Concentrations can also be divided in terms of their function, according to whether they act as an opponent to desirous attachment, hatred, ignorance, pride, jealousy, conceptual thoughts, or delusions in general. For example, if we have a problem of strong desirous attachment we emphasize the meditations on repulsiveness – seeing our own body, the bodies of others, our environment, and our enjoyments as unclean. When we meditate on our own body or the bodies of others as unclean we meditate on the body as a collection of thirty-two impure substances. When we meditate on the environment as unclean we visualize the whole ground composed of the bones of corpses, mud, and excrement. In the *Vinaya Sutras* many such meditations are explained to help us to develop strong renunciation, and we can apply these according to whatever is the object of our attachment.

If we have a problem of strong hatred we emphasize the meditations on love and compassion. To overcome ignorance we meditate on dependent relationship. Meditating in great detail on the divisions of each of the external and internal elements, trying to identify each object, how it develops, its source, its causes, and so on, exposes how little we really know, and thereby reduces our pride. Jealousy can be countered by meditation on rejoicing. Meditation on the breath is useful whenever our mind is very busy and distracted. To overcome the root of all delusions and suffering we meditate on emptiness.

If we practise any of these concentrations with the motivation of renunciation or bodhichitta we are practising higher concentration.

HOW TO PRACTISE HIGHER WISDOM

Wisdom is a virtuous, intelligent mind that functions to recognize objects unmistakenly. Analytical meditation is a practice of wisdom because through investigation and analysis we come to know our object more fully. Whenever we do analytical meditation with the motivation of renunciation or bodhichitta we are practising higher wisdom. In the beginning, the wisdom of analysis helps us to develop placement meditation. Eventually, when our concentration becomes very stable and we attain tranquil abiding, our concentration improves our wisdom. By means of tranquil abiding we attain the special wisdom called 'superior seeing', and with superior seeing our meditation becomes very powerful.

Generally, wisdom helps all our spiritual practices, not only our meditation. In the *Condensed Perfection of Wisdom Sutra* Buddha says:

Wisdom goes before the practice of giving.
Likewise, it goes before the practice of moral
    discipline, patience, effort, and concentration.

To develop the desire to practise giving we first need to understand the benefits, and to understand the benefits we need wisdom. Thus, wisdom is a prerequisite for all our virtuous practices.

There are three types of wisdom: wisdom arisen from listening, wisdom arisen from contemplation, and wisdom arisen from meditation. We develop the first type of wisdom when we listen to someone explaining Dharma and understand what they are saying, or when we read a book and understand its meaning. We develop wisdom arisen from contemplation when we think for ourself, applying our own lines of reasoning and analysis to arrive at a deeper understanding of our object. For example, if we pause while reading a Dharma book and begin to investigate for ourself, checking the meaning that we have understood, we shall develop wisdom arisen from contemplation. If we then meditate on the object and gain a special experience, this is wisdom arisen from meditation.

We improve our wisdom arisen from listening by listening to Dharma discourses or reading Dharma books, and we improve our wisdom arisen from contemplation by repeatedly reflecting on the meaning of what we have listened to or read. We improve our wisdom arisen from meditation by repeatedly engaging in meditation on the Dharma we have received. In this way our Dharma wisdom will improve day by day, month by month, year by year. Since all problems and all suffering arise from ignorance, the wisdom that overcomes ignorance and reveals clearly what is to be abandoned and what is to be practised is our best friend, leading us finally to full enlightenment.

PART THREE

The Great Scope

Entering the Mahayana

TRAINING THE MIND IN THE STAGES OF THE PATH OF A PERSON OF GREAT SCOPE

All the stages of the path to enlightenment can be divided into common and uncommon paths. The stages of the path that have been explained so far are common to both Hinayana and Mahayana paths; but the stages that follow – the stages of the path of a great being – are uncommon Mahayana paths. Training the mind in the stages of the path of a person of great scope is explained in five parts:

1 Why we need to enter the Mahayana
2 The benefits of bodhichitta
3 How to develop bodhichitta
4 How to engage in a Bodhisattva's actions
5 The final result, full enlightenment

WHY WE NEED TO ENTER THE MAHAYANA

Since we can attain liberation by practising only the stages of the path of small and middle beings, we may wonder why it is necessary to enter the Mahayana. We need to enter the Mahayana path because liberation is surpassed by the full enlightenment of Buddhahood. Only a Buddha's mind is omniscient, directly understanding all objects of knowledge, and only Buddhas have abandoned all faults and attained all good qualities. Those who have attained only liberation have not completed their own purpose and cannot work extensively for the benefit of other living beings because they still have many subtle levels of obstruction. Since Hinayana paths do not include methods for eliminating subtle levels of obstruction, if we wish to become completely free from faults we need to accomplish the Mahayana paths. These alone can eliminate faults completely and develop every good quality. Although all living beings possess the seed of full enlightenment, this seed is brought to perfect fruition only through the complete practice of the Mahayana path. If this is the case, why did Buddha teach Hinayana paths? Buddha taught these for disciples who cannot immediately follow Mahayana paths, which are more difficult to understand and practise. He taught Hinayana paths as preparations for Mahayana paths. It was his main intention to lead all disciples, Hinayana and Mahayana, to Mahayana paths, and hence to the full enlightenment of Buddhahood.

From the point of view of our own welfare we need to enter the Mahayana path because it is only by attaining full enlightenment that we can fulfil all our own desires and realize the ultimate purpose of our human life. From the point of view of others' welfare as well we need to enter the Mahayana path because it is only by becoming a Buddha that we become perfectly capable of helping all other living beings.

If a mother and her son were both trapped in prison and the son were to make plans for his own escape without thinking about his mother, we would consider his attitude to be very callous and selfish. Since all living beings are our mothers, and all of them are trapped in the prison of samsara, it would be cruel of us to turn our back on them and think of attaining only our own happiness. We must abandon the inferior attitude of concern for our own welfare alone and make a firm decision to enter the Mahayana path for the sake of others.

THE BENEFITS OF BODHICHITTA

To enter the Mahayana path we must first generate bodhichitta. This is a spontaneous wish to attain enlightenment in order to benefit all living beings. It is born from great compassion – a mind that cannot bear others to experience pain and that wants to release all living beings from every kind of suffering. At present it is our own suffering that we cannot bear, but when we gain the realization of great compassion the suffering of others is unbearable to us. Seeing how many and how great their sufferings are, we have a spontaneous and continuous wish, 'How wonderful it would be if all living beings were entirely free from every kind of suffering.'

Having generated great compassion, when we become determined to attain enlightenment for the sake of others and this determination is spontaneous and continuous all day and all night, we have realized bodhichitta. Bodhichitta is the supreme motivation, the door through which we enter the stages of the Mahayana path.

It has been explained that bodhichitta has two parts or two aspirational thoughts. The primary aspiration is to release all living beings from their sufferings, and the secondary aspiration is to attain enlightenment so as to be able to do this. Since such sublime aspirations do not arise naturally and spontaneously in our mind, we have to cultivate them. In the beginning they will seem foreign and unnatural and we shall have to encourage them in ways that feel artificial. When we begin to experience some success we shall have to protect and enhance our small realizations until, in time, these special intentions become more and more familiar to us. Eventually they will become entirely natural. For this to happen we need to apply steady, continuous effort. With effort we can fulfil all our wishes. Without it we give in to laziness, we develop dislike for the practices and a reluctance to listen to or read the instructions, we feel discouraged, depressed, and incapable of doing the meditations, or we let ourself give in to inclinations to engage in non-virtuous actions.

The method for overcoming our laziness and generating the power of effort is to meditate on the benefits of bodhichitta. These are countless, but are all contained within ten:

1 We enter the gateway to the Mahayana
2 We become a Son or Daughter of the Buddhas
3 We surpass Hearers and Solitary Realizers
4 We become worthy to receive offerings and prostrations from humans and gods

5 We easily accumulate a vast amount of merit
6 We quickly destroy powerful negativities
7 We fulfil all our wishes
8 We are free from harm by spirits and so forth
9 We accomplish all the spiritual grounds and paths
10 We have a state of mind that is the source of peace
and happiness for all beings

WE ENTER THE GATEWAY TO THE MAHAYANA

When we generate bodhichitta we become a Bodhisattva and enter into Mahayana paths; therefore bodhichitta is called the 'gateway to the Mahayana'. To become a Mahayanist we need to develop bodhichitta. Without bodhichitta, even if we practise Highest Yoga Tantra we are not Mahayanists; and even if we have studied extensively and deeply and received many Mahayana instructions, this alone does not make us a Mahayanist. To enter the gateway to the Mahayana means to develop the inner experience of bodhichitta, not merely to hold Mahayana tenets. It is quite possible to hold Mahayana tenets and yet have a Hinayana motivation, just as it is possible to hold Hinayana tenets and have a Mahayana motivation. We should not develop pride just because we are studying Mahayana scriptures or because we are attending a Mahayana Centre; rather we should put effort into generating the precious mind of bodhichitta and become a true Mahayanist.

WE BECOME A SON OR DAUGHTER OF THE BUDDHAS

In *Guide to the Bodhisattva's Way of Life* Shantideva says:

The moment bodhichitta is generated
Even in pitiful beings bound within the prison
of samsara,
They become Bodhisattvas – a 'Son or Daughter
of Buddha'.

We become a Son or Daughter of the Buddhas when our Buddha lineage ripens and we enter Mahayana paths. Even if we have many other good qualities such as clairvoyance, miracle powers, or a direct realization of emptiness, if we have not developed bodhichitta we are not yet an heir to the throne of Buddhahood. A Bodhisattva is like a prince and a Buddha is like a king. Just as people consider a prince to be very precious and offer him the same respect they offer the king, knowing that the prince will become a king, so a Bodhisattva is in line for the throne of Buddhahood. He or she is known as a 'being bound for enlightenment'.

WE SURPASS HEARERS AND SOLITARY REALIZERS

Hearers and Solitary Realizer Foe Destroyers are far superior to ordinary beings who have not yet entered spiritual paths because they have realized renunciation, completed the three higher trainings of Hinayana paths, and gained the realizations of the four noble truths. They have realized emptiness directly and thereby abandoned all delusions and attained liberation. They have attained tranquil abiding and superior seeing, and they possess clairvoyance and miracle powers. However, compared with Bodhisattvas, Hearers and Solitary Realizers are like candlelight against the brilliance of the sun. At night a candle shines brightly, but in the morning the sun far outshines it. In *Perfect Liberation of Maitreya Sutra* Buddha says:

> Son of the lineage, it is like this. For example, immediately a prince is born, because he bears the name of a king he outshines the entire retinue of elder and principal ministers through the greatness of his lineage. In the same way, immediately a novice Bodhisattva generates the mind of enlightenment, because he is born into the lineage of the Tathagatas he outshines Hearers and Solitary Realizers who have been practising pure deeds for a long time, through the power of his compassion and bodhichitta.

It is said that bodhichitta is supreme amongst all good qualities as the diamond is supreme amongst gems. The good qualities of Hearers and Solitary Realizers are like ornaments made of gold, but bodhichitta is like a diamond.

WE BECOME WORTHY TO RECEIVE OFFERINGS AND PROSTRATIONS FROM HUMANS AND GODS

It is easy to understand why Buddhas are worthy to receive offerings and prostrations, but why should Bodhisattvas receive the same honour? The reason is that it is only by first becoming a Bodhisattva that one can become a Buddha. Thus it is said that Buddhas become enlightened in dependence upon the kindness of Bodhisattvas. It is even more appropriate to pay respect to the cause of enlightenment than to the effect. Buddha Shakyamuni said:

Those who have faith in me should prostrate and make offerings to the Bodhisattvas rather than to the Tathagatas.

WE EASILY ACCUMULATE A VAST AMOUNT OF MERIT

With bodhichitta we draw closer to Buddhahood with every moment. With bodhichitta as our motivation, everything we do creates limitless merit because we engage in all our actions for the sake of limitless beings. Actions performed in this way are very powerful and they complete our collection of merit very quickly.

Buddha said:

A person with merit will have all his wishes fulfilled and will easily subdue evil spirits. Such a person will soon attain full enlightenment. However, a person who lacks merit will be surrounded by external and internal hindrances. Such a person's wishes will not be fulfilled.

With bodhichitta our merit increases continuously, even while we are sleeping. In the *Perfection of Wisdom Sutra in Eight Thousand Lines* Buddha says:

If someone who is motivated by bodhichitta commits some seemingly improper action, that action will still be a cause for enlightenment.

With bodhichitta, if we recite just one mantra such as OM MANI PÄME HUM, if we offer just one candle to Buddha, or if we offer just one morsel of food to a dog, our merit will be as great as the number of living beings upon whose behalf we perform the action. In this way bodhichitta multiplies the merit of any action by the number of countless beings.

If a Bodhisattva engages in an action that benefits only one other living being, that action makes the Buddhas very happy and is vastly greater in merit than any action, such as making a large offering to the Buddhas, performed while we are harbouring any harmful intention towards another living being. Just as a mother is not happy to receive friendship from someone who beats her child, so the Buddhas are not happy to receive offerings from anyone who harms another living being, because they regard even those who are weak and miserable as extremely precious.

It is said that actions motivated by other virtuous states of mind are like a banana tree whose fruits, once ripe, are finished; whereas actions motivated by bodhichitta are limitless and everlasting. These actions are like a wish-granting tree that produces the fruits of all our aspirations.

WE QUICKLY DESTROY POWERFUL NEGATIVITIES

Shantideva says that just as the fire that consumes the world at the end of an aeon is the hottest and most intense, so bodhichitta is the most powerful method for consuming our negativities. Even non-virtuous actions that cannot be purified by other methods are purified when we develop the realization of bodhichitta. When we generate great compassion and bodhichitta our karmic obstructions are quickly destroyed and we swiftly accomplish all good qualities and realizations.

Arya Asanga meditated for twelve years in retreat trying to see Buddha Maitreya directly, but due to his karmic obstructions he was unable to do so. He finally left his retreat cave and set off down the mountain track. As he was walking he came across a dog, who was an emanation of Buddha Maitreya. The dog had collapsed by the roadside and was slowly being eaten alive by maggots. When he saw this, Asanga developed such strong compassion that this purified all the karmic obstructions preventing him from seeing Buddha directly. Then he saw Buddha Maitreya.

WE FULFIL ALL OUR WISHES

Any wish a Bodhisattva has is easily fulfilled. Since Bodhisattvas have superior intention they never wish for harmful things and they never want to commit non-virtuous actions. All they seek is to attain enlightenment so that they can help others. This wish is accomplished through the power of bodhichitta.

With bodhichitta all Dharma actions are powerful and effective. When Bodhisattvas visualize a Deity, recite mantras, engage in actions to protect others, or perform pacifying, increasing, controlling, and wrathful actions, all these actions are powerful and effective only because they are performed with the motivation of bodhichitta. Without bodhichitta even the practices of Secret Mantra have no power and do not bring great results. For example, if we meditate on the mandala of a Deity without generating bodhichitta it will be like taking a visit to a museum. When we go to a museum we may experience some temporary pleasure and wonderment as we wander about gazing at the objects through the glass, but when we leave the museum we do not take home any lasting benefit.

If even the smallest realizations of the Mahayana path depend upon bodhichitta for their development, it goes without saying that full enlightenment is attained only in dependence upon bodhichitta. Secret Mantra is like the fastest vehicle on the road to enlightenment, but bodhichitta is like the road itself. Without it even the fastest vehicle cannot go anywhere.

WE ARE FREE FROM HARM BY SPIRITS AND SO FORTH

Dharma Protectors and powerful worldly guardians who respect Dharma safeguard anyone who has generated bodhichitta because they cherish such a person as a future Buddha.

Externally these Dharma Protectors and worldly guardians prevent Bodhisattvas from being harmed by evil spirits, and internally bodhichitta protects Bodhisattvas from harm because it destroys self-cherishing, which is the basis for receiving every kind of harm. Because Bodhisattvas regard others as more precious than themselves, they have removed from their minds the means for receiving harm from humans and non-humans. For the sake of others Bodhisattvas happily accept any difficulties or pains that are inflicted upon them and so they do not experience such things as harmful. Since Bodhisattvas wish to take the sufferings of others upon themselves they remain peaceful and untroubled no matter what the circumstances may be. In this way bodhichitta averts every kind of harm.

In a town called Phenbo, near Lhasa, there once lived a Geshe called Khampa Lungpa. When he first arrived in the town some local guardians and spirits became very jealous and decided to injure him. However, when they came into his presence they found him weeping. The chief malevolent spirit was clairvoyant and saw that the Geshe was meditating on bodhichitta. This undermined all his evil intentions and he said to the others 'It is completely impossible for us to harm this man because he loves us more than he loves himself.' Then they heard the Geshe exclaim aloud 'How wonderful it would be if all living beings were free from their sufferings!', and they watched as tears of compassion rolled down his cheeks. The chief spirit said 'Those tears are for us! This Geshe really cares about us! How could we possibly harm him?' The spirits' bad designs were defeated by the Geshe's compassion.

When Buddha Shakyamuni was about to attain enlightenment many demons tried to harm him by firing weapons at him, but through the power of his mental stabilization on love he remained unharmed. He did not retaliate, but his meditation was powerful enough to disarm all his enemies. Similarly, if we ourself realize great compassion, great love, and bodhichitta, we shall be protected from every harm.

WE ACCOMPLISH ALL THE SPIRITUAL GROUNDS
AND PATHS

In general, Secret Mantra is the quick path to enlightenment, but without bodhichitta there is no quick path. Without bodhichitta, even if we practise Secret Mantra for aeons we shall not even enter the Mahayana path.

Bodhichitta brings us swiftly to Buddhahood because it helps us quickly to complete the collections of merit and wisdom, and thus attain the Form Body and Truth Body of a Buddha. It has already been explained how bodhichitta helps us to complete our collection of merit. It also helps us to complete our collection of wisdom because we can abandon obstructions to omniscience only by meditating on emptiness with bodhichitta motivation. Without bodhichitta, even if we gain a direct realization of emptiness this eliminates only the obstructions to liberation.

Obstructions to omniscience are like the trunk of a tree, wisdom realizing emptiness is like an axe, and bodhichitta is like the hands that wield the axe. No matter how sharp the wisdom realizing emptiness may be, it cannot cut the obstructions to omniscience unless it is wielded by the powerful hands of a Bodhisattva.

WE HAVE A STATE OF MIND THAT IS THE SOURCE OF PEACE
AND HAPPINESS FOR ALL BEINGS

All the peace and happiness of living beings arise in dependence upon their own virtuous actions; virtuous actions arise in dependence upon the instructions, blessings, and inspiration of Buddhas; Buddhas arise in dependence upon the paths of Bodhisattvas; and Bodhisattvas arise in dependence upon bodhichitta. Therefore, all peace and happiness arise in dependence upon bodhichitta.

It is said that if an action is virtuous it is necessarily the result of a Buddha's inspiration because directly or indirectly Buddhas cause us to engage in virtuous actions. By engaging in these actions we create the cause to take higher rebirth and enjoy the happiness of humans and gods. All these happinesses come from bodhichitta, the cause of all Buddhas.

In *Guide to the Middle Way* Chandrakirti says that all Hearers and Solitary Realizers depend upon bodhichitta. This means that even Hinayana practitioners depend upon bodhichitta because they can practise their paths only by relying upon the teachings of Buddhas, and Buddhas are born from Bodhisattvas who in turn are born from bodhichitta, the source of all good results.

Only when we actually realize bodhichitta shall we really understand its benefits, because the only way to know these perfectly is by direct experience, just as the only way to know the excellence of a particular type of chocolate is by actually tasting it. Nevertheless, if we meditate with faith on the benefits of bodhichitta we shall create virtuous potentialities within our mind. If we have practised like this in the past, our meditations will be fruitful and we shall easily develop bodhichitta later in this life.

There was once a king called Ajatashatru who had very little time to practise Dharma and engaged in many non-virtuous actions. One day he invited Manjushri to lunch, after which he intended to offer him an exquisite cloth worth one thousand gold coins. However, when the lunch was finished and the king was about to make his offering, Manjushri vanished. It occurred to the king that he should wear the cloth himself. As this thought developed in his mind he felt as if he too was vanishing into emptiness, and he quickly realized emptiness. He was able to gain this realization without doing meditation because he carried within his mind good potentialities that were caused to ripen by the blessings of Manjushri. In a similar way, if we now meditate on the benefits of bodhichitta we may attain realizations very quickly. We shall at least create the potentiality to develop bodhichitta easily in the future.

Some people think that bodhichitta is so profound that it is out of reach and so they give up, believing themselves incapable of such altruism. Others become enthusiastic about Secret Mantra but look down on the methods for developing bodhichitta because they think that these are only Sutra practices. There are very few people who avoid both of these mistaken attitudes and who actually put the methods into practice. It is said that if we neglect the practice of bodhichitta while at the same time seeking enlightenment, it is like searching for a jewel where none are to be found and neglecting to look in a place where they are plentiful.

Atisha's Spiritual Guide Rahulagupta said that it is not so unusual to find people who have developed strong concentration, who have seen the face of their Deity, or who have developed clairvoyance or miracle powers. What is truly extraordinary is to find someone who has generated great compassion and bodhichitta. These uncommon minds are the real wonders to admire. Many times in the past we have all developed tranquil abiding and have taken rebirth in the form and formless realms where concentration comes effortlessly. In the bardo we have all experienced contaminated clairvoyance and our bodies have been so supple that we have been able to fly and walk through walls. We have been able to cross huge distances with great speed, but what good has come of all these experiences? In the past we have accomplished many things but we have never before accomplished spontaneous bodhichitta. Had we done so, we might have been enlightened by now. When Kadampa Geshes were asked 'Which would you prefer, miracle powers and clairvoyance or bodhichitta?', they all used to answer without hesitation 'Bodhichitta'.

If we meditate on bodhichitta again and again we shall come to understand how precious it is. Bodhichitta is the best method for bestowing happiness, the best method for eliminating suffering, and the best method for dispelling confusion. There is no virtue equal to it, no better friend, no greater merit. Bodhichitta is the very essence of all eighty-four thousand instructions of Buddha. In *Guide to the Bodhisattva's Way of Life* Shantideva says:

It is the quintessential butter that arises
When the milk of Dharma is churned.

Just as by stirring milk, butter emerges as its essence, so by stirring the entire collection of Buddha's scriptures, bodhichitta emerges as its essence. For aeons Buddhas have been investigating what is the most beneficial thing for us. They have seen that it is bodhichitta because bodhichitta brings every living being to the supreme bliss of full enlightenment.

Developing Bodhichitta

HOW TO DEVELOP BODHICHITTA

The way to develop bodhichitta is explained in two parts:

1 The stages of actually training the mind in bodhichitta
2 Maintaining bodhichitta by means of ritual

THE STAGES OF ACTUALLY TRAINING THE MIND IN BODHICHITTA

Traditionally, two methods are taught for generating bodhichitta:

1 Training the mind in the sevenfold cause and effect
2 Training the mind in equalizing and exchanging self with others

The first method was taught by Buddha Shakyamuni and passed down through Maitreya to Masters such as Asanga. The second was taught by Buddha Shakyamuni and passed down through Manjushri to Masters such as Shantideva.

Although the two methods have the same purpose, the second method is more powerful and profound than the first. According to the first method we hold others as dear as we hold our own mother, but according to the second method we hold others as dear as we hold ourself. Since we cherish ourself more dearly than we cherish even our mother, the attitude of cherishing others that comes from practising the second method is stronger and deeper than the attitude of cherishing others that comes from practising the first. Similarly, the great compassion we develop from practising the second method is stronger and deeper than the great compassion we develop from practising the first because our compassion for ourself exceeds our compassion for our mother. Therefore the bodhichitta that results from practising the second method is more profound than the bodhichitta that results from practising the first.

It is possible that the bodhichitta developed by meditating on the sevenfold cause and effect instructions may degenerate because Bodhisattvas who rely only upon the first method may still have some self-cherishing. This is because their bodhichitta is based on their cherishing of their own mother, which is often coloured by self-cherishing. However, the bodhichitta that arises from meditating on equalizing and exchanging self with others will never degenerate because Bodhisattvas who rely upon this method totally abandon self-cherishing in the very process of generating bodhichitta.

The most skilful way to practise is by combining both methods, but before we can do this we need to study and practise each method separately.

TRAINING THE MIND IN THE SEVENFOLD CAUSE AND EFFECT

Although this method is called the 'sevenfold cause and effect', in practice this method has eight stages of meditation. The first stage is a preparation, the next six stages are meditations to generate the causes of bodhichitta, and the eighth stage is meditation on their effect, bodhichitta itself. The stages of meditation are as follows:

1 Developing equanimity
2 Recognizing that all living beings are our mothers
3 Remembering the kindness of all mother beings
4 Developing the wish to repay the kindness of all mother beings
5 Developing affectionate love
6 Developing great compassion
7 Developing superior intention
8 Developing bodhichitta

DEVELOPING EQUANIMITY

This meditation on equanimity is an essential preparation for meditation on the sevenfold cause and effect. The realization of equanimity is the basis for all the subsequent realizations because we need to reduce our strong attachment and aversion before we can recognize all other beings as our mother. Je Tsongkhapa said:

On the ground of equanimity pour the water of love and sow the seed of compassion. From these the harvest of bodhichitta will arise.

Most of us at present have some people whom we hold very close and dear, some people whom we hate and try to avoid, and some people towards whom we have no particular feeling of either attachment or aversion. To eliminate such an unbalanced attitude we need to gain the realization of equanimity.

To do this meditation we imagine three groups of people sitting in front of and facing towards us. The central group comprises people for whom we have no strong attachment or aversion; to their left is a group of people for whom we have strong attachment; and to their right is a group of people whom we hate or dislike. The aim of the meditation is to arrive at a balanced state of mind that is free from attachment and aversion, so that when we observe the people in the left and the right groups we have the same balanced feeling that we have when we observe the people in the central group. When we regard the people in the centre our mind is at peace, undisturbed by the delusions of attachment or anger.

The meditation has four parts, or rounds. First we focus our attention on the group of people whom we dislike, and we meditate as follows:

Because of my ignorance I perceive these people as my enemies, but in fact they have all been my dear friends earlier in this life or in previous lives. When each one was my friend we loved and cared for one another, but now I dislike them and like others instead. Since the only difference between these people and my present friends is a matter of time, there is no valid reason for me to dislike these people.

As a result of meditating in this way we should make the strong determination, 'From now on I will never develop anger towards these people.' Then we meditate on this determination single-pointedly for as long as possible.

We begin the second round of meditation by focusing our attention on the group of people for whom we have strong attachment, and we meditate:

It is only due to my inappropriate attention that I have attachment to these people. At one time or another, either earlier in this life or in previous lives, they have all been my enemies or they have been the objects of my aversion. Since we have fought each other over long periods of time and have destroyed each other's possessions and lives many times, there is no valid reason for me to have attachment towards these people.

As a result of meditating in this way we should make the strong determination, 'From now on I will never develop strong attachment towards these people.' Then we meditate on this determination single-pointedly for as long as possible.

We begin the third round of meditation by focusing our attention on both groups of friends and enemies, and we meditate:

From my own point of view there is no significant difference between these two groups because sometimes my friends become my enemies and my enemies become my dear friends. Both are impermanent and can change very quickly. From their own point of view there is no big difference either because both of them experience suffering and both of them want happiness. Therefore I will cease to make such false discriminations between them, favouring some and rejecting others. From now on I will maintain equanimity, free from strong attachment and strong aversion. I will avoid unbalanced attitudes of feeling very close to some and very distant from others.

When this determination arises clearly and definitely in our mind we take it as our object of placement meditation.

We begin the fourth round of meditation by focusing our attention on the people in the central group of our visualization, and we meditate:

Although each person has at some time been my friend and at some time my enemy, I do not at present feel any attachment or hatred for them. When I meet them my mind remains undisturbed and at ease. This is how it should be when I meet other people as well because everyone has been both enemy and friend to me. Therefore, I will regard all of them with the same balanced attitude I have towards the people in this group, knowing that there is no good reason to discriminate between them. All of them are just living beings who suffer and search for happiness.

When this determination arises clearly and definitely in our mind we take it as our object of placement meditation.

We should train our mind in these four rounds of meditation until we develop a balanced mind free from strong attachment and aversion towards all people. Most of our daily problems arise from unbalanced minds such as strong attachment and anger. All such problems can be prevented through gaining experience of equanimity.

Even if we have some success with this meditation we may still find that when we are out of meditation and confronted with our enemy face to face we forget all our good resolutions and all the reasonable trains of thought that we have been cultivating in our meditation sessions. Then we may develop some doubt, thinking 'The past is past. These people are my enemies now. What does it matter how kind they were to me in the past?' If we allow such a thought to take hold of our mind it will destroy all the good habits we have been cultivating. At such times we need to persuade ourself, asking inwardly:

If one person gave me a gift last year and another person gave me a gift this year, can I say that the second person is kinder than the first? In the same way all beings are equally kind to me, no matter how they may be treating me right now.

When we contemplate these instructions we may object 'By a similar line of reasoning everyone has been equally hateful to me in the past and so why should I develop liking for them now?' It is true that others have harmed us in the past but it is still appropriate for us to love them because when they harmed us they did so in ignorance, not recognizing us as their friend and relative. When they inflicted harm on us they were not in charge of their actions because they mistakenly apprehended us as their enemy. It was their ignorance that was to blame because it was their ignorance that drove them to act harmfully. On the other hand, whenever they helped us in the past they did so freely, without being controlled by ignorance. On those occasions they correctly apprehended us as their friend and relative. When they were our mother they knew us as their children and cared for us. Since the harm we have received from others has come from their ignorance we should always relate to them with warmth and kindness.

The equanimity we are cultivating here is a type of immeasurable equanimity because we are developing equanimity towards immeasurable living beings. In general there are three types of equanimity: equanimity of feeling, compositional equanimity, and immeasurable equanimity. Equanimity of feeling is any feeling that is neither pleasant nor unpleasant, and it can be of varying intensity. An example of strong equanimity of feeling is the feeling we have when we see someone walking down the street in outlandish clothes that we neither like nor dislike. Compositional equanimity is a state of mind that is attained in meditation. It is a mind that abides unmoving with flawless mental stabilization. Such a mind is natural and relaxed and does not require effort to maintain. There are two types of immeasurable equanimity: the type that we cultivate when we do the above meditation, and the type that is included within the four immeasurables that are part of the six preparatory practices. With the first type we observe immeasurable living beings and develop equanimity towards them. With the second type we observe immeasurable living beings and wish for them to develop equanimity towards each other. This latter wish arises from compassion and a wisdom realizing that the sufferings of living beings come from the attachment and aversion they have towards each other.

When we gain the realization of equanimity our mind becomes peaceful and we do not feel disturbed whatever our circumstances. This does not mean that we have just made ourself callous and uncaring. As explained before, equanimity is far removed from indifference or apathy. It does not reduce our love and compassion, nor our ability to rejoice in others' good fortune. Quite the opposite – it is the very foundation for increasing all these good qualities. Equanimity reduces our attachment and hostility, but it does not reduce our liking and our love for others. Bodhisattvas, who have developed equanimity, have great liking for other living beings, and they have unusually pleasant, agreeable feelings towards them. When they see someone in pain they do not feel unmoved, but develop a strong wish to remove the pain; and if they can actually do this they feel overjoyed. Although Bodhisattvas have great liking for others they remain undisturbed by attachment because their minds have the nature of love and peace. Therefore, we cannot say that someone does not have equanimity just because they make friends or because they behave differently towards different people. Bodhisattvas observe the conventions of their societies. For example, in England they do not hug and kiss everyone they see just because they feel so pleasantly disposed towards them. It is impossible to tell from external behaviour whether someone has equanimity.

If we become excited or depressed when we meet other people we shall keep encountering problems, but if we can maintain a well-balanced mind our meetings with our friends will be pleasant and our friendships will be long-lasting. Outwardly we should try to have a constant and agreeable expression, one that always verges on smiling, never elated and never depressed. The Tibetans say that someone who has a constant, warm smile and who is well-disposed to others and even-tempered, not exuberant one day then miserable the next, is like gold whose colour remains stable without varying from day to day.

When we have developed equanimity towards all other living beings by training our mind in this meditation it will be very easy to maintain equanimity with regard to inanimate objects such as the weather.

RECOGNIZING THAT ALL LIVING BEINGS ARE OUR MOTHERS

Buddha said:

> I have not seen a single living being who has not been the mother of all the rest.

If we have faith in the infallible word of Buddha we can develop a realization of this just by meditating on its meaning. Otherwise we need to develop conviction by reasoning 'It is definite that all living beings have been my mother because they have all been my mother in past lives.' If someone asks 'How is it possible that countless beings have been my mother?' we can answer 'Because our births have been countless, so we have had countless mothers.' There is no method to prove that any living being has not been our mother.

We can correctly infer that we have taken countless rebirths because the continuum of our mind is beginningless and our body is impermanent. For example, a barley seed comes from a crop that in turn grew from a seed. If we trace it back we can never find the beginning of the continuum of the barley seed. Even before this planet developed, the continuum of the barley seed existed in some other universe. Similarly, the mind of today arises from the mind of yesterday, and the continuum of the mind has no beginning. The mind we have right now does not arise independently, without causes and conditions. The mind of a newborn baby arises from the mind of the baby in its mother's womb, and the mind of the baby in its mother's womb arises from the mind that entered the fertilized ovum at conception. Where did that mind come from? It came from the mind that existed before conception, the mind of the previous life. This mind itself came from the mind of the previous life, and so on without beginning. It follows that we have had countless different bodies and countless different mothers.

If someone objects that our mothers of the past are not our mother now, we can consider that if our mother of this life were to die we would still think of her as our mother. Her death does not alter the fact that she is our mother, and it does not make her any less kind. It is the same with all our past mothers and with anyone who has been kind to us in the past. We still regard the kindness we received last year or yesterday as kindness and we want to repay it, even though the time when it was shown has passed away.

Furthermore, if someone is our mother it does not follow that we can recognize her. Many people do not even know their mother of this life. For example, the great Lama Kachen Yeshe Gyaltsen was brought up in his father's house without his mother because his parents separated when he was very young. His father later sent him to Tashi Lhunpo Monastery. When his mother heard that he was there she went to see him, but neither could recognize each other. When an older monk introduced the mother to her son, she wept.

If our mother of this life were to die and take rebirth as our neighbour's son, and someone with clairvoyance were to introduce us to this boy and tell us that he is our mother, we would develop very different feelings towards that child. This is not mere fantasy because all living beings can rightly be introduced to us as our own mother.

If our mother of this life were to enter the room in disguise, once we saw through the disguise we would know without any doubt that it had been our mother all along. The appearance of our mother of this life changes completely during the time we identify her as our mother. When we were a baby she was young and beautiful. If she is now eighty years old her appearance will be completely transformed by age, and yet we shall still recognize her as our mother. In a similar way, the appearance of all our past mothers has changed and yet they remain, in essence, our mothers.

By meditating on these points we shall gain understanding through our own experience. The measurement that we have realized all living beings as our mother is that we naturally and spontaneously recognize everyone we meet as our mother, no matter what their present appearance may be. This goes even for small animals and insects. For example, when we see a mouse, if we recognize it as in essence our own mother, and remember how much kindness we have received from her, this is a sign that we have developed the realization that all living beings are our mothers. If our house is painted yellow, whenever we think of our house we simultaneously think of its yellow colour. In a similar way, whenever we think of another living being, if we simultaneously remember that it is our mother this indicates that we have realized that all living beings are our mother.

When we do this meditation we are not just pretending because it is a fact that all living beings have been our mother. This is not a new idea invented by Buddhists. We are simply rediscovering what has been true all along. If we study and meditate on this repeatedly we shall gain conviction and always recognize mother living beings.

REMEMBERING THE KINDNESS OF ALL MOTHER BEINGS

The next stage of meditation is to remind ourself of the great kindness of all our mothers. We begin by remembering the kindness of our mother of this life, and then, by extension, we remember the kindness of all our other mothers. If we cannot appreciate the kindness of our present mother, how shall we ever be able to appreciate the kindness of all our previous mothers? Since it is easy to forget this kindness, or to take it for granted and to remember only the times when we think our mother harmed us, we need to remember in detail how kind our mother has been from the very beginning of this life.

In the beginning our mother was kind in offering us a place of rebirth. Before we were conceived in her womb we wandered about from place to place as a bardo being with nowhere to rest. We were blown by the winds of our karma without freedom to choose where we would go, and all our acquaintances were fleeting. We experienced great pain and fear, but from this state we were able to enter the safety of our mother's womb. Although we were an uninvited guest, when she knew that we had entered her womb our mother let us stay there. If she had wanted to evict us she could have done so and we would not have been alive today to enjoy all our present opportunities. We are now able to develop the aspiration to attain enlightenment only because our mother was kind enough to let us stay in her womb. In winter, when it is cold and stormy outside, if someone invites us into their warm home and entertains us well, we consider this person to be extremely kind. How much kinder is our mother, who let us enter her own body and offered us such good hospitality there!

When we were in our mother's womb she protected us carefully, more carefully than she would guard a most precious jewel. In every situation she thought of our safety. She consulted doctors, exercised, ate special foods, and nurtured us day and night for nine months; and she was also mindful not to do anything that might damage the development of our physical and mental faculties. Because she looked after us so well we were born with a normal and healthy body that we can use to accomplish so many good things.

At the time of our birth our mother experienced great pain, but when she saw us she felt happier than if someone had presented her with a superb treasure. Even during the agony of childbirth our welfare was foremost in her mind. When we were newly born, although we looked more like a frog than a human being, our mother loved us dearly. We were completely helpless, even more helpless than a new-born foal, who can at least stand up and feed as soon as it is born. We were as if blind, unable to identify our parents, and we could not understand anything. If someone had been preparing to kill us we would not have known. We had no idea what we were doing. We could not even tell when we were urinating. Who cared for and protected this scarcely human thing? It was our mother. She clothed it, cradled it, and fed it with her own milk. She removed the filth from its body without feeling any disgust. Sometimes mothers remove the mucus from their baby's nose by using their own mouths because they do not want to cause the baby any pain by using their rough hands. Even when our mother had problems she always showed us a loving expression and called us sweet names. While we were small our mother was constantly watchful. If she had forgotten us for even a short time, we might have met our death or been disabled for life. Each day of our early childhood our mother rescued us from many disasters, and she always considered things from the point of view of our own safety and well-being.

In the winter she would make sure that we were warm and had good clothing, even when she herself was cold. She always selected the best things for us to eat and took the worst for herself, and she would rather have been sick herself than see us sick. She would rather have died herself than see us die. Our mother naturally behaves towards us like someone who has gained the realization of exchanging self with others. She is able to put our welfare before her own, and she does so perfectly and spontaneously. If someone were to threaten to kill us she would offer herself to the killer instead. She has such compassion for us.

When we were small our mother would not sleep well. She slept lightly, waking every few hours and remaining alert for our cry. As we grew older our mother taught us how to eat, drink, speak, sit, and walk. She sent us to school and encouraged us to do good things in life. If we have any knowledge and skills now, it is solely as a result of her kindness. When we grew older and became adolescent we preferred to be with our friends and we would completely forget our mother. While we enjoyed ourself it was as if our mother had ceased to exist, and we would remember her only when we needed something from her. Although we were forgetful and allowed ourself to become completely absorbed in the pleasures we enjoyed with our friends, our mother remained continuously concerned for us. She would often become anxious, and in the back of her mind there was always some worry about us. She had the kind of worry we normally have only for ourself. Even when we are grown up and have a family of our own, our mother does not cease to care for us. She may be old and weak and scarcely able to stand on her feet, and yet she never forgets her children.

By meditating in this way, recalling the kindness of our mother in great detail, we shall come to cherish our mother very dearly. When we have this feeling from the depths of our heart, we should extend it to all other living beings, remembering that every one of them has shown us the same kindness.

We then meditate on the kindness of our mother when we took other types of rebirth, considering, for example, how attentively a mother bird protects her eggs from danger and how she shields her young beneath her wings. When a hunter comes she does not fly away and leave her babies unprotected. All day long she searches for food to nourish them until they are strong enough to leave the nest.

There was once a robber in Tibet who stabbed a horse who was carrying a foal in her womb. His knife penetrated so deeply into the side of the horse that it cut open her uterus and the foal emerged through its mother's side. As she was dying, the mother spent her last strength licking her off-spring with great affection. Seeing this, the robber was filled with remorse. He was amazed to see how, even in the pains of death, this mother had such compassion for her foal and how her only concern was for its welfare. He then ceased his non-virtuous way of life and began to practise Dharma purely.

Every single living being has shown us the same selfless concern, the perfect kindness of a mother. By meditating in this way we become determined never to forget the kindness of mother beings.

DEVELOPING THE WISH TO REPAY THE KINDNESS OF ALL MOTHER BEINGS

It is natural for us to want to repay any kindness we have received. Even when we receive a short letter we want to respond. Thus it is perfectly natural to want to repay the kindness of all our mothers. To enhance this wish we can follow Shantideva's advice in *Compendium of Trainings* where he said that we should visualize our present mother as old, blind, and senile, and imagine that she is about to fall down. We should try to imagine how we would feel, how we would automatically reach out to help her. Then we should meditate:

Although my mother's physical eyesight is unimpaired, her spiritual eyes are blind. She does not know actions and their effects. She does not know correct spiritual paths and she does not know the ultimate nature of phenomena. She does not experience pure happiness although that is what she seeks. Instead of creating the causes for happiness she creates the causes for future suffering, and without choice she engages in actions that conflict with her own desires. Inwardly she suffers from delusions and so she acts wrongly and follows mistaken paths. As a result her mind is really like the mind of someone who is senile. Because of her ignorance she is about to fall from human life to the lower realms. If I do not help her, who will? I am much more fortunate than my mother because I have received Dharma teachings and have some wisdom because I have learnt what to practise and what to abandon. Since I can distinguish between what is virtuous and what is non-virtuous, if I apply effort I shall be able to attain the realizations of renunciation, bodhichitta, and the correct view of emptiness. Provided I apply effort there is no reason why I should not attain full enlightenment. Since I enjoy such good fortune I have a great opportunity to repay the kindness of my mother. I will do whatever I can to repay her kindness.

When we have developed this determination we can extend it so that it includes all our mothers, seeing no difference between our present mother and those who have been our mothers in the past. When the determination to repay the kindness of all our mothers arises strongly in our mind we do placement meditation until this thought pervades our whole mind and we never lose it.

Then we do further analytical meditation:

> *What is the best way to repay the kindness of my mothers? Surely the best way is to give them everlasting pure happiness? It is not enough to give them only the imperfect happiness of samsara because they have experienced this kind of happiness countless times but now have nothing to show for it. They have experienced every kind of contaminated happiness but they remain unhappy now because contaminated happiness is in the nature of changing suffering. Therefore, the best way to repay the kindness of my mothers is to give them the supreme and everlasting bliss of liberation.*

When we have developed a strong determination to exert effort in leading all our mothers to the bliss of liberation we do placement meditation to make this thought continuous. To have such an intention for even just a few moments brings countless benefits and accumulates a vast amount of merit. It is extremely rare for any ordinary being to have the desire to give perfect happiness to all other beings. It is unusual even for mothers to have this thought towards their own children. They do not usually think 'How wonderful it would be if my children were to become free from the sufferings of samsaric rebirth. How wonderful it would be if they could find release from all contaminated aggregates and enjoy the bliss of liberation.' In *Guide to the Bodhisattva's Way of Life* Shantideva says:

> Does our father or mother
> Have such a beneficial intention as this?
> Do the gods or the sages?
> Does even Brahma himself?

Only pure practitioners of the Mahayana have the intention to benefit all mother beings by leading them to perfect bliss.

We need to contemplate and meditate repeatedly on these three stages of the meditation on the sevenfold cause and effect. If we can recognize all living beings as our mother and remember their kindness we shall naturally wish to repay it. The success of the subsequent stages depends upon our gaining a clear and definite experience of these stages.

DEVELOPING AFFECTIONATE LOVE

A woman once asked Geshe Potowa 'What is affectionate love?' He replied, 'What do you feel when you see your own son? You are delighted to see him and he appears pleasant to you. If we regard all beings in the same way, feeling close to them and holding them dear, we have developed affectionate love.'

Our own mother may not be very beautiful or wear very elegant clothes, but because we have a good relationship with her, in our eyes she is beautiful. We love her and feel compassion for her. If we have this same tender regard for all other living beings we have affectionate love. With this affectionate love for all it is impossible to develop jealousy and anger towards them. If we improve our awareness of the kindness of others we shall develop this warm heart and tenderness, and we shall naturally cherish others. Even though they may possess many faults we shall see their beauty, just as a mother sees the beauty of her children no matter what they do.

From affectionate love develops the love that cherishes others, and from cherishing love develops wishing love – the love that wishes all other living beings to be perfectly happy. When we develop wishing love for all living beings, at the same time we develop great compassion – a mind that cannot bear others to experience any pain and desires their complete freedom from every kind of suffering. The realizations of wishing love and great compassion are like two sides of the same coin. Both depend upon affectionate love.

To develop affectionate love three things are necessary:

(1) Contemplating the benefits of affectionate love
(2) Having all the conducive conditions for developing affectionate love
(3) Eliminating all the obstacles to developing affectionate love

CONTEMPLATING THE BENEFITS OF AFFECTIONATE LOVE

Love is very beneficial even when it is mixed with desirous attachment. It is the foundation for all harmonious and lasting relationships. If we love our friends and our family we shall be happy even if we have no material wealth, but without love no amount of wealth or resources will make our relationships lasting and fruitful.

When we first meet someone whom we find attractive we feel happy and we easily develop loving-kindness towards them. In time, if our love decreases, we experience problems and unhappiness, but if our love increases we continue to be happy even when we are experiencing problems and are without many possessions. Since love is so beneficial even when it is mixed with desirous attachment, what need is there to say how fruitful love is when it is completely free from attachment? If we meditate on love towards all living beings, even for only a short time, we shall accumulate a vast amount of merit and receive many benefits.

In *Precious Garland of Advice for the King* Nagarjuna says that there are eight main benefits of affectionate love:

(1) By meditating on love for just one moment we accumulate more merit than we do by offering food to all living beings three times every day.
(2) We become someone loved by humans and gods. Some people are naturally loved by others. They make others feel happy to see them and they receive gifts and hospitality. The reason why they are so loved is that they have practised love in the past.
(3) We shall be protected by humans and gods even in our sleep. Since we have no clear mindfulness or

memory while we are asleep, it is easier for spirits to harm us at that time. It is said that spirits who want to harm us are more numerous than human beings. They can inflict mental suffering by destroying our positive states of mind, and they can disturb our mind and make it crazy. They can inflict disease and discomfort, and they can interfere with virtuous actions we wish to perform. They can prevent our wishes from being fulfilled, they can interfere with our Dharma practice, and they can cause disharmony and unhappiness in our relationships with others.

(4) We shall become happy. When our mind has the nature of love we naturally feel happy and peaceful. With such a state of mind it is impossible to become disturbed or depressed or to develop anger or jealousy. If we have love for others now and we work to bring them happiness, we ourself shall definitely experience happiness in the future.

(5) We shall experience physical comfort in the future.

(6) By developing strong concentration on love we shall be protected from harm by poison, weapons, and other instruments of harm.

(7) Our wishes will be easily fulfilled.

(8) We shall take rebirth in the realms of gods such as Brahma, and finally we shall attain enlightenment.

There are countless benefits besides these. One special benefit of developing affectionate love is that because affectionate love is the direct opponent to anger it eliminates all the pains and problems we bring upon ourself as a result of anger. Although we love our friends and family we still sometimes get angry with them due to forgetting loving-kindness, and so we create unhappiness for ourself and our loved ones. Our anger hinders our spiritual practice and robs us of our peace of mind. It even takes away our physical beauty, making us look so ugly that others become frightened when they see us. With affectionate love we shall be free from these problems because anger and jealousy will not arise in our mind. External conditions will not disturb us, and our friends, our family, and the people with whom we live and work will become happier. Thus we need to exert effort to cultivate and enhance our love. Effort is a mind that is pleased to engage in virtuous actions. Here it is generated by understanding the benefits of developing affectionate love. With this firm understanding our effort is natural and joyous.

HAVING ALL THE CONDUCIVE CONDITIONS FOR DEVELOPING AFFECTIONATE LOVE

With a strong wish to develop affectionate love we need to recognize what conditions are conducive. The conducive conditions are the three stages of meditation on the seven-fold cause and effect – recognizing all living beings as our mother, remembering their kindness, and wishing to repay it. If we recognize all living beings as our mother and remember their great kindness we shall wish to repay their kindness, and affectionate love for them will arise in our heart spontaneously.

ELIMINATING ALL THE OBSTACLES TO DEVELOPING AFFECTIONATE LOVE

The main obstacle to developing affectionate love is the feeling of dislike towards others. We cannot have affectionate love towards all mother living beings whilst we continue to feel glad to meet some people and irritated or annoyed when meeting others. Therefore, whenever we become aware of feelings of dislike we should meditate:

I feel dislike for this person but my attitude is incorrect and my perception is mistaken. He appears to be unpleasant but this appearance has arisen only because I am paying inappropriate attention to the faults he seems to possess. By developing such inappropriate attention I myself have created my feeling of dislike.

If there is someone whom we find particularly unpleasant we can meditate:

Is this person really so disagreeable? If so, I am right to perceive him or her as I do, and my dislike is based upon unmistaken awareness. However, not everyone sees this person in the same way. He has friends who find him very agreeable. Whose perception is correct? This person's friends and I cannot both be right because our attitudes are contradictory and yet we are both observing the same person.

If we continue to investigate we shall see that it is our own attitude that is incorrect. The other person is not unattractive from his or her own side. The way he appears to us is a reflection of our own deluded state of mind – an appearance created by our own anger or confusion. Therefore, when we see someone as unattractive or displeasing we need to recognize that what we are seeing is a projection of our own mind, arising from our own deluded thoughts. We need to meditate:

This dislike is non-virtuous and it will cause me to develop many unhappy states of mind. It can never bring any benefit. If I feel such dislike for others it is not surprising that I have other non-virtuous states of mind.

Most of us at present are not in the habit of frequently examining our own thoughts. We do not usually stop to ask ourself 'What thoughts are arising in my mind right now?' Yet we need to keep watch on our mind in this way if we are to succeed in eliminating the non-virtuous states of mind that cause us to suffer. Whenever we develop dislike we need to become aware of it and eliminate it as soon as we can. If we let it remain in our mind it will turn into anger and bring unfortunate results. We must overcome whatever displeasure we feel when we see another person before we can feel affectionate love for them. The more successful we are in identifying and overcoming our dislike, the easier it will be to realize affectionate love. Developing this realization is a gradual process. First we need to enhance our love for our own family and friends. If we continue to feel any anger or dislike towards them, how can we possibly develop affectionate love towards all other living beings? When we have accustomed ourself to developing affectionate love towards those who are close to us, we can gradually extend our practice so that it includes our neighbours, our community, and so on, until our feeling of love includes all living beings.

DEVELOPING GREAT COMPASSION

When we see that someone we like is experiencing pain we feel compassion and sympathy for them, but this feeling is not the great compassion we need to cultivate in order to enter Mahayana paths. Great compassion observes all living beings. Seeing that they all experience suffering it wishes all of them, without exception, to be free from their misery.

Since bodhichitta is generated in dependence upon great compassion, the power of our bodhichitta depends upon the power of our compassion. Bodhisattvas who have very strong compassion attain enlightenment quickly. They cannot bear to see others suffer and they want to release them from their pain as soon as possible. Therefore they seek a quick path to enlightenment and enter into the practices of Secret Mantra. Just as a mother who sees her child fall into a fire has an extremely urgent wish to rescue him or her, so a Bodhisattva who has very strong compassion urgently wishes to release all living beings from their suffering as quickly as possible. He or she thinks 'How wonderful it would be if I could free all living beings from the prison of samsara right now.'

Great compassion is important even after attaining full enlightenment. When Bodhisattvas become Buddhas they have become free from all faults, they have accomplished all good qualities, and they enjoy eternal happiness. If Buddhas lacked great compassion they would abide in this state of happiness just as Hinayana Foe Destroyers abide peacefully in the state of liberation. Because they have not developed great compassion, Hinayana Foe Destroyers do not exert effort to help others; but the great compassion of the Buddhas compels them to work for the sake of others. Therefore it is said that great compassion is important at the beginning of our practice, throughout our practice, and at the end of our practice. At the beginning of *Guide to the Middle Way* Chandrakirti pays homage to great compassion and not to the Buddhas and Bodhisattvas, although homage to the Buddhas and Bodhisattvas is more usual at the beginning of such a text. He departs from this convention to indicate and emphasize that great compassion is important at the beginning, the middle, and the end of the path to enlightenment. At the beginning of our practice great compassion is like a seed; throughout our practice great compassion is like the water, sunlight, and other nurturing conditions; and at the end of our practice great compassion is like the fully ripened crop that allows us to reap the good harvest of benefiting others.

To generate great compassion we first develop affectionate love for all living beings and then meditate on the sufferings they experience. With the realization of affectionate love, whenever we see, remember, or contemplate the sufferings of others we develop great compassion naturally and spontaneously. We shall have no choice, just as a mother has no choice in feeling compassion for her child when she sees it in pain. With affectionate love we easily understand how it is possible to develop great compassion, because all living beings experience suffering. Although we do not see their sufferings all the time, it is certain that all beings within samsara have problems and are bound to suffer the pains of sickness, ageing, and death. When we have developed affectionate love, if we consider again and again the sufferings others endure, our compassion will increase day by day, and we shall become closer and closer to Avalokiteshvara, who is the manifestation of the great compassion of all the Buddhas.

Great compassion is not easy to generate; we have to cultivate it gradually. We can begin by contemplating the sufferings that animals endure, remembering how many of them will die violently at the hands of a slaughterer. We remember the physical pain they will experience and the dreadful fear they will have when they realize that their life is in danger.

When human beings are in fear of their life they can often find protection or receive help from nurses and doctors, but when animals are in danger they are completely vulnerable and unprotected. By meditating on the sufferings of animals we shall develop compassion, thinking 'How wonderful it would be if all these beings were free from samsaric sufferings and their causes.'

We then meditate on the sufferings of human beings, such as the pains of those who are in hospital and the sufferings of the aged and dying. If we find it hard to develop compassion for people who do not seem to be experiencing manifest suffering but who seem to be enjoying good fortune we can recall the stages of meditation for a middle being. We can remember that although these people may be enjoying the good life right now, their experience of happiness will soon change and they have no freedom. Even now they are experiencing various sufferings, such as the sufferings of uncertainty, discontent, and so on. Just as a bird eventually has to return to the ground no matter how far and high it may soar, so all living beings bound within samsara must eventually experience a fall to lower states no matter how much good fortune they may temporarily enjoy. Knowing that samsaric beings have no choice in what they experience helps us to develop compassion for them. An animal that is to be slaughtered next year is as much an object of compassion as one who is to be slaughtered tomorrow. In the same way, human beings who are bound to experience suffering in the future are objects of compassion just as much as those who are experiencing suffering right now. We particularly need to develop compassion for those who are committing negative actions because they are creating the cause to experience suffering in the future. Their situation is actually worse than the situation of those who are experiencing suffering right now. People who are at present experiencing the results of their past negativities will not have to experience them again in the future, whereas those who are now engaging in negative actions can look forward only to future misery.

By meditating in this way we try to develop compassion for all living beings. When this special feeling of compassion arises clearly and definitely in our mind we do placement meditation to become more and more familiar with it. When we are out of meditation we try to maintain compassion in all that we do. Again, our practice is gradual. We begin by enhancing the compassion we naturally feel towards our friends and family, and then we extend our compassion until it includes all living beings.

The sign that we have realized great compassion is that whenever we see another living being we have the spontaneous wish for them to be free from their sufferings. Just as when her child is ill a mother naturally wants it to become well again, we shall have generated great compassion when we have this same feeling towards all living beings day and night, thinking 'How wonderful it would be if all living beings were separated from suffering and its causes.'

DEVELOPING SUPERIOR INTENTION

When we have generated great compassion we meditate:

Is it sufficient merely to have the wish that all living beings become free from suffering? Surely not! I must actually do something to bring this about. I myself must take responsibility to help all living beings find release from their sufferings.

If a mother were to see her child fall into a fire she would not rest content merely wishing her child were safe. She would swiftly and spontaneously act to rescue her child. If our own mother is experiencing pain we do not just pray for her to be relieved of pain but we do everything we can to ease her suffering. In a similar way, once we have generated great compassion we cultivate superior intention – the determination to take responsibility to release others from suffering and lead them to perfect happiness. Superior intention is the promise to liberate all living beings, recognizing that they are all our mothers and that they all wish to avoid suffering and experience happiness. Seeing the need to take personal responsibility, we assume the task of benefiting others and we carry out our intention at all times.

This state of mind is called 'superior intention' because it is superior to the minds of mere love and mere compassion. Whereas the practices of developing love and compassion are common to both Hinayana and Mahayana trainings, superior intention is exclusively a practice of the Mahayana. Superior intention, the sixth cause of bodhichitta, is more than just the wish to repay the kindness of all our mothers, which is the third cause. When we have that wish, although we wish to lead all beings to liberation we have not yet made a personal commitment to do so; but when we have superior intention we have made a firm decision actively to engage in the means of accomplishing our aim. The wish to repay the kindness of others is motivated by the recognition of how kind others have been to us in the past, whereas superior intention is motivated by great compassion. Wishing to repay the kindness of others is like wanting to purchase something we have seen in a shop, but developing superior intention is like actually deciding to buy what we want.

DEVELOPING BODHICHITTA

The stages of meditation explained so far lead us actually to generate bodhichitta. The explanation of bodhichitta is in three parts:

1 The basis for generating bodhichitta
2 The nature of bodhichitta and how it is generated
3 The divisions of bodhichitta

THE BASIS FOR GENERATING BODHICHITTA

Although bodhichitta can be generated by non-human beings such as gods and nagas who have the opportunity to receive Dharma, a human life with all the freedoms and endowments is the best basis for developing this special mind. Human beings can generate bodhichitta more powerfully because the human realm has more objects of compassion.

There is much more suffering in the human realm and there is a greater opportunity to receive Dharma. Therefore human beings can more easily develop renunciation and compassion. Recognizing that the opportunity we now have is the best one for studying and practising Mahayana paths, we should meditate:

> Since I have taken a perfect human rebirth and have now come into contact with pure Mahayana teachings there is no better time for me to generate bodhichitta. If I do not make use of the present opportunity, when shall I ever find such an opportunity again? It is so rare. I must use it well while I can. Although these are degenerate times, for me they are fortunate because I have a wonderful opportunity that I have never had before.

There was once a Tibetan man called Drukku Shewo who had no legs. One day he fell from a cliff's edge onto the back of a wild horse. The horse was so astonished that it took off at a gallop and Drukku Shewo had to hang on for his life. When the horse finally began to tire and slow down some people shouted to Drukku Shewo to dismount quickly, but he shouted back 'No way! When does a legless man ever get the chance to ride a wild horse? I may never get this opportunity again and so I am going to stay right here for as long as I can.'

We are like Drukku Shewo because by the greatest good fortune we have come across pure Mahayana teachings. These were previously unknown in the West, and they may not be around for long. How can we be sure that we shall ever have this opportunity again? Conditions change quickly and no one can say how much longer the pure Mahayana teachings will remain in this world. Before Tibet was invaded by the Chinese many Tibetans thought that Dharma would remain there for centuries, and they expected to return to their monasteries in future lives. They never imagined that these monasteries, centuries old, would be completely destroyed in that very lifetime; but this happened and in a very short time Buddhadharma has virtually disappeared from Tibet.

It has been said that Buddhadharma is like a precious golden yoke tossed on the waves of time, never remaining fixed in one place. It may disappear from this country or from this world and appear in other realms. No one can say that this will not happen. Since at present we are so fortunate, we should seize the opportunity and use our time wisely to gain stable experiences of Dharma and create the causes to experience good fortune in the future.

THE NATURE OF BODHICHITTA AND HOW IT IS GENERATED

Bodhichitta is a spontaneous wish, motivated by great compassion, to attain enlightenment to benefit all living beings. It has been explained that bodhichitta has two aspirations: the aspiration to attain enlightenment oneself, and the aspiration to lead all other living beings to the same state. It should be emphasized that the first aspiration is not the wish to attain enlightenment for oneself alone, but the wish to attain enlightenment oneself as the only perfectly effective means for fulfilling our main wish, which is to bring all living beings to the same state. Attaining enlightenment oneself is only a means to an end. For example, when we want to drink a cup of tea our real wish is to drink tea. We want to obtain a cup only because it is the implement we require to drink tea. The aspiration to benefit others is like our wish to drink tea, whereas the aspiration to attain enlightenment oneself is like our wish to obtain a teacup.

When we have generated superior intention we are determined to lead all living beings to full enlightenment. We meditate:

Am I at present able to accomplish what I have promised? Even Hinayana Foe Destroyers who have attained liberation do not have this ability to bring others to the fully awakened state of Buddhahood. Worldly gods such as Brahma and Ishvara cannot lead others to enlightenment, and even Bodhisattvas on the four learning paths do not have this ability because they are not yet Buddhas. Who is able to perform such a task? Only Buddhas have all the qualities that are needed. Therefore to fulfil my promise I must attain enlightenment.

By meditating in this way we develop bodhichitta – the spontaneous wish to attain enlightenment for the sake of others. The sign that we have realized bodhichitta is that we never lose this thought; all day and all night we wish to become enlightened for the sake of others. We have now entered the Mahayana path.

THE DIVISIONS OF BODHICHITTA

There are many types of bodhichitta, which are all included in the following four divisions:

1 The twofold division
2 The threefold division
3 The fourfold division
4 The twenty-twofold division

The twofold division is from the point of view of the nature of bodhichitta; the threefold division is from the point of view of the way in which we generate bodhichitta; and the fourfold and twenty-twofold divisions are from the point of view of the basis for developing bodhichitta.

THE TWOFOLD DIVISION

The many levels of bodhichitta are all included within the two: aspiring bodhichitta and engaging bodhichitta. Aspiring bodhichitta is any bodhichitta we generate before taking the Bodhisattva vows. When we have aspiring bodhichitta we have the wish to attain Buddhahood for the sake of others, but we have not yet actually engaged in the paths that lead to Buddhahood. Aspiring bodhichitta is like a decision to go to a particular destination.

Engaging bodhichitta is the bodhichitta we generate after taking the Bodhisattva vows. By taking the Bodhisattva vows we have the commitment to follow the paths of a Bodhisattva, the paths to Buddhahood. In this way we transform our aspiring bodhichitta into engaging bodhichitta. To have engaging bodhichitta is like actually embarking upon the journey to our destination. While we have only aspiring bodhichitta it is still possible to lose it or to give it up, but once we have taken the Bodhisattva vows we draw closer to Buddhahood every moment, even while we are asleep.

THE THREEFOLD DIVISION

Bodhichitta can also be divided into king-like bodhichitta, shepherd-like bodhichitta, and boatman-like bodhichitta. A Bodhisattva who has king-like bodhichitta wishes to lead all living beings to Buddhahood in the way that a king serves his subjects – first by becoming powerful and wealthy himself, and then by using his resources to help his subjects. A Bodhisattva who has shepherd-like bodhichitta wishes to lead all living beings to Buddhahood in the way that a shepherd leads his sheep to safety. Just as shepherds first supply all the needs of their flock and attend to their own needs last of all, so some Bodhisattvas want to lead all living beings to Buddhahood first and then attain enlightenment for themselves last of all. They have this wish because they have the least concern for their own welfare and they cherish all others before themselves. This type of bodhichitta arises from practising exchanging self with others. It is said that this is the attitude Manjushri developed. A Bodhisattva who has boatman-like bodhichitta wishes to bring all living beings to Buddhahood in the way that a boatman brings people to the opposite shore – by travelling along with them. This Bodhisattva has the wish for all living beings to attain enlightenment simultaneously with himself or herself.

In reality, the second two types of bodhichitta are wishes that are impossible to fulfil because it is only possible to lead others to enlightenment once we have attained enlightenment ourself. Therefore, only king-like bodhichitta is actual bodhichitta. Je Tsongkhapa says that although the other Bodhisattvas wish for that which is impossible, their attitude is sublime and unmistaken. If a child has a strong wish to protect its parents, this attitude is admirable even though the child is actually incapable of providing protection. Similarly, the sublime thoughts of a shepherd-like Bodhisattva and a boatman-like Bodhisattva are greatly to be admired.

THE FOURFOLD DIVISION

Bodhichitta can also be divided into the mind generation of imaginary engagement, the mind generation of pure superior intention, the mind generation of full maturation, and the mind generation of abandoned obstructions.

The mind generation of imaginary engagement is the bodhichitta of Bodhisattvas on the Mahayana paths of accumulation and preparation. On these paths Bodhisattvas meditate on both bodhichitta and emptiness because to attain enlightenment a Bodhisattva needs method and wisdom, just as a bird needs both wings to fly. Meditating on bodhichitta increases their merit and meditating on emptiness increases their wisdom. When Bodhisattvas attain superior seeing observing emptiness they enter the path of preparation. On this path their bodhichitta and their wisdom realizing emptiness are more powerful than on the path of accumulation. Bodhisattvas on these first two paths are ordinary Bodhisattvas because they have not yet realized emptiness directly. They apprehend their object, emptiness, by means of a generic image. Therefore they are said to have the 'mind generation of conceptual, or imaginary, engagement'.

When Bodhisattvas realize emptiness directly they enter the Mahayana path of seeing and the first ground of a Superior Bodhisattva. Bodhisattvas on the first to the seventh grounds are said to have the 'mind generation of pure superior intention' because their meditations on emptiness and bodhichitta are superior to those of Bodhisattvas on the paths of accumulation and preparation. Bodhisattvas on the eighth, ninth, and tenth grounds have the mind generation of full maturation. The mind generation of abandoned obstructions is the bodhichitta of a Buddha.

THE TWENTY-TWOFOLD DIVISION

Bodhichitta can be divided into twenty-two types from the point of view of the basis for developing bodhichitta. The first of the twenty-two types is called 'earth-like bodhichitta'. This is another name for aspiring bodhichitta. Just as trees, houses, and huge cities depend upon the earth, so all the other levels of bodhichitta depend upon aspiring bodhichitta, which is the necessary foundation for taking the Bodhisattva vows. When Bodhisattvas develop engaging bodhichitta they attain the second of the twenty-two types, called 'gold-like bodhichitta'. This is so called because like gold it will never degenerate. From this level a Bodhisattva's bodhichitta improves until it becomes the cloud-like bodhichitta of a Bodhisattva on the tenth ground. Just as from clouds rain falls to nourish the earth, so from the cloud-like bodhichitta of a Bodhisattva on the tenth ground the rain of Dharma falls to nourish living beings.

Extensive explanations of the twenty-two types of bodhichitta can be found in commentaries to the *Perfection of Wisdom Sutras*. For our present purposes it is sufficient to concentrate on generating the first, earth-like bodhichitta.

TRAINING THE MIND IN EQUALIZING AND EXCHANGING SELF WITH OTHERS

Training the mind in equalizing and exchanging self with others and the practice of taking and giving are the two main practices in the Kadam training the mind tradition, called 'Lojong' in Tibetan. These instructions were passed from Buddha Shakyamuni in unbroken succession to Atisha, from Atisha to Dromtonpa, and from Dromtonpa in unbroken lineage to Geshe Potowa, Geshe Langri Tangpa, Geshe Sharawa, and Geshe Chekhawa. Before the time of Geshe Chekhawa the instructions were known as 'secret Dharma' because they were taught only to disciples with special wisdom whilst the other stages of the path were taught openly. In *Guide to the Bodhisattva's Way of Life* Shantideva says:

> Thus, whoever wants to swiftly protect
> Both themselves and others
> Should practise this holy secret
> Of exchanging self with others.

Geshe Chekhawa was the first Teacher to spread these instructions openly and extensively in Tibet, and as a result many people developed the realization of bodhichitta. Geshe Chekhawa wrote a root text called *Training the Mind in Seven Points*, which includes all the main practices of Kadam training the mind. The special method for generating bodhichitta according to this tradition is now explained under the following five headings:

1 Equalizing self and others
2 Contemplating the disadvantages of self-cherishing
3 Contemplating the advantages of cherishing others
4 Exchanging self with others
5 Taking and giving

EQUALIZING SELF AND OTHERS

We cannot immediately convert self-cherishing, the attitude of regarding ourself as most precious and important, into the opposite attitude of cherishing others, regarding them as most precious and important. Therefore we need to begin by equalizing ourself and others, learning to regard ourself and others as equally dear. To do this we meditate:

I myself do not have the slightest wish to experience suffering and I am not content with the happiness I enjoy, but this is equally true for everyone else. Therefore it is inappropriate for me to consider myself to be more important than everyone else. I want happiness, but so do others. I want freedom from misery, but so do others. Since we all want the same thing, I will regard others in the same way as I regard myself.

When this determination arises we should hold it in placement meditation to become thoroughly acquainted with it. If we have wisdom we shall not have to employ many different lines of reasoning to arrive at the determination to cherish others as we cherish ourself, but if we find it hard to make a clear decision we need to engage in reasoning to remove our doubt. However, there is no guarantee that this will enable us to reach such a decision because our ability to do this comes from experience. If we can take this step without hesitation, this is wonderful because it is a step we must definitely take if we are to attain full enlightenment.

CONTEMPLATING THE DISADVANTAGES
OF SELF-CHERISHING

It has been explained that self-grasping ignorance observes the mere I and grasps it as inherently existent. For ordinary beings, self-cherishing is a mind that holds the inherently existent self conceived by self-grasping to be supremely important. Self-cherishing arises in dependence upon self-grasping. These two are like inseparable friends and are the source of all our problems. Due to our self-cherishing mind we develop a strong desire to secure our own welfare, but to do this we sometimes have to engage in non-virtuous actions that cause us to experience suffering and dissatisfaction. In this way all our problems, external and internal, arise directly or indirectly from our attitude of self-cherishing and cannot be traced to any other source. In *Guide to the Bodhisattva's Way of Life* Shantideva says that every single suffering that is experienced in this world arises as a result of self-cherishing.

In one of his former lives Buddha Shakyamuni was a Bodhisattva called Powerful Heart. One day he went into a forest with a group of friends and saw there a starving tigress with many cubs. It had been so long since this tigress had been able to find any food that she was preparing to kill and eat one of her cubs. When he saw this, Powerful Heart declared: 'This clearly demonstrates that there is not one good thing that can be said about samsara since even a mother can be driven to do this! How? It is only her self-cherishing mind that could lead her to do such a thing.'

What causes a criminal to experience all the miseries of imprisonment? The real criminal is the self-cherishing mind that drove him to commit his crime. Similarly, when a mouse is caught in a trap, its own self-cherishing is what really traps it because self-cherishing drives the mouse to snatch the cheese. Again, when a fish is caught, its own self-cherishing is what drives it to bite the fisherman's bait and become impaled upon the hook.

What causes us to experience suffering if someone comes to take our possessions or to kill us? It is our self-cherishing mind alone that is directly or indirectly responsible for our pain and fear. The miseries we experience in this life, such as the sorrow of losing those who are dear to us, the miseries of poverty, or the pains of illness, all arise in dependence upon our taking samsaric rebirth; and samsaric rebirth comes as a result of past actions we have committed out of self-cherishing. If someone comes to inflict harm upon us they do so as a result of our own past negative actions, and as they approach us we feel frightened only because we continue to cherish ourself and value our own welfare so highly. The misfortunes we experience now come as a result of our past self-cherishing, and our present feelings of pain or fear come from the self-cherishing that we have right now. Thus it is extremely dangerous to encourage and enhance this enemy of self-cherishing or to allow ourself to be dominated by it.

When someone speaks harshly to us we feel hurt and unhappy. Why? Only because we think we are so important. If we did not think so, words of criticism, blame, or mockery could not hurt us. All the different kinds of hurtful speech have power to inflict pain upon us only by virtue of our own self-cherishing. With self-cherishing such words lacerate our mind as they are spoken, and we rub salt into the wound by remembering them over and over again. Then we feel angry and hold a grudge against the other person, all because we feel we are so precious. Again, if we lend our possessions to someone and they neglect to return them we become agitated and keep thinking about how the person has not returned our possessions; but if our self-cherishing were not so strong we would not worry so much about what others do with our possessions.

Self-cherishing makes us feel upset every time our wishes are not fulfilled and we do not get what we want or what we expected to receive; but when someone else's wishes are not fulfilled we have no such feeling. If a businessman does not get what he wants, if someone else has to live in poverty, or if an animal is taken off to be slaughtered, these things do not cause us the pain we feel when our own desires are frustrated.

Both the smallest and the greatest sufferings arise from self-cherishing. If we eat too much food, or if our food is bad and we become sick, we are inclined to blame the food for our suffering. If we check we shall find that it is our own self-cherishing that inflicts our suffering because we ate the food in the first place with an attitude of self-cherishing. Even the minor irritation of having an insect or a mouse in our room arises from our attitude of self-cherishing. Any discomfort we experience while we are meditating comes from self-cherishing. If something disturbs us we become upset and inwardly we shout in protest 'I am trying to meditate!' We feel it is supremely important that our own meditation sessions go very well, and find it hard to tolerate any interruption, but we do not attach the same importance to other people's spiritual practice. Just as these small sufferings come about as a result of self-cherishing, so too do the greatest sufferings people can experience, such as the sufferings of war.

In the texts on training the mind the self-cherishing mind is called by many names. It is said to be a slaughterer that destroys the life of liberation by causing us to commit unskilful actions; it is a thief that steals our virtuous potentialities by causing us to become angry; it is a farmer that plants the seeds of negative actions in the field of our consciousness so that the fruit of suffering will ripen in our lives; and it is a possessor because it is covetous. With self-cherishing we are like a businessman who out of covetousness deals with a man who is known to be dangerous and who may try to kill him; or we are like a soldier who out of lust for victory recklessly disregards the fact that at any moment he may be killed. Self-cherishing causes all kinds of recklessness. It is also said to be inconsideration because it makes us inconsiderate towards others, creating problems for them, telling them lies, taking their possessions, or neglecting to show them respect; and it is said to be shamelessness because it causes us to disregard our conscience and act recklessly.

In *Guide to the Bodhisattva's Way of Life* Shantideva says that although we have been pursuing our own welfare since

428

beginningless time, we have succeeded in obtaining only suffering. In this life and in all our countless past lives we have struggled hard to be happy and successful, and all our efforts have been motivated by self-cherishing; but having worked in this way for aeons we still have nothing to show for it. We have made no real progress. All we have brought with us from our former lives is suffering.

To become convinced of the great dangers of self-cherishing we need to check thoroughly to see if we can find any example of physical or mental suffering that is not directly or indirectly caused by self-cherishing. If we cannot, we should recognize clearly that all problems and miseries, and all external and internal faults, arise from self-cherishing. With this recognition we can make a firm decision, 'Since I do not want to experience problems and unhappiness I will abandon self-cherishing.' When we have made this decision we take it as our object of placement meditation.

We need to keep this resolution at all times. Whenever we encounter problems we should think 'This very problem is the result of my self-cherishing.' In this way we can use the opportunity to strengthen our resolution.

CONTEMPLATING THE ADVANTAGES OF CHERISHING OTHERS

In his Lamrim, Gyalwa Ensapa says that if we cherish others we shall want to benefit them and with this motivation we shall engage in positive actions and create the cause for future happiness. Shantideva said that all the happiness of this world comes from the mind desiring others to be happy.

It is this wish for others to be happy that motivated us in the past to create the causes for a precious human life by practising the moral discipline of abandoning negative actions of body, speech, and mind. Our human life with all its freedoms and endowments provides us with the opportunity to experience the joys and happiness of human existence. The favourable conditions we enjoy as a human being also come from our past attitude of cherishing others, because this attitude is what motivated us to benefit others by practising giving, patience, and other virtues. If others now regard us with warmth and love, and if they take good care of us, it is because we have cherished them in the past. All the kindness we have received from our parents and all the help we have received in this life come as a result of cherishing others.

In *Guide to the Bodhisattva's Way of Life* Shantideva says:

But what need is there to speak at length?
The childish work only for themselves,
Whereas the Buddhas work only for others –
Just look at the difference between them!

Here 'the childish' refers to ordinary beings who have worked for lifetimes without gaining anything of lasting value. Since beginningless time we have been motivated by self-cherishing and we have received only suffering, whereas the Buddhas have been motivated by cherishing others and they have gained ultimate happiness.

In *Stories of Rebirth* and in many of the Sutras it is told how in his past lives Buddha Shakyamuni abandoned self-cherishing and worked for the welfare of others. There is one text called *The Wishfulfilling Tree of One Hundred and Eight Deeds* with one hundred and eight chapters extracted from the Sutras. Each chapter tells of one life spent for the sake of others. In one of these lives the future Buddha was a king called Pema Chen. At that time in many countries of this world people suffered from a disease that caused them to experience severe headaches. Doctors conferred to see if they could find a remedy, but none could be found. Eventually one doctor discovered an antidote, but he explained to the others, 'To cure this disease we need to gather many potent ingredients. I have all of these except one – the flesh of a rohita fish. I cannot obtain this ingredient because the rohita fish is now extinct.' When he heard this, King Pema Chen called the doctor to him and told him that there was one special place where rohita fish could be found, and he told the doctor to go and search there in a few days' time. The doctor was sceptical at first because he had already searched thoroughly in the place indicated by the king, but he was prepared to look again. Very soon afterwards King Pema Chen died and took rebirth in that place as a rohita fish. When the doctor arrived he found the fish. Then he made the medicine and cured all the people. This Bodhisattva, Pema Chen, who was to become Buddha Shakyamuni, took many rebirths as a rohita fish and gave his life for the benefit of others.

Whenever we cherish anything, we do so because we recognize and appreciate its good qualities. Therefore, if we recognize and appreciate the good qualities, especially the great kindness, of other living beings, we shall naturally cherish them and want to return their kindness. Everything we possess is ours only through the kindness of others. If it were not for others we would not be able to call our possessions our own. We did not manufacture them on our own, nor did they arise miraculously of their own accord. They were all produced in dependence upon the kindness of others. For example, take the bread we eat each day. Where does it come from? Many people labour in the fields to produce the wheat, and many people work to turn the wheat into loaves of bread and transport it to the shop where we buy it. We may think that the bread is ours simply because we paid for it, but money cannot produce bread. If we sow coins in the ground they will not produce a harvest. It is the kindness of others and not our own cash that provides the bread we need.

Even our money comes through the kindness of others. We do not manufacture it ourself. We may think 'This money is mine because I earned it. It has nothing to do with anyone else.' But who provided us with the job we do to earn the money? Who is it that makes sure our work is in demand? Others employ us and create our jobs.

Even the smallest things we take for granted are ours only through the kindness of others. A cup of tea takes two minutes to prepare, but if we were to consider how many people have laboured to grow, to pick, to pack, and to transport the tea, and how many people have laboured to help them, we would be amazed to see how our cup of tea depends directly or indirectly upon the kindness of the whole world. The same applies with the sugar and the milk we stir into the tea. Just think of the kindness of the cow who has given us milk that was intended for her calf!

Our houses, our offices, our cities all arise in dependence upon living beings who work hard to build them. Generations have laboured to make the environments we call our own and to build the roads we use to travel from place to place. When we stay in hotels or go shopping we take all these services for granted, but it takes thousands of people to provide them.

All the temporary happiness and possessions of this life, including our own body, are obtained in dependence upon the kindness of others; and all the happiness of future lives will arise in dependence upon the kindness of others because we depend upon others to practise giving, moral discipline, patience, and effort, which are the causes of higher rebirths. All ultimate happiness also depends upon the kindness of others because we need others in order to develop great compassion and bodhichitta, the causes of full enlightenment.

In *Guide to the Bodhisattva's Way of Life* Shantideva says that living beings and Buddhas are of equal importance for our attainment of Buddhahood. We usually say that Buddhas lead others to enlightenment, but so do all other living beings because we can develop the cause of enlightenment, bodhichitta, only by taking all other living beings as our object of practice. Since others are of such supreme benefit to us we should cherish them most dearly. In *Eight Verses of Training the Mind* Geshe Langri Tangpa says:

With the intention to attain
The ultimate, supreme goal
That surpasses even the wish-granting jewel,
May I constantly cherish all living beings.

EXCHANGING SELF WITH OTHERS

This is presented in three parts:

1 Recognizing why we need to exchange self with others
2 Recognizing that we can exchange self with others
3 How to exchange self with others

RECOGNIZING WHY WE NEED TO EXCHANGE SELF WITH OTHERS

Shantideva said that we need to convert our self-cherishing into the attitude of cherishing others because if we do not there is no way we can attain enlightenment; and it is certainly necessary for us to attain enlightenment because there is no lasting happiness to be found anywhere in samsara. If we do not cherish others, even our wishes for this life will not be fulfilled, let alone our wishes for future lives. We can see for ourself that even in the most mundane situations we are not successful if we do not cherish others. For example, when an employer has no respect for his employees, or the employees have no respect for their employer, they cannot work well together. The employees may go on strike and lose their wages, while the employer's enterprise will not prosper. The same goes for any relationship between people. If there is no mutual care and respect, no one will get what they want. If a wife does not cherish her husband he will lose his interest in fulfilling her wishes. He will eventually cease to care for her and there will be nothing to hold the marriage together. If a Teacher does not respect his or her students they will misbehave and frustrate his wishes; and if the students do not respect their Teacher they will not be able to learn anything. If people are living in a community and the individual members of the community do not cherish one another, the community will fall apart; and if the community as a whole does not respect its members it will become weak and unharmonious. If its members do not offer one another mutual support, a community will experience many problems and no one's wishes will be fulfilled. Again, if we rent a house but feel no respect for the landlord we shall neglect the property and as a result we shall be asked to leave. In many ways such as these we inflict difficulties upon ourself by failing to cherish others. If our main concern is for our own welfare we can be certain that we shall experience problems.

By thinking like this we can make a strong determination: 'I must cherish others so that I can develop great compassion and bodhichitta and thereby experience all the benefits of bodhichitta.' We then meditate on this determination single-pointedly.

RECOGNIZING THAT WE CAN EXCHANGE SELF WITH OTHERS

We may understand that we need to exchange self with others, giving up self-cherishing and cherishing only others, and yet we may still feel incapable of actually doing so. For example, we may start to think 'Living beings are countless, I cannot possibly love all of them.' We can overcome this discouragement and develop conviction by considering the reasons why it is possible for us to cherish others.

Shantideva said that if we make an effort to change the object of our cherishing it will not be difficult for us to cherish even our enemies. The more familiar we are with the practice the easier it will be. We can see for ourself that people who dislike one another so much that they cannot bear the sight of each other often become friends later on. Sometimes they even get married, and their names, once so unbearable to hear, become a source of delight to one another. Within our one short lifetime we have many experiences similar to this.

In fact it is quite easy for us to change the object of our cherishing. Right now we are cherishing very dearly something that really belongs to others. What is it? Our own body. In reality, this body does not belong to us because it developed from the union of our father's sperm and our mother's ovum. Although our body was produced from the bodies of our parents and belongs to them, we still hold it as our own and cherish it. Why? Only because we are so familiar with it. It follows that when we become familiar with others we shall cherish them just as dearly. We only need to change the object of our cherishing, and this is what we are doing all the time. Take for example a novice monk. Before taking novice vows this person cherished the body of a layman as his own, but now he cherishes the body of a novice, and when he takes full ordination he will cherish the body of a fully ordained monk. Similarly, a young man cherishes the body of a youth, when he is thirty he cherishes the body of a thirty-year-old, and when he is eighty he cherishes the body of an old man. The observed object of our self-cherishing changes continuously. The body we cherished yesterday has ceased to exist. Although the continuum of our body remains, the body we cherish one moment is different from the body we cherish the next.

Our body is like the house in which we live. We may stay in our house for a few years and call it our own, but the house is actually owned by others. Even if we have purchased it and do not have a mortgage we still have to pass it on to others or give it up at the time of death. Understanding this we shall see how we can give up our special regard for our own body right now and take others as our object of cherishing.

We think 'I am this, I am that', but the person of whom we feel so proud frequently changes identity. Moment by moment the self we cherish changes. If we understand subtle impermanence we shall easily understand how the object of our self-cherishing is changing all the time. If this is so, why should it be hard to shift our cherishing to others?

Je Tsongkhapa explained that self and other are not different in the way that yellow and blue are different, but they are different in the way that 'this mountain' is different from 'that mountain'. If something is yellow it cannot correctly be apprehended as blue, and if something is blue it cannot correctly be apprehended as yellow. The object of a mind correctly apprehending yellow and the object of a mind correctly apprehending blue are completely different; but 'this mountain' can correctly be apprehended as 'that mountain', and 'that mountain' can correctly be apprehended as 'this mountain'. If we stand on the top of one mountain and look at another mountain, the mountain we are standing on will be 'this mountain', and the other mountain will be 'that mountain'; but if we climb down 'this mountain' and then climb up 'that mountain', 'that mountain' will be 'this mountain', and 'this mountain' will be 'that mountain'.

Self and other are like 'this mountain' and 'that mountain'. We can observe another person and cherish them as our self or I. To do this we climb down from the mountain of self and cross over to the mountain of other. If we do this we shall put the mountain of self at a distance so that it is, in our view, the least important and most faraway thing.

HOW TO EXCHANGE SELF WITH OTHERS

If we know why we need to cherish others, and we are convinced that we can do it, we shall arrive at a firm decision to exchange self with others and it will be easy to engage in the actual practice.

In every situation we must take the opportunity to train our mind in exchanging self with others. When we are not in meditation we shall meet many people and it will seem that some are easy to cherish while with others it is virtually impossible. We cannot expect instant success but, as before, we need to train gradually, starting with those who are already close to us and then extending the scope of our cherishing others to include more and more people. It may take many years to complete this training and we need to persevere patiently. When we are actually in meditation we take all living beings as our object and develop a mind that cherishes all of them, but we need to meditate like this over and over again without expecting our attitude towards others to change in only a few sessions.

What is the sign that we have completed this training? Until now we have thought very highly of ourself and have neglected and looked down upon others. If we find that by practising exchanging self with others this attitude is reversed, so that when we see others we spontaneously cherish them in the same way that we used to cherish ourself, this indicates that we have realized exchanging self with others. With this realization, whenever we see someone suffering we feel it is as unbearable as if it were our own suffering, and whenever we see someone without happiness we feel love, wishing them to enjoy happiness everlastingly.

TAKING AND GIVING

It is not unusual to be able to exchange self with others for a short time – a few minutes, a few hours, or even a few days – but what we are aiming for is a lasting experience, a stable realization. Once we have some familiarity with exchanging self with others we can engage in the practice of taking and giving to increase and stabilize our experience. The main purpose of this practice is to improve our compassion and love. It also transforms adversities that we experience into the spiritual path and it accumulates great and powerful merit. We first practise taking the miseries and sufferings of others and then we practise giving them happiness and health. We practise taking and giving in this order because it is difficult for others to receive happiness while they are burdened with sorrow.

TAKING

This practice is motivated by compassion wishing to take the suffering, fear, unhappiness, and faults of others. We can practise taking in two ways: either taking the sufferings of all beings collectively, or taking the sufferings of individuals or groups of individuals.

If we are practising in the first way we imagine that we are surrounded by all living beings who inhabit the six realms and we contemplate their sufferings. In this way we generate compassion, thinking 'How wonderful it would be if all living beings were free from their sufferings right now. I myself will make this happen.' Then we visualize all the sufferings of living beings in the form of black smoke which we draw into our heart where our self-cherishing mind is concentrated. As it dissolves into our heart this smoke consumes our self-cherishing. When we have taken all the black smoke of others' suffering we think: 'Now this black smoke has completely extinguished my self-cherishing and all other living beings are released from their suffering. Their bodies have become pure and their minds have transformed into uncontaminated great bliss.' Then we do placement meditation on this feeling.

If we are practising in the second way we do separate rounds of meditation, focusing in turn upon the sufferings of beings within each realm of samsara. When we have concluded the six rounds of meditation we imagine that all the beings of the six realms are completely released from every kind of suffering. Their bodies have become pure and their minds have transformed into uncontaminated great bliss. If we wish we can also do this practice of taking by focusing on just one other person or a number of people individually.

It is possible to misunderstand the purpose of this practice of taking and to think 'I have enough misery of my own; I cannot take on the suffering of the whole world.' The purpose of this practice is not to accumulate an intolerable burden of suffering, but to increase our compassion, stabilize our experience of exchanging self with others, and accumulate merit. We cannot say that as a direct result of our engaging in this practice of taking all living beings will be released from their suffering, but if we do the meditation it is certain that we ourself shall increase our compassion. Since compassion is the cause of enlightenment we can be sure that our practice of taking creates the cause for us to become enlightened and thereby fully capable of helping others to find freedom from their suffering.

If it is hard to begin by taking the sufferings of others we can follow the advice of Geshe Chekhawa in *Training the Mind in Seven Points* where he suggests that we begin by taking our own future sufferings. It is definite that we shall experience the sufferings of ageing, sickness, death, and many other miseries in the future. If we take these sufferings upon ourself now, we shall become familiar enough with the practice to take the sufferings of others as well. Furthermore, we shall indirectly release ourself from our future suffering by creating the cause to eliminate our self-cherishing, which is the source of all future unhappiness. The practice of taking our own future suffering can be done with the motivation to purify our negativities, to overcome our self-cherishing, or to be able to take on the sufferings of others. Having generated such a motivation we visualize our own future sufferings in the aspect of black smoke which gathers and dissolves into our heart, purifying the negative karma that causes us to experience future suffering. We then think 'Now I have released myself from my future suffering', and we generate great joy. We need to repeat this practice many times.

The practice of taking others' suffering enables us to transform adversities into the spiritual path because, when we are practising taking, our own adversities seem relatively insignificant. We are able to endure them because we have dedicated ourself to enduring the sufferings of all living beings. If we think in this way, our own difficulties will not seem like big problems and we can accept whatever situation arises. If our practice of taking is sincere, our own sufferings cannot make us depressed. When we are concerned solely for our own welfare we easily become excited or depressed. With such an unbalanced mind it is hard to practise Dharma, but if we cherish others and take their sufferings upon ourself we shall be able to maintain a more even state of mind with regard to our own personal circumstances. In this way we shall be able to transform distractions and other unfavourable conditions into the spiritual path.

GIVING

This practice is motivated by love wishing all living beings to have happiness. We again visualize all living beings surrounding us and we consider, 'Everyone wants pure happiness but no one possesses it. How wonderful it would be if everyone had pure happiness. I myself will make this happen.' We then imagine that our body transforms into a wishfulfilling jewel, which radiates light in all directions reaching every single living being. When it touches beings suffering in the hot hells it is like cooling water; when it touches beings suffering in the cold hells it is like the warmth of the sun; when it touches hungry ghosts it is like nourishing food and drink; when it touches human beings it becomes all the objects they desire; and when it touches gods it becomes objects to delight their five senses. We imagine in this way that we are giving benefit to all the beings of the six realms. When we have completed this visualization we think 'Now all beings are experiencing satisfaction and joy', and we hold this feeling in placement meditation.

When we gain high realizations we shall be able to emanate all that is wished for by others. Our potentialities to develop such powers are nourished by this practice of giving, which acts as a cause for us to be able to give real happiness in the future. By doing this meditation every day we shall develop a warm and loving regard for the people we meet. Eventually we shall generate spontaneous love, compassion, and bodhichitta. No other qualities are needed to become a Bodhisattva. We do not have to be good-looking, well-dressed, or unusual in any other respect. Bodhisattvas may appear to be ordinary, but inwardly they have profound, uncommon understanding.

At the completion of each session of the practice of taking and giving we dedicate our merit so that others may become free from suffering and hindrances and find lasting peace and happiness. In our meditation break we should hold the feeling of wishing to practise taking and giving, and try to accept difficulties and offer happiness to others as much as possible. To help us do this we can recite lines that remind us of the practice while we engage in any of our daily activities. There are two lines by Nagarjuna that are easy to remember:

May the sufferings and negativities of living beings ripen upon me,
And may my happiness and virtue ripen upon them.

Or we can recite these two lines from *Eight Verses of Training the Mind* by Geshe Langri Tangpa:

May I take defeat upon myself
And offer them the victory.

Or we can recite the verse from *Offering to the Spiritual Guide*:

Therefore, O Compassionate, Venerable Guru, I seek your
*   blessings*
So that all the suffering, negativities, and obstructions
*   of mother sentient beings*
Will ripen upon me right now;
And through my giving my happiness and virtue to
*   others,*
May all migrating beings be happy.

When meditating on taking and giving we can also recite these lines purely and gently as a preliminary after visualizing the Field for Accumulating Merit and offering the mandala.

The practice of taking and giving is similar to the Secret Mantra practice called 'bringing the result into the path', and quickly ripens our potentiality to attain Buddhahood. When we practise taking we imagine that we have purified the world and the minds of all living beings. When we practise giving we imagine that we have endowed the world and the minds of all living beings with all good qualities. Practising in this way helps us to overcome ordinary appearance. In this respect as well the practices of taking and giving are like the practices of Secret Mantra, and this is another reason why the instructions are known as 'secret Dharma'.

Those who have some experience of the practice described so far can practise taking and giving mounted upon the breath. With the motivation of compassion and love, as we gently inhale we imagine that we are taking upon ourself the sufferings and obstructions of others, and as we gently exhale we imagine that we are giving our happiness and virtuous actions to them. Someone who can practise like this does not need to waste a single breath. It is a very powerful practice because our breath and our mind are closely related.

Je Tsongkhapa was skilled at taking and giving. His disciple Khädrubje said to him:

O Protector, even your daily breath causes infinite migrators to receive benefit. What need is there to say how wise and compassionate are all your other actions?

When we have practised the two ways of developing bodhichitta – meditating on the sevenfold cause and effect and exchanging self with others – we can combine the two practices and meditate in eleven rounds as follows:

(1) Developing equanimity
(2) Recognizing that all living beings are our mothers
(3) Remembering the past and present kindness of all mother beings
(4) Developing the wish to repay the kindness of all mother beings
(5) Equalizing self and others
(6) Contemplating the disadvantages of self-cherishing
(7) Contemplating the advantages of cherishing others
(8) Exchanging self with others by practising taking
(9) Exchanging self with others by practising giving
(10) Developing superior intention
(11) Developing bodhichitta

MAINTAINING BODHICHITTA BY MEANS OF RITUAL

This has two parts:

1 Maintaining the aspiring mind by means of ritual
2 Maintaining the engaging mind by means of ritual

MAINTAINING THE ASPIRING MIND BY MEANS OF RITUAL

When each of the one thousand Buddhas first generated bodhichitta they did so while presenting offering substances of various kinds to the Field for Accumulating Merit. Buddha Shakyamuni, the fourth of the one thousand Buddhas, first generated bodhichitta in a previous life when he was the son of a Brahmin. The Buddha who was giving teachings at that time was called Tathagata Shakya Mahamuni. The future Buddha filled a begging bowl with food, generated bodhichitta, and then offered the bowl to Tathagata Shakya Mahamuni, thinking 'May I attain enlightenment for the sake of all living beings.' Tathagata Shakya Mahamuni then prophesied that this Brahmin's son would become a Buddha called Shakyamuni, and he made fifteen predictions about him which all came true. Among them were predictions of the place where Prince Siddhartha would be born, his parents' qualities, the place of his enlightenment, the number of his disciples, and so on.

The way of maintaining aspiring bodhichitta by means of ritual is by taking the precepts of aspiring bodhichitta. To do this we first develop either artificial or spontaneous bodhichitta, and then in front of all the holy beings we make the promise never to give up the mind of bodhichitta. We can make this promise in front of a Spiritual Guide, or in front of a symbol or representation of Buddha, or by visualizing all the Buddhas in front of us. We begin by offering the prayer of seven limbs and a mandala. Then we go for refuge, generate bodhichitta, and take the precepts with the following prayers:

I and all sentient beings, until we achieve enlightenment,
Go for refuge to Buddha, Dharma, and Sangha.
Through the virtues I collect by giving and other
  perfections,
May I become a Buddha for the benefit of all.   (3x)

From this time forth until I become a Buddha,
I shall keep even at the cost of my life
A mind wishing to attain complete enlightenment
To free all living beings from the fears of samsara and
  solitary peace.   (3x)

When we take these precepts directly from a Spiritual Guide we have to repeat these two verses after him or her. When we take them before a representation of Buddha or before a visualized assembly we imagine that we are repeating the words after Buddha. When we have received the precepts we keep them as our daily practice.

The eight precepts are:

(1) To remember the benefits of bodhichitta six times a day
(2) To generate bodhichitta six times a day
(3) Not to abandon any living being
(4) To accumulate merit and wisdom
(5) Not to cheat or deceive our Preceptors or Spiritual Guides
(6) Not to criticize those who have entered the Mahayana
(7) Not to cause others to regret their virtuous actions
(8) Not to pretend to have good qualities or hide our faults without a special, pure intention

Keeping the first four precepts prevents our bodhichitta from degenerating in this lifetime, and keeping the second four precepts prevents our bodhichitta from degenerating in future lifetimes.

MAINTAINING THE ENGAGING MIND BY MEANS OF RITUAL

We maintain engaging bodhichitta by means of ritual by taking the actual Bodhisattva vows. Initially we need to receive these from a qualified Spiritual Guide. Once we have received them we can take them on our own again at any time and as often as we wish. When we do so, we visualize the Field for Accumulating Merit and repeat three times the promise to keep the moral discipline of a Bodhisattva, avoiding all downfalls by engaging in the practice of the six perfections. We can renew or strengthen this promise by reciting the following verse three times:

O Gurus, Buddhas, and Bodhisattvas
Please listen to what I now say.
Just as all the previous Sugatas
Generated the mind of enlightenment

And accomplished all the stages
Of the Bodhisattva training,
So will I too for the sake of all beings
Generate the mind of enlightenment
And accomplish all the stages
Of the Bodhisattva training.

At the conclusion of the third recitation we should consider that we have now stabilized and enhanced our Bodhisattva vows.

Je Tsongkhapa

Jampel Gyatso   *Khedrubje*

Engaging in a
Bodhisattva's Actions

HOW TO ENGAGE IN A BODHISATTVA'S ACTIONS

Once we have generated bodhichitta and taken the Bodhisattva vows we enter into the actions of a Bodhisattva. Maintaining the Bodhisattva vows is the basis for training in a Bodhisattva's actions, which consist of the practice of the six perfections, the path to enlightenment. If we wish to become enlightened but do not engage in these actions, we are like someone who wants to go to India but who does not actually make the journey.

In the *Condensed Perfection of Wisdom Sutra* it is said that all the Buddhas of the past, present, and future practised the six perfections, which are like the main road to enlightenment. All the Mahayana practices of Sutra and Tantra are included within the six perfections. They are exclusively the practices of Bodhisattvas because they are all motivated by bodhichitta. Any action of giving that is not motivated by bodhichitta is not the perfection of giving. In the same way, any practice of moral discipline, patience, effort, mental stabilization, or wisdom is not the practice of a perfection unless it is motivated by bodhichitta.

The main purpose of practising the six perfections is to complete the collections of merit and wisdom. Whereas the impure bodies of ordinary beings arise from impure causes – contaminated actions and delusion – the pure bodies of a Buddha arise from the collections of merit and wisdom. The practices of the first five perfections complete the collection of merit, and the practice of the sixth perfection, the perfection of wisdom, completes the collection of wisdom. The collection of merit is the main cause of a Buddha's Form

Body and the collection of wisdom is the main cause of a Buddha's Truth Body.

Engaging in a Bodhisattva's actions is explained in two parts:

1 Training in the six perfections to ripen our own mental continuum
2 Training in the four ways of gathering to ripen the mental continuum of others

TRAINING IN THE SIX PERFECTIONS TO RIPEN OUR OWN MENTAL CONTINUUM

This has four parts:

1 The six perfections in general
2 The perfections of mental stabilization and wisdom in particular
3 How to progress through the spiritual grounds and paths in dependence upon a union of tranquil abiding and superior seeing
4 Training in Vajrayana paths

THE SIX PERFECTIONS IN GENERAL

All the countless actions of a Bodhisattva are included within the six perfections:

1 The perfection of giving
2 The perfection of moral discipline
3 The perfection of patience
4 The perfection of effort
5 The perfection of mental stabilization
6 The perfection of wisdom

THE PERFECTION OF GIVING

Giving is a virtuous mental decision to give, or a bodily or verbal action of giving that is motivated by a virtuous state of mind. Giving practised with bodhichitta motivation is a perfection of giving. There are three types of giving:

(1) Giving material things
(2) Giving Dharma
(3) Giving fearlessness

GIVING MATERIAL THINGS

Giving material things is a virtuous thought to give our possessions, our enjoyments, or our body. It is impossible to develop the wish to give our body to others if we cannot even develop the wish to give away our possessions and enjoyments. Therefore we need to train first in giving away our possessions.

To practise giving away our possessions we first need to contemplate the benefits of giving and the disadvantages of miserliness so that we develop the wish to give. Then we need to engage in the actual practice of giving our things away to others. We meditate:

If I do not practise giving now, in the future I shall take rebirth in poverty and shall not be able to practise giving material possessions to others; thus I shall not be able to create the cause to receive resources again in the future. In this way I shall be bound to experience many future lifetimes of poverty. Therefore it does not matter if I leave myself with few resources in this life and give the rest away, because I shall be creating the cause to receive plenty in the future.

When we go on holiday we take care to carry enough money to see us through the whole holiday, but how much more important it is to ensure that we travel to future lives with enough virtue to provide us with all the resources we shall need. Our practice of giving is the best insurance against future poverty. If we have strong attachment to our possessions we need to consider what Buddha says in the *Condensed Perfection of Wisdom Sutra* – that misers are reborn in the land of hungry ghosts, and when reborn as humans they experience poverty. We should meditate:

In former lives I had great wealth. I have often possessed the wealth of a monarch and enjoyed the fabulous riches of gods such as Brahma. If all my previous wealth were gathered together it would cover the whole globe, but now I am not able to use even the smallest amount of my past wealth. If I do not give my possessions away right now, I shall have to let others take them when I die, and then I shall not only fail to receive the benefits of having given them away freely but I shall also have to suffer all the disadvantages of my miserliness – the experience of repeated deprivations in the future. There is no real benefit in holding tightly to possessions because they are all impermanent, subject to loss and decay. They gain meaning only in being given away. In themselves my possessions are valueless, but they become precious when I offer them to others. At that time they are the means of gaining lasting happiness.

The amount of merit we accumulate through the practice of giving depends upon many factors. One important factor is the recipient to whom we make the gift. Amongst all the objects of giving it is most meritorious to give to Buddhas. Other especially powerful objects of giving are our Spiritual Guides, our parents, and those who are in great need.

If we have few possessions to give we can still practise this kind of giving. For example, we can give small portions of food to insects, birds, and fish, or we can offer fresh water to the Buddhas. If we give large or expensive gifts it does not follow that our merit is greater than if we give small ones, because the strength of our virtuous motivation is another important factor in determining the merit of our actions of giving. For example, if we give just one crumb to an insect with pure compassion, this is more meritorious than giving a diamond to someone whilst taking pride in the great rarity of our gift. Again, our actions of giving are less powerful if they are attended by a feeling of loss or if we later regret our generosity. Such regret deprives our virtuous action of all its power.

Some actions of so-called giving are completely without merit, and some are even non-virtuous, as in the case of giving with a bad motivation. Actions of this kind are not really actions of giving because giving is necessarily motivated by a virtuous state of mind. When large and powerful nations supply smaller nations with arms or with material aid they do so out of arrogance or greed, wishing to dominate and control the smaller country or to improve their international reputation. These are not real actions of giving. When we give, our mind should be free from strong delusions such as pride, and we should have a beneficial intention. The best motivation is bodhichitta. With bodhichitta, if we give even the tiniest morsel to an insect, this is the perfection of giving.

When we are very familiar with giving away our possessions we can practise giving away our body. In *Compendium of Trainings* Shantideva explains four ways of giving away our body:

(1) Giving
(2) Keeping
(3) Purifying
(4) Increasing

GIVING

To practise giving away our body all the appropriate conditions must be assembled. For all the conditions to be right there must be no obstacles, and we must have developed the ability to give away our body with a motivation of pure compassion. It must also be certain that the person for whose sake we are giving our body will receive great benefit from our action.

KEEPING

This way of giving our body is by keeping and protecting it when the conditions are not right for giving it away. If we cannot give our body with perfect compassion, if there are obstacles, or if the recipient will not greatly benefit from our action, we must on no account give our body away. When the time is not right to give our body we must protect it because by doing so we shall bring much greater benefit to others. Since we can attain enlightenment with this body we should do whatever we can to protect it whenever it is in danger. If Bodhisattvas protect their bodies in this way it is not because they have strong self-cherishing but because they cherish others so much that they want to use their own body in the best way for the benefit of all. Shantideva said that if we lack pure compassion we should not give away our body because we shall not benefit ourself or others by such an action. Therefore, until the time is right to give it away we should practise the generosity of keeping it.

PURIFYING

This way of practising giving is by using our body, while we are keeping and protecting it, to engage only in virtuous actions and to refrain from non-virtuous actions. We purify our body by disengaging it from any negativity.

INCREASING

This way of practising giving is by using our body, while we are keeping and protecting it, to increase the causes to attain a human rebirth with the eight special attributes. We should not give up our body until we have accumulated many causes to attain such a good human rebirth in the future.

These four ways of giving are also to be applied with respect to the practice of giving away our possessions. We should give away our possessions only when the time is right, that is, when it would not cause any hindrances to our spiritual practice or endanger our life, and when the person to whom we are giving will derive some significant benefit from it. Otherwise we should not give away our possessions even if someone asks for them. For example, if we can see that a gift will cause harm to others we should not offer it. We need to consider all the implications of our action, including how it will affect others besides the person who is to receive the gift. We also need to keep those things that are necessary for our Dharma practice. If we were to give these away we would be indirectly harming others because we would be creating obstacles to our progress towards enlightenment for their sake. An example of such misguided giving would be for us to give away our Dharma books to someone who has no real interest in them. It would also be inappropriate to give money to someone who is wealthier than we are and who has no need for our gift. We should either keep our possessions until we find someone who really needs them, or we should offer them to Buddha or the Sangha.

It is impossible to tell whether or not someone is practising giving by the number of their possessions. We can consider the example of Marpa. Through collecting and keeping many things, which he eventually sold for gold, he accumulated a lot of wealth. With this he travelled to India and received instructions from many Spiritual Guides. When he had used up all his wealth he returned to Tibet as a poor man bearing many Dharma texts. Then he repeated the whole process several times. Marpa's real purpose in accumulating wealth was to benefit others, for he knew the Tibetans were in great need of Dharma. While people watched him labouring in the fields Marpa was practising the generosity of keeping. Afterwards he practised giving. He eventually gave everything for the sake of Buddhadharma. If he had never practised keeping but had always given away everything he owned he would never have been able to bring so much benefit to so many people. Marpa's practice of keeping his possessions is benefiting living beings even now.

There may be some things that are appropriate to give away at any time because giving them away could never hinder our spiritual practice or bring harm to others. Just as a successful businessman uses his resources in the most suitable way to gain the maximum profit, so we should practise giving in the way that brings the greatest spiritual advantage to ourself and others.

With respect to giving our possessions, the practices of purifying and increasing are to avoid using our possessions as a means of committing non-virtuous actions and to use them only to do good. We must use our wealth and resources to create the causes for increased resources in future lives and to bring benefit to others.

GIVING DHARMA

There are many ways to give Dharma. If with a good motivation we teach even just one word of Dharma to others we are giving Dharma. Whenever we whisper mantras into the ears of animals or dedicate our virtue so that all living beings may enjoy peace and happiness we are giving Dharma. If with a good motivation we offer even just one verse of pure Dharma teachings to someone else, this is much more beneficial than any kind of material gift, because material gifts help others only in this life whereas the gift of Dharma helps them in this and all their future lives.

GIVING FEARLESSNESS

To give fearlessness is to protect other living beings from fear or danger. For example, if we rescue someone from a fire or from some other natural disaster, if we protect others from physical violence, or if we save animals and insects who have fallen into water or who are trapped, we are practising giving fearlessness. If we are not able to rescue those in danger we can still give fearlessness by making prayers and offerings so that they may be released from danger. We can also practise giving fearlessness by praying for others to become free from their delusions, especially the delusion of self-grasping, which is the ultimate source of all fear.

THE PERFECTION OF MORAL DISCIPLINE

Moral discipline is a virtuous mental determination to abandon any fault, or it is a bodily or verbal action motivated by such a determination. Moral discipline practised with bodhichitta motivation is a perfection of moral discipline. There are three types of moral discipline:

(1) The moral discipline of restraint
(2) The moral discipline of gathering virtuous Dharmas
(3) The moral discipline of benefiting living beings

THE MORAL DISCIPLINE OF RESTRAINT

This is the moral discipline of abstaining from non-virtue. To practise this moral discipline we need to understand the dangers of committing negative actions, make a promise or vow to abandon them, and then keep that promise or vow. Thus we cannot be said to be practising the moral discipline of restraint if we unknowingly avoid committing negative actions, since even babies can do this.

Any spiritual discipline that avoids or overcomes either mental faults or negative actions of body or speech is included within the moral discipline of restraint. For example, if we understand the dangers of the ten non-virtuous actions, promise to refrain from them, and keep that promise, we are practising the moral discipline of restraint.

It is not necessary to take vows in front of our Spiritual Guide or in front of the visualized Field for Accumulating Merit. We can take them by ourself by recognizing the faults of the actions we want to abandon and promising to refrain from them for whatever length of time we can. When we make a promise or take a vow we should be skilful in determining for how long we undertake to observe it. Even if we promise to refrain from just one negative action for only a short time, for example if we promise to abandon only killing for just one week, and we keep that promise, we are practising the moral discipline of restraint. However, as our capacity increases we should gradually extend the duration of our restraint, and also promise to abandon other non-virtuous actions.

When we take the Bodhisattva vows we must have the intention to keep them continuously until we are enlightened. If we are to fulfil our wish to attain enlightenment quickly for the sake of others, we need to overcome our faults as soon as we can. For a Bodhisattva the main object to be abandoned is the intention to work solely for one's own sake. Bodhisattvas see clearly the dangers of self-cherishing and they realize that it is the principal obstacle to developing bodhichitta and to attaining enlightenment. In the *Condensed*

Perfection of Wisdom Sutra Buddha says that the moral discipline of a Bodhisattva does not degenerate if he or she enjoys beautiful forms, sounds, tastes, or other objects of the senses, but if a Bodhisattva develops concern for his own welfare, both his moral discipline and his bodhichitta degenerate. If we generate bodhichitta and later think that it would be better to seek only our own liberation, we incur a root Bodhisattva downfall and break our moral discipline of restraint.

With the motivation of bodhichitta no action can be non-virtuous because bodhichitta eliminates self-cherishing, which is the root of all non-virtuous actions. Even if a Bodhisattva has to kill, this action is not non-virtuous because it is performed solely for the benefit of all living beings. Although others may condemn them, Bodhisattvas incur no negative karma when they perform such actions because their bodhichitta ensures that all their actions are pure.

THE MORAL DISCIPLINE OF GATHERING VIRTUOUS DHARMAS

The moral discipline of gathering virtuous Dharmas includes practices such as the moral discipline of sincerely engaging in the practice of the six perfections and the moral discipline of engaging in the ten Dharma activities. These are: writing Dharma books, reading Dharma books, memorizing words of Dharma, reciting words of Dharma, making offerings to Dharma, giving Dharma books, explaining the meaning of Dharma, listening to Dharma, contemplating the meaning of Dharma, and meditating on the meaning of Dharma. Even if we do not understand what we hear or read, our actions of listening to and reading Dharma are never a waste of time because they create good potentialities within our mind.

THE MORAL DISCIPLINE OF BENEFITING LIVING BEINGS

This is the moral discipline of helping others in whatever way we can. If we cannot offer practical help to someone, we can at least make prayers for them and maintain a continuous intention to give assistance when an opportunity arises.

Arya Asanga explained that there are eleven main ways of helping others:

(1) Alleviating the suffering of others and offering them assistance in their work.

(2) Teaching others skills when they do not know how to accomplish tasks. We can help others by teaching worldly skills such as how to read and write and by teaching spiritual skills such as how to meditate.

(3) Returning the kindness we have received. If we cannot actually do anything we can at least remember the kindness we have received and pay due respect.

(4) Removing dangers that threaten others, and eliminating whatever causes them fear. If we cannot do anything practical we can at least make prayers for them.

(5) Consoling others when they are in grief. For example, when others are separated from their family, they lose their job, or their hopes are not fulfilled, we can try to remove their unhappiness and offer them sound advice.

(6) Giving material assistance to those who are destitute.

(7) Helping those who experience problems that come when they have strong delusions such as anger or desirous attachment.

(8) Helping others in a way that is appropriate to their own views and customs. When we help others we should be tactful and sensitive. We should try to understand the other person's experience and point of view, and then offer help that is relevant to them, and in such a way that they can accept it. We cannot help others if we attack their values and beliefs, or if we ignore their temperament and their personal circumstances. We have to adapt our own behaviour so that it suits the other person and makes them feel at ease. We need both flexibility of mind and flexibility of behaviour. For example, even if we do not drink, it may at times be helpful to others if we go to a pub with them and talk to them there.

Since Bodhisattvas have great compassion they do whatever is necessary to help others. In effect, Bodhisattvas will do whatever needs to be done to make someone else happy because when others are happy their minds are more open and receptive to advice and example. If we wish to influence others we can do so only if we do not antagonize them or make them feel uncomfortable or frightened. Just as a mother will play with her child to keep it happy even when she herself has no interest in the game, so Bodhisattvas will go along with others to keep them happy and to provide the opportunity to help them whenever they can.

A woman who had recently given birth to a baby girl was frightened that she would lose her baby because she had already given birth to one child who had died in infancy. The woman expressed her anxiety to her mother, who told her that children given into the care of Geshe Langri Tangpa would not die. Later, when the little girl fell ill, the woman took her to see Geshe Langri Tangpa, but when she arrived she found him sitting on a throne giving a discourse to a thousand disciples. The woman began to worry that her child would die before the end of the discourse. She knew that Geshe Langri Tangpa was a Bodhisattva and would show patience, and so she walked up to the throne and in a loud, affronted tone of voice declared 'Here, take your baby. Now you look after her!' She turned to the audience and said 'This is the father of my child', and then turned back to Geshe Langri Tangpa and pleaded softly 'Please don't let her die.' Geshe Langri Tangpa just nodded his head in acceptance. As if he really were the father of the child, he wrapped it tenderly in his robes and continued his discourse. His disciples were astonished and asked him 'Are you really the father of that child?' Knowing that if he were to deny it, the woman would have been thought crazy and the people would have ridiculed her, Geshe Langri Tangpa replied that he was.

Although he was a monk, Geshe Langri Tangpa acted like a real father for the child, delighting in her and caring for her. After some time the mother returned to see if her daughter was well. When she saw how healthy the child was she asked Geshe Langri Tangpa if she could have her back again. The Geshe then kindly returned the girl to her mother. When his disciples realized what had happened they said 'So you are not really the father after all!' and Geshe Langri Tangpa replied 'No, I am not.' In this way Geshe Langri Tangpa responded to the woman's actions with pure compassion, and acted in accordance with the needs of the time.

(9) Benefiting those who have entered correct spiritual paths by praising and encouraging them, paying due respect, and helping them to continue their practice in whatever way we can.

(10) Benefiting those who have entered wrong paths by helping them to see their error and by helping them to enter correct spiritual paths. We need to talk to people who hold mistaken views and try to help them gradually change their views into correct ones.

(11) Helping others by using whatever miracle powers we possess. By using his miracle powers Maudgalyanaputra helped Nanda to overcome his desirous attachment. One day Maudgalyanaputra invited Nanda for a walk in the forest, and as they were walking Maudgalyanaputra magically emanated a hell realm and led Nanda through it. Nanda was so terrified that all his desirous attachment was eliminated and he was able to practise Dharma purely and develop renunciation. If we have such powers we must use them to help those who are engaging in negative actions to abandon them and to develop faith.

THE PERFECTION OF PATIENCE

Patience is a virtuous mind that is able to bear any kind of suffering or harm. Patience practised with bodhichitta motivation is a perfection of patience. With patience we can accept any pain that is inflicted upon us and we can easily endure our usual troubles and indispositions. With patience nothing upsets our peace of mind and we do not experience problems. We need to cultivate patience even if we have no interest in spiritual development because without it we remain vulnerable to anxiety, frustration, and disquiet. If we lack patience it is difficult for us to maintain peaceful relationships with others.

Patience is the opponent to anger, the most potent destroyer of virtue. We can see from our own experience how much suffering arises from anger. It prevents us from judging a situation correctly, and it causes us to act in regrettable ways. It destroys our own peace of mind, and it disturbs everyone else we meet. Even people who are normally attracted to us are repelled when they see us angry. Anger can make us reject or insult our own parents, and when it is intense it can even drive us to kill the people we love, or even to take our own life. Although we usually find it unbearable to receive any wound, our anger hurts us much more than any physical injury.

If we were asked 'Who caused all the wars in which so many people have died?', we would have to reply that they were caused by angry minds. If nations were full of calm, peace-loving people, how could wars ever arise? Anger is the greatest enemy of living beings. It harmed us in the past, it harms us now, and, if we do not overcome it through the practice of patience, it will continue to harm us in the future. It has been causing pain and distress since beginningless time. If we do not overcome this inner enemy it will defeat us over and over again. As Shantideva said:

This enemy of anger has no function
Other than to cause me harm.

External enemies harm us in slower and less subtle ways, and if we practise patience with them we can even win them over and turn them into our friends; but there can be no reconciliation with anger. If we try to treat it gently its fury grows worse. It takes advantage of our lenience to hurt us even more. There is no external enemy who can be so vicious as our own anger because other people can harm us only in this life whereas our anger harms us for many future lives.

Therefore, we need to eliminate anger as soon as we become aware that it has entered our mind. Since anger is like a blazing fire that quickly consumes our virtuous potentialities, as soon as the match of anger is struck we must quickly extinguish it with patience.

Patience, on the other hand, helps us in this life and in all future lives. Chandrakirti said that if we practise patience we shall have a beautiful form in the future and we shall become a holy being with high realizations. There are three types of patience:

(1) The patience of not retaliating
(2) The patience of voluntarily enduring suffering
(3) The patience of definitely thinking about Dharma

THE PATIENCE OF NOT RETALIATING

To practise this type of patience we need to remain continuously mindful of the dangers of anger and the benefits of patient acceptance, and whenever anger is about to arise in our mind we need immediately to apply the methods for eliminating it. If we want to control our anger in all situations it is not enough just to remember its faults and the benefits of patient acceptance. We also need to have experience of putting into effect the methods we have learnt for eliminating our anger.

There was once a teacher who had a very bad-tempered assistant. This teacher taught his assistant how to meditate on patience. While he was in meditation the assistant would see clearly the dangers of anger and the great importance of practising patience, but when he was out of meditation he would completely forget about patience. His teacher advised him to put a huge sign saying PATIENCE on his door, and this usually helped the assistant to maintain his mindfulness when he was out of meditation. However, one day a thief came into the assistant's room and stole some of his possessions. When the assistant caught the thief he lost his temper and began to thrash him vigorously. The teacher saw this and told him 'Don't beat him like that!', but the assistant was so engrossed in his revenge that he could not hear his teacher's words. The teacher ran inside, fetched the sign saying PATIENCE, and thrust it right in front of his assistant's face. When the disciple saw the sign he immediately remembered all the instructions on patience and he released the thief. When we are out of meditation we can benefit by using methods such as this because our mind changes easily, like a candle flame flickering in the breeze.

When we are meditating on patience we can use many different lines of reasoning. For example, in *Guide to the Bodhisattva's Way of Life* Shantideva says that if someone hits us with a stick we do not get angry with the stick, because the stick is being wielded by the hands of our attacker and has no freedom; and we do not get angry with the hands, because they are not in control of their own movements. In the same way, we should feel no anger towards the person who is attacking us because he also has no choice. He is driven by anger and is not in charge of his own actions. If we are going to get angry with anything, we should get angry with anger itself.

If we are about to get angry with someone who has spoken to us harshly, or criticized or mocked us, we should ask ourself:

Why am I getting angry? These words cannot hurt my body and they cannot hurt my mind, but the anger I am generating does harm my mind. In themselves the words are merely empty and cannot affect me. If someone calls me an ass I am not thereby transformed into an ass!

If someone tries to harm us physically or tries to interfere with our life we should try to solve such problems skilfully, without anger. If we fail to overcome our problems we should not get angry, but think:

I myself created the cause to receive this harm and so I am the one who is really responsible for the suffering that I am now experiencing. Even now I am partly at fault because I am the object of this person's anger. Just as without fuel there could be no fire, so without me there would be no anger in

462

this person's mind. Therefore I have no reason to get angry or to blame the other person for this situation.

If someone who is mentally ill speaks harshly to his doctor, the doctor does not lose his temper because he understands that the patient is not in control of his mind. Instead he develops compassion and seeks a cure for his patient's illness. In the same way, if a child becomes mentally unbalanced, its mother does not feel angry. No matter how violent or difficult the child becomes, its mother always sees it as the fault of the child's illness and thinks 'How wonderful it would be if my child were to become well again.' Whenever someone becomes angry they fall completely under the control of delusion and so they are temporarily insane. There is no reason for us to respond by becoming insane ourself.

We can meditate:

If I put my hand into a fire and get burnt I do not lose my temper with the fire because I know that it is the nature of fire to burn. Similarly, if someone who is angry inflicts harm upon me I should not get angry because it is the nature of anger to inflict harm; it is not that person's fault. The anger is only temporary. It will not last for very long.

When snow falls we do not get angry with the sky. We think 'It is winter and so it is snowing.' When it rains it would be foolish to hurl abuse at the clouds, because when the clouds are black and heavy with moisture it is natural for them to shed rain. Similarly, it is natural for an angry person to issue blows and abuse. Why should we be angry with people and not with the clouds or the sky in winter?

We grasp at our world and our problems as if they were fixed, solid, and permanent. Since we conceive of them in this way we often become upset and angry; but all our anger comes from our own mistaken conceptions.

By meditating on these lines of thought over and over again we shall develop a special wisdom. If we then combine our wisdom with mindfulness, never forgetting what we have understood, we shall find it easy to be patient.

THE PATIENCE OF VOLUNTARILY ENDURING SUFFERING

If we do not have the patience of voluntarily enduring suffering we become discouraged whenever we encounter obstacles and whenever our wishes go unfulfilled. We find it hard to complete our tasks because we feel like abandoning them as soon as they become difficult, and our miseries are further aggravated by our impatience. However, it is possible to accept and endure pain if we have a good reason to do so, and whenever we practise such patience we actually reduce our sufferings. For example, if someone were to stick a sharp needle into our flesh we would find the pain unbearable, but if the needle contained a vaccine that we needed, our tolerance would increase considerably.

If we are able to endure adversities we shall reap great rewards. Our present sufferings will diminish, and we shall accomplish both our temporary and our ultimate wishes. By voluntarily enduring suffering businessmen gain worldly success and spiritual practitioners are able to complete all that needs to be done to attain enlightenment.

If two people are suffering in hospital and one of them practises voluntary endurance but the other does not, their experiences will be very different even if their bodies are afflicted with the same disease. The one who practises patient endurance will not feel upset, lonely, or irritated. His or her mind will remain peaceful and at ease, but the other person will experience frustration and discomfort, and may even experience unbearable torment. There are some people in hospital with severe illnesses who are able to smile. If we ask them how they are, they will say that they are well.

All the sufferings of sickness, old age, and death, and all the other sufferings of our life are to be endured. How? We should meditate in this way:

Although my circumstances are not what I really want, there is no point in feeling frustrated. The situation I find myself in is one that I have created myself through my past actions. I experience this situation as unsatisfactory, but it comes as a result of samsaric rebirth. If I were not subject to uncontrolled rebirth I would not find myself in difficult and unpleasant situations such as this. My own condition is not such a great disaster because every living being inhabits a place where sufferings are to be endured, and most of them experience much worse difficulties than the ones I experience. Therefore, instead of getting tense and frustrated I must use these experiences of pain and dissatisfaction to generate renunciation and compassion.

If we realize that every living being is trapped in a situation that is painful and unsatisfactory, instead of feeling self-pity we shall develop compassion, thinking 'How wonderful it would be if all living beings were free from suffering.' To transform our experiences of pain and frustration into the attitudes of renunciation and compassion is the essence of patiently enduring suffering. With such a practice we remain happy in the very midst of circumstances that others would regard as big problems and great miseries. Renunciation and compassion are virtuous minds that bring only peace and happiness.

When we confront problems, instead of becoming discouraged we need to put more effort into making good use of the situation. Then we shall quickly gain results. If soldiers were to lose heart and run for their lives as soon as they heard the sound of the first attack, they would never win any battles. In the same way, if we are easily discouraged or depressed we shall never succeed in our spiritual practice; but if we persevere and gather strength and courage from our adversities we shall easily accomplish our aims.

If we lack material resources we can meditate:

For the time being I can put up with these discomforts because I know that my conditions will improve if I practise Dharma sincerely. By patiently accepting bad conditions now, I shall be creating the cause for better conditions in the future. The long-term advantage is better than the short-term advantage. If I had all material comforts now, I would lack this opportunity to practise patience and create the cause for good things in the future. What is more, if I were to gain all the comforts I desire they would only bring me further problems.

They cannot bring me any ultimate benefit because their nature is deceptive.

There is no guarantee that material wealth will bring greater happiness. It often brings great misery. There was once a man who found a large quantity of gold. He was so thrilled that he went to show it to Buddha, but Buddha spoke just two lines to him: 'Your wealth is like poison. To you it is deadly poison.' To the man these words seemed incomprehensible and he concluded that Buddha must be jealous of his fortune. What he did not know was that the gold had been stolen by thieves from a government official and that the official was still looking for it. All the people who were with Buddha at that time caught sight of the gold, and the word quickly spread that this man who a few days before had been poor was now suddenly very wealthy. When the official heard this he accused the man of theft, and everyone believed the accusation to be just. The man was thrown into prison and sentenced to death. As he waited to die he remembered the words of Buddha and realized their meaning.

At present, if everyone were offered the choice of a thousand pounds or enlightenment, most people would choose a thousand pounds. It is important to overcome attachment to possessions and discouragement at our lack of material things because these states of mind are great obstacles to our spiritual practice.

In some texts it is said that there are six kinds of situation in which we need to practise the patience of voluntarily enduring suffering:

(1) When we hear unpleasant words such as words of criticism or words spoken unkindly
(2) When we are meditating or listening to Dharma instructions
(3) When we are engaged in virtuous actions such as prostrations
(4) When we lack material resources
(5) When we experience mental or physical suffering
(6) When our wishes are not fulfilled

THE PATIENCE OF DEFINITELY THINKING ABOUT DHARMA

If we listen to, contemplate, or meditate on Dharma with a patient and joyful mind so as to gain a special experience of it, we are practising the patience of definitely thinking about Dharma. Such patience is important because if our mind is impatient or unhappy when we are engaging in Dharma practice, this will prevent us from improving our Dharma wisdom. When we listen to, contemplate, and meditate on Dharma, even if the meaning is difficult to understand we still need to apply ourself to it happily. There are three types of patience of definitely thinking about Dharma, which correspond to the three types of being: small being, middle being, and great being.

THE PERFECTION OF EFFORT

Effort is a mind that delights in virtue. Effort practised with bodhichitta motivation is a perfection of effort. Applying ourself energetically to non-virtuous or neutral actions, however, is not a practice of effort.

In *Ornament for Mahayana Sutras* Maitreya says that effort is supreme amongst virtues because with effort we can attain all good qualities. With effort we can gain all temporary worldly happiness, the bliss of suppleness, and all mundane and supramundane attainments. We can purify all our negativities of body, speech, and mind, and we can eliminate our obstructions and attain the ultimate happiness of liberation and full enlightenment. In the *Condensed Perfection of Wisdom Sutra* Buddha says that with effort we can attain all the good qualities we wish for. Without effort, even if we possess wisdom we shall be unable to complete our spiritual practices. Therefore, in *Guide to the Middle Way* Chandrakirti says that all good qualities follow upon effort.

To generate effort we need to overcome laziness, which is its main opponent. There are three types of laziness:

(1) The laziness of procrastination
(2) The laziness of attraction to what is meaningless or non-virtuous
(3) The laziness of discouragement

THE LAZINESS OF PROCRASTINATION

This laziness is a reluctance or unwillingness to put effort into our spiritual practice right now. For example, if we are interested in Dharma, believe it to be worthwhile, and intend to practise it, but we think that the time to practise is some time in the future, we are suffering from the laziness of procrastination. This attitude is very harmful because time passes quickly, our opportunities are soon lost, and the duration of our life is uncertain.

It is dangerous to think that we shall practise when we have finished our present job because there are always other jobs to be done. Gungtang Rinpoche said that worldly activities are like an old man's beard – though he may shave it off in the morning, it has grown again by the evening. Since worldly work is endless we need to practise Dharma while we are engaged in all our daily tasks.

Meditations on this precious human life, and on death and impermanence, are powerful methods for overcoming the laziness of procrastination, because these meditations make us come to a firm decision to practise pure Dharma right now.

THE LAZINESS OF ATTRACTION TO WHAT IS MEANINGLESS
OR NON-VIRTUOUS

Most of us are very familiar with this type of laziness. We give in to it whenever we watch television for hours on end without caring what comes on, when we indulge in prolonged conversations with no purpose, or when we become engrossed in sports or business ventures for their own sake. Activities such as these dissipate the energy we have for practising Dharma. When we are immersed in them it seems that our spiritual practice is an obstacle to our pleasures and addictions. If we do not overcome this laziness we can gradually become so involved in meaningless activities that we give up our Dharma practice completely. Therefore we need to meditate again and again on the dangers of samsara, remembering that all the entertainments of worldly life are deceptive because in reality they serve only to bind us within samsara and cause us even more suffering.

Worldly enjoyments are like a flame and we are like moths. When a moth sees a flame it becomes so attracted, so fascinated, that it draws closer and closer, playing with it until it is killed. The moth sees the flame as a wonderful place to be. In fact, it is a place of destruction. In a similar way we become fascinated by worldly pursuits and enjoyments and want to become more and more closely involved with them, but they are strong claws that hold us within the Wheel of Life and condemn us to suffer. If we are to generate effort that overcomes the laziness of attraction to what is meaningless or non-virtuous we need to remember again and again how such activities waste our precious human life and destroy its essence.

THE LAZINESS OF DISCOURAGEMENT

In these degenerate times there are many things that can make us feel discouraged with our spiritual practice. Since we cannot see with our own eyes living examples of enlightened beings, and since our spiritual progress is often much slower than we expect it to be, we may begin to doubt whether Buddhahood is possible, or we may conclude that it must be so rare that there is almost no hope of attaining it. We may also see faults in our Spiritual Guide and in those who are practising Dharma, and conclude that they have no realizations and that effort put into Dharma practice is wasted. If we find we are becoming discouraged in this way, we need to remember that every appearance to the minds of ordinary beings is mistaken because it is contaminated by ignorance. What appears to our mind does not actually exist in the way it appears. Appearances to our mind are like hallucinations – they are not true. We believe that what appears to our mind is true because we assume that our mind is unmistaken. We think that enlightened beings do not exist because the only beings who appear to our mind are imperfect. However, if we understand what causes the hallucinations of ordinary appearance we shall not cling so strongly to the view that what does not appear to our mind, such as Buddhas and realized beings, does not exist. If we abandon this view there will be no basis for becoming discouraged in our spiritual practice.

There are two causes of hallucinations, external and internal. External causes are numerous. For example, our face in front of a mirror is an external cause of hallucination because when we look into the mirror there seems to be a real face there. If we shout 'Hello' in a rocky canyon, this is an external cause of hallucination because the echo appears to be the voice of someone else responding to our greeting. Taking a drug called 'dhatura' is an external cause of hallucination because it makes the whole ground appear to be golden. These types of hallucination help us to understand how things that do not exist can appear to our mind.

The internal cause of hallucination is self-grasping ignorance. This ignorance makes all phenomena appear to be truly existent when in fact they are not. As long as we have strong self-grasping we do not perceive things the way they are. Therefore, we need to consider 'If I cannot see living examples of enlightened beings right now, that does not prove anything because I cannot expect to see Buddhas until I have purified my mind.' For example, if the surface of a pond is covered with scum it cannot reflect the moon even when the moon is full and shining straight above it, but as soon as the scum is removed the moon's reflection is bright and clear. In a similar way, although Buddhas are everywhere – directly in front of us, at our crown, and at our heart – we are prevented from seeing them by the obstructions within our mind.

To understand this further we can meditate on the view of the Chittamatra system, according to which no objects exist external to the mind and all objects that appear to the mind are the nature of the mind itself. According to this view, appearances to the minds of ordinary beings are not reliable, certain, or true, because external objects appear to their minds and such objects do not exist. Gaining an experience of the Chittamatrin view is the best way to approach an understanding of the supreme view held by the Madhyamika-Prasangika system, according to which all objects lack inherent existence. In the third chapter of *Commentary to Valid*

Cognition Dharmakirti explains the Chittamatrin view and in the sixth chapter of *Guide to the Middle Way* Chandrakirti explains the Madhyamika view. Je Tsongkhapa said that we need to realize the view that unites both.

It is helpful to consider what happens to our mind when we fall asleep. While we are awake we perceive and remember many things, but when we fall asleep these appearances cease, and when we reawaken everything that appears to our mind is new. If we understand subtle impermanence – the momentary disintegration of things – we shall understand that what appeared to our mind yesterday has ceased to exist and that what appears to our mind right now is completely new. In the same way, when we die the appearances of this life cease, and when we take rebirth the appearances of our next life are entirely new. This indicates that what appears to our mind comes from the mind itself. If all appearances arise from the mind there is no need to become discouraged when we cannot see living examples of enlightened beings because it is certain that when our mind becomes pure we shall perceive pure objects.

With effort we can accomplish everything. We gain experience of Dharma and our problems become fewer. With fewer problems our progress towards enlightenment is easier and we are able to accomplish many deeds, such as the Bodhisattva's giving of his or her own body. We have the seed of enlightenment and we have found perfect methods for attaining enlightenment. Now all we need is to apply effort. It is not necessary to undergo unusual hardships. So what reason is there to become discouraged? There are three types of effort:

(1) Armour-like effort
(2) The effort of gathering virtuous Dharmas
(3) The effort of benefiting others

ARMOUR-LIKE EFFORT

This is the effort we have when we are confident and think 'No matter what difficulties I might face or how long it might take, I will complete my task and attain Buddhahood for the sake of others', or, 'Even if it takes me a very long time to bring just a small amount of benefit to one other living being, I will complete my spiritual task.'

Armour-like effort is so called because it protects us from laziness as armour protects a soldier from his enemy. If we generate this type of effort at the beginning of our practice, deciding to persevere throughout our life, we shall not feel discouraged even if we practise for a long time without perceiving any results.

When we get up in the morning we need to put on this armour-like effort, deciding to persevere throughout the day no matter what difficulties we may have to endure. In the same way, whenever we do retreat we need to begin by putting on this armour-like effort, making a firm decision not to be overwhelmed or depressed by the difficulties we encounter. We must decide to complete our retreat no matter what happens. Armour-like effort must always be present when we are applying other types of effort.

THE EFFORT OF GATHERING VIRTUOUS DHARMAS

This is the effort we have when we put energy into virtuous actions. It is not the same as the moral discipline of gathering virtuous Dharmas. The moral discipline of gathering virtuous Dharmas is principally the wish or intention to engage in virtue, whereas the effort of gathering virtuous Dharmas is the actual exertion of effort towards any virtue.

THE EFFORT OF BENEFITING OTHERS

This is the effort we have whenever we act to benefit others. Again, it is not the same as the moral discipline of benefiting others. The moral discipline of benefiting others is principally the wish or intention to benefit others, whereas the effort of benefiting others is the actual exertion of effort towards that end.

There are four methods for increasing our effort, known as the 'four powers':

(1) The power of aspiration
(2) The power of steadfastness
(3) The power of joy
(4) The power of relaxation

THE POWER OF ASPIRATION

The power of aspiration is the wish to engage in virtue. If we are to exert effort in any virtuous practice we need to begin by having the aspiration to accomplish its aim. Strong aspiration induces strong effort. For example, if we want to develop strong effort in our practice of bodhichitta we need to have a strong wish to gain the realization of bodhichitta, and if we want to realize emptiness we need to have the wish 'How wonderful it would be if I were to realize the correct view of emptiness.' We generate the aspiration to engage in virtuous actions by contemplating their benefits and the dangers of non-virtuous actions. Aspiration is said to be a power because it makes our effort powerful.

THE POWER OF STEADFASTNESS

Once we have generated effort we need to maintain it continuously. It is not hard to generate effort for just a few days, or even for a few weeks or months, but if we are to accomplish our goal our effort needs to be constant. Some people at first develop great enthusiasm for Dharma practice and for a time they think of nothing else, even neglecting to eat. They exert tremendous effort for a short time and while they are doing so they have great hopes and expectations, thinking 'I can realize emptiness soon', or 'I am going to become very learned and famous for my knowledge of Buddhist philosophy', or 'I am going to become a Buddha shortly.' However if we overexert ourself and develop overenthusiastic ideas about our progress we shall exhaust ourself and, having failed to attain great results, we shall become discouraged and may even decide to abandon our practice. This kind of effort is foolish and damaging because it leads to a reaction that is worse than having no effort at all. It makes us inert and depressed. With such a frame of mind we develop aversion for spiritual practice. The lethargy that comes from overexertion can be as powerful or even more powerful than our initial zeal. Therefore we need to be very skilful and apply effort that is firm, stable, and continuous. It is far better to apply a small amount of effort consistently than to apply a huge amount of effort for only a few days. It is said that our effort should be like water in a wide river, gently flowing day and night, year after year. Foolish effort is like a waterfall caused by a sudden storm. It cascades noisily and releases tremendous energy for a while, and then it trickles away to nothing.

As long as our effort is consistent there is no doubt that we shall attain results. It is said that with stable, indestructible effort all good qualities and realizations will increase day by day. Je Tsongkhapa said that with such effort we shall complete our spiritual practice.

THE POWER OF JOY

When we put effort into our Dharma practice we need to have a calm and joyful mind. This joy is said to be a power because it enables us to accomplish our spiritual tasks quickly and easily. It makes our effort strong and courageous. If we are anxious or depressed our effort will be blocked and frustrated. If others see us miserable while we are practising Dharma they will not believe that Dharma brings peace and happiness. When we practise Dharma we should be like a child at play. When children are engrossed in their games they feel completely contented and nothing can distract them. Even if they are offered sweets they have no interest because the pleasure of their game is so great.

Sometimes, when our mind is overexcited, we need to calm it down by doing meditations such as the meditations on death and impermanence or the meditations on true sufferings. At other times, when we are feeling sad or depressed, we need to encourage ourself by meditating on our precious human life.

THE POWER OF RELAXATION

It is very important not to become overtired through exerting too much effort. If we relax at the right time we shall soon be able to apply new effort again. Timely relaxation maintains the constancy of our practice. If we neglect the need for rest we become overtired and we are not able to apply effort again with joy. Relaxation is said to be a power because it protects and supports our effort.

We all know that when effort is applied even to tasks that have no spiritual benefit, unheard of things can be accomplished. For example, human beings have landed on the moon even though this was once thought impossible. If such a thing can be done with ordinary worldly motivations there is no doubt that with effort we can accomplish all spiritual tasks and attain enlightenment, because enlightenment is not unheard of but has been attained countless times.

Asanga once went into retreat to gain a vision of Maitreya. After three years he was still unsuccessful and so he became discouraged and decided to abandon his retreat. As he was walking down the road from his cave he came across a man who was repeatedly stroking a huge iron block with a feather. Asanga asked him what he was doing, and the man said that he was cutting the iron block in two. Asanga said 'How can you expect to cut through a block of iron with a feather?' The man replied 'Of course I can! Look! I have already made a mark. I am bound to do it as long as I keep applying effort.' Asanga then thought to himself, 'If this man can apply such consistent effort to a task like that, surely I can persevere in my retreat to attain a much more meaningful goal.' Then he returned to his cave and eventually attained a vision of Maitreya.

By meditating on these points we shall become determined to generate effort that is strong, steadfast, and joyous.

THE PERFECTION OF MENTAL STABILIZATION

Mental stabilization, or concentration, is a mind whose nature is to be single-pointedly placed on a virtuous object and whose function is to prevent distraction. Mental stabilization practised with bodhichitta motivation is a perfection of mental stabilization.

For ordinary beings, concentration functions mainly by means of mental awareness. Our sense awarenesses can behold and remain single-pointedly on their objects, but these are not concentrations. For example, when our eye awareness stares single-pointedly at a candle flame we are not practising concentration. For us, the main object of concentration is the generic image of an object, and this generic image is grasped by our mental awareness.

There are many different types of concentration. There are two types of concentration from the point of view of their nature, mundane and supramundane. Mundane concentrations are motivated merely by mundane wishes such as the wish to attain clairvoyance and miracle powers, the wish to attain a rebirth in the god realms, or the wish to increase worldly happiness. Supramundane concentrations are motivated either by renunciation or bodhichitta. They are attained only by pure practitioners of Buddhadharma because only Buddhist scriptures contain correct and precise explanations of pervasive suffering, and we need to understand pervasive suffering in order to realize renunciation. If we know that our own appropriated aggregates are the very basis for all our suffering we shall make a strong decision to cut the continuum of our appropriated aggregates. This decision is necessary if we are to attain supramundane concentrations. Everyone knows manifest suffering and wants to be free from it. Some non-Buddhists also know changing suffering. They know that worldly happiness is changeable and has the nature of suffering, and so they meditate to attain a cessation of all pleasant and unpleasant feelings. However only Buddhists realize pervasive suffering.

If we have not yet realized renunciation or bodhichitta but we wish to attain liberation or enlightenment, and we meditate to fulfil this wish, any concentration we attain is said to be in the aspect of supramundane concentration. These concentrations resemble actual supramundane concentrations and they go in the same direction.

Mental stabilizations can also be divided into those of the desire realm, those of the form realm, and those of the formless realm. As our concentrations improve, our mind becomes more and more subtle. The mind of the form realm is more subtle than the mind of the desire realm, and the mind of the formless realm is more subtle than the mind of the form realm.

It is said that human beings who lived in this world during its first aeon could easily attain strong concentration. They did not need to exert great effort to attain the nine mental abidings that lead to tranquil abiding. By contrast, we have to spend a lot of time and effort to attain even the first of the nine mental abidings, and we find it hard to attain the later stages. We have to remain on the second mental abiding for a long time, and we have to remain on the third and fourth mental abidings even longer. The human beings of the first aeon descended from the form realm and so they retained very strong powers of concentration. In time their powers decreased and their minds became more and more gross. Their distractions and conceptual minds became stronger and more numerous, and it became harder and harder for them to attain concentration. At the time of Buddha Shakyamuni thousands of people were able to develop the concentration of tranquil abiding whenever he gave discourses. In these degenerate times it is hard to find anyone with such a powerful mind. Our delusions are becoming stronger and our merit is decreasing, and so it is more difficult to gain spiritual realizations.

Concentrations can also be divided into those that are principally directed towards attaining tranquil abiding, those that are principally directed towards attaining superior seeing, and those that are principally directed towards attaining the union of tranquil abiding and superior seeing. These will be explained in more detail below.

There are three types of concentration from the point of view of their function: those that produce the bliss of mental and physical suppleness; those that help us to realize renunciation, bodhichitta, and the correct view of emptiness; and those that provide us with the means of benefiting others. All concentrations have the first function. Suppleness makes our body light and free from tension, and it helps to eliminate mental disturbances. If we have perfect concentration we shall experience joy continuously and all our meditations will be successful. We shall easily and powerfully eliminate mental hindrances, and we shall quickly apprehend the nature of any object we set ourself to understand. Mental stabilization brings the mind closer and closer to its object until the mind and its object mix. In this way, concentration induces spontaneous realizations of all the stages of the path such as renunciation, bodhichitta, and the correct view of emptiness. If we lack good concentration it takes a long time to accomplish anything. We have to listen to or read the instructions over and over again and spend a lot of time in meditation, and yet we still experience many difficulties. Without the power of concentration our mind is weak, like a candle flame in the wind, and we are unable to muster much strength of mind when we engage in virtuous actions.

If we train in the nine mental abidings and attain tranquil abiding we shall gradually develop clairvoyance and miracle powers, and these will enable us greatly to benefit others. Any concentration that provides us with these means of helping others is called a 'concentration of benefiting others'. If we lack clairvoyance and miracle powers we may sometimes harm others even when we have the wish to benefit them. Atisha said that just as a bird cannot fly without wings, so we cannot benefit others without clairvoyance.

According to the Mahayana tradition, if we are practising Dharma purely we have no reason to develop these powers for our own sake. Our main aim must always be to attain liberation and full enlightenment for the sake of others. If we are to fulfil this aim we definitely have to develop mental stabilization, and, by improving our powers of mental stabilization, clairvoyance and miracle powers will come naturally. If we have the motivation of bodhichitta and we have taken the Bodhisattva vows we should have a strong interest in improving our mental stabilization as a means of fulfilling our wish to help others. If we have taken the Bodhisattva vows but we have no wish to improve our mental stabilization, we are indirectly breaking one of our commitments.

THE PERFECTION OF WISDOM

Wisdom is a virtuous mind that functions mainly to dispel doubt and confusion by understanding its object thoroughly. Wisdom practised with bodhichitta motivation is a perfection of wisdom.

In the *Condensed Perfection of Wisdom Sutra* Buddha says that just as a blind man cannot reach his destination unless he has a guide, the other five perfections cannot, without wisdom, take us to our destination of full enlightenment. In fact it is impossible to perform any virtuous action without wisdom because wisdom distinguishes between what is virtuous and what is non-virtuous, discriminating the benefits of the one and the dangers of the other. Our wish to do what is virtuous arises in dependence upon this wisdom, and this wish in turn gives rise to all the effort we apply in our practice. The more wisdom we have, the stronger our practice will be. Therefore, all good qualities and spiritual realizations come from wisdom. Mental stabilization and wisdom are closely related; greater wisdom brings stronger mental stabilization, and stronger mental stabilization brings greater wisdom.

There are many types of wisdom. Four of the most important are: profound wisdom, clear wisdom, quick wisdom, and great wisdom. Profound wisdom is wisdom that easily understands subtle topics such as subtle impermanence or emptiness. Even if someone has great knowledge and skill and understands many technical subjects, if that person cannot easily understand deeper topics when they are explained, this indicates that they lack profound wisdom. Clear wisdom is wisdom that discerns its object clearly and precisely. If we can understand with ease whatever we attempt to understand, if we have a clear memory and imagination, and if we can distinguish the subtlest topics, this indicates that we possess clear wisdom. With clear wisdom we can clearly recall what has been understood. Clear wisdom brings clear concentration. Quick wisdom is wisdom that quickly understands objects of contemplation without the need for further investigation. Great wisdom is wisdom that easily understands objects of contemplation without the need for explanation. If we can understand what we read in a Dharma book and we have no need for anyone to explain it to us, this indicates that we possess great wisdom. With great wisdom Dharma books can become our Spiritual Guide because we can clear away all our doubts without needing further instructions.

Wisdom can also be divided into wisdom arisen from listening, wisdom arisen from contemplation, and wisdom arisen from meditation. To increase our wisdom arisen from listening we need to listen to correct instructions from fully qualified Spiritual Guides, read authentic Dharma books, and discuss what we have heard. Wisdom arisen from contemplation arises from reflecting again and again upon what we have heard and understood, and wisdom arisen from meditation arises from meditating on what we have heard and contemplated. We need to keep increasing these three wisdoms continuously until we attain enlightenment.

Wisdom can also be divided into wisdom realizing conventional truths and wisdom realizing ultimate truths. These will be explained below.

Since Bodhisattvas wish to become enlightened as quickly as possible, they have a strong wish to accumulate powerful merit quickly; therefore they practise each of the six perfections in conjunction with all the others. For example, when Bodhisattvas practise the perfection of giving they do so in such a way that they are able to practise all the other perfections at the same time. When they practise giving they do so without self-interest, expecting nothing in return. In this way they practise in accordance with their Bodhisattva vows and combine the perfection of giving with the perfection of moral discipline. By patiently accepting any hardships involved, and not allowing anger to arise if no gratitude is shown, they combine the perfection of giving with the perfection of patience. By giving joyfully they combine the perfection of giving with the perfection of effort; and by concentrating their minds, thinking 'May this gift bring real benefit to this person', they combine it with the perfection of mental stabilization. Finally, by realizing that the giver, the gift, and the action of giving all lack inherent existence, they combine the perfection of giving with the perfection of wisdom.

The other perfections can also be practised in this way, with each perfection being practised in conjunction with all the others. This is the armour-like skilful action of a Bodhisattva that hastens the completion of the two collections – the collection of merit and the collection of wisdom.

Training the Mind in Tranquil Abiding

This section has two parts:

1 How to train the mind in tranquil abiding, the
   essence of concentration
2 How to train the mind in superior seeing, the
   essence of wisdom

HOW TO TRAIN THE MIND IN TRANQUIL ABIDING, THE ESSENCE OF CONCENTRATION

The Tibetan term for tranquil abiding is 'zhi nä', in which 'zhi' means tranquil or pacified and 'nä' means abiding or remaining. Tranquil abiding, therefore, is a mind that has pacified distractions and that remains single-pointedly on one object. The definition of tranquil abiding is a concentration that possesses the special bliss of physical and mental suppleness that is attained in dependence upon completing the nine mental abidings. With effort it is not difficult to attain a mind that can remain for a short time on one object single-pointedly without distraction, but this is not tranquil abiding. Actual tranquil abiding is attained only by improving this mind until it induces the special bliss of suppleness.

We need to develop tranquil abiding both for our own sake and for the sake of others. Since we do not want to experience suffering we need to eliminate its root cause, self-grasping. To do this we need to realize emptiness directly, but we cannot realize emptiness directly unless we first attain tranquil abiding. This is because emptiness is a very subtle object and to realize it directly we need the special wisdom of superior seeing; and this wisdom arises only from tranquil abiding. At present our mind is wild and easily distracted, and it has the nature of movement. To realize emptiness directly our mind must become stilled and refined through the power of tranquil abiding.

Before we develop concentration we feel some kind of mental and physical discomfort more or less all the time. Our state of mind quickly changes. For a short while we are happy, but then we are sad. Our physical condition also changes quickly. In the morning we may feel well, but by the evening we may be feeling sick. When we attain tranquil abiding we do not experience any mental or physical discomfort. Our mind becomes peaceful and we are always able to generate virtuous thoughts and feelings and create the causes for happiness.

When we attain tranquil abiding we not only receive these benefits for ourself but we also become capable of greatly benefiting others, because tranquil abiding gives rise to attainments such as the various types of clairvoyance. There are five types of clairvoyance: the clairvoyance of divine eye, the clairvoyance of divine ear, the clairvoyance of knowing others' minds, the clairvoyance of knowing previous lives, and the clairvoyance of miracle powers. With the clairvoyance of divine eye we can see what others far away from us are experiencing, and with the clairvoyance of knowing others' minds we can know what others are thinking and what their problems are.

A king once tested Arya Asanga to discover whether or not he had clairvoyance. The king asked Asanga to answer his questions in front of a large crowd, but instead of asking the questions out loud he simply formulated them in his mind. The questions concerned the *Perfection of Wisdom Sutras*, and with his clairvoyance Asanga was able to answer all the king's silent questions.

While he was giving his discourses Buddha Shakyamuni would read the minds of those attending, and sometimes he would expose their distractions in public, saying 'Don't think like that!' Other renowned Teachers would do the same.

Once, while Je Tsongkhapa was giving a discourse on emptiness to a thousand disciples in a place called Sera Chodhing above Sera monastery, one of the monks called Sherab Senge realized emptiness. His realization was so powerful that he felt he had entirely disappeared. To reassure himself that conventionally he still existed he started to tug at his upper robe. With his clairvoyance Je Tsongkhapa understood what was happening and he declared 'Sherab Senge has found the conventional I.' He was delighted with his disciple's achievement.

With the attainment of tranquil abiding we also attain the clairvoyance of miracle powers, which enables us to manifest animate and inanimate objects. On one occasion Milarepa's disciple Rechungpa became rather proud of his learning and skills, and so Milarepa invited him for a walk. As they walked Milarepa manifested a hailstorm. Rechungpa lost sight of Milarepa and could not find anywhere to take shelter. Eventually he discovered Milarepa inside the horn of a dead yak. He saw that Milarepa had not become any smaller and the horn had not become any larger. Nevertheless, from inside the horn Milarepa beckoned to his disciple, saying 'Son, if you feel that you are equal with me, your spiritual father, come inside this horn. It is very comfortable and very spacious in here.' However Rechungpa had no power to do as Milarepa had done, and so his pride was eliminated.

No one wants to have faults but it is only Buddhas who are faultless. Therefore, if we are to become free from faults and fulfil our desire to be perfect we need to become enlightened by progressively attaining higher and higher spiritual grounds and paths, and gaining the realizations of generation and completion stages of Secret Mantra. To gain these advanced realizations we need tranquil abiding. In fact, to accomplish any virtuous action we need some degree of concentration because concentration overcomes obstacles to our practice such as mental and physical discomfort. With tranquil abiding we can easily gain any realization because our mind can remain focused on any object we choose until our mind and the object mix.

At present, when we engage in any virtuous action and wish to keep our mind focused on it we still have many distractions and negative thoughts and so our virtue is weak and impure. Our mind is constantly troubled by delusions such as anger, jealousy, and desirous attachment. Our memory is unclear and unstable, and our intelligence is dull. However, with tranquil abiding we gain the bliss of mental and physical suppleness, and all our previous obstacles to concentration disappear. Our body is supple and healthy and feels as light as cotton wool, as if it could float through solid walls. We experience no physical discomfort and we have the physical power to engage in any virtuous action. We have no need for physical exercise to develop a fit and supple body and we are able to spend long periods in concentration without pain. We have no laziness and we can accomplish any spiritual task without problems, no matter how long it may take. We feel calm all the time because our mind is completely free from tension. It is always supple and flexible.

With tranquil abiding we can endure difficult circumstances and deprivations with ease. We can live for a long time without food and yet experience no discomfort. In Tibet there are still some monks in remote caves who have remained undiscovered since the Chinese invasion of 1959. They have survived in solitary retreat without the food and drink they used to receive from lay people. How have they managed? They have been able to continue their practice in comfort because of their attainment of tranquil abiding. They may not be renowned scholars, but they are serious practitioners with great inner strength and realizations. These have been their nourishment and their protection.

We need to contemplate these benefits of developing tranquil abiding until we generate a strong wish to engage in the practice. Once this wish arises clearly in our mind we should do placement meditation to acquaint ourself with it.

The explanation of how to attain tranquil abiding has two parts:

1 The necessary conditions for attaining tranquil abiding
2 How to attain tranquil abiding

THE NECESSARY CONDITIONS FOR ATTAINING TRANQUIL ABIDING

To attain tranquil abiding all our conditions, external and internal, need to be right. If we have not prepared ourself properly and we try to do retreat to attain tranquil abiding we may spend years in retreat without success. In *Lamp for the Path to Enlightenment* Atisha says:

One who neglects the branches of tranquil abiding
Will never attain concentration
Even if he meditates with great effort
For a thousand years.

There are six 'branches' or necessary conditions for attaining tranquil abiding:

1 A suitable place for retreat
2 Little desire
3 Contentment
4 No distracting activities
5 Pure moral discipline
6 No distracting conceptions

A SUITABLE PLACE FOR RETREAT

When we engage in retreat to attain tranquil abiding we need to find a suitable place. In *Ornament for Mahayana Sutras* Maitreya explains that a place suitable for retreat is one that has the following five qualities:

(1) It is a place where it is easy to obtain necessities such as food and clothing.
(2) Buddhas and highly realized beings have blessed it or our Spiritual Guide has visited it. If we cannot find such a place we should at least find one where there has been no transgression of commitments and

no disharmony amongst spiritual practitioners. If we do retreat in a place where spiritual practitioners have been in conflict we shall find it hard to gain realizations.

(3) The environment is healthy, the climate is good – neither too hot nor too cold – and the water supply is clean.

(4) There are spiritual friends nearby to offer us their support. Practitioners who are very experienced and who have special realizations can meditate in complete solitude, but if we are not greatly experienced in meditation we need to be able to contact others easily if we need their help.

(5) It is quiet. When we have some degree of concentration, if there is a loud noise like a motorcycle passing or a dog barking this will pierce our concentration like a thorn piercing our flesh. Thus we need to find a place where there are no disturbing noises during the day or the night – for example, disturbing noises made by human beings, animals, or the environment, such as the crashing of a waterfall.

LITTLE DESIRE

In *Guide to the Bodhisattva's Way of Life* Shantideva says:

I should first strive to attain tranquil abiding
By gladly forsaking attachment to worldly life.

If we cannot abandon attachment to objects of desire when we do retreat, it will be very difficult to abandon other distractions and it will be impossible to develop pure concentration. Therefore, one of the necessary conditions for doing tranquil abiding retreat is to reduce our attachment to objects of worldly concern such as wealth and reputation.

CONTENTMENT

During our retreat, if we are not content with what we have – the accommodation, the food, and so forth – we shall keep seeking to change and improve our external circumstances, and this will cause our distractions and conceptual thoughts to increase. These are the very enemies of concentration. Furthermore, if we are not content we shall experience physical and mental discomfort and we shall become discouraged and want to give up our retreat. To overcome our discontent we should repeatedly consider:

It does not matter that for a few months or a few years my conditions are poor. My main goal is the attainment of liberation and enlightenment, and I can accomplish this goal only by attaining tranquil abiding.

NO DISTRACTING ACTIVITIES

If we are to attain completely pure concentration we need to disengage from all worldly activities and discipline ourself to do only the things that will help us to develop and maintain a calm mind. We must leave aside all harmful and meaningless activities. For example, during our meditation breaks we need to avoid reading books that are unrelated to our practice. Instead we should read explanations of the stages of the path to develop a strong motivation to improve our experience, and in particular we should study explanations of the stages of tranquil abiding. In our meditation breaks we should engage in activities that will increase our collection of merit and purify our negativities.

PURE MORAL DISCIPLINE

In this context pure moral discipline means conscientiousness with regard to our actions of body, speech, and mind. If we engage in reckless activities, distractions will naturally occur. Therefore we need to protect ourself against any tendency towards negative actions, and we need to guard against incorrect attitudes and defiled conceptions. To keep pure moral discipline it is not necessary to take vows. If we have powerful mindfulness this will protect us from negative actions of body, speech, and mind, and it will ensure that all our activities are pure. With mindfulness we can overcome gross distractions and maintain moral discipline. If we do not over-come gross distractions we shall not be able to develop the concentration which, by applying mindfulness and alertness while we are meditating, overcomes the more subtle distrac-tions. Therefore, keeping moral discipline is a prerequisite for attaining tranquil abiding. It is like a fence that keeps out the enemies of distraction in the way that a garden fence keeps out unwanted animals.

NO DISTRACTING CONCEPTIONS

During retreat on tranquil abiding we have to stop distract-ing conceptions such as recalling previous activities and worldly experiences, or thinking about and planning future activities.

HOW TO ATTAIN TRANQUIL ABIDING

How to attain tranquil abiding will now be explained under the following six headings:

1 The five obstacles to attaining tranquil abiding
2 The eight opponents to the five obstacles
3 How to attain the nine mental abidings
4 The six forces
5 The four attentions
6 The measurement of having attained tranquil abiding

We need to have a complete understanding of the instruc-tions on how to attain tranquil abiding before we start our retreat. Otherwise we may have to leave our retreat to seek advice, or we may become confused and develop doubts about what we are doing. If we know these instructions well we shall know how to prepare for our retreat and how to attain each level of concentration. We shall be able to identify the obstacles to tranquil abiding and we shall know what methods to use to overcome them.

If we wish to build a house we first receive full instruc-tions on how to prepare, how to construct the building, and how to solve any problems we may encounter. If we do not receive these instructions we shall make mistakes and waste a lot of time, and we may even give up in despair. It is the same with tranquil abiding. If we wish to succeed we need to make inner preparations and receive complete and correct instructions on how to accomplish our goal.

Maitreya gave correct and explicit instructions on tranquil abiding in his treatises such as *Ornament for Mahayana Sutras* and *Discrimination of the Middle and the Extremes*. Asanga extracted these instructions and incorporated them in his *Five Sets on the Spiritual Grounds*, where he explains in detail how to attain tranquil abiding. The great Yogi Kamalashila also gave perfect instructions in *Stages of Meditation*. Later, Je Tsongkhapa extracted the essence of all the instructions and compiled them in his *Great Exposition of the Stages of the Path*. The lineage of these instructions and the lineage of these practitioners remain unbroken. Therefore, if we rely upon these instructions there is great hope that we shall attain tranquil abiding in this lifetime.

THE FIVE OBSTACLES TO ATTAINING TRANQUIL ABIDING

These are explained in Maitreya's text *Discrimination of the Middle and the Extremes*. They are:

1 Laziness
2 Forgetfulness
3 Mental sinking and mental excitement
4 Non-application
5 Unnecessary application

LAZINESS

In general, laziness is a mind that is displeased to engage in virtuous actions. In this context it is a mind that is displeased to train in tranquil abiding. We can develop this laziness at any time, either before we begin our retreat or while our retreat is in progress. There are many types of laziness. For example, attachment to worldly activities makes us reluctant to train in tranquil abiding and is therefore a type of laziness. If we become depressed or discouraged, thinking that tranquil abiding is too hard for us to attain, or if we procrastinate, thinking that we should do our retreat some time in the future when actually the time is right for us to do it now, these are also types of laziness. At the beginning of our practice, laziness is the greatest obstacle because it prevents us from exerting effort to attain tranquil abiding. While we are not happy to apply effort, the door of tranquil abiding remains closed.

FORGETFULNESS

This refers to forgetting our object while we are meditating or forgetting the instructions that we have received from our Spiritual Guide. Forgetfulness makes our meditation useless – we become like a rider who has fallen off his horse. While we are meditating we need to hold our object firmly in the reins of mindfulness.

MENTAL SINKING AND MENTAL EXCITEMENT

Once we have begun our training in tranquil abiding, mental sinking and mental excitement are the two greatest obstacles that we encounter because they destroy perfect concentration. Perfect concentration has two characteristics: it remains on its object single-pointedly, and it perceives its object clearly, holding it firmly. Mental excitement destroys the single-pointedness of concentration because it occurs when distractions develop. Mental sinking destroys the clarity of concentration and its firm hold upon the object.

Mental excitement occurs when the mind wanders to an object of attachment. While we are concentrating, if part of our mind remembers an object of attachment such as a friend or some delicious food, this is mental excitement because our mind has wandered to an object of attachment. If we do not quickly become aware of this and return our mind to the object of meditation we shall lose this object completely. Since we are so familiar with objects of attachment we develop mental excitement frequently at the beginning of our practice.

There are two types of mental excitement, gross and subtle. If we first gain a clear appearance of our object and hold it firmly, remaining on it single-pointedly, and then while we are in this concentration we remember something we desire such as food, we shall not necessarily forget our object of meditation all at once. Part of our mind will remain on its object while part of it wanders away. If this happens we are experiencing subtle mental excitement. Subtle mental excitement is like the movement of a small fish under water – the surface of the water remains still while the fish moves underneath. When the mind has subtle excitement it still holds the object of concentration but part of it has moved away. If we continue to remember the object of desire, mental excitement will grow stronger until our object is completely lost. When this happens we are experiencing gross mental excitement. Mental excitement can develop at other times, not just in meditation. For example, while we are listening to a discourse we may remember some object of attachment and lose part of our attention to the discourse. In fact we experience mental excitement very frequently, whereas mental sinking occurs only when we are in meditation.

Mental excitement is a special type of distraction or mental wandering. When our mind is distracted by any object other than an object of desirous attachment, this is mental wandering and an obstacle to perfect concentration, even when the object is virtuous. For example, if we are meditating on our breath and we remember the form of Buddha Shakyamuni, we have incurred the fault of mental wandering because even distraction by virtuous objects interrupts our concentration and must be eliminated from our mind if we are to make progress in developing tranquil abiding.

There are also two types of mental sinking, gross and subtle. If we develop good concentration, holding the object clearly, and then the clarity reduces, this is gross mental sinking. If the clarity remains but our grip on the object loosens, this is subtle mental sinking. With subtle sinking the mind remains single-pointedly on its object and it perceives the object clearly, but the hold on the object, the intensity of the concentration, decreases. Mindfulness is what keeps our hold on the object firm. If the power of our mindfulness decreases, our hold slackens. If subtle sinking develops and remains uncorrected we may lose the object entirely. When this happens we have developed gross sinking.

We first need to understand subtle mental sinking intellectually, but to understand it perfectly we need to identify it in meditation and observe what happens. If we do not detect subtle mental sinking our concentration will become faulty. Since the mind continues to remain on its object single-pointedly and continues to perceive its object clearly even when subtle mental sinking has occurred, it is hard to identify the fault. Indeed, some people remain for a long time with subtle mental sinking, believing that they are abiding in faultless concentration. However, with mental sinking it is impossible to develop tranquil abiding. Therefore we need to learn how to identify subtle mental sinking as soon as it occurs and take the appropriate remedial action.

NON-APPLICATION

We incur the fault of non-application when we fail to apply the correct remedies to mental excitement and mental sinking. Most people develop this fault when they are meditating. For example, during a meditation session when we remember something that we desire we often let the object remain in our mind without making a firm decision to eliminate it. We let thoughts that arise in our mind remain there and so, even though we may look as if we are meditating, inwardly our mind is wandering everywhere, planning holidays, visiting people, going shopping, and so on. Since non-application can become a strong habit of mind we need to detect and abandon irrelevant thoughts as soon as they arise, and repeatedly return our attention to the object of concentration. If gross sinking occurs and we forget our object completely due to non-application, we enter a state that is neither meditation nor sleep. Our mind is just vacant, waiting for thoughts to occur in it. This condition may be quite good for relaxation, but it is not meditation.

UNNECESSARY APPLICATION

In the beginning of our practice of concentration it is impossible for us to develop this fault because it arises only after we have attained perfect concentration. When we have attained the seventh or eighth mental abiding and overcome the obstacles of sinking and excitement, but nevertheless still continue to apply the remedies for these faults, this inappropriate application of remedies will disturb the single-pointedness of our concentration.

THE EIGHT OPPONENTS TO THE FIVE OBSTACLES

In *Discrimination of the Middle and the Extremes* Maitreya explains eight opponents to the five faults:

1 Faith
2 Aspiration
3 Effort
4 Suppleness
5 Mindfulness
6 Alertness
7 Application
8 Non-application

The first four are opponents to laziness; and the second four are opponents to forgetfulness, mental sinking and mental excitement, non-application, and unnecessary application respectively.

FAITH, ASPIRATION, EFFORT, AND SUPPLENESS: THE OPPONENTS TO LAZINESS

Faith and aspiration are indirect opponents to laziness, and effort and suppleness are direct opponents. Effort here refers specifically to a mind that delights in the practice of concentration, and whenever we apply it we are free from laziness. Suppleness is attained through effort, and when we develop complete suppleness we become completely free from laziness.

Faith here refers to faith in the attainment of tranquil abiding. We generate this faith by understanding the great benefits of tranquil abiding and the good things that can be accomplished in dependence upon it. Of the three types of faith, this is an example of admiring faith. With this faith we develop the aspiration to attain tranquil abiding, and with such an aspiration we naturally generate joyful effort in the practices that lead to our goal. In this way the indirect opponents, faith and aspiration, induce the direct opponents, effort and suppleness.

When the good qualities of a product are advertised on television we naturally develop the wish to purchase it. Similarly, when we know the excellences of tranquil abiding we shall naturally aspire to attain it and want to put effort into our practice.

If we do not now aspire to attain tranquil abiding it will be difficult to generate such an aspiration in future lives. We may not even hear the term 'tranquil abiding' in our next life. In this world there are many people who have not heard it. Thus, while we have the chance we must cherish our good fortune and generate a strong aspiration to attain tranquil abiding, remembering that it is easier to practise concentration when we are young. When we are strong and healthy it is easier to endure any difficulties we may encounter, our mind is clearer, and we have a better memory and more stable mindfulness.

MINDFULNESS: THE OPPONENT TO FORGETFULNESS

Mindfulness is the opponent to forgetfulness. Its nature is to remember and hold its object firmly, and its function is to overcome and prevent distractions. The object of mindfulness is one with which we are already familiar and which we have previously understood. In *Compendium of Abhidharma* Asanga explains three characteristics of mindfulness: its object is already known, its nature is not to forget its object, and its function is to overcome distractions.

While we are training in concentration we need to eliminate forgetfulness by renewing mindfulness over and over again so that the object becomes more and more familiar. If we keep renewing our mindfulness we shall prevent it from degenerating. While our mindfulness is functioning well we shall not forget our object of concentration.

ALERTNESS: THE OPPONENT TO MENTAL SINKING AND MENTAL EXCITEMENT

Alertness is the opponent to mental sinking and mental excitement. It is an aspect of wisdom that examines the concentration and knows whether or not the faults of sinking or excitement are developing. It is like a spy because it specializes in detecting the presence of these two enemies of concentration and in warning us if they are about to interfere. As we train in concentration we need to use alertness skilfully. If we overapply alertness it will turn into an obstacle because it will disturb the single-pointedness of our concentration. On the other hand, if we underapply it the enemies of sinking and excitement will creep in.

The way to use alertness can be understood by the following analogy. If we are walking along a road carrying a lot of money and we become aware of someone following us who may be a thief, we shall proceed cautiously, keeping our main attention on the road ahead but out of the corner of our eye checking regularly to see what this person is doing. In a similar way, when we are training in concentration our main mind should be on our object, but part of our mind should be watching out for sinking and excitement. This surveillance needs to be conducted very smoothly so that it does not disrupt our concentration. Just as a person who is being followed by a suspected thief does not suddenly stop in his tracks and stare straight into the face of his follower, so while we are meditating we should check inconspicuously, glancing with part of our mind but never abandoning our concentration. Spies complete their task by just checking and reporting what they know – they do not actually take up arms. Once they have given their information to their commanding officer the army is sent to eliminate the danger. In a similar way, alertness counters mental sinking and mental excitement by warning us that these faults are developing and urging us to apply the direct opponents.

The direct opponent to subtle mental sinking is to grip the object more firmly because subtle sinking slackens our hold on the object. If we are holding a ball and our grip loosens there will be a danger of dropping the ball altogether. Subtle sinking has the same kind of effect on our concentration. If we leave mental sinking uncorrected our object will eventually slip from our grasp.

There are many direct opponents to gross mental sinking. When gross sinking occurs, our object appears less clearly to our mind. We can remedy this fault by doing further analytical meditation. For example, if our object is the visualized form of Buddha Shakyamuni we can return to analytical meditation, remembering the various features of the object from head to foot. Since gross sinking occurs when our mind becomes heavy, as if it has slumped or gathered density, we can overcome gross mental sinking by making our mind lighter and more energetic. We can do this by remembering earlier meditations, such as the meditation on this precious human life or on the great benefits of attaining tranquil abiding.

There is a more forceful method for eliminating gross mental sinking. We visualize our root mind at our heart in the aspect of white light in the shape of a tiny egg. Then we loudly utter the syllable PHAT (pronounced peh). As we do so we imagine that our root mind in the aspect of a tiny ball of light shoots up through our central channel, out through the top of our head, and far into space. We then imagine that our mind has mixed inseparably with space and hold this recognition in single-pointed meditation.

The direct opponent to subtle mental excitement is to relax slightly the intensity of our concentration. Subtle excitement arises when we try too hard to behold our object clearly and we apply more effort than is needed to maintain single-pointedness. If we apply too much effort and hold the object too tightly we lose single-pointedness and our concentration wavers. When this happens part of our mind wanders to another object. We can regain single-pointedness by gently relaxing the intensity of our hold on the object.

The direct opponent to gross mental excitement is to forget the object of attachment. To overcome gross excitement we have to meditate again and again on impermanence and the dangers of samsara and try to generate renunciation. If this does not work, we can do breathing meditation to reduce conceptual thoughts and temporarily remove our attention from the object of attachment.

Pure concentration is like a two-edged sword; it has the edge of single-pointedness or stability, and it has the edge of clarity and intensity. To attain single-pointedness at the beginning we have to make great effort, but if we apply too much effort we lose our single-pointedness and our mind begins to waver towards another object. On the other hand, if we do not apply enough effort we lose our grip on the object and mental sinking sets in. The great meditator Chandragomin said:

> When I depend upon effort mental excitement occurs,
> but when I reduce that effort mental sinking sets in.

We have to learn to adjust our effort so that it is not too tight and not too loose, rather as a musician has to adjust the strings of an instrument.

APPLICATION: THE OPPONENT TO NON-APPLICATION

When we are practising concentration, application of the correct remedy to whatever fault arises is the opponent to non-application. To apply the correct remedy we have to remember what it is and we have to make a strong determination actually to apply it.

NON-APPLICATION: THE OPPONENT TO UNNECESSARY APPLICATION

When our concentration is perfect, non-application of remedies is the opponent to unnecessary application. Abiding naturally in perfect concentration is called 'equanimity of application'. The mind is peaceful and the concentration has no faults.

The more realized we become, the better our concentration will be. When we attain medium levels of concentration we have to know exactly when to apply the opponents to sinking and excitement, but when we attain the eighth mental abiding we shall not need to apply further effort. Thereafter our concentration remains faultless. At that level our concentration is strong and its hold on the object is firm, and so the effort of applying opponents is relaxed.

Although mental sinking and mental excitement are the most common obstacles to concentration, there are many others. As already explained, any distraction is an obstacle because our mind at present cannot hold two objects at once, and so as soon as we remember another object our concentration is damaged. Sleep and dullness are big obstacles to concentration. It is easy to understand how sleep interferes! If we are sleepy when we settle down to meditate we need to make sure that our room has plenty of light and fresh air. We should sit straight with our eyes slightly more open than usual, and we should not wear very heavy clothing. When we are familiar with concentration we can eliminate sleepiness just by recalling our object and concentrating on it. Concentration itself then acts as an opponent to sleepiness. When we attain tranquil abiding our sleep itself becomes concentration.

Dullness is also an obstacle to concentration. It is a type of confusion that makes the mind and body feel heavy, and it causes mental sinking and sleep. Dullness is one of the causes of mental sinking and although sometimes the two are confused they are not the same. If the strength of our concentration is slightly diminished by dullness we experience subtle mental sinking. If dullness destroys the strength of our concentration and we cannot perceive the object clearly, we experience gross mental sinking.

Concentration is like a seed, and overcoming obstacles and accumulating necessary conditions are like the water and so forth that nourish the seed. Tranquil abiding is like the fruit that is produced when the seed and all the nourishing conditions are gathered together.

HOW TO ATTAIN THE NINE MENTAL ABIDINGS

This explanation is presented in two parts:

1 The object of meditation
2 The nine mental abidings

THE OBJECT OF MEDITATION

Before we begin our retreat on tranquil abiding we need to decide what is to be our object of meditation, and then keep this as our sole object throughout the retreat. The object should be one best suited to us, and once we have chosen it we should familiarize ourself with it both during our meditation sessions and during our meditation breaks. Even now we can begin to prepare for our tranquil abiding retreat by doing short retreats to become familiar with our chosen object. We can also train in concentration as we are doing our daily meditation sessions. If we quietly apply effort in practising concentration we can accomplish the first four mental abidings before doing our retreat. Some monks have even been able to attain tranquil abiding by practising at night while remaining in their monasteries.

In *Essence of the Middle Way* it is said that we need to bind our elephant-like mind to the stake of our virtuous object with the strong rope of mindfulness and use the hook of alertness to subdue it. At present our mind is like a crazy wild elephant. Our delusions are strong, they drive us to commit many harmful actions, and we have been governed by them since beginningless time. Training in tranquil abiding is the method for taming and gaining control over our wild elephant-like mind, and our object of concentration is like a fixed stake to which we tie our mind. Without such a virtuous object our mind will not abide peacefully but will continue to wander to objects of delusion.

There are many objects suitable to take as our object of tranquil abiding. Buddha mentioned four types:

1 Pervasive objects
2 Objects for abandoning individual delusions

3 Object for abandoning delusions in general
4 Objects for scholars

PERVASIVE OBJECTS

Pervasive objects are the two truths, conventional truths and ultimate truths. They are called 'pervasive objects' because they pervade all objects of tranquil abiding meditation.

OBJECTS FOR ABANDONING INDIVIDUAL DELUSIONS

Objects for abandoning individual delusions are objects of concentration that are opponents to specific delusions. For example, repulsiveness is such an object for someone who has strong desirous attachment. By taking repulsiveness as their object of concentration they will attain tranquil abiding and eliminate desirous attachment at the same time. Impermanence is such an object for those who suffer from anxiety concerning the welfare of this life. By taking impermanence as their object they will attain tranquil abiding and overcome their anxiety at the same time. In a similar way, those whose main problem is anger can take love as their object; those who want to develop renunciation can take the sufferings of samsara as their object; those who want to attain enlightenment by entering the Mahayana can take great compassion or bodhichitta as their object; those who have many distractions can take their breath as their object; those who have received a Tantric empowerment can take their body generated as the body of a Deity as their object; and those who are practising completion stage can take seed-letters, channels, winds, drops, and so forth as their object.

In *King of Concentration Sutra* it is recommended that we take the form of a Buddha as our object of concentration. If we focus upon the form of a Buddha, even if our concentration is not clear we shall develop special virtuous potentialities, accumulate merit, and purify negativities. If we have become very familiar with the form of a Buddha, keeping it always in mind, we shall remember it at the time of our death and we shall definitely attain a higher rebirth.

Some people gain tranquil abiding more quickly by practising according to Mahamudra, taking their own subtle mind as their object of concentration. Practising in this way brings less danger of mental sinking and mental excitement, and causes practitioners to gain the realization of completion stage easily.

OBJECT FOR ABANDONING DELUSIONS IN GENERAL

Emptiness is the object for abandoning delusions in general because by meditating on emptiness we finally abandon self-grasping, the root of all delusions.

OBJECTS FOR SCHOLARS

Our object is said to be an object for scholars if by concentrating on it our wisdom and our concentration both improve. For both our wisdom and concentration to improve we need to meditate with a sharp mind and great skill. Examples of objects for scholars are the five aggregates, the eighteen elements, the twelve sources, the twelve dependent-related links, and the two truths.

Each phenomenon's own nature is its element. There are two types of element, external and internal. Scientists know a lot about external elements. They know the constituents and potential power of external substances, and what happens when they are combined. Since scientists have specialized in knowing external elements, they have learnt how to manipulate the material world, make great technological advances, and produce many wonderful things.

To know subtle elements precisely – their natures and their functions – we need to study the inner science of Buddhadharma. If we master the subjects of inner science we shall attain special realizations which are the inner fruits of our study. When we have a complete understanding of inner science we shall attain enlightenment. All the realizations we gain as a result of Dharma practice are inner powers. Inner science brings only peace and never any danger. By comparison, external science, for all its great benefits, brings many dangers and conflicts. In fact at present its dangers greatly outweigh its benefits because our technological advancement has brought us nuclear weapons, and these have a destructive power many times greater than the creative power of all our other inventions. Now external science is endangering the welfare of the whole world. Therefore, of the two, it is more important to learn inner science.

Elements can be divided into eighteen. If we take the eighteen elements as our object of concentration, we first do analytical meditation until we develop a special experience, and then we take this experience as our actual object of concentration. In a similar way, if we take the twelve dependent-related links as our object, we first do analytical meditation until we develop a strong determination to attain liberation, and then we take this special thought as our actual object of concentration.

The eighteen elements are the six objects of consciousness – visual forms, sounds, smells, tastes, tactile objects, and phenomena; the six powers – the eye sense power, the ear sense power, the nose sense power, the tongue sense power, the body sense power, and the mental power; and the six consciousnesses – the eye consciousness, the ear consciousness, the nose consciousness, the tongue consciousness, the body consciousness, and the mental consciousness. The five sense powers are not the gross physical sense organs themselves but the subtle inner energy powers that directly generate sense consciousnesses. The mental power is the previous moment of any mental consciousness. The six powers give their respective consciousnesses power to apprehend their objects. The physical organs alone cannot empower the sense consciousnesses to know their objects. If they could, a blind person who still possesses an eye organ would be able to see.

How do we take these eighteen elements as our object of concentration? First we should try to understand that all objects of knowledge are included within the eighteen elements. The eighteen elements are included within the twelve: the six powers, and the six objects of the six consciousnesses. When we take the eighteen elements as our object of concentration we first do extensive analytical meditation on them, dividing the eighteen elements into their countless parts. When we analyze the elements it is as if our mind has divided into countless parts. Having distinguished the parts of each element we investigate to know the power, the nature, the function, and so forth of each one. Meditating in this way greatly increases our wisdom. Then we gather the countless parts into the eighteen elements, the eighteen into the twelve, and the twelve into the six objects of consciousness. Finally these six are all included in one category – the objects of mental consciousness, or the element of phenomena. Then we take this as our object of mental stabilization. Meditating in this way is called 'gathering the mind'. If we have any experience of emptiness we remember that this object is empty, and we meditate on emptiness. Emptiness itself is included within the element of phenomena.

Objects can be divided into objects that are not minds and objects that are minds, or subjects. The way of meditating on each of these is different. When we meditate on objects that are not minds, such as emptiness, impermanence, or the form of a Buddha, we first need to find the object by doing analytical meditation. Having found it, we hold it and remain on it single-pointedly in placement meditation. For example, if we take gross impermanence as our object we first get a mental image of impermanence, thinking of ourself as impermanent and remembering the nine rounds of the death meditation. When we have a strong feeling of our own impermanence we hold this by means of concentration.

When we meditate on subjects we do analytical meditation to transform our mind into that subject, and then we hold that mind single-pointedly in placement meditation. We begin by actually transforming our mind into its object, such as equanimity, compassion, or bodhichitta, and then we maintain and enhance that mind by means of concentration. In this case we never think of the object as external to us. Our mind is actually turning into its object rather than just observing it. When the state of mind that is our object of concentration becomes spontaneous and continuous, at the same time we have attained tranquil abiding. For example, if our object is bodhichitta, when that mind becomes spontaneous, at that time we have also attained tranquil abiding.

When we are doing Lamrim meditations other than meditation on the stages of tranquil abiding we are not training specifically in tranquil abiding, but our meditations are similar because, as explained before, in all of them we first find our object by doing analytical meditation and then we hold it by doing placement meditation. In this way all our meditations are preparing us to attain tranquil abiding.

THE NINE MENTAL ABIDINGS

To attain tranquil abiding we need to gain in succession nine levels of concentration on one object. These are called:

1 Placing the mind
2 Continual placement
3 Replacement
4 Close placement
5 Controlling
6 Pacifying
7 Completely pacifying
8 Single-pointedness
9 Placement in equipoise

As a child grows up he or she becomes stronger and more mature each year. Similarly, our concentration grows stronger and more powerful with each level until we attain tranquil abiding. There now follows an explanation of what characterizes each level and how they are attained in succession.

PLACING THE MIND

When we start our training in tranquil abiding we sit in the seven-point posture of Buddha Vairochana, or as close to it as we can, and then we generate bodhichitta motivation – deciding to train in tranquil abiding to fulfil our wish to benefit others.

At this stage of training, our goal is to find our object and focus, or place, our mind on it. When we attain placing the mind we are not yet able to hold the object continuously for any length of time. We can just focus our mind on it.

We find the object by examining it in detail. For example, if our object is the visualized form of Buddha we find it by remembering the various aspects of its appearance. To begin with we visualize the object about thumb-size, but as our training progresses we visualize our object as small as possible. If we have many distractions we can visualize the object at the level of our navel because this helps reduce mental excitement and other distractions. Visualizing the object higher will help reduce mental sinking. We need to experiment to find out which is the best position for us, although in general the best position is level with our eyebrows.

Before doing our meditation and during our meditation break we can examine images of Buddha. By recollecting these in our meditation session we try to perceive a clear generic image. We try to establish this image in our mind's eye by remembering its various aspects, from head to foot, thinking 'The hair is like this, the face is like this . . . ', and so on. Then we check in reverse, from the feet to the crown of the head. This process of checking is called 'seeking' the object. After a while we shall be able to establish a rough generic image of the whole form. Then we take this rough generic image as our object and try to place our mind on it without attempting to make it any clearer. If we can perceive the whole image clearly at this stage we are very fortunate, but if we can establish only a vague image that is sufficient for the time being. We are still ready to practise placing the mind. When we have found or established the object well, and we are able to focus our mind on it and hold it singlepointedly, we have attained the first mental abiding. It may take a few months to reach this level.

On the level of placing the mind we still have more distractions than concentration during our meditation session. We may even feel that we have more distractions than usual. In fact this is not the case. It seems that way only because our mind has become slightly clearer and more inwardly gathered. In our daily life we have more distractions than when we are meditating, but since we are mostly unaware of these distractions it can seem to us that they are fewer than those we experience when we sit down to meditate.

CONTINUAL PLACEMENT

After attaining placing the mind we continue to meditate on the same object over and over again until we can hold our object single-pointedly for about five minutes. When we can do this we have reached the second level, continual placement. On this level we still have many conceptual thoughts and other distractions, but they are fewer than on the first level. The distractions are less busy and it is as if they are ready to retire. Our concentration is stronger. There are times when our mind is free from conceptual thoughts and there are times when it is not.

REPLACEMENT

After attaining continual placement, if we continue to meditate over and over again we shall eventually reach the third level, replacement. On the second level we can hold our object for about five minutes before we lose it, and when we lose it we cannot immediately regain it. We need to return to analytical meditation each time we lose the object. However, on the third level, whenever we lose the object we can immediately retrieve it without having to begin our search all over again. On the second level we are like a child who has dropped a ball and cannot easily pick it up again. On the third level we are like an adult who can immediately retrieve the ball whenever it is dropped. When we attain replacement our mindfulness becomes much stronger and we can meditate for an hour without ever completely losing our object. During that time we drop our object many times, but we are always able to regain it immediately.

CLOSE PLACEMENT

After attaining replacement, if we continue to meditate over and over again we shall reach the fourth level, close placement. On this level the power of our mindfulness is complete and so we do not forget our object of meditation at any time during the session. This level is called 'close placement' because the object is always close to us.

CONTROLLING

After attaining close placement we continue to meditate over and over again, and our concentration improves until we reach the fifth level, controlling. On this level there is no danger of any mental excitement or gross mental sinking, but due to the power of stable concentration our mind may become too inwardly gathered and so there is a great danger of developing subtle mental sinking. With alertness we can control subtle mental sinking and, by applying the appropriate opponent, eliminate it immediately. At this stage alertness is applied principally to overcome this obstacle.

PACIFYING

After attaining controlling, if we continue to improve our concentration we shall reach the sixth level, pacifying. On this level there is no danger of any mental sinking or gross mental excitement, but due to applying the remedy to mental sinking on the level of controlling we run the risk of slight overapplication, which induces subtle mental excitement. We identify this obstacle through the force of alertness, and overcome it by applying the appropriate opponent.

COMPLETELY PACIFYING

After attaining pacifying, if we continue to improve our concentration we shall reach the seventh level, completely pacifying. On this level, because we have perfected the powers of mindfulness and alertness, there is no great danger of either subtle mental excitement or subtle mental sinking.

In the case of either obstacle arising it can immediately be eliminated through the power of effort.

SINGLE-POINTEDNESS

By continuing our practice of concentration we reach the eighth level, single-pointedness. On this level it is impossible for any mental sinking or mental excitement to develop during our meditation. However, although we are able to focus and remain single-pointedly on our object for as long as we like, we still need to exert effort to maintain concentration.

PLACEMENT IN EQUIPOISE

By continuing our practice of concentration we reach the ninth level, placement in equipoise. On this level, as soon as we have engaged in concentration it is effortless to sustain. Initially, when we decide to engage in concentration we have to make some slight effort to move the mind to its object, but once we have done this no further effort is needed to maintain our concentration. Just as we effortlessly fall asleep once we have gone to bed and lain down, so on this level, once we have decided to practise concentration and remembered our object, concentration comes naturally and spontaneously. Any living being needs to apply at least a minimum effort to perform any action; only Buddhas have completed the perfection of effort and can accomplish all tasks effortlessly.

THE SIX FORCES

The six forces are methods for attaining and improving the nine mental abidings. They are:

1 The force of listening
2 The force of contemplating
3 The force of mindfulness
4 The force of alertness
5 The force of effort
6 The force of complete familiarity

The force of listening refers to listening to the instructions on how to find our object of concentration. We need to receive these instructions from a qualified Teacher if we are to attain the first mental abiding, placing the mind.

We attain the second mental abiding, continual placement, in dependence upon the force of contemplating. This involves contemplating our object of concentration over and over again until we have become familiar with it. We do this both during our meditation session and during our meditation break. We should try to contemplate our object even in our dreams. In this way we shall become very familiar with it, just as we become familiar with objects of attachment by dreaming about them. It is easy for us to bring to mind an object of attachment and to remain fixed on it single-pointedly. We can contemplate desired objects even while we are doing other things like eating our food. When we bring these to mind it feels as if our mind has absorbed into its object. This resembles real concentration induced by contemplation, but it is not actual concentration because the object is non-virtuous.

The force of mindfulness enables us to attain the third and fourth mental abidings – replacement and close placement; and the force of alertness enables us to attain the fifth and sixth mental abidings – controlling and pacifying. Through the force of alertness, mental sinking is largely overcome on the level of controlling, and mental excitement is largely overcome on the level of pacifying.

The force of effort enables us to attain the seventh and eighth mental abidings – completely pacifying and single-pointedness. The force of effort subdues sinking and excitement whenever they arise on the level of completely pacifying, and it maintains our concentration on the level of single-pointedness.

The force of complete familiarity with our object enables us to attain the ninth mental abiding – placement in equipoise.

THE FOUR ATTENTIONS

Attention is an all-accompanying mental factor that functions to move, direct, and focus the mind single-pointedly on its object. For example, if there are many objects on a table, attention is the mental factor that directs and focuses our mind on one of them and then moves it to another. If attention were not functioning we would not be able to single out each object one by one.

There are four types of attention:

1 Tight attention
2 Interrupted attention
3 Uninterrupted attention
4 Spontaneous attention

On the first two levels of concentration we use tight attention to keep renewing our effort. On the next five levels we use interrupted attention because our concentration is occasionally interrupted by mental sinking or mental excitement. On the eighth level we use uninterrupted attention because our concentration is never interrupted by any faults. On the ninth level we have spontaneous attention because our concentration is effortless. When we are training in tranquil abiding these four attentions arise naturally at the right times; we do not need to make a special effort to cultivate them.

THE MEASUREMENT OF HAVING ATTAINED
TRANQUIL ABIDING

When we attain complete suppleness, which is induced by the attainment of the ninth mental abiding, placement in equipoise, we have attained tranquil abiding. On the second mental abiding we develop a slight suppleness which is hard to recognize, and on the third and fourth levels our suppleness is more developed. Those who are familiar with meditation can recognize suppleness while they are on the first two levels, but complete suppleness is attained some time after gaining placement in equipoise. The time it takes depends on the person. Some meditators advance quickly, but others have to continue meditating for several weeks after attaining placement in equipoise before they attain tranquil abiding.

When we attain the special suppleness of tranquil abiding we become free from all mental and physical inflexibility and heaviness, our mind becomes clear, and we do not experience obstacles to engaging in virtuous actions. Physical suppleness develops in dependence upon mental suppleness, and our body becomes light, healthy, and tireless. This is because when we attain mental suppleness this induces suppleness in the subtle winds that flow through our body. Physical suppleness pervades our whole body and this induces a feeling of bliss. In dependence upon the bliss of physical suppleness we experience the bliss of mental suppleness. When we first experience the bliss of physical suppleness it is so intense that we feel a kind of shock, and this makes our concentration quiver, making the bliss slightly less intense. When the experience of bliss becomes more stable we attain the unchangeable bliss of concentration. This is the sign that we have attained tranquil abiding. At this stage it is as if our mind has dissolved into its object. The mind is extremely clear and it feels as if we could count the atoms in a wall. When we attain tranquil abiding our mind is transformed from a mind of the desire realm into a mind of the upper realms. Subsequently, we use our attainment of tranquil abiding to gain higher and higher spiritual grounds and paths until we attain liberation and full enlightenment.

Training the Mind in Superior Seeing

HOW TO TRAIN THE MIND IN SUPERIOR SEEING, THE ESSENCE OF WISDOM

How to attain superior seeing in dependence upon tranquil abiding will now be explained in three parts:

1 The nature of superior seeing
2 The function of superior seeing
3 The object of superior seeing

THE NATURE OF SUPERIOR SEEING

The nature of superior seeing is wisdom. Just as tranquil abiding is a special and superior kind of concentration, so superior seeing is a superior wisdom arising in dependence upon tranquil abiding. When we have attained tranquil abiding our concentration cannot be disturbed by conceptual thoughts. It is unshakeable, like a huge mountain that cannot be moved by the wind. With such stable concentration we can investigate our observed object more thoroughly. Through the power of repeated investigation we shall eventually gain a superior knowledge or insight into the nature of our object of meditation. This wisdom of investigation induces a special suppleness. Wisdom that is qualified by such suppleness is superior seeing.

The suppleness of superior seeing and the suppleness of tranquil abiding are alike in that they are both supplenesses, but they differ with respect to their causes. The suppleness of tranquil abiding is principally induced by concentration, whereas the suppleness of superior seeing is principally induced by wisdom. The nature of analytical meditation is wisdom and the nature of placement meditation is concentration. Superior seeing is so called because a meditator who has attained superior seeing sees the nature of the observed object more clearly, and hence in a way superior to the way in which it is seen by a meditator who has attained only tranquil abiding.

At present we do not have strong concentration and so when we engage in meditation our one mind cannot do both analytical and placement meditation at the same time. However, when we attain tranquil abiding we can investigate our object without disturbing our concentration. According to the Mahamudra system, tranquil abiding is like clear water and superior seeing is like a small fish that swims skilfully through the water without disturbing the tranquillity of the surface. A meditator who has attained a union of tranquil abiding and superior seeing is able to advance quickly to higher grounds and paths.

THE FUNCTION OF SUPERIOR SEEING

The superior seeing of the perfection of wisdom is a path to liberation and full enlightenment. Its main function is to eliminate all faults and delusions. When we have attained tranquil abiding we can examine deeply the nature of our object of meditation. For example, if our object is the visualized form of a Buddha we can use our wisdom to investigate it, and eventually we shall discover that it has two natures – a conventional nature and an ultimate nature. Through further investigation we shall see the ultimate nature of the object, emptiness, more and more clearly until, finally, we realize it directly.

THE OBJECT OF SUPERIOR SEEING

In general, all the objects of tranquil abiding can also be used as objects of superior seeing. Among these, ultimate truth, emptiness, is the best object of superior seeing because we need to realize emptiness directly to attain liberation and full enlightenment. Superior seeing itself is a mind, but since its principal object is emptiness, emptiness will now be explained.

In *The Three Principal Aspects of the Path* Je Tsongkhapa says:

> But, even though you may be acquainted with
>   renunciation and bodhichitta,
> If you do not possess the wisdom realizing the way
>   things are,
> You will not be able to cut the root of samsara;
> Therefore strive in the means for realizing dependent
>   relationship.

In *Commentary to Valid Cognition* Dharmakirti says:

> We shall be released from samsara by the view of emp-
> tiness. The other meditations assist this view.

Buddha Shakyamuni said that the reason why beings continue to wander in samsara is that they have not yet realized emptiness. In the *Condensed Perfection of Wisdom Sutra* he says that without the wisdom realizing emptiness all the other perfections are blind.

In *Guide to the Bodhisattva's Way of Life* Shantideva says:

> Buddha taught all the method practices explained above
> To enable us to complete the training in wisdom
>   realizing emptiness.

Here the 'method practices' refer to all the other practices taught by Buddha. They all assist the wisdom realizing emptiness, which is the principal tool for cutting through the two obstructions.

To attain enlightenment it is necessary to understand the correct view of emptiness. This ultimate view has been realized and explained by practitioners since the time of Buddha Shakyamuni. There is no other ultimate view. Although there has not been much disagreement among Indian and Tibetan Buddhists concerning Buddha's teachings on method – the instructions on renunciation, bodhichitta, and so forth – there is disagreement concerning Buddha's teachings on wisdom.

The correct view, and the one that Buddha intended everyone to know, is the view taught by Nagarjuna in his system, the Madhyamika-Prasangika.

Before Buddha Shakyamuni passed away he predicted that four hundred years later a monk called Bhikkshu Palden would come to a town called Bendra in Southern India. This man would later be known as Nagarjuna, and he would give perfect explanations of the correct view free from the extremes of existence and non-existence. Nagarjuna would cause the perfect doctrine to flourish throughout the world. If we are Buddhists and we do not trust these words of Buddha, whose can we trust? Nagarjuna came as predicted. In *Six Collections of Reasonings* he explains the correct view of emptiness, revealing the meaning of all the topics set forth in the twelve volumes of the *Perfection of Wisdom Sutra in One Hundred Thousand Lines*. Among these six treatises it is mainly in *Fundamental Wisdom of the Middle Way* that Nagarjuna explains emptiness. In this work Nagarjuna explains all the stages of the profound path using many ways of reasoning. Later, Nagarjuna's disciple Chandrakirti composed a commentary to this text entitled *Guide to the Middle Way*. When Atisha was teaching in Tibet he gave this advice for disciples of the future:

> Chandrakirti is the disciple of Nagarjuna. There is Buddhahood in this lineage. Apart from this lineage there is no Buddhahood.

His meaning is that it is impossible to attain enlightenment by following a view that contradicts the system of Nagarjuna and Chandrakirti.

By the time of Je Tsongkhapa many different interpretations of emptiness were being taught in Tibet. Je Tsongkhapa asked Manjushri, 'Which works should I rely upon to gain a perfect understanding of Buddha's ultimate view?' Manjushri replied that he should rely principally upon the works of the glorious Chandrakirti. Chandrakirti, he said, was a high Bodhisattva who came from a Pure Land to teach the correct view of emptiness as explained by Nagarjuna.

In *Guide to the Middle Way* Chandrakirti says that without realizing emptiness as explained by Nagarjuna there is no way to attain liberation. If we hold a contradictory view we do not have the practice of the two truths and so we have no way of attaining liberation. Therefore, if we have wisdom but forsake the view of Nagarjuna and Chandrakirti for another view, we are like someone who walks off a high cliff with their eyes wide open.

It has already been explained that the *Perfection of Wisdom Sutras* explicitly teach emptiness and implicitly teach all the stages of the vast path. Nagarjuna's *Fundamental Wisdom of the Middle Way* gives a detailed commentary on the Sutras' explicit teachings, and his *Precious Garland of Advice for the King* gives a detailed commentary on the Sutras' implicit teachings. In the *Perfection of Wisdom Sutra in One Hundred Thousand Lines* Buddha teaches emptiness extensively. He names all the bases of emptiness, such as the five aggregates, the twelve sources, the eighteen elements, the twelve dependent-related links of samsara, and so forth. He explains in detail how all of these are empty and he gives reasons establishing their emptiness. He lists one hundred and eight categories that include all objects of knowledge, from form to omniscient mind, and he proves that each one lacks inherent existence. These one hundred and eight emptinesses can be condensed into sixteen emptinesses, the sixteen into four, and the four into two – the emptiness of persons and the emptiness of phenomena other than persons. Since all bases of emptiness, all objects of knowledge, are divisible into persons and other phenomena, if we realize perfectly the emptiness of persons and the emptiness of phenomena we shall realize all emptinesses. For this reason the explanation of emptiness, the object of superior seeing, is presented under the following two headings:

1 The emptiness of persons
2 The emptiness of phenomena

THE EMPTINESS OF PERSONS

This has two parts:

1 How to sustain space-like meditative equipoise on
   the emptiness of persons
2 How to sustain illusion-like subsequent attainment

HOW TO SUSTAIN SPACE-LIKE MEDITATIVE EQUIPOISE ON
THE EMPTINESS OF PERSONS

To understand the meaning of the words 'emptiness of persons' we need to examine how it is that a person is empty.
If we first understand how a person is empty we shall easily
understand how other phenomena are empty. If possible we
should study Nagarjuna's *Fundamental Wisdom of the Middle
Way* and Chandrakirti's *Guide to the Middle Way* together
with their commentaries, especially the commentaries by Je
Tsongkhapa. A commentary to *Guide to the Middle Way* can
be found in the book *Ocean of Nectar*. The texts by Nagarjuna
and Chandrakirti are like doors that open the meaning of the
Perfection of Wisdom Sutras, and Je Tsongkhapa's texts are like
keys to those doors. However if we cannot study so extensively we should study and practise according to the following Lamrim instructions because they contain the essential
meaning of all the other great texts.

There are many methods for gaining a clear understanding
of the emptiness of persons. The method presented here has
four essential steps:

1 Ascertaining the negated object
2 Ascertaining the pervasion
3 Ascertaining the absence of oneness
4 Ascertaining the absence of difference

ASCERTAINING THE NEGATED OBJECT

Emptiness is a non-affirming negative phenomenon that
negates inherent existence and does not affirm any positive
phenomenon. It is a mere absence of inherent existence. Not

all empties are emptinesses. For example, when a wine bottle is empty, this empty is not an emptiness because in this case the negated object is wine, whereas in the case of emptiness the negated object is always inherent existence. It is essential to identify what inherent existence is if we are to understand emptiness. When it is said that inherent existence is the negated object of emptiness, this does not mean that it is put out of existence by emptiness, because inherent existence has never existed. Nevertheless, because we believe that inherent existence really exists we need to examine this object and get a clearer idea of it.

It is possible to get a very clear idea of an object that does not exist. For example, even though a horn on a rabbit's head does not exist, we can imagine clearly what it would look like if it did exist. In fact, to know beyond any doubt that a rabbit's head is empty of horns we need to know exactly what is absent. In other words, we need to have a clear idea of the negated object. Similarly, if we are to realize the emptiness of a person we need to have a clear idea of what an inherently existent person would be like if such a being were to exist. If we cannot correctly identify the negated object of emptiness we cannot establish its non-existence, and if we cannot establish its non-existence we cannot realize emptiness.

If we want to overcome our enemy we have to identify him clearly, otherwise we may overcome our friend. Similarly, if we make a mistake in identifying the negated object of emptiness our understanding will be incorrect and we shall not realize emptiness. Many mistakes have been made on this point because the negated object is subtle and hard to discern. One Chinese monk called Hashang read in Buddha's scriptures that all objects of knowledge are empty of inherent existence and he concluded that all objects of knowledge do not exist. When he read 'There is no form . . . ' he understood this to mean that form has no mode of existence whatsoever. Then he instructed his disciples to aim at realizing nothingness. There are still people today who cannot discriminate between emptiness and nothingness, and who train their minds to become like stones, apprehending nothing.

The clearest description of the negated object of emptiness – inherent existence – is given by Chandrakirti in his commentary to Aryadeva's *Four Hundred*, where he says:

For things to exist inherently means that things are not dependent upon other factors for their existence; but because things do depend upon other factors there can be no inherently existent objects.

Because a rose depends upon its causes and conditions it does not exist inherently. If we can find an independent object we have found an inherently existent object, but such an object is unfindable because every object of knowledge depends upon its parts. According to Nagarjuna and his followers, understanding dependent-related phenomena is the best way to realize emptiness.

The first step in realizing the emptiness of persons is to identify the negated object – an independent person. Upon investigation, if we can find such a person, that person exists inherently. When we are conducting this investigation we begin by meditating upon our I. An inherently existent I is always appearing to our mind, and there is never a time when we are not grasping it, even when we are asleep. We begin our meditation by considering, 'How am I grasping at self? What is the I that appears to my mind?' Enquiring in this way, we try to establish a clear image of the inherently existent I. If someone describes their holiday house to us we can perceive a clear image of it even though we may never have seen it. Our image of the house is the generic image of the house. Similarly, by considering the I that usually appears to our mind – the object of our self-grasping – we can get a clear generic image of the inherently existent I.

If we do not investigate we assume that an inherently existent I actually exists. Although we do not go about asserting 'I exist inherently', whenever we think about ourself or talk about ourself, the inherently existent I is the object to which we refer. However, we do not usually have a very clear idea of this I and so we need to begin by emphasizing it so that we can then focus our attention upon it. We can think

'I am reading this book', and then ask ourself, 'How does the I that is reading this book appear to my mind?' If we consider in this way we shall observe that this I appears to be something different from, and independent of, our body and mind. We do not feel that 'I am reading this book' means the same as 'My body is reading this book' or 'My mind is reading this book.' The I appears to exist from its own side. This independent I, if it exists, is the inherently existent I, the I we cherish.

When we investigate the negated object of emptiness it is important not to jump to conclusions, thinking: 'I have heard that there is no inherently existent I and so there is no need to think about it.' Instead, we should deliberately cultivate a strong sense of I and establish a rough generic image of it. Then we can concentrate on it, thinking: 'This is the I that I cherish. This is the I reading this book. This is the I that works and sleeps. This is the I that gets hurt. This is the independent, inherently existent I.' At this stage we have to be content with just a rough generic image. If we try to push the investigation further, the image will become unclear and we shall lose it. As soon as we have established a rough generic image of the I, we need to do placement meditation to become more familiar with it. We spend as long as necessary at this stage of the meditation. It may even take years to perceive a clear generic image of the inherently existent I, but it does not matter how long it takes because this step is an essential foundation for the other stages of the meditation. If we build this foundation well it will be easy to gain a realization of the subsequent steps.

It is not possible to give a clearer explanation of how to identify the negated object. Once we have understood this explanation, the only way to proceed is by contemplating and meditating on the instructions and gaining our own experience. There is plenty of scope for observing the inherently existent I both during our meditation sessions and during our meditation breaks because we grasp at this I all the time. Therefore, we can use these instructions to challenge repeatedly our habitual sense of an inherently existent I. If we find we cannot easily make progress with this practice, it is not because the explanations are inadequate but because we lack wisdom and familiarity with the subject matter. In this respect we are like old people with bad eyesight who complain that they cannot read books with especially large print, even though the print itself is clear.

During our meditation breaks we need to continue to contemplate the negated object of emptiness. When we read authoritative explanations such as those presented in the ninth chapter of Shantideva's *Guide to the Bodhisattva's Way of Life* and the sixth chapter of Chandrakirti's *Guide to the Middle Way*, we need to read carefully, contemplating each sentence well. We may spend two hours reading just one page, but it is time well spent because such texts are not to be read like newspapers. In *Guide to the Bodhisattva's Way of Life* Shantideva spends much time refuting incorrect views of emptiness. If we read these pages carefully we shall be able to eliminate our own wrong views and understand the essential points of the Madhyamika-Prasangika system; but such understanding takes time. In *Guide to the Middle Way* Chandrakirti explains that when he refutes the views of others and establishes his own he does not do so merely for the sake of debate but in order to reveal correct paths to those who seek liberation. Since they are written with this great purpose and beneficial intention, we should study such explanations with patience and care.

There is something quite strange about the inherently existent I. If we do not investigate it, it will appear all the time and even in our dreams we shall grasp at it; but as soon as we actually examine it, it becomes very unclear. As we search for it, instead of being able to locate it we lose it. This very experience is a sign that the I does not exist from its own side, because if it did exist from its own side investigation would reveal it more and more clearly. The same applies to external objects. For example, if we do not look at a rose too closely, whenever we glance in its direction the rose will appear to us. However, if we start to analyze it, trying to find what is the rose, we shall find many parts of the rose but we shall not find the rose itself. The more closely we investigate, the more difficult it becomes to see the rose. Usually if someone says 'Where is the rose?' we point in its direction and say 'There it is!'; but if through investigation we look more closely we shall not be able to locate the rose itself. This kind of experience is a sign indicating that phenomena other than persons also lack inherent existence or true existence. Persons and phenomena do not exist from their own side.

ASCERTAINING THE PERVASION

As a result of practising the first step of the meditation, when we apprehend the generic image of the object of negation – the inherently existent I – we proceed with our investigation without prejudice to see whether or not such an I actually exists. If such an I does exist, then through our investigation it will appear more and more clearly to us, and we shall have correct reasons proving its existence. If it does not exist, this will also become apparent through investigation. The next step is to ascertain the pervasion:

If the I that we always perceive as existing from its own side actually exists, it must be either one with or separate from the aggregates. There is no third possibility.

If we want to conduct a conclusive search for the inherently existent I, we have to be sure that our search covers every place where an inherently existent I could possibly be. If we are not sure that our search has covered every possibility, we shall not be able to arrive at a firm conclusion. To draw an analogy, if we think that there is a fish in our house, there are only two places where it could be. Either it is inside the aquarium or it is outside the aquarium. There is no third place where it could be. If we establish that there is no fish inside the aquarium and no fish outside the aquarium we can firmly conclude that there is no fish in our house.

ASCERTAINING THE ABSENCE OF ONENESS

The next step of the meditation is to find out whether or not the inherently existent I is one with the aggregates. We meditate on the following reasons:

If this I is one with the aggregates it follows that one person has five I's because there are five aggregates.

If the I is one with the aggregates it must either be one with the body or one with the mind. If it is one with the body it follows that when our body is cremated the I becomes non-existent. If this is so, there is no next rebirth because the I is destroyed along with the body.

Furthermore, the I cannot be one with the body because we refer to 'my body', clearly indicating that we believe the body to be in the possession of the I.

Similarly, the I cannot be one with the mind because we refer to 'my mind', clearly indicating that we regard the mind as being in the possession of the I.

If the I and the mind are one, it follows that one person has many I's because there are many minds – the main mind, the secondary minds, virtuous minds, non-virtuous minds, and so forth.

For these reasons it follows that the I is not one with the aggregates or with any one of the aggregates. When our analytical meditation leads us to this firm conclusion we do placement meditation.

ASCERTAINING THE ABSENCE OF DIFFERENCE

The fourth step of the meditation is to investigate the remaining possibility, that the inherently existent I is separate from the aggregates. We meditate on the following reasons:

If the I is separate from the mind and body it would not make sense to say 'I am getting old' when our body is ageing. It would make just as much sense to say 'I am getting old' when our dog's body is ageing, because both bodies would be equally different from our I. Likewise, if the I were separate from the mind and body it would be nonsense to say 'I have a headache.' In fact, most of our ordinary speech would be nonsense.

Chandrakirti said that there is no I separate from the aggregates because without perceiving the aggregates the I cannot be perceived. Unless the aggregates appear to the mind there is no way to apprehend the I.

If it were possible to apprehend the I without the aggregates appearing to our mind, self-grasping could exist where the aggregates are absent, just as a donkey can exist where a horse is absent because a donkey and a horse are different and do not necessarily exist together.

Furthermore, if the I were separate from the aggregates we would be able to find it apart from the aggregates. For example, take someone called Peter. If Peter's I were separate from his aggregates we would be able to find Peter apart from his body and mind, because the name 'Peter' refers to Peter's I and not to his body and mind. However, apart from his body and mind it is impossible to find Peter.

For these reasons it follows that the I does not exist separate from the body and mind. When our analytical meditation leads us to this firm conclusion we do placement meditation.

When we have ascertained the absence of difference we are close to realizing that the inherently existent I does not exist at all. At this point in the meditation we need to recall the generic image of the inherently existent I and meditate:

Until now I have believed this I to exist, but upon thorough investigation I have seen that no such I exists. Having checked the two possibilities – that it is one with the aggregates or separate from the aggregates – I have found it to be neither.

As a result of engaging in this analytical meditation we become aware that the inherently existent I we usually perceive does not exist. We ascertain the emptiness of our I. We perceive an absence where we used to perceive an I. This absence is the non-affirming negative that is the negation of the inherently existent I. At this point we do not need to think specifically 'This is emptiness'; we just meditate single-pointedly on the absence of such an I.

Experiencing the absence of the inherently existent I as a result of careful analytical meditation is similar to the experience we have when we conduct a thorough search for a particular object in our house and, having looked in every possible place where it could be, realize that it is not there.

When we perceive the generic image of an emptiness that is the negation of the inherently existent I, we are realizing emptiness conceptually. Only space-like emptiness appears to our mind. The generic image of the emptiness of the I is the object of space-like meditative equipoise. What is understood at this stage is the mere absence of the inherently existent I. We feel that there is no I to cherish. By repeated meditation on emptiness our self-grasping and other delusions will lessen and our sufferings and problems will become fewer. Eventually we shall realize emptiness directly and eliminate the root of all our problems.

The concentration that has as its object the mere absence of an inherently existent I has two characteristics: it perceives only space-like emptiness, and it remains single-pointedly on its object, eliminating all distractions. With the mere absence of an inherently existent I as our object we try to attain at least the second mental abiding, continual placement. Whenever we forget our object we need to renew our mindfulness, remembering with one part of our mind how an inherently existent I does not exist. By applying the appropriate opponents, if we are able to remain with concentration on this space-like emptiness this is called 'sustaining space-like meditative equipoise on emptiness'.

We meditate on space-like emptiness in the way that an eagle soars gently through the sky, only occasionally flapping its wings to sustain its flight. We fix our mind single-pointedly upon space-like emptiness, from time to time applying effort to maintain our mindfulness. In this way we gently sustain and improve our meditative equipoise on emptiness.

Some meditators experience great joy when they arise from this meditation in which they have realized emptiness. They feel like a poor man who has found a priceless treasure. Other meditators experience fear. They feel that they have lost something very precious; but with further meditation they realize the conventional I and their fear lessens and then disappears. Of the two, the first response indicates that the meditator has greater wisdom; but both responses are signs of faultless meditation on emptiness.

After realizing the emptiness of the I we need to improve our understanding so that we realize the subtle conventional I – the I that is merely imputed by conception. Having firmly concluded that there is no inherently existent I we need to consider 'How does the I exist?' When we realize that the I exists as mere name we have realized both its subtle conventional nature and the union of the two truths. There is then no danger of our falling to the extreme of non-existence or to the extreme of existence. By understanding its subtle conventional nature, our understanding of emptiness is enhanced.

When we understand the name given to a thing and we do not engage in investigation, we accept the name and proceed to use the object appropriately. For example, if we are introduced to someone and told that this person is called Peter, we say 'Hello Peter, how are you?' We do not go searching for Peter, wondering 'Where is Peter?', as if Peter were something different from the name given to a set of human aggregates. Once we have realized the subtle conventional nature of things we shall accept only names and use them appropriately, just as worldly people do. For example, we shall not feel the need to make further analysis to find out where Peter is because we shall know that if we were to conduct such an investigation at this point we would never find Peter.

The correct view of emptiness does not invalidate names as they are commonly used in the world. We understand this when we have understood the union of conventional and ultimate truths. When we understand the union of the two truths we see that functioning things exist as mere imputation, and that it is the merely imputed I that creates karma, experiences suffering, and so forth. The merely imputed I means the I merely imputed by conception. This conception is a mind that conceives I and clings to it. If someone accuses us falsely, for example, we develop the thought 'I am wrongly accused.' The mind clinging to the I is a conceiver. The I is merely what is conceived by that mind. Since we conceive an I we say 'I'. This I is merely stated by speech or imputed by a conceiver, just like the things we dream about. Suppose we dreamt last night that we were being pursued by a tiger. This dream tiger is merely conceived by our mind. We may become frightened in our dream, but only because we believe the tiger to be real when in fact it is the creation of our mind. Our I is like this dream tiger. Whenever the I appears to our mind we believe that it truly exists, and we develop anxiety, discontent, and so forth; but apart from the mere conception of the I there is no I. The same applies to any other object we investigate. We never find anything existing from its own side. All we ever find is emptiness.

If we understand that our own I is empty of true existence we shall understand the selflessness of other persons. While we apprehend ourself and others to exist inherently we discriminate strongly between self and others and commit many non-virtuous actions that cause us to continue experiencing suffering within samsara. Through realizing the emptiness of self and others we shall cease to commit these non-virtuous actions.

The way to meditate on the emptiness of other persons is to follow the same procedure as before, this time identifying the negated object as an inherently existent friend, stranger, or enemy. For example, when we search for our inherently existent friend we shall find that our friend is not the body or the mind of our friend, and that apart from these there is no friend. Usually, if we see just the back of our friend's head we say 'There is my friend', and we have a strong sense of an inherently existent friend; but if we investigate we shall lose this sense of a substantially existent friend and we shall apprehend only emptiness.

HOW TO SUSTAIN ILLUSION-LIKE SUBSEQUENT ATTAINMENT

When we arise from the meditation in which we have realized that the I is empty of inherent existence, the I will still continue to appear to us as if it were inherently existent.

It has appeared in this way since beginningless time, and this appearance does not immediately cease as soon as we have negated inherent existence in our meditation. For a long time afterwards the I still appears to be inherently existent. Therefore, our practice during the meditation break is to disbelieve this appearance. We should remember continuously our realization of emptiness and recognize the appearance of inherent existence as false.

When a magician creates the illusion of a horse, the horse appears to his mind but he knows that the horse is unreal. Similarly, when we arise from meditation on emptiness we know that the inherently existent I that appears to our mind is an illusion. If we look into a mirror we can see our face reflected, but the face in the mirror is just a reflection and not a real face existing from its own side. In a similar way, knowing that the I also does not exist from its own side and holding such understanding at all times is called 'sustaining illusion-like subsequent attainment'. Sustaining illusion-like subsequent attainment is like watching television with the continuous understanding that although many things appear on the screen, none of them really exist inside the box.

THE EMPTINESS OF PHENOMENA

In the *Condensed Perfection of Wisdom Sutra* Buddha says:

> Whatever we have understood with respect to ourself we should apply to all other living beings, and whatever we have understood with respect to all other living beings we should apply to all phenomena.

If we have realized that both we ourself and others lack inherent existence we have realized selflessness of persons. We should then investigate other phenomena. By understanding the emptiness of one object we indirectly understand the emptiness of all objects because we can apply the same reasoning to all other bases of emptiness. For example, if we meditate on our own body we first try to identify the negated object, asking ourself 'What is it that appears to my mind when I think "my body"?' When we grasp at our own body, its parts appear to our mind, but these are not what we are grasping at as our body. We have a mental image of our body as something different from its parts. When we think 'My body is attractive' we are not thinking 'My feet are attractive, my elbows are attractive, my forehead is attractive . . . ', and so forth, but we apprehend an independent body.

As before, we should not be in haste to arrive at any conclusions. We first try to get a clear generic image of our inherently existent body. Such a body appears to us all the time and, provided we do not investigate further, we always grasp onto it as existing in the way that it appears. If our body has special features, for example if it is tall, we should think 'My tall body', to provoke a strong sense of our inherently existent body. When we have a clear generic image we think 'This is the body I cherish. This is the body I think about when I think "My body is beautiful".' Then we investigate in the same way as before, using the following lines of reasoning:

> *If my body exists in the way that it appears to me, it must be either one with the parts of the body or separate from the parts of the body.*
>
> *If the body is one with the parts of the body it follows that one person must have many bodies because there are many parts.*
>
> *Furthermore, the parts of the body cannot be the body because they are the parts of the body, and a thing cannot be part of itself.*
>
> *If the body were separate from the parts of the body it would be possible to find the body existing elsewhere, but we cannot point to anything outside the limbs and the other parts of the body and say 'There is my body.'*
>
> *Furthermore, if the body were separate from the parts of the body it would not make sense to say 'My body is hurt' when our foot is injured.*

If we check in this way we shall not be able to find our body and we shall have to conclude that our body does not exist from its own side. Our sense of an inherently existent body that is independent of everything else will become unclear and we shall eventually lose it, apprehending only emptiness. At that time we are realizing the emptiness of our own body. We can then proceed to examine each part of our body in the same way. For example, we can search for our face until we find only emptiness. Finally, even the atoms of our body will be found to be empty.

If our body has the nature of emptiness, why do we perceive it as solid and substantial? In *Guide to the Bodhisattva's Way of Life* Shantideva says that although there is no body we develop the mind apprehending body because due to ignorance we develop the mind apprehending hands and so forth. We do so not because our body actually exists in that way, but because we have always had ignorance grasping at our body as inherently existent. The parts of the body and the collection of the parts are the basis of imputation for the body, and the body is the imputed object. What we see directly are the parts of the body, and seeing these we mistakenly apprehend an independent body that exists from its own side over and above the parts of the body. The mind that apprehends the body in this way is self-grasping of phenomena. We have had this ignorance since beginningless time.

When we have realized the emptiness of our own body we need to sustain this realization in space-like meditative equipoise. Again, in our meditation break we practise illusion-like subsequent attainment. Then we try to understand the emptiness of all other phenomena so that, eventually, we can meditate with space-like meditative equipoise on the emptiness of all phenomena. After meditating in this way, we improve our understanding so that we realize the subtle conventional nature of all phenomena – that they are merely imputed by conception, existing merely as names. What remains after negating all negated objects are mere names. For example, when we meditate on the emptiness of our body we strongly refute the inherently existent body and perceive only emptiness. When we arise from our meditation, if we check 'What remains?', only the name 'body' remains. Accepting the mere name we can talk sensibly about our body, saying such things as 'My body is strong', and we can carry on our usual work and communicate and function just like everyone else; but our understanding is different because we know that if we check behind the mere name we cannot find the thing to which it refers.

If we understand how on a clear, cloudless night the moon is reflected in water, whenever we see such a reflection this in itself will remind us that there is no moon actually in the water. Similarly, when we arise from meditation on emptiness, whenever inherently existent phenomena appear to our mind this very appearance will remind us that there are no inherently existent phenomena. The very appearance of inherently existent phenomena will help us to maintain our realization of emptiness at all times.

Buddha Shakyamuni said that whatever we are doing – travelling about, working in the city, having a good time, or having a bad time – we should always remember emptiness. If we practise like this, our whole life will become meaningful and all our actions will be causes of attaining liberation.

Manjushri told Je Tsongkhapa that there are four conditions necessary for realizing emptiness:

(1) Reliance upon a qualified and experienced
     Spiritual Guide who can explain emptiness clearly
(2) Purification of negativity
(3) Accumulation of merit
(4) Frequent meditation on emptiness

Meditation on emptiness is like a seed and the other three conditions are like water that nourishes the seed. We begin by reading carefully and listening to instructions on emptiness, and by contemplating them repeatedly so that our understanding becomes clearer and clearer. We may have to meditate for a long time, but eventually we shall realize emptiness and experience greater joy than if we had found a priceless treasure. When we have this experience we enter the door to liberation, the door to peace. Aryadeva said that there is only one door to liberation – the wisdom realizing emptiness – and that without this wisdom no other practice will open the door to liberation.

Realizing emptiness is a universal remedy, a panacea, because it is the only experience that alone solves all our problems. It removes the physical and mental torment of this life and future lives because it completely destroys self-grasping, which is the root cause of all suffering.

Kyabje Phabongkha Rinpoche

Trijang Rinpoche　　　　　　　　　*Kelsang Gyatso Rinpoche*

Progressing through the Spiritual Grounds and Paths

To attain full enlightenment we need to attain a union of tranquil abiding and superior seeing and complete all the Mahayana paths. There are five Mahayana paths:

(1) The Mahayana path of accumulation
(2) The Mahayana path of preparation
(3) The Mahayana path of seeing
(4) The Mahayana path of meditation
(5) The Mahayana Path of No More Learning

These are called 'paths' because just as external paths lead us to our destination, so these internal paths lead us to our ultimate destination, full enlightenment. They can also be called 'grounds' because just as the ground acts as the basis for the growth of plants, trees, and crops, so spiritual grounds are the basis for all spiritual qualities.

We enter the Mahayana path of accumulation when we generate spontaneous bodhichitta and become a Bodhisattva. All the virtuous minds of a Bodhisattva at this stage, such as the minds of love, compassion, bodhichitta, and the wisdom realizing emptiness, are Mahayana paths of accumulation. By virtue of the spontaneous attainment of bodhichitta, the realizations of method and wisdom within the mind of a Bodhisattva are greatly superior to the realizations of Hinayanists.

The Mahayana path of accumulation has three stages: small, middling, and great. When we attain spontaneous aspiring bodhichitta before taking the Bodhisattva vows, we have the mind of earth-like bodhichitta and we enter the small stage of the path of accumulation. After taking the Bodhisattva vows, earth-like bodhichitta, which is the basis for all the subsequent realizations of the Mahayana, transforms into gold-like bodhichitta, and we enter the middling stage of the path of accumulation. When we have attained this path our realization of bodhichitta will not deteriorate. We then attain the concentration of the Dharma continuum. With this attainment we can remember all that we studied and understood in past lives, and we do not forget what we have learnt in this life. With this concentration we are able to see directly the Supreme Emanation Bodies of Buddhas and we are able to receive teachings directly from them. At this stage we have entered the great stage of the path of accumulation.

Bodhisattvas on the path of accumulation improve their realizations of method and wisdom and thereby progress to the Mahayana path of preparation. They advance to the path of preparation while in meditative equipoise on emptiness. While on the path of accumulation Bodhisattvas meditate on emptiness with tranquil abiding. Through repeated meditation their wisdom analyzing emptiness induces a special suppleness. When this special suppleness develops they have attained superior seeing observing emptiness. When Bodhisattvas have a union of tranquil abiding and superior seeing observing emptiness they advance to the Mahayana path of preparation. On this path they have a greater experience of emptiness than before and they have attained a special wisdom realizing emptiness.

The Mahayana path of preparation is so called because the Bodhisattva is now preparing for a direct realization of emptiness. At this point the Bodhisattva's meditation on emptiness is still conceptual, that is, emptiness still appears to his or her mind mixed with a mental image. Because of this he still has dualistic appearance. The goal of the Mahayana path of preparation is to bring the mind and its object, emptiness, closer and closer together until eventually they mix completely, the mental image dissolves, and all dualistic appearance subsides into emptiness. This is accomplished through repeated meditation on emptiness with a union of tranquil abiding and superior seeing.

The Mahayana path of preparation has four stages: heat, peak, patience, and supreme Dharma. When Bodhisattvas attain the first stage of the path of preparation they have a special experience of emptiness that is a sign pointing to their future attainment of the fire-like wisdom of the Mahayana path of seeing. The experience of emptiness of Bodhisattvas on the path of preparation is not the actual fire of wisdom, but it is the beginning of that fire. The first stage is called 'heat' because at this stage Bodhisattvas begin to generate the heat that will become the actual fire of wisdom on the path of seeing.

Bodhisattvas at the heat stage of the path of preparation meditate on emptiness single-pointedly. In their meditation breaks they engage in method practices such as giving Dharma. They go in and out of meditation many times until eventually, while in meditative equipoise, their experience of emptiness becomes stronger, and they move to the peak stage of the path of preparation. At this stage the heat increases and reaches its peak. It is on the verge of becoming a blazing fire. When Bodhisattvas are at the heat stage they have strong concentration on emptiness and it is as if their mind is mixed with emptiness, although this is not yet the case. When Bodhisattvas move to the peak stage their mind mixes with its object more closely and so the experience of emptiness is more intense.

Bodhisattvas at the peak stage also engage in method practices while they are out of meditation. They go in and out of meditation many times until eventually, while in meditative equipoise, their experience of emptiness becomes stronger, and they move to the patience stage of the path of preparation. Bodhisattvas at this stage have attained the special patience of definitely thinking about Dharma, and their patience is especially fine with regard to emptiness. At this stage, during meditation, the Bodhisattva's mind is even more closely mixed with emptiness than before. The Bodhisattva feels that there is no dualistic appearance of mind and its object. Nevertheless, subtle dualistic appearance still remains, and as long as any degree of dualistic appearance remains the mind is not completely mixed with its object, emptiness.

The aim of meditating on emptiness with a union of tranquil abiding and superior seeing is to bring the mind and its object closer and closer until they become inseparably mixed. Before this happens many degrees of mixing are experienced. The more closely the mind is mixed with emptiness the less dualistic appearance there will be. On the Mahayana path of seeing dualistic appearance ceases completely during meditation, and the mind and emptiness mix like water pouring into water. The mind and its object feel the same. Only emptiness is perceived, and no other phenomenon, not even the mind, appears. All dualistic appearance disappears.

At the patience stage of the path of preparation dualistic appearance is less than before and the experience of emptiness is more refined. Gross dualistic appearance has virtually disappeared but there is still subtle dualistic appearance. Because it is subtle, the meditator is unaware of it and thinks that the mind has completely mixed with emptiness. When Bodhisattvas at the patience stage rise from meditation they engage in method practices to benefit others. They go in and out of meditation many times until eventually, while in meditative equipoise on emptiness, they move to the next stage.

At the stage of supreme Dharma the Bodhisattva's mind and emptiness are nearly mixed and the experience of emptiness excels that of the patience stage. The stage of supreme Dharma is so called because it is the highest experience of an ordinary Bodhisattva. All the experiences of Bodhisattvas at this stage are supreme Dharma paths of preparation. Again, Bodhisattvas at this stage engage in method practices during their meditation breaks. Eventually, while they are in meditative equipoise on emptiness, their mind becomes completely mixed with emptiness like water mixed with water, and there is no longer any dualistic appearance. At this point emptiness is realized directly, and the stage of supreme Dharma transforms into the Mahayana path of seeing. The Bodhisattva thus attains the first Bodhisattva ground, called Very Joyful, and becomes a Superior Bodhisattva. The first moment of the path of seeing arises in the same meditation session as the last moment of the stage of supreme Dharma of the path of preparation. This first moment is called the 'uninterrupted path' of the path of seeing because it acts uninterruptedly as the direct antidote to intellectually-formed self-grasping. It is like an axe that cuts down the tree of such ignorance.

The nature of this path of seeing is wisdom. It is a wisdom that meditates on emptiness single-pointedly. When, in meditative equipoise, Bodhisattvas abandon intellectually-formed self-grasping and all other intellectually-formed delusions, the uninterrupted path of the path of seeing transforms into the released path of the path of seeing. The released path is the result of having abandoned intellectually-formed delusions. Both the uninterrupted path and the released path are attained within the same meditation session. When Bodhisattvas arise from this meditation they have great power to benefit others. At this stage they attain the surpassing perfection of giving, being able to give away even their own bodies for the sake of others.

Altogether there are ten Bodhisattva grounds. These are also known as 'causal grounds' because they are the cause of the resultant ground of Buddhahood. All ten grounds are realizations of Superior Bodhisattvas on the Mahayana paths of seeing and meditation. The first Bodhisattva ground has two levels: the path of seeing, and the uninterrupted path of the path of meditation of the first ground. On the path of seeing Bodhisattvas abandon intellectually-formed delusions and self-grasping but still have to overcome innate self-grasping. There are nine levels of innate self-grasping: big-big, middling-big, small-big, big-middling, middling-middling, small-middling, big-small, middling-small, and small-small. Bodhisattvas on the path of seeing enter meditative equipoise on emptiness to overcome big-big innate self-grasping.

When their wisdom of meditative equipoise becomes powerful enough to act as the direct antidote to big-big innate self-grasping, it has transformed into the wisdom of meditative equipoise of the uninterrupted path of the path of meditation of the first ground. At this point the Bodhisattva advances to the Mahayana path of meditation. In the same session the Bodhisattva abandons big-big innate self-grasping. When this abandonment has occurred, the Bodhisattva has attained the released path of the second Bodhisattva ground, Stainless. The good qualities of a Bodhisattva on this ground are multiplied one thousand times. These Bodhisattvas then arise from meditation and work to help others. Later, they enter meditation again to abandon middling-big innate self-grasping.

When Bodhisattvas have abandoned middling-big innate self-grasping they advance to the third Bodhisattva ground. When Bodhisattvas on the third ground arise from meditation they perform actions to help others, and then they enter meditation again to abandon small-big innate self-grasping. When they have abandoned small-big innate self-grasping they advance to the fourth ground, and in their meditation breaks they continue to work for the benefit of others. This process continues in a similar way as Bodhisattvas abandon the next three levels of innate self-grasping. Bodhisattvas on the seventh ground, having worked for the benefit of others while out of meditation, again enter meditation and abandon the last three levels of innate self-grasping all in one session, thus advancing to the eighth ground.

On the eighth ground Bodhisattvas have abandoned all self-grasping and all delusions, but they still have obstructions to omniscience. They once again enter meditation on emptiness, and when they have abandoned the gross obstructions to omniscience they advance to the ninth ground. Bodhisattvas on the ninth ground again enter meditative equipoise and abandon the subtle obstructions to omniscience, thus advancing to the tenth ground.

When Bodhisattvas on the tenth ground enter meditative equipoise on emptiness their wisdom becomes powerful enough to act as the direct antidote to the very subtle obstructions to omniscience. This concentration is known as the 'vajra-like concentration of the path of meditation'. It is also called the 'exalted wisdom of the final continuum' because it is the last moment of the mind of a sentient being. In the next moment the Bodhisattva becomes a Buddha. In one session, Bodhisattvas free themselves from the very subtle obstructions to omniscience and attain the final released path, the Mahayana Path of No More Learning. When this path is attained, the Bodhisattva has become a Buddha and has gained the exalted omniscient wisdom. At this time the meditator attains the four bodies of a Buddha. Bodhisattvas on the tenth ground have many emanations, and when they become Buddhas all their emanations become Buddhas and work for the benefit of all living beings.

The Vajrayana Paths

If we wish to become enlightened in this very lifetime we need to enter the Vajrayana, or Tantric, path because only the Vajrayana teaches methods for attaining Buddhahood in one life. It is very rare to receive the teachings of Vajrayana; of the one thousand Buddhas of this Fortunate Aeon it is said that only three teach Vajrayana, and one of these is Buddha Shakyamuni. Furthermore, the teachings move quickly from place to place. Now that we have the opportunity to receive them and put them into practice we should do so, recognizing how very rare it is to receive such precious instructions.

Vajrayana means, literally, 'Vajra Vehicle'. 'Vajra' refers to the non-duality of method and wisdom, and 'Vehicle' refers to a spiritual path. It is the quick path to enlightenment because by practising Vajrayana we accumulate both the collection of merit and the collection of wisdom within one concentration on emptiness, and thus create simultaneously all the causes for the Form Body and the Truth Body of a Buddha. Because the collections of merit and wisdom are both accumulated within one concentration they are said to be indivisible, like a vajra. Such a practice of concentration is revealed only in the Vajrayana.

Buddha taught four classes of Tantra, in accordance with the various inclinations of his disciples. These are:

(1) Action Tantra
(2) Performance Tantra
(3) Yoga Tantra
(4) Highest Yoga Tantra

542

Action Tantra is so called because it principally stresses external actions; Performance Tantra places equal emphasis on both external and internal actions; Yoga Tantra emphasizes mainly internal actions; and Highest Yoga Tantra is the supreme class of Tantra.

Action Tantra has four main root texts: *General Secret Tantra*, *Excellent Establishment Tantra*, *Tantra Requested by Subahu*, and *Concentration Continuum Tantra*. There are also many branch Tantras. All Action Tantras are included within three lineages: the Tathagata lineage, the Lotus lineage, and the Vajra lineage. Each of these has further divisions, and are described in texts such as Je Tsongkhapa's *Great Exposition of the Stages of Secret Mantra*, where the practices of all the Tantras are explained.

By comparison with Action Tantra there are fewer texts of Performance Tantra translated into Tibetan. The main Tantra of Performance Tantra is *Vairochanabhisambodhitantra*. Besides this, only *Condensed Vairochana Tantra*, which is a branch of the previous Tantra, and *Vajrapani Empowerment Tantra* are translated into Tibetan, although there are many Tibetan commentaries to these Tantras.

The main Tantras of Yoga Tantra are *Condensation of Thatness Tantra* and its autocommentary, *Vajra Peak Explanatory Tantra*.

There are two divisions of Highest Yoga Tantra: Father Tantra and Mother Tantra. Father Tantras such as *Guhyasamaja Tantra* mainly emphasize developing the illusory body, and Mother Tantras such as *Heruka Tantra* mainly emphasize developing clear light. Only Highest Yoga Tantra has a complete method for attaining enlightenment in this short life. Some practitioners of the three lower Tantras can extend their life spans, but to attain enlightenment in one lifetime they need to enter the practices of Highest Yoga Tantra. Without relying upon Highest Yoga Tantra it is impossible to attain full enlightenment.

The practice of Highest Yoga Tantra is very extensive, but all the practices are included within five:

(1) Generating special bodhichitta
(2) Receiving an empowerment
(3) Maintaining the vows and commitments purely
(4) Practising the yogas of generation stage
(5) Practising the yogas of completion stage

If we practise the Vajrayana path, or Secret Mantra, without the motivation of bodhichitta we cannot attain enlightenment. Therefore, the first thing we need to do if we wish to practise Secret Mantra is to gain experience of all the preceding stages of the path leading to the realization of bodhichitta. Bodhichitta is like the outer door to Secret Mantra and receiving an empowerment is like the inner door. This is why the Bodhisattva vows are always given before an empowerment is granted. When we receive a Tantric empowerment, which empowers us to engage in the actual practices, we take a number of vows and commitments such as the Bodhisattva vows and the Tantric vows. Subsequent success in our Tantric practices depends upon maintaining these vows and commitments purely. Just as crops cannot grow easily in a field that is full of stones and weeds, so it is difficult for us to gain the special realizations of Secret Mantra when our moral discipline is impure.

These first three practices are preparations. The actual practices of Highest Yoga Tantra are the yogas of generation stage and completion stage. Generation stage meditations are paths that lead to completion stage and cause the realizations of completion stage to ripen. Thus, if we meditate well on generation stage our practice of completion stage will progress easily. It is the yogas of completion stage that actually liberate us from samsara and lead us to Buddhahood.

To understand how Tantric practices lead to Buddhahood it is necessary to understand the basis, the path, and the result. The basis is the object to be purified, the path is the means of purifying, and the result is the pure effect. The basis to be purified is samsara – that is, ordinary death, intermediate state, and rebirth. Usually these follow one upon the other, condemning us to one samsaric rebirth after another. By practising the yogas of generation stage and completion stage we can purify these and transform them into the three bodies of a Buddha: the Truth Body, the Enjoyment Body, and the Emanation Body. The yogas of generation stage purify ordinary death, intermediate state, and rebirth indirectly, and the yogas of completion stage purify them directly.

To gain realizations of generation stage we need to do generation stage meditation. This has the following three features:

(1) Bringing the three bodies of a Buddha into the path
(2) Meditating on clear appearance and divine pride
(3) Overcoming ordinary appearances and ordinary conceptions in dependence upon clear appearance and divine pride.

The first of these consists of three yogas: bringing ordinary death into the path of the Truth Body, bringing ordinary intermediate state into the path of the Enjoyment Body, and bringing ordinary rebirth into the path of the Emanation Body. With these yogas we generate ourself as the Deity and then, with concentration, train in clear appearance and divine pride. Through training in clear appearance we overcome ordinary appearances, and through training in divine pride we overcome ordinary conceptions.

Highest Yoga Tantra sadhanas include these three practices, as well as other secondary practices such as mantra recitation. All three features must be present for a practice to be actual generation stage. Generating ourself as a Deity alone is not a yoga of generation stage, because even some non-Buddhists perform similar practices, generating themselves as gods such as Ishvara for example. A more extensive explanation of the yogas of generation stage can be found in *Guide to Dakini Land*.

The main function of the yogas of generation stage and completion stage is to purify ordinary death, intermediate state, and rebirth, and to transform them into the three bodies of a Buddha. The yogas of generation stage purify these indirectly, and the yogas of completion stage purify them directly. Ordinary death, intermediate state, and rebirth follow one upon the other relentlessly, like a wheel spinning, keeping ordinary beings bound within samsara. In Secret Mantra, ordinary death, intermediate state, and rebirth are called the 'three basic bodies'. Ordinary death is known as the 'basic truth body'. It is not the actual Truth Body, but it is the basis of the Truth Body. Similarly, ordinary intermediate state is known as the 'basic enjoyment body' because it is the basis of the Enjoyment Body, and ordinary rebirth is known as the 'basic emanation body' because it is the basis of the Emanation Body. In Secret Mantra these three basic bodies are the basis to be purified.

In completion stage there are three corresponding path bodies. The two stages of the completion stage yoga of clear light – ultimate example clear light and meaning clear light – are known as the 'path truth body'. These two clear lights purify ordinary death directly. The meditator initially becomes free from ordinary death with the attainment of ultimate example clear light of isolated mind. The impure illusory body and the pure illusory body are known as the 'path enjoyment body', and these purify ordinary intermediate state directly. The gross physical Deity bodies of those who have attained either the impure or the pure illusory body are known as the 'path emanation body', and these purify ordinary rebirth directly. The practices of clear light, illusory body, and the Deity's gross body are the main yogas of completion stage. More extensively, completion stage has five main stages which are explained in detail by Je Tsong-khapa in *Clear Lamp of the Five Stages*. A further explanation of the five stages can be found in *Clear Light of Bliss* and *Tantric Grounds and Paths*.

The three path bodies purify ordinary death, intermediate state, and rebirth directly. After that we attain the three resultant bodies of a Buddha – the Emanation Body, the Enjoyment Body, and the Truth Body. The ultimate result of practising Secret Mantra is the attainment of these three resultant bodies, accomplished in dependence upon completion stage practices, which in turn depend upon gaining the realizations of generation stage.

It is impossible to attain Buddhahood without relying upon these yogas of generation stage and completion stage. They are the quick path Buddha taught in his Tantric scriptures and are not newly invented. An authentic Tantra is one that has been taught by Buddha. All the authoritative Tantras were practised by the Buddhist Mahasiddhas such as Saraha, Nagarjuna, and Tilopa, who explained the two Tantric stages in their writings and revealed what they themselves had experienced. Furthermore, in *Great Exposition of the Stages of Secret Mantra* Je Tsongkhapa gives extensive explanations of the four classes of Tantra. Everything he writes was expressed in the Tantras by Buddha; Je Tsongkhapa quotes the words of Buddha and gives scriptural authority for everything he writes in his commentary.

We should try to become familiar with the life and works of Je Tsongkhapa and develop faith in him. He is not praised here just because he was the founder of the Gelug tradition, but on account of his excellence. If we were to study his works we would be astounded by their clarity and beauty, and we would understand that they are the works of a realized Master who has written honestly and sincerely about his own experiences. His teachings are said to have two special qualities: his teaching of Secret Mantra reveals the meaning of the Tantras unmistakenly and more clearly than others; and his special way of presenting the profound view cannot be found elsewhere. We cannot become convinced of this simply by listening to others; these special qualities can be understood only through study and practice.

Full Enlightenment

Any being who has become completely free from the two obstructions, which are the roots of all faults, has attained full enlightenment. If we consider our own experience we shall gain conviction that we ourself can abandon all faults and become a Buddha. Sometimes we have great faults and many of them, but at other times we have very few faults and those we have are quite small. Since even without applying any effort our faults and delusions sometimes decrease, this indicates that with effort we can definitely abandon them completely.

As explained, there are two types of obstruction: delusion-obstructions and obstructions to omniscience. The latter prevent us from knowing all objects directly and simultaneously, that is, from gaining the all-knowing mind of a Buddha. Since delusions – the obstructions preventing liberation – can be reduced and abandoned, it follows that the imprints of delusions – the obstructions preventing omniscience – can also be completely abandoned. However, for this to happen we need to exert effort in applying the methods for training our mind in all the stages of Sutra and Tantra. If we put effort into training our mind in all the methods that have been explained, our mind will transform into the omniscient mind of a Buddha.

Buddha Shakyamuni said:

If you realize your own mind you will become a Buddha; you should not seek Buddhahood elsewhere.

Here, to realize our own mind means to experience our own mind as pure and free from the two obstructions.

When we become fully enlightened we attain the four bodies of a Buddha. As explained, a Buddha's main body is the Truth Body which is of two types: the Wisdom Truth Body and the Nature Body. The Wisdom Truth Body is the omniscient mind of a Buddha, and the Nature Body is the ultimate nature of a Buddha's mind which is free from the two obstructions. The other two bodies of a Buddha – the Enjoyment Body and the Emanation Body – together constitute the Form Body. Of the two, the Enjoyment Body is the more subtle.

If Buddhas were to remain with their Truth Body alone other beings would not receive benefit because only Buddhas can perceive the Truth Body. Therefore from the Truth Body Buddhas manifest an Enjoyment Body and, since only Superior Bodhisattvas can perceive this, from the Enjoyment Body they manifest Emanation Bodies. The Supreme Emanation Body can be seen only by those who have pure karma. For those with impure karma, Buddhas manifest as ordinary beings. To help others they can assume any aspect, Buddhist or non-Buddhist, and they can assume any form, animate or inanimate. Since the minds of those who perceive them are obstructed by ignorance they do not suspect that these ordinary looking forms are the Emanation Bodies of Buddhas. In fact it is very difficult for us to know who is an emanation of Buddha. The only person whom we can say for sure is not a Buddha is ourself. Buddha said 'Someone such as I can know people but others cannot.' His meaning is that someone who is a Buddha can know whether or not another person is a Buddha, but others who are not Buddhas cannot.

A Buddha's body has many marvellous good qualities, such as being free from birth, ageing, sickness, and death. It is immutable, a vajra body. It is said that a Buddha's body can understand and expound Dharma, and that discourses have been delivered from a Buddha's crown protusion. Similarly, a Buddha's speech is unlike that of ordinary beings. Its volume does not vary, no matter how close or distant the listener may be; and whatever a Buddha says is understood by the listener in his or her own language. Just hearing the speech of a Buddha pacifies delusions in the mind of whoever listens. A Buddha's speech can expound Dharma that cannot be expounded by others and so it frees living beings from samsara. Our liberation and full enlightenment depend upon the speech of Buddha, for if Buddha had not taught Dharma there would be no method for freeing ourself from samsara. From listening to, contemplating, and meditating on Buddha's words, all good qualities and realizations are attained.

The extraordinary qualities of a Buddha's mind are summarized in the scriptures as the ten forces, the eighteen unshared qualities, the four fearlessnesses, and the four correct, specific cognizers.

The ten forces of a Buddha are:

(1) The force knowing source and non-source. A Buddha knows directly all causes and their effects.

(2) The force knowing full ripening of actions. A Buddha knows directly all actions and their effects.

(3) The force knowing the various desires. A Buddha knows directly every single desire of each and every living being.

(4) The force knowing the various elements. A Buddha knows directly all gross and subtle elements.

(5) The force knowing supreme and non-supreme powers. A Buddha knows directly all the powers, as well as their ability to support each other.

(6) The force knowing all paths that lead to samsara and solitary peace. A Buddha knows directly all correct and incorrect paths.

(7) The force knowing the mental stabilizations, concentrations of perfect liberation, concentrations, absorptions, and so forth. A Buddha knows directly all concentrations.

(8) The force knowing recollections of previous lives. A Buddha knows directly all the previous rebirths of every living being.

(9) The force knowing death and birth. A Buddha knows directly the whole process of death and birth of every living being.

(10) The force knowing the cessation of contaminations.
A Buddha knows directly the three types of enlightenment – a Hearer's enlightenment, a Solitary Realizer's enlightenment, and a Buddha's enlightenment.

The eighteen unshared qualities of a Buddha are the six
unshared activities, the six unshared realizations, the three
unshared deeds, and the three unshared exalted awarenesses.
They are called 'unshared' because they are not shared by
living beings; they are uncommon qualities belonging only
to Buddhas.

(1) Not possessing mistaken activities of body.
(2) Not possessing mistaken activities of speech.
(3) Not possessing mistaken activities of mind.
Buddhas have perfect mindfulness.
(4) Not possessing a mind not in meditative equipoise.
Only Buddhas can be in meditative equipoise and
subsequent attainment at the same time.
(5) Not possessing conceptuality.
(6) Not possessing neutrality. All Buddhas' actions
are virtuous, never negative or neutral. They
regard all beings as their children, regarding
them with perfect equanimity, compassion, and
love, and not being indifferent to anyone.
(7) Not possessing degeneration of aspiration.
(8) Not possessing degeneration of effort.
(9) Not possessing degeneration of mindfulness.
(10) Not possessing degeneration of concentration.
(11) Not possessing degeneration of wisdom.
(12) Not possessing degeneration of perfect liberation.
(13) Deeds of body preceded by and followed by exalted
awareness, and thus completely pure and limitless.
(14) Deeds of speech preceded by and followed by exalted
awareness, and thus completely pure and limitless.
(15) Deeds of mind preceded by and followed by exalted
awareness, and thus completely pure and limitless.
(16) Unobstructed exalted awareness that knows all
the past directly and without obstruction.

(17) Unobstructed exalted awareness that knows all the future directly and without obstruction.

(18) Unobstructed exalted awareness that knows all the present directly and without obstruction.

The four fearlessnesses of a Buddha are:

(1) Fearlessness in revealing the Dharma of renunciation

(2) Fearlessness in revealing the Dharma of overcoming obstructions

(3) Fearlessness in revealing the Dharma of excellent abandonments

(4) Fearlessness in revealing the Dharma of excellent realizations

The four correct, specific cognizers of a Buddha are:

(1) Correct cognizers of specific phenomena
(2) Correct cognizers of specific meanings
(3) Correct cognizers of specific, definite words
(4) Correct cognizers of specific confidence

Even very highly realized Bodhisattvas are unable to express adequately the good qualities of a Buddha. If a bird flies high in the sky it must eventually come down somewhere, no matter how far it soars. This is not because the bird has arrived at the end of space, but because it has run out of energy to fly. Space is vast and endless and the bird's power is exhausted before it has travelled throughout space. The good qualities of a Buddha are like space and our understanding is like this bird. If we were to try to describe all the good qualities of a Buddha, our wisdom and skill would run out before we could finish describing them. They are beyond our imagination.

TRAINING IN THE FOUR WAYS OF GATHERING TO RIPEN THE MENTAL CONTINUUM OF OTHERS

The main reason why Bodhisattvas train in the six perfections to ripen their own mental continuum is because they wish to help all living beings. In general, there are countless ways of benefiting others in accordance with their aspirations. However, there are four essential ways, called the 'four ways of gathering':

(1) Pleasing others by giving them material things or whatever they need
(2) Teaching Dharma to lead others to liberation
(3) Helping others in their Dharma practice by giving them encouragement
(4) Showing a good example by always practising what we teach

In this way Bodhisattvas gather many disciples and lead them into the spiritual path. Once we have taken the Bodhisattva vows we must never lose the intention to benefit others. We need always to think how we can help others; and to bring them the greatest benefit we must constantly be intent upon attaining full enlightenment. The way to attain the final result of full enlightenment is by training the mind in all the stages of the path as they have been explained. If we also receive an empowerment into the practices of Highest Yoga Tantra, maintain our vows and commitments purely, and practise sincerely the yogas of generation stage and completion stage, we shall attain full enlightenment in this very lifetime.

In conclusion, our attainment of full enlightenment depends upon our practice of the stages of the path of Secret Mantra; our practice of the stages of the path of Secret Mantra depends upon our practice of the stages of the path of Sutra; and our practice of the stages of the path of Sutra depends upon wholehearted reliance upon our Spiritual Guide, the root of the path.

Dedication

Through the virtues I have collected by reading, contemplating, and practising these instructions, may all living beings find the opportunity to practise the stages of the path.

May all living beings develop great wisdom like that of Manjushri, great compassion like that of Avalokiteshvara, and great power like that of Vajrapani; and may they all attain the great enlightenment of Buddha Shakyamuni.

Appendix I
The Condensed Meaning
of the Text

The Condensed Meaning
of the Text

The instructions on the stages of the path to enlightenment, Lamrim, has four parts:

1 Explanation of the pre-eminent qualities of the author, showing that the instructions of Lamrim are authentic
2 Explanation of the pre-eminent qualities of Lamrim to inspire faith and respect for the Lamrim instructions
3 Explanation of how to listen to and teach Dharma
4 Explanation of the actual instructions of the stages of the path to enlightenment

Explanation of the pre-eminent qualities of the author, showing that the instructions of Lamrim are authentic, has three parts:

1 Atisha's birth into a royal family and his early life
2 Atisha's attainments of knowledge and spiritual realizations
3 Atisha's work of spreading Buddhadharma in India and Tibet

Explanation of the pre-eminent qualities of Lamrim to inspire faith and respect for the Lamrim instructions has two parts:

1 The pre-eminent characteristics of Lamrim
2 The pre-eminent attributes of Lamrim

The pre-eminent characteristics of Lamrim has three parts:

1 The Lamrim teaching is the condensation of all Buddhadharma
2 The instructions of Lamrim are easy to put into practice
3 The presentation of the instructions of Lamrim is superior to other traditions

The pre-eminent attributes of Lamrim has four parts:

1 We shall understand that none of Buddha's teachings are contradictory
2 We shall take all Buddha's teachings as personal advice and put them into practice
3 We shall easily realize Buddha's ultimate intention
4 We shall naturally become free from the great fault and from all other faults

Explanation of how to listen to and teach Dharma has three parts:

1 How to listen to Dharma
2 How to teach Dharma
3 The concluding stage common to the Teacher and the student

How to listen to Dharma has three parts:

1 Considering the benefits of listening to Dharma
2 Developing respect for Dharma and its Teacher
3 The actual way of listening to Dharma

The actual way of listening to Dharma has two parts:

1 Abandoning three faults
2 Cultivating six recognitions

Abandoning three faults has three parts:

1 The fault of being like a pot turned upside-down
2 The fault of being like a bad-smelling pot
3 The fault of being like a leaky pot

Cultivating six recognitions has six parts:

1 Regarding ourself as a sick person because we suffer from desirous attachment, hatred, ignorance, and other diseases of the mind.
2 Regarding Dharma as supreme medicine for our mental sickness.
3 Regarding our Dharma Teacher as a supreme doctor.
4 Regarding putting Dharma into practice as the way to become cured of our mental disease.
5 Developing conviction in Buddha Shakyamuni as a holy being who is completely reliable.

6 Developing a strong wish that Dharma will flourish and remain for a long time.

How to teach Dharma has four parts:

1 Considering the benefits of teaching Dharma.
2 Increasing faith and respect for Dharma and its Teacher.
3 The attitudes to cultivate and the way to conduct ourself whilst teaching Dharma.
4 Recognizing whom should be taught and whom should not be taught.

Explanation of the actual instructions of the stages of the path to enlightenment has two parts:

1 How to rely upon a Spiritual Guide, the root of spiritual paths
2 How to take the essence of our human life

How to rely upon a Spiritual Guide, the root of spiritual paths, has two parts:

1 How to train the mind during the meditation session
2 How to train the mind during the meditation break

How to train the mind during the meditation session has three parts:

1 Preparing for meditation
2 The actual meditation
3 Concluding the meditation

Preparing for meditation has six parts:

1 Cleaning the meditation room and setting up a shrine with representations of Buddha's body, speech, and mind.
2 Arranging suitable offerings.
3 Sitting in the correct meditation posture, going for refuge, generating and enhancing bodhichitta.
4 Visualizing the Field for Accumulating Merit.
5 Accumulating merit and purifying negativity by offering the practice of the seven limbs and the mandala.
6 Requesting the Field for Accumulating Merit in general and the Lamrim lineage Gurus in particular to bestow their blessings.

The actual meditation has two parts:

1 The qualifications of a Mahayana Spiritual Guide and
   a Mahayana disciple
2 The actual meditation on relying upon our Spiritual
   Guide

The actual meditation on relying upon our Spiritual Guide has
four parts:

1 The benefits of relying completely upon our Spiritual
   Guide
2 The dangers of breaking our commitment to our
   Spiritual Guide
3 How to rely upon our Spiritual Guide by developing
   faith and respect
4 How to rely upon our Spiritual Guide by engaging in
   actions of service and devotion

The benefits of relying completely upon our Spiritual Guide
has eight parts:

1 We progress towards enlightenment
2 We delight all the Buddhas
3 We are not harmed by demons and other evil
   influences
4 We easily overcome our faults and delusions
5 Our experiences and realizations of spiritual grounds
   and paths greatly increase
6 We never lack spiritual friends in all our future lives
7 We do not take rebirth in the lower realms
8 All our wishes, temporary and ultimate, are easily
   fulfilled

The dangers of breaking our commitment to our Spiritual
Guide has eight parts:

1 Since our Spiritual Guide is an emanation of all the
   Buddhas, if we forsake or show contempt for him or
   her, this action will have the same effect as forsaking
   or showing contempt for all the Buddhas.
2 Every moment of anger that arises in our mind towards
   our Spiritual Guide destroys all the good karma that
   we can create in one aeon and causes us to take
   rebirth in hell for one aeon.

3 Even though we may practise Secret Mantra for aeons, if we have forsaken our Spiritual Guide it will be impossible to gain realizations.

4 With a critical or angry mind towards our Spiritual Guide our practice of Secret Mantra will become the cause of rebirth in hell.

5 It will be impossible to gain new realizations, and the realizations that we have already gained will degenerate.

6 We shall be afflicted with misfortunes such as disease, fear, and possession by evil spirits.

7 We shall take rebirth in the lower realms repeatedly.

8 In many future lives we shall not meet well-qualified Spiritual Guides and we shall be without Dharma, and whenever we do meet Spiritual Guides we shall continue to lack faith and respect for them.

How to rely upon our Spiritual Guide by developing faith and respect has two parts:

1 How to develop faith that our Spiritual Guide is a Buddha, which is the root of all attainments

2 How to develop respect for our Spiritual Guide by remembering his or her kindness

How to develop faith that our Spiritual Guide is a Buddha, which is the root of all attainments, has three parts:

1 Why it is necessary to regard our Spiritual Guide as a Buddha

2 How it is possible to regard our Spiritual Guide as a Buddha

3 How to develop conviction that our Spiritual Guide is a Buddha

How to develop conviction that our Spiritual Guide is a Buddha has four parts:

1 Buddha Vajradhara said that Spiritual Guides are Buddhas

2 Our Spiritual Guide performs the enlightened actions of a Buddha

3 In these degenerate times Buddhas continue to work for the benefit of all living beings

4 Appearances are deceptive and our own opinions are
unreliable

How to develop respect for our Spiritual Guide by remembering
his or her kindness has two parts:

1 Remembering that our Spiritual Guide is kinder than
all the Buddhas
2 Remembering that our Spiritual Guide is kinder even
than Buddha Shakyamuni

How to rely upon our Spiritual Guide by engaging in actions
of service and devotion has four parts:

1 Offering actions of bodily or verbal respect such as
making prostrations or reciting praises
2 Offering material things
3 Offering service
4 Offering our own practice of Dharma

How to take the essence of our human life has two parts:

1 How to develop the determination to take the essence
of our precious human life
2 Training the mind in the actual methods for taking
the essence of our precious human life

How to develop the determination to take the essence of our
precious human life has three parts:

1 Recognizing that we now possess a precious human
life
2 Meditating on the great value of our precious human
life
3 Meditating on the great rarity of our precious human
life

Recognizing that we now possess a precious human life has
two parts:

1 The eight freedoms
2 The ten endowments

The eight freedoms has eight parts:

1 Freedom from being born as a hell being
2 Freedom from being born as a hungry spirit

3 Freedom from being born as, an animal
4 Freedom from being born as an ordinary god
5 Freedom from being born and remaining in a country where there is no religion
6 Freedom from being born and remaining in a country where there is no Buddhadharma
7 Freedom from being born and remaining with mental or physical disabilities
8 Freedom from holding wrong views denying Dharma

The ten endowments has ten parts:

1 Being born human
2 Being born and remaining in a country where Dharma is flourishing
3 Being born and remaining with complete powers, free from mental and physical disabilities
4 Not having committed any of the five actions of immediate retribution
5 Having faith in the three sets of Buddha's teachings
6 Taking human rebirth in a world where Buddha has appeared
7 Taking human rebirth in a world where Buddha has taught Dharma
8 Taking human rebirth in a world where pure Dharma is still being taught
9 Taking human rebirth in a world where there are people practising pure Dharma
10 Taking human rebirth in a world where there are benefactors and sponsors for Dharma practitioners

Meditating on the great value of our precious human life has three parts:

1 The great value of our precious human life from the point of view of our temporary goal
2 The great value of our precious human life from the point of view of our ultimate goal
3 The great value of every moment of our precious human life

Meditating on the great rarity of our precious human life has three parts:

1 Recognizing the rarity of our precious human life in terms of its cause
2 Recognizing the rarity of our precious human life by analogy
3 Recognizing the rarity of our precious human life in terms of numbers

Training the mind in the actual methods for taking the essence of our precious human life has three parts:

1 Training the mind in the stages of the path of a person of initial scope
2 Training the mind in the stages of the path of a person of intermediate scope
3 Training the mind in the stages of the path of a person of great scope

Training the mind in the stages of the path of a person of initial scope has two parts:

1 Developing the aspiration to experience the happiness of higher states in future lives
2 The actual methods for gaining the happiness of higher states of existence in future lives

Developing the aspiration to experience the happiness of higher states in future lives has two parts:

1 Meditating on death
2 Meditating on the sufferings of the lower realms

Meditating on death has three parts:

1 Considering the dangers of forgetting about death
2 Considering the benefits of remaining mindful of death
3 The actual meditation on death

Considering the dangers of forgetting about death has six parts:

1 We shall easily forget Dharma
2 Even if we do not forget Dharma we shall not be likely to put it into practice

JOYFUL PATH OF GOOD FORTUNE

3 Even if we do not forget Dharma and we put it into practice, our practice will not be pure

4 Even if we do not forget Dharma and we put it into practice purely, we shall lack persistent effort in our practice

5 We shall continue to perform non-virtuous actions

6 We shall die full of regret

Considering the benefits of remaining mindful of death has six parts:

1 We engage in Dharma practice sincerely and energetically

2 Our Dharma practice becomes very powerful and very pure

3 It is important at the beginning of our practice

4 It is important throughout our practice

5 It is important in attaining the final goal of our practice

6 We shall have a happy mind at the time of death

The actual meditation on death has two parts:

1 Meditating on death using nine ways of reasoning

2 Meditating on death imagining that the time of our death has come

Meditating on death using nine ways of reasoning has three parts:

1 Using three ways of reasoning to gain conviction that death is certain

2 Using three ways of reasoning to gain conviction that the time of death is uncertain

3 Using three ways of reasoning to gain conviction that at the time of death and after death only our practice of Dharma is of benefit to us

Using three ways of reasoning to gain conviction that death is certain has three parts:

1 Death will definitely come and nothing can prevent it

2 Our life span cannot be increased and it decreases continuously

3 Death will come regardless of whether or not we have made the time to practise Dharma

Using three ways of reasoning to gain conviction that the time of death is uncertain has three parts:

1 The life span of beings living in this world is not fixed
2 There are many more conditions conducive to death than to survival
3 The human body is very fragile

Using three ways of reasoning to gain conviction that at the time of death and after death only our practice of Dharma is of benefit to us has three parts:

1 At the time of death our wealth cannot help us
2 At the time of death our friends and relatives cannot help us
3 At the time of death even our own body is of no use

Meditating on the sufferings of the lower realms has three parts:

1 The sufferings of hell beings
2 The sufferings of hungry spirits
3 The sufferings of animals

The sufferings of hell beings has two parts:

1 Gaining conviction that hell exists
2 The actual meditation on the sufferings of hell beings

Gaining conviction that hell exists has two parts:

1 Reasoning using external signs
2 Reasoning using internal signs

Reasoning using internal signs has three parts:

1 Considering the law of karma in general
2 Considering dreams
3 Considering how the world as it appears to us depends upon karma

The actual meditation on the sufferings of hell beings has four parts:

1 The sufferings of beings in the great hells
2 The sufferings of beings in the neighbouring hells
3 The sufferings of beings in the cold hells
4 The sufferings of beings in the resembling hells

The sufferings of hungry spirits has six parts:

1 Intense heat
2 Intense cold
3 Intense hunger
4 Intense thirst
5 Great fatigue
6 Great fear

The sufferings of animals has five parts:

1 Ignorance and stupidity
2 Heat and cold
3 Hunger and thirst
4 Exploitation by human beings for labour, food, resources, and entertainment
5 Being prey to one another

The actual methods for gaining the happiness of higher states of existence in future lives has two parts:

1 Going for refuge, the gateway to Buddhadharma
2 Gaining conviction in the law of karma, the root of all good qualities and happiness

Going for refuge, the gateway to Buddhadharma, has seven parts:

1 The causes of going for refuge
2 The objects of refuge
3 The way of going for refuge
4 The measurement of going for refuge perfectly
5 The benefits of going for refuge
6 The commitments of going for refuge
7 How to go for refuge by practising three rounds of meditation

The objects of refuge has two parts:

1 Identifying the objects of refuge
2 Understanding why the Three Jewels are suitable objects of refuge

Identifying the objects of refuge has three parts:

1 The Buddha Jewel
2 The Dharma Jewel
3 The Sangha Jewel

Understanding why the Three Jewels are suitable objects of refuge has four parts:

1 Buddha is free from all fear
2 Buddha is very skilful in liberating living beings
3 Buddha has compassion for all living beings without discrimination
4 Buddha benefits all living beings whether or not they have helped him

The way of going for refuge has four parts:

1 Going for refuge understanding the good qualities of the Three Jewels
2 Going for refuge differentiating the qualities of each of the Three Jewels
3 Going for refuge by promising to go for refuge
4 Going for refuge by abandoning going for ultimate refuge to other objects

Going for refuge differentiating the qualities of each of the Three Jewels has six parts:

1 Going for refuge understanding the different natures of the Three Jewels
2 Going for refuge understanding the different functions of the Three Jewels
3 Going for refuge differentiating the Three Jewels by an analogy
4 Going for refuge distinguishing the time of going for refuge
5 Going for refuge understanding the different ways in which merit is increased by going for refuge to each of the Three Jewels
6 Going for refuge understanding the different ways in which the Three Jewels help our practice

The benefits of going for refuge has eight parts:

1 We become a pure Buddhist
2 We establish the foundation for taking all other vows
3 We purify the negative karma that we have accumulated in the past
4 We daily accumulate a vast amount of merit
5 We are held back from falling into the lower realms

6 We are protected from harm inflicted by humans and non-humans

7 We fulfil all our temporary and ultimate wishes

8 We quickly attain the full enlightenment of Buddhahood

The commitments of going for refuge has two parts:

1 The special commitments

2 The general commitments

The special commitments has three parts:

1 One abandonment and one acknowledgement with regard to the Buddha Jewel

2 One abandonment and one acknowledgement with regard to the Dharma Jewel

3 One abandonment and one acknowledgement with regard to the Sangha Jewel

The general commitments has six parts:

1 To go for refuge to the Three Jewels again and again, remembering their good qualities and the differences between them

2 To offer the first portion of whatever we eat and drink to the Three Jewels, remembering their kindness

3 With compassion, always to encourage others to go for refuge

4 Remembering the benefits of going for refuge, to go for refuge at least three times during the day and three times during the night

5 To perform every action with complete trust in the Three Jewels

6 Never to forsake the Three Jewels even at the cost of our life, or as a joke

Gaining conviction in the law of karma, the root of all good qualities and happiness, has four parts:

1 The general characteristics of karma

2 Particular types of action and their effects

3 The eight attributes of a fully endowed human life

4 How to practise moral discipline having gained conviction in the law of karma

The general characteristics of karma has four parts:

1 The results of actions are definite
2 The results of actions increase
3 If an action is not performed its result cannot be experienced
4 An action is never wasted

Particular types of action and their effects has four parts:

1 Non-virtuous actions and their effects
2 Virtuous actions and their effects
3 Factors in the power of any action
4 Throwing actions and completing actions

Non-virtuous actions and their effects has three parts:

1 The ten non-virtuous actions and factors in their completion
2 Factors in the severity of non-virtuous actions
3 The effects of non-virtuous actions

The ten non-virtuous actions and factors in their completion has ten parts:

1 Killing
2 Stealing
3 Sexual misconduct
4 Lying
5 Divisive speech
6 Hurtful speech
7 Idle chatter
8 Covetousness
9 Malice
10 Holding wrong views

Factors in the severity of non-virtuous actions has six parts:

1 The nature of the action
2 The intention
3 The method
4 The object
5 How often the action is committed
6 The application or non-application of an opponent

The effects of non-virtuous actions has three parts:

1 The ripened effect
2 The effects similar to the cause
3 The environmental effect

The effects similar to the cause has two parts:

1 Tendencies similar to the cause
2 Experiences similar to the cause

Virtuous actions and their effects has three parts:

1 The ten virtuous actions and factors in their completion
2 Factors in the beneficial power of virtuous actions
3 The effects of virtuous actions

The ten virtuous actions and factors in their completion has ten parts:

1 Abandoning killing
2 Abandoning stealing
3 Abandoning sexual misconduct
4 Abandoning lying
5 Abandoning divisive speech
6 Abandoning hurtful speech
7 Abandoning idle chatter
8 Abandoning covetousness
9 Abandoning malice
10 Abandoning holding wrong views

Factors in the power of any action has four parts:

1 The person who is the object of the action
2 The vows taken
3 The object that is instrumental in the action
4 The motivation

The eight attributes of a fully endowed human life has three parts:

1 Their advantages
2 Their functions
3 Their causes

Training the mind in the stages of the path of a person of intermediate scope has three parts:

1 Developing the wish to attain liberation
2 A preliminary explanation for establishing the path that leads to liberation
3 How to practise the path that leads to liberation

Developing the wish to attain liberation has two parts:

1 Introduction to the four noble truths
2 Meditating on true sufferings

Introduction to the four noble truths has four parts:

1 True sufferings
2 True origins
3 True cessations
4 True paths

Meditating on true sufferings has three parts:

1 The general sufferings of samsara
2 The particular sufferings of each state of samsaric rebirth
3 The three types of suffering

The general sufferings of samsara has six parts:

1 Uncertainty
2 Having no satisfaction
3 Having to leave our body over and over again
4 Having to take rebirth over and over again
5 Having to lose status over and over again
6 Having no companionship

The particular sufferings of each state of samsaric rebirth has two parts:

1 The sufferings of the lower realms
2 The sufferings of the higher realms

The sufferings of the higher realms has three parts:

1 The sufferings of human beings
2 The sufferings of demi-gods
3 The sufferings of gods

The sufferings of human beings has seven parts:

1 Birth
2 Ageing
3 Sickness
4 Death
5 Having to part with what we like
6 Having to encounter what we do not like
7 Failing to satisfy our desires

Birth has five parts:

1 The extreme pains experienced in the womb and during birth
2 The unceasing pains we experience after birth
3 Birth is the basis for all the sufferings of life
4 Birth is the foundation for all delusions
5 Birth changes into death

Ageing has five parts:

1 Loss of beauty and health
2 Loss of physical strength and vitality
3 Loss of power in our sense and mental faculties
4 Loss of enjoyments
5 Loss of life span

Sickness has five parts:

1 Loss of power and control over the functions of our body
2 Increasing unhappiness
3 Loss of enjoyments
4 Having to experience what we do not want to experience
5 Knowing that our sickness is incurable and that our life is coming to an end

Death has five parts:

1 Departing from our possessions
2 Departing from our friends
3 Departing from those who live and work with us
4 Departing from our body
5 Experiencing mental and physical pain

The three types of suffering has three parts:

1 The suffering of manifest pain
2 Changing suffering
3 Pervasive suffering

A preliminary explanation for establishing the path that leads to liberation has two parts:

1 The development of delusions and actions, death and rebirth
2 An explanation of the twelve dependent-related links

The development of delusions and actions, death and rebirth, has six parts:

1 Identifying the delusions
2 The stages by which delusions develop
3 The causes of delusions
4 The dangers of delusions
5 How actions are created in dependence upon delusions
6 The way we die and take rebirth

Identifying the delusions has two parts:

1 Definition of delusion
2 The six root delusions

The six root delusions has six parts:

1 Desirous attachment
2 Anger
3 Deluded pride
4 Ignorance
5 Deluded doubt
6 Deluded view

Deluded view has five parts:

1 View of the transitory collection
2 Extreme view
3 Holding false views as supreme
4 Holding wrong moral disciplines and conduct as supreme
5 Wrong view

The causes of delusions has six parts:

1 The seed
2 The object
3 Distraction and being influenced by others
4 Bad habits
5 Familiarity
6 Inappropriate attention

The way we die and take rebirth has three parts:

1 The way we die
2 The way we enter the intermediate state
3 The way we take rebirth

The way we die has five parts:

1 The signs of death
2 The causes of death
3 The conditions of death
4 The minds of death
5 The sign that dying has ended

The way we enter the intermediate state has three parts:

1 How to gain conviction that the bardo exists by considering the analogy of the dream state
2 The attributes of the body of a bardo being
3 What appears to a bardo being

The way we take rebirth has three parts:

1 The causes and conditions of taking rebirth
2 How we take rebirth
3 The nature of rebirth

An explanation of the twelve dependent-related links has four parts:

1 A general explanation of dependent-related phenomena
2 The twelve dependent-related links
3 An explanation of the diagram of the Wheel of Life
4 The actual meditation on the twelve dependent-related links

The twelve dependent-related links has twelve parts:

1 Dependent-related ignorance
2 Dependent-related compositional actions
3 Dependent-related consciousness
4 Dependent-related name and form
5 Dependent-related six sources
6 Dependent-related contact
7 Dependent-related feeling
8 Dependent-related craving
9 Dependent-related grasping
10 Dependent-related existence
11 Dependent-related birth
12 Dependent-related ageing and death

An explanation of the diagram of the Wheel of Life has three parts:

1 The benefits of contemplating and meditating on the diagram
2 The origin of the diagram
3 The symbolism of the diagram

The actual meditation on the twelve dependent-related links has four parts:

1 Meditation in serial order on the dependent relationship of the side of delusion
2 Meditation in reverse order on the dependent relationship of the side of delusion
3 Meditation in serial order on the dependent relationship of the perfectly purified side
4 Meditation in reverse order on the dependent relationship of the perfectly purified side

How to practise the path that leads to liberation has two parts:

1 The bodily basis we need to attain liberation
2 The paths we need to follow to attain liberation

The paths we need to follow to attain liberation has three parts:

1 The three higher trainings
2 Why we need to practise the three higher trainings to attain liberation
3 How to practise the three higher trainings

The three higher trainings has three parts:

  1 Training in higher moral discipline
  2 Training in higher concentration
  3 Training in higher wisdom

How to practise the three higher trainings has three parts:

  1 How to practise higher moral discipline
  2 How to practise higher concentration
  3 How to practise higher wisdom

Training the mind in the stages of the path of a person of great scope has five parts:

  1 Why we need to enter the Mahayana
  2 The benefits of bodhichitta
  3 How to develop bodhichitta
  4 How to engage in a Bodhisattva's actions
  5 The final result, full enlightenment

The benefits of bodhichitta has ten parts:

  1 We enter the gateway to the Mahayana
  2 We become a Son or Daughter of the Buddhas
  3 We surpass Hearers and Solitary Realizers
  4 We become worthy to receive offerings and prostrations from humans and gods
  5 We easily accumulate a vast amount of merit
  6 We quickly destroy powerful negativities
  7 We fulfil all our wishes
  8 We are free from harm by spirits and so forth
  9 We accomplish all the spiritual grounds and paths
  10 We have a state of mind that is the source of peace and happiness for all beings

How to develop bodhichitta has two parts:

  1 The stages of actually training the mind in bodhichitta
  2 Maintaining bodhichitta by means of ritual

The stages of actually training the mind in bodhichitta has two parts:

  1 Training the mind in the sevenfold cause and effect
  2 Training the mind in equalizing and exchanging self with others

Training the mind in the sevenfold cause and effect has eight parts:

1 Developing equanimity
2 Recognizing that all living beings are our mothers
3 Remembering the kindness of all mother beings
4 Developing the wish to repay the kindness of all mother beings
5 Developing affectionate love
6 Developing great compassion
7 Developing superior intention
8 Developing bodhichitta

Developing bodhichitta has three parts:

1 The basis for generating bodhichitta
2 The nature of bodhichitta and how it is generated
3 The divisions of bodhichitta

The divisions of bodhichitta has four parts:

1 The twofold division
2 The threefold division
3 The fourfold division
4 The twenty-twofold division

Training the mind in equalizing and exchanging self with others has five parts:

1 Equalizing self and others
2 Contemplating the disadvantages of self-cherishing
3 Contemplating the advantages of cherishing others
4 Exchanging self with others
5 Taking and giving

Exchanging self with others has three parts:

1 Recognizing why we need to exchange self with others
2 Recognizing that we can exchange self with others
3 How to exchange self with others

Maintaining bodhichitta by means of ritual has two parts:

1 Maintaining the aspiring mind by means of ritual
2 Maintaining the engaging mind by means of ritual

How to engage in a Bodhisattva's actions has two parts:

1 Training in the six perfections to ripen our own mental continuum
2 Training in the four ways of gathering to ripen the mental continuum of others

Training in the six perfections to ripen our own mental continuum has four parts:

1 The six perfections in general
2 The perfections of mental stabilization and wisdom in particular
3 How to progress through the spiritual grounds and paths in dependence upon a union of tranquil abiding and superior seeing
4 Training in Vajrayana paths

The six perfections in general has six parts:

1 The perfection of giving
2 The perfection of moral discipline
3 The perfection of patience
4 The perfection of effort
5 The perfection of mental stabilization
6 The perfection of wisdom

The perfections of mental stabilization and wisdom in particular has two parts:

1 How to train the mind in tranquil abiding, the essence of concentration
2 How to train the mind in superior seeing, the essence of wisdom

How to train the mind in tranquil abiding, the essence of concentration, has two parts:

1 The necessary conditions for attaining tranquil abiding
2 How to attain tranquil abiding

The necessary conditions for attaining tranquil abiding has six parts:

1 A suitable place for retreat
2 Little desire
3 Contentment
4 No distracting activities

5 Pure moral discipline
6 No distracting conceptions

How to attain tranquil abiding has six parts:

1 The five obstacles to attaining tranquil abiding
2 The eight opponents to the five obstacles
3 How to attain the nine mental abidings
4 The six forces
5 The four attentions
6 The measurement of having attained tranquil abiding

The five obstacles to attaining tranquil abiding has five parts:

1 Laziness
2 Forgetfulness
3 Mental sinking and mental excitement
4 Non-application
5 Unnecessary application

The eight opponents to the five obstacles has eight parts:

1 Faith
2 Aspiration
3 Effort
4 Suppleness
5 Mindfulness
6 Alertness
7 Application
8 Non-application

How to attain the nine mental abidings has two parts:

1 The object of meditation
2 The nine mental abidings

The object of meditation has four parts:

1 Pervasive objects
2 Objects for abandoning individual delusions
3 Object for abandoning delusions in general
4 Objects for scholars

The nine mental abidings has nine parts:

1 Placing the mind
2 Continual placement
3 Replacement

4 Close placement
5 Controlling
6 Pacifying
7 Completely pacifying
8 Single-pointedness
9 Placement in equipoise

The six forces has six parts:

1 The force of listening
2 The force of contemplating
3 The force of mindfulness
4 The force of alertness
5 The force of effort
6 The force of complete familiarity

The four attentions has four parts:

1 Tight attention
2 Interrupted attention
3 Uninterrupted attention
4 Spontaneous attention

How to train the mind in superior seeing, the essence of wisdom, has three parts:

1 The nature of superior seeing
2 The function of superior seeing
3 The object of superior seeing

The object of superior seeing has two parts:

1 The emptiness of persons
2 The emptiness of phenomena

The emptiness of persons has two parts:

1 How to sustain space-like meditative equipoise on the emptiness of persons
2 How to sustain illusion-like subsequent attainment

How to sustain space-like meditative equipoise on the emptiness of persons has four parts:

1 Ascertaining the negated object
2 Ascertaining the pervasion
3 Ascertaining the absence of oneness
4 Ascertaining the absence of difference

Appendix II
Sadhanas

CONTENTS

Liberating Prayer

PRAISE TO BUDDHA SHAKYAMUNI

O Blessed One, Shakyamuni Buddha,
Precious treasury of compassion,
Bestower of supreme inner peace,

You, who love all beings without exception,
Are the source of happiness and goodness;
And you guide us to the liberating path.

Your body is a wishfulfilling jewel,
Your speech is supreme, purifying nectar,
And your mind is refuge for all living beings.

With folded hands I turn to you,
Supreme unchanging friend,
I request from the depths of my heart:

Please give me the light of your wisdom
To dispel the darkness of my mind
And to heal my mental continuum.

Please nourish me with your goodness,
That I in turn may nourish all beings
With an unceasing banquet of delight.

Through your compassionate intention,
Your blessings and virtuous deeds,
And my strong wish to rely upon you,

May all suffering quickly cease
And all happiness and joy be fulfilled;
And may holy Dharma flourish for evermore.

Colophon: This prayer was composed by Venerable Geshe Kelsang Gyatso. It is recited regularly at the beginning of sadhanas in Kadampa Buddhist Centres throughout the world.

Essence of Good Fortune

PRAYERS FOR THE SIX PREPARATORY
PRACTICES FOR MEDITATION ON
THE STAGES OF THE PATH TO
ENLIGHTENMENT

Essence of Good Fortune

Mentally purifying the environment

May the whole ground
Become completely pure,
As level as the palm of a hand,
And as smooth as lapis lazuli.

Mentally arranging pure offerings

May all of space be filled
With offerings from gods and men,
Both set out and imagined,
Like offerings of the All Good One.

Visualizing the objects of refuge

In the space in front, on a lion throne, on a cushion
of lotus, sun, and moon, sits Buddha Shakyamuni,
the essence of all my kind Teachers, surrounded by
the assembly of direct and indirect Gurus, Yidams,
Buddhas, Bodhisattvas, Hearers, Solitary Conquerors,
Heroes, Dakinis, and Dharma Protectors.

Generating the causes of going for refuge

I and all my kind mothers, fearing samsara's torments,
turn to Buddha, Dharma, and Sangha, the only sources of
refuge. From now until enlightenment, to the Three Jewels
we go for refuge.

Short prayer of going for refuge

I and all sentient beings, until we achieve enlightenment,
Go for refuge to Buddha, Dharma, and Sangha.

(7x, 100x, etc.)

Generating bodhichitta

Through the virtues I collect by giving and other perfections,
May I become a Buddha for the benefit of all.   (3x)

Purifying and receiving blessings

From the hearts of all refuge objects, lights and nectars
stream down and dissolve into myself and all living
beings, purifying negative karma and obstructions,
increasing our lives, our virtues, and Dharma realizations.

Generating the four immeasurables

May everyone be happy,
May everyone be free from misery,
May no one ever be separated from their happiness,
May everyone have equanimity, free from hatred and
  attachment.

Inviting the Field for Accumulating Merit

You, Protector of all beings,
Great Destroyer of hosts of demons,
Please, O Blessed One, Knower of All,
Come to this place with your retinue.

Prayer of seven limbs

With my body, speech, and mind, humbly I prostrate,
And make offerings both set out and imagined.
I confess my wrong deeds from all time,
And rejoice in the virtues of all.
Please stay until samsara ceases,
And turn the Wheel of Dharma for us.
I dedicate all virtues to great enlightenment.

Offering the mandala

The ground sprinkled with perfume and spread with
    flowers,
The Great Mountain, four lands, sun and moon,
Seen as a Buddha Land and offered thus,
May all beings enjoy such Pure Lands.

I offer without any sense of loss
The objects that give rise to my attachment, hatred, and
    confusion,
My friends, enemies, and strangers, our bodies and
    enjoyments;
Please accept these and bless me to be released directly
    from the three poisons.

IDAM GURU RATNA MANDALAKAM NIRYATAYAMI

Requests to the Field for Accumulating Merit and the Lamrim lineage Gurus

So now my most kind root Guru,
Please sit on the lotus and moon on my crown
And grant me out of your great kindness,
Your body, speech, and mind's attainments.

*Visualize that your root Guru comes to the crown of your
head and makes the following requests with you:*

I make requests to you, Buddha Shakyamuni,
Whose body comes from countless virtues,
Whose speech fulfils the hopes of mortals,
Whose mind sees clearly all existence.

I make requests to you, Gurus of the lineage of extensive
    deeds,
Venerable Maitreya, Noble Asanga, Vasubandhu,
And all the other precious Teachers
Who have revealed the path of vastness.

I make requests to you, Gurus of the lineage of profound
    view,
Venerable Manjushri, Nagarjuna, Chandrakirti,
And all the other precious Teachers
Who have revealed the most profound path.

I make requests to you, Gurus of the lineage of Secret
    Mantra,
Conqueror Vajradhara, Tilopa, and Naropa,
And all the other precious Teachers
Who have revealed the path of Tantra.

I make requests to you, Gurus of the Old Kadam lineage,
The second Buddha Atisha, Dromtonpa, Geshe Potowa,
And all the other precious Teachers
Who have revealed the union of vast and profound
    paths.

I make requests to you, Gurus of the New Kadam
    lineage,
Venerable Tsongkhapa, Jampel Gyatso, Khedrubje,
And all the other precious Teachers
Who have revealed the union of Sutra and Tantra.

I make requests to you, Venerable Kelsang Gyatso,
Protector of a vast ocean of living beings,
Unequalled Teacher of the paths to liberation and
    enlightenment,
Who accomplish and explain everything that was
    revealed
By the Fourth Deliverer of this Fortunate Aeon.

I make requests to you, my kind precious Teacher,
Who care for those with uncontrolled minds
Untamed by all the previous Buddhas,
As if they were fortunate disciples.

Requesting the three great purposes

Please pour down your inspiring blessings upon myself
and all my mothers so that we may quickly stop all
perverse minds, from disrespect for our kind Teacher
to the most subtle dual appearance.

Please pour down your inspiring blessings so that we may
quickly generate pure minds, from respect for our kind
Teacher to the supreme mind of Union.

Please pour down your inspiring blessings to pacify all
outer and inner obstructions.   (3x)

Receiving blessings and purifying

From the hearts of all the holy beings, streams of light
and nectar flow down, granting blessings and purifying.

Prayer of the Stages of the Path

The path begins with strong reliance
On my kind Teacher, source of all good;
O Bless me with this understanding
To follow him with great devotion.

This human life with all its freedoms,
Extremely rare, with so much meaning;
O Bless me with this understanding
All day and night to seize its essence.

My body, like a water bubble,
Decays and dies so very quickly;
After death come results of karma,
Just like the shadow of a body.

With this firm knowledge and remembrance
Bless me to be extremely cautious,
Always avoiding harmful actions
And gathering abundant virtue.

Samsara's pleasures are deceptive,
Give no contentment, only torment;
So please bless me to strive sincerely
To gain the bliss of perfect freedom.

O Bless me so that from this pure thought
Come mindfulness and greatest caution,
To keep as my essential practice
The doctrine's root, the Pratimoksha.

Just like myself all my kind mothers
Are drowning in samsara's ocean;
O So that I may soon release them,
Bless me to train in bodhichitta.

But I cannot become a Buddha
By this alone without three ethics;
So bless me with the strength to practise
The Bodhisattva's ordination.

By pacifying my distractions
And analyzing perfect meanings,
Bless me to quickly gain the union
Of special insight and quiescence.

When I become a pure container
Through common paths, bless me to enter
The essence practice of good fortune,
The supreme vehicle, Vajrayana.

The two attainments both depend on
My sacred vows and my commitments;
Bless me to understand this clearly
And keep them at the cost of my life.

By constant practice in four sessions,
The way explained by holy Teachers,
O Bless me to gain both the stages,
Which are the essence of the Tantras.

May those who guide me on the good path,
And my companions all have long lives;
Bless me to pacify completely
All obstacles, outer and inner.

May I always find perfect Teachers,
And take delight in holy Dharma,
Accomplish all grounds and paths swiftly,
And gain the state of Vajradhara.

You may do your meditation here or at any appropriate point within the Prayer of the Stages of the Path.

Mantra recitation

After our meditation we contemplate that from the heart of Buddha Shakyamuni, the principal Field of Merit in front of us, infinite light rays emanate, reaching all environments and all beings. These dissolve into light and gradually gather into the Field of Merit. This dissolves into the central figure, Buddha Shakyamuni, who then dissolves into our root Guru at the crown of our head, instantly transforming him into the aspect of Guru Buddha Shakyamuni. He then diminishes in size, enters through our crown, and descends to our heart. His mind and our mind become one nature. We recite the mantra:

OM MUNI MUNI MAHA MUNIYE SÖHA　　　(7x, 100x, etc.)

Dedication prayers

Through the virtues I have collected
By practising the stages of the path,
May all living beings find the opportunity
To practise in the same way.

However many living beings there are
Experiencing mental and physical suffering,
May their suffering cease through the power of my merit,
And may they find everlasting happiness and joy.

May everyone experience
The happiness of humans and gods,
And quickly attain enlightenment,
So that samsara is finally extinguished.

For the benefit of all living beings as extensive as space,
May I attain great wisdom like that of Manjushri,
Great compassion like that of Avalokiteshvara,
Great power like that of Vajrapani.

The Buddhadharma is the supreme medicine
That relieves all mental pain,
So may this precious Dharma Jewel
Pervade all worlds throughout space.

May there arise in the minds of all living beings
Great faith in Buddha, Dharma, and Sangha,
And thus may they always receive
The blessings of the Three Precious Gems.

May there never arise in this world
The miseries of incurable disease, famine, or war,
Or the dangers of earthquakes, fires,
Floods, storms, and so forth.

May all mother beings meet precious Teachers
Who reveal the stages of the path to enlightenment,
And through engaging in this path
May they quickly attain the ultimate peace of full
    enlightenment.

Through the blessings of the Buddhas and Bodhisattvas,
The truth of actions and their effects,
And the power of my pure superior intention,
May all my prayers be fulfilled.

*If we are unable to recite all these prayers for the six prepara-
tory practices in every meditation session, we should at least
always remember Guru Buddha Shakyamuni at the crown
of our head, recalling that his mind is the synthesis of all
Buddha Jewels, his speech the synthesis of all Dharma Jewels,*

and his body the synthesis of all Sangha Jewels. Then with strong faith we should go for refuge by reciting the short prayer of going for refuge, generate bodhichitta with the words 'Through the virtues . . . for the benefit of all', offer the mandala, request the three great purposes, and receive blessings and purify.*

If we perform these three practices every time we sit down to meditate – namely, accumulating merit, purifying negative karma, and making requests to receive blessings and inspiration – we shall have accomplished the three purposes of engaging in preparatory practices. At the conclusion of every meditation session we should dedicate our merit.

Colophon: These prayers were compiled from traditional sources by Venerable Geshe Kelsang Gyatso. The verse of request to Geshe Kelsang Gyatso was composed by the Dharma Protector Duldzin Dorje Shugden and included in the prayers at the request of Geshe Kelsang's faithful disciples.

Prayers for Meditation

BRIEF PREPARATORY PRAYERS
FOR MEDITATION

Prayers for Meditation

Going for refuge

I and all sentient beings, until we achieve enlightenment,
Go for refuge to Buddha, Dharma, and Sangha.

(3x, 7x, 100x, or more)

Generating bodhichitta

Through the virtues I collect by giving and other perfections,
May I become a Buddha for the benefit of all.   (3x)

Generating the four immeasurables

May everyone be happy,
May everyone be free from misery,
May no one ever be separated from their happiness,
May everyone have equanimity, free from hatred and
    attachment.

Visualizing the Field for Accumulating Merit

In the space before me is the living Buddha Shakyamuni
surrounded by all the Buddhas and Bodhisattvas, like the
full moon surrounded by stars.

Prayer of seven limbs

With my body, speech, and mind, humbly I prostrate,
And make offerings both set out and imagined.
I confess my wrong deeds from all time,
And rejoice in the virtues of all.
Please stay until samsara ceases,
And turn the Wheel of Dharma for us.
I dedicate all virtues to great enlightenment.

Offering the mandala

The ground sprinkled with perfume and spread with
    flowers,
The Great Mountain, four lands, sun and moon,
Seen as a Buddha Land and offered thus,
May all beings enjoy such Pure Lands.

I offer without any sense of loss
The objects that give rise to my attachment, hatred, and
    confusion,
My friends, enemies, and strangers, our bodies and
    enjoyments;
Please accept these and bless me to be released directly
    from the three poisons.

IDAM GURU RATNA MANDALAKAM NIRYATAYAMI

Prayer of the Stages of the Path

The path begins with strong reliance
On my kind Teacher, source of all good;
O Bless me with this understanding
To follow him with great devotion.

This human life with all its freedoms,
Extremely rare, with so much meaning;
O Bless me with this understanding
All day and night to seize its essence.

My body, like a water bubble,
Decays and dies so very quickly;
After death come results of karma,
Just like the shadow of a body.

With this firm knowledge and remembrance
Bless me to be extremely cautious,
Always avoiding harmful actions
And gathering abundant virtue.

Samsara's pleasures are deceptive,
Give no contentment, only torment;
So please bless me to strive sincerely
To gain the bliss of perfect freedom.

O Bless me so that from this pure thought
Come mindfulness and greatest caution,
To keep as my essential practice
The doctrine's root, the Pratimoksha.

Just like myself all my kind mothers
Are drowning in samsara's ocean;
O So that I may soon release them,
Bless me to train in bodhichitta.

But I cannot become a Buddha
By this alone without three ethics;
So bless me with the strength to practise
The Bodhisattva's ordination.

By pacifying my distractions
And analyzing perfect meanings,
Bless me to quickly gain the union
Of special insight and quiescence.

When I become a pure container
Through common paths, bless me to enter
The essence practice of good fortune,
The supreme vehicle, Vajrayana.

The two attainments both depend on
My sacred vows and my commitments;
Bless me to understand this clearly
And keep them at the cost of my life.

By constant practice in four sessions,
The way explained by holy Teachers,
O Bless me to gain both the stages,
Which are the essence of the Tantras.

May those who guide me on the good path,
And my companions all have long lives;
Bless me to pacify completely
All obstacles, outer and inner.

May I always find perfect Teachers,
And take delight in holy Dharma,
Accomplish all grounds and paths swiftly,
And gain the state of Vajradhara.

Receiving blessings and purifying

From the hearts of all the holy beings, streams of light
and nectar flow down, granting blessings and purifying.

*At this point we begin the actual contemplation and medi-
tation. After the meditation we dedicate our merit while
reciting the following prayers:*

Dedication prayers

Through the virtues I have collected
By practising the stages of the path,
May all living beings find the opportunity
To practise in the same way.

May everyone experience
The happiness of humans and gods,
And quickly attain enlightenment,
So that samsara is finally extinguished.

Colophon: These prayers were compiled from traditional
sources by Venerable Geshe Kelsang Gyatso.

Glossary

Action mudra A Highest Yoga Tantra consort who assists in developing great bliss. See *Clear Light of Bliss* and *Tantric Grounds and Paths*.

Aggregate In general, all functioning things are aggregates because they are an aggregation of their parts. In particular, a person of the desire realm or form realm has five aggregates: the aggregates of form, feeling, discrimination, compositional factors, and consciousness. A being of the formless realm lacks the aggregate of form but has the other four. A person's form aggregate is his or her body. The remaining four aggregates are aspects of his mind. See *Heart of Wisdom*.

Alertness A mental factor which is a type of wisdom that examines our activity of body, speech, and mind and knows whether or not faults are developing. See *Understanding the Mind*.

All Good One An English name for Samantabhadra, a Bodhisattva renowned for his extensive offerings. See *Great Treasury of Merit*.

Amitayus A Buddha who increases our lifespan, merit, and wisdom. He is the Enjoyment Body aspect of Buddha Amitabha.

Analysis A mental factor that examines an object to gain an understanding of its subtle nature. See *Understanding the Mind*.

Asanga A great Indian Buddhist Yogi and scholar of the fifth century, author of *Compendium of Abhidharma*. See *Living Meaningfully, Dying Joyfully*.

Avalokiteshvara 'Chenrezig' in Tibetan. The embodiment of the compassion of all the Buddhas. At the time of Buddha Shakyamuni, he manifested as a Bodhisattva disciple. See *Living Meaningfully, Dying Joyfully*.

Basis of emptiness Any phenomenon with respect to which inherent existence is negated in realizing its emptiness. Since all phenomena, including emptiness itself, are empty of inherent existence, all phenomena are bases of emptiness. In the *Perfection of Wisdom Sutra in One Hundred Thousand Lines*, Buddha explains that all phenomena are included within one hundred and eight categories, from form to omniscient mind, all of which are bases of emptiness. See *Heart of Wisdom* and *Ocean of Nectar*.

Basis of imputation All phenomena are imputed upon their parts; therefore, any of the individual parts, or the entire collection of the parts, of any phenomenon is its basis of imputation. A phenomenon is imputed by mind in dependence upon its basis of imputation appearing to that mind. See *Heart of Wisdom* and *Ocean of Nectar*.

Blessing 'Jin gyi lob pa' in Tibetan. The transformation of our mind from a negative state to a positive state, from an unhappy state to a happy state, or from a state of weakness to a state of strength, through the inspiration of holy beings such as our Spiritual Guide, Buddhas, and Bodhisattvas.

Buddha family There are five main Buddha families: the families of Vairochana, Ratnasambhava, Amitabha, Amoghasiddhi, and Akshobya. They are the five purified aggregates – the aggregates of form, feeling, discrimination, compositional factors, and consciousness, respectively; and the five exalted wisdoms – the exalted mirror-like wisdom, the exalted wisdom of equality, the exalted wisdom of individual realization, the exalted wisdom of accomplishing activities, and the exalted wisdom of the Dharmadhatu, respectively. See *Great Treasury of Merit*.

Buddha lineage/seed The root mind of a sentient being, and its ultimate nature. Buddha lineage, Buddha seed, and Buddha nature are synonyms. All sentient beings have Buddha lineage and therefore the potential to attain Buddhahood. See *Mahamudra Tantra*.

Buddha Shakyamuni The fourth of one thousand founding Buddhas who are to appear in this world during this Fortunate Aeon. The first three were Krakuchchanda, Kanakamuni, and Kashyapa. The fifth Buddha will be Maitreya. See *Introduction to Buddhism*.

Chandrakirti (circa 7th century AD) A great Indian Buddhist scholar and meditation master who composed, among many other books, the well-known *Guide to the Middle Way*, in which he clearly elucidates the view of the Madhyamika-Prasangika school according to Buddha's teachings given in the *Perfection of Wisdom Sutras*. See *Ocean of Nectar*.

Channels Subtle inner passageways of the body through which flow subtle drops moved by inner winds. See *Clear Light of Bliss*.

Chittamatra The lower of the two schools of Mahayana tenets. 'Chittamatra' means 'mind only'. According to this school, all phenomena are the same nature as the mind that apprehends them. They also assert that dependent phenomena are truly existent but do not exist external to the mind. A Chittamatrin is a proponent of Chittamatra tenets. See *Meaningful to Behold* and *Ocean of Nectar*.

Clairvoyance Abilities that arise from special concentration. There are five principal types of clairvoyance: the clairvoyance of divine eye (the ability to see subtle and distant forms), the clairvoyance of divine ear (the ability to hear subtle and distant sounds), the clairvoyance of miracle powers (the ability to emanate various forms by mind), the clairvoyance of knowing previous lives, and the clairvoyance of knowing others' minds. Some beings, such as bardo beings and some human beings and spirits, have contaminated clairvoyance that is developed due to karma, but these are not actual clairvoyance.

Clear appearance Generally, a clear perception of the object of meditation. More specifically, a Secret Mantra practice whereby the practitioner, having generated himself or herself as a Deity and the environment as the Deity's mandala, tries to attain clear appearance of the whole object to his or her concentration. It is the antidote to ordinary appearance. See *Guide to Dakini Land*.

Clear light A manifest very subtle mind that perceives an appearance like clear, empty space. See *Clear Light of Bliss, Mahamudra Tantra* and *Tantric Grounds and Paths*.

Collection of merit A virtuous action motivated by bodhichitta that is a main cause of attaining the Form Body of a Buddha. Examples are: making offerings and prostrations to holy beings with bodhichitta motivation, and the practice of the perfections of giving, moral discipline, and patience.

Collection of wisdom A virtuous mental action motivated by bodhichitta that is a main cause of attaining the Truth Body of a Buddha. Examples are: listening to, contemplating, and meditating on emptiness with bodhichitta motivation.

Collective karma The karma we create when we act in association with others. Those who create karma together also experience its effects together.

Commitment being A visualized Buddha or ourself visualized as a Buddha. A commitment being is so called because in general it is the commitment of all Buddhists to visualize or remember Buddha, and in particular it is a commitment of those who have received an empowerment into Highest Yoga Tantra to generate themselves as a Deity.

Completion stage Highest Yoga Tantra realizations developed in dependence upon the winds entering, abiding, and dissolving within the central channel through the force of meditation. See *Clear Light of Bliss, Tantric Grounds and Paths* and *Mahamudra Tantra*.

Conceived object The apprehended object of a conceptual mind. It need not be an existent object. For example, the conceived object of the view of the transitory collection is an inherently existent I, but this does not exist. See *Understanding the Mind*.

Concentration being A symbol of Buddha's Truth Body, usually visualized as a seed-letter at the heart of a commitment being or a wisdom being. It is so called because it is generated through concentration.

Conscientiousness A mental factor that, in dependence upon effort, cherishes what is virtuous and guards the mind from delusion and non-virtue. See *Meaningful to Behold* and *Understanding the Mind*.

Consideration for others A mental factor that functions to avoid inappropriate actions for reasons that concern others. See *Understanding the Mind*.

Contaminated phenomenon Any phenomenon that gives rise to delusions or that causes them to increase. Examples are the environments, beings, and enjoyments of samsara.

Contentment Being satisfied with one's inner and outer conditions, motivated by a virtuous intention.

Conventional truth Any phenomenon other than emptiness. Conventional truths are true with respect to the minds of ordinary beings, but in reality they are false. See *Heart of Wisdom*.

Dakinis/Dakas Dakinis are female Tantric Buddhas and those women who have attained the realization of meaning clear light. Dakas are the male equivalent. See *Guide to Dakini Land*.

Degenerate times A period when spiritual activity degenerates.

Deity 'Yidam' in Sanskrit. A Tantric enlightened being.

Demon 'Mara' in Sanskrit. Anything that obstructs the attainment of liberation or enlightenment. There are four principal types of demon: the demon of the delusions, the demon of contaminated aggregates, the demon of uncontrolled death, and the Devaputra demons. Of these, only the last are actual sentient beings. The principal Devaputra demon is wrathful Ishvara, the highest of the desire realm gods, who inhabits Land of Controlling Emanations. Buddha is called a 'Conqueror' because he or she has conquered all four types of demon. See *Heart of Wisdom*.

Desire realm The environment of hell beings, hungry spirits, animals, human beings, demi-gods, and the gods who enjoy the five objects of desire.

Dharma Buddha's teachings and the inner realizations that are attained in dependence upon practising them. 'Dharma' means 'protection'. By practising Buddha's teachings, we protect ourself from suffering and problems.

Dharma Protector A manifestation of a Buddha or Bodhisattva, whose main function is to eliminate obstacles and gather all necessary conditions for pure Dharma practitioners. Also called 'Dharmapala' in Sanskrit. See *Heart Jewel.*

Divine pride A non-deluded pride that regards oneself as a Deity and one's environment and enjoyments as those of the Deity. It is the antidote to ordinary conceptions. See *Guide to Dakini Land.*

Drops There are two types of drop in the body: white drops and red drops. These are the pure essence of sperm and blood. When the drops melt and flow through the inner channels, they give rise to an experience of bliss. See *Clear Light of Bliss* and *Tantric Grounds and Paths.*

Element 'Kham' in Tibetan. The nature of any phenomenon. All phenomena hold their own natures, which are all included within the eighteen elements. See also *Elements, four.* See *Heart of Wisdom* and *Ocean of Nectar.*

Elements, four 'Jung wa' in Tibetan. Earth, water, fire, and wind. All matter can be said to be composed of a combination of these elements. There are four inner elements (those that are conjoined with the continuum of a person), and four outer elements (those that are not conjoined with the continuum of a person). These elements are not the same as the earth of a field, the water of a river, and so forth. Rather, the elements of earth, water, fire, and wind in broad terms are the properties of solidity, liquidity, heat, and movement respectively.

Foe Destroyer 'Arhat' in Sanskrit. A practitioner who has abandoned all delusions and their seeds by training on the spiritual paths, and who will never again be reborn in samsara. In this context, the term 'Foe' refers to the delusions. See also *Hearer.*

Form realm The environment of the gods who possess form.

Formless realm The environment of the gods who do not possess form.

Fortunate Aeon The name given to this world age. It is so called because one thousand founding Buddhas will appear during this aeon. Buddha Shakyamuni was the fourth and Buddha Maitreya will be the fifth. An aeon in which no Buddhas appear is called a 'Dark Aeon'.

Four schools of Buddhist tenets See *Schools of Buddhist tenets.*

Gelug The tradition established by Je Tsongkhapa. The name 'Gelug' means 'Virtuous Tradition'. A Gelugpa is a practitioner who follows this tradition. The Gelugpas are sometimes referred to as the 'new Kadampas'. See *Heart Jewel.*

Generation stage A realization of a creative yoga prior to attaining the actual completion stage, which is attained through the practice of bringing the three bodies into the path, in which one mentally generates oneself as a Tantric Deity and one's surroundings as the Deity's mandala. Meditation on generation stage is called a 'creative yoga' because its object is created, or generated, by correct imagination. See *Tantric Grounds and Paths* and *Mahamudra Tantra*.

Generic image The appearing object of a conceptual mind. A generic image, or mental image, of an object is like a reflection of that object. Conceptual minds know their object through the appearance of a generic image of that object, not by seeing the object directly. See *Heart of Wisdom* and *Understanding the Mind*.

Geshe A title given by Kadampa monasteries to accomplished Buddhist scholars. Contracted form of the Tibetan 'ge wai she nyen', literally meaning 'virtuous friend'.

Golden age A time when sentient beings have abundant merit and when Dharma activities flourish. It is contrasted with degenerate times.

Ground/Spiritual ground A clear realization that acts as the foundation of many good qualities. A clear realization is a realization held by spontaneous renunciation or bodhichitta. The ten grounds are the realizations of Superior Bodhisattvas: Very Joyful, Stainless, Luminous, Radiant, Difficult to Overcome, Approaching, Gone Afar, Immovable, Good Intelligence, and Cloud of Dharma. See also *Path/Spiritual path*. See *Ocean of Nectar* and *Tantric Grounds and Paths*.

Guide to the Bodhisattva's Way of Life A classic Mahayana Buddhist text composed by the great Indian Buddhist Yogi and scholar Shantideva, which presents all the practices of a Bodhisattva from the initial generation of bodhichitta through to the completion of the practice of the six perfections. For a translation, see *Guide to the Bodhisattva's Way of Life*. For a full commentary, see *Meaningful to Behold*.

Guide to the Middle Way A classic Mahayana Buddhist text composed by the great Indian Buddhist Yogi and scholar Chandrakirti, which provides a comprehensive explanation of the Madhyamika-Prasangika view of emptiness as taught in the *Perfection of Wisdom Sutras*. For a translation and full commentary, see *Ocean of Nectar*.

Guru See *Root Guru* and *Spiritual Guide*.

Hearer One of two types of Hinayana practitioner. Both Hearers and Solitary Realizers are Hinayanists, but they differ in their motivation, behaviour, merit, and wisdom. In all these respects, Solitary Realizers are superior to Hearers. See *Ocean of Nectar*.

Heart Sutra One of several *Perfection of Wisdom Sutras* that Buddha taught. Although much shorter than the other *Perfection of Wisdom Sutras*, it contains explicitly or implicitly their entire meaning. Also known as the *Essence of Wisdom Sutra*. For a translation and full commentary, see *Heart of Wisdom*.

Hero and Heroine A Hero is a male Tantric Deity generally embodying method. A Heroine is a female Tantric Deity generally embodying wisdom. See *Guide to Dakini Land*.

Heruka A principal Deity of Mother Tantra, who is the embodiment of indivisible bliss and emptiness. He has a blue-coloured body, four faces, and twelve arms, and embraces his consort Vajravarahi. See *Essence of Vajrayana*.

Hidden object An object whose initial realization by a valid cognizer depends upon correct logical reasons. See *Understanding the Mind*.

Hinayana Sanskrit word for 'Lesser Vehicle'. The Hinayana goal is to attain merely one's own liberation from suffering by completely abandoning delusions.

Illusory body The subtle divine body that is principally developed from the indestructible wind. When a practitioner of Highest Yoga Tantra rises from the meditation of the isolated mind of ultimate example clear light, he or she attains a body that is not the same as his or her ordinary physical body. This new body is the illusory body. It has the same appearance as the body of the personal Deity of generation stage except that it is white in colour. It can be perceived only by those who have already attained an illusory body. See *Clear Light of Bliss* and *Tantric Grounds and Paths*.

Impermanent phenomenon Phenomena are either permanent or impermanent. 'Impermanent' means 'momentary'; thus an impermanent phenomenon is a phenomenon that is produced and disintegrates within a moment. Synonyms of impermanent phenomenon are 'functioning thing', 'thing, and 'product'. There are two types of impermanence: gross and subtle. Gross impermanence is any impermanence that can be seen by a ordinary sense awareness – for example the ageing and death of a sentient being. Subtle impermanence is the momentary disintegration of a functioning thing. See *Heart of Wisdom*.

Imprint There are two types of imprint: imprints of actions and imprints of delusions. Every action we perform leaves an imprint on the mental consciousness, and these imprints are karmic potentialities to experience certain effects in the future. The imprints left by delusions remain even after the delusions themselves have been abandoned, rather as the smell of garlic lingers in a container after the garlic has been removed. Imprints of delusions are obstructions to omniscience, and are completely abandoned only by Buddhas.

Indestructible drop The most subtle drop, which is located at the heart. It is formed from the essence of the white and red drops received from our parents at conception, and encloses the very subtle mind and its mounted wind. These red and white drops do not separate until the time of death, when they open and allow the very subtle mind and its mounted wind to depart to the next life. See *Tantric Grounds and Paths* and *Clear Light of Bliss*.

Indra A worldly god. See *Heart of Wisdom*.

Inner winds Special subtle winds related to the mind that flow through the channels of our body. Our body and mind cannot function without these winds. See *Clear Light of Bliss* and *Tantric Grounds and Paths*.

Intention A mental factor that functions to move its primary mind to the object. It functions to engage the mind in virtuous, non-virtuous, and neutral objects. All bodily and verbal actions are initiated by the mental factor intention. See *Understanding the Mind*.

Ishvara A god who abides in the Land of Controlling Emanations, the highest state of existence within the desire realm. Ishvara has limited, contaminated miracle powers that make him more powerful than other beings in the desire realm. If we entrust ourself to Ishvara we may receive some temporary benefit in this life, such as an increase in wealth or possessions, but wrathful Ishvara is the enemy of those who seek liberation and he interferes with their spiritual progress. He is therefore said to be a type of Devaputra demon.

Jealousy A deluded mental factor that feels displeasure when observing others' enjoyments, good qualities, or good fortune. See *Understanding the Mind*.

Je Phabongkhapa (AD 1878-1941) A great Tibetan Lama who was an emanation of Heruka. Phabongkha Rinpoche was the holder of many lineages of Sutra and Secret Mantra. He was the root Guru of Yongdzin Trijang Dorjechang (Trijang Rinpoche).

Je Tsongkhapa (AD 1357-1419) An emanation of the Wisdom Buddha Manjushri, whose appearance in fourteenth-century Tibet as a monk, and the holder of the lineage of pure view and pure deeds, was prophesied by Buddha. He spread a very pure Buddhadharma throughout Tibet, showing how to combine the practices of Sutra and Tantra, and how to practise pure Dharma during degenerate times. His tradition later became known as the 'Gelug', or 'Ganden Tradition'. See *Heart Jewel* and *Great Treasury of Merit*.

Kadampa A Tibetan term in which 'Ka' means 'word' and refers to all Buddha's teachings, 'dam' refers to Atisha's special Lamrim instructions known as the 'stages of the path to enlightenment', and 'pa' refers to a follower of Kadampa Buddhism who integrates all the teachings of Buddha that they know into their Lamrim practice. See also *Kadampa Buddhism* and *Kadampa Tradition*.

Kadampa Buddhism A Mahayana Buddhist school founded by the great Indian Buddhist Master Atisha (AD 982-1054). See also *Kadampa*, *Kadampa Tradition*, and *New Kadampa Tradition*.

Kadampa Tradition The pure tradition of Buddhism established by Atisha. Followers of this tradition up to the time of Je Tsongkhapa are known as 'Old Kadampas', and those after the time of Je Tsongkhapa are known as 'New Kadampas'. See also *Kadampa*, *Kadampa Buddhism*, and *New Kadampa Tradition*.

Khädrubje (AD 1385-1438) One of the principal disciples of Je Tsongkhapa, who did much to promote the tradition of Je Tsongkhapa after he passed away. See *Great Treasury of Merit*.

Lama Losang Tubwang Dorjechang A special manifestation of Je Tsongkhapa revealed directly to the great Yogi Dharmavajra. In this manifestation, Je Tsongkhapa appears as a fully ordained monk wearing a long-eared Pandit's hat, with Buddha Shakyamuni at his heart, and Conqueror Vajradhara at his heart. In the practice of *Offering to the Spiritual Guide*, we visualize our Spiritual Guide in this aspect. See *Great Treasury of Merit*.

Land of the Thirty-three Heavens One of the six abodes of desire realm gods. These are, in sequence: Land of the Four Great Kings, Land of the Thirty-three Heavens, Land Without Combat, Joyful Land, Land of Enjoying Emanations, and Land of Controlling Emanations.

Langri Tangpa, Geshe (AD 1054-1123) A great Kadampa Teacher who was famous for his realization of exchanging self with others. He composed *Eight Verses of Training the Mind*. See *Eight Steps to Happiness*.

Lord of Death Although the demon of uncontrolled death is not a sentient being, it is personified as the Lord of Death, or 'Yama'. The Lord of Death is depicted in the diagram of the Wheel of Life clutching the wheel between his claws and teeth.

Madhyamika A Sanskrit term, literally meaning 'Middle Way'. The higher of the two schools of Mahayana tenets. The Madhyamika view was taught by Buddha in the *Perfection of Wisdom Sutras* during the second turning of the Wheel of Dharma and was subsequently elucidated by Nagarjuna and his followers. There are two divisions of this school, Madhyamika-Svatantrika and Madhyamika-Prasangika, of which the latter is Buddha's final view. See *Meaningful to Behold* and *Ocean of Nectar*.

Mahamudra A Sanskrit term, literally meaning 'great seal'. According to Sutra, this refers to the profound view of emptiness. Since emptiness is the nature of all phenomena, it is called a 'seal', and since a direct realization of emptiness enables us to accomplish the great purpose – complete liberation from the sufferings of samsara – it is also called 'great'. According to Secret Mantra, or Tantra, great seal is the union of spontaneous great bliss and emptiness. See *Great Treasury of Merit*, *Clear Light of Bliss* and *Mahamudra Tantra*.

Mahasiddha A Sanskrit term for 'Greatly Accomplished One', which is used to refer to Yogis or Yoginis with high attainments.

Maitreya The embodiment of the loving kindness of all the Buddhas. At the time of Buddha Shakyamuni, he manifested as a Bodhisattva disciple. In the future, he will manifest as the fifth founding Buddha.

Manjushri The embodiment of the wisdom of all the Buddhas. At the time of Buddha Shakyamuni, he manifested as a Bodhisattva disciple. See *Great Treasury of Merit* and *Heart Jewel*.

Mantra A Sanskrit term, literally meaning 'mind protection'. Mantra protects the mind from ordinary appearances and conceptions. There are four types of mantra: mantras that are mind, mantras that are inner wind, mantras that are sound, and mantras that are form. In general, there are three types of mantra recitation: verbal recitation, mental recitation, and vajra recitation. See *Tantric Grounds and Paths*.

Meditative equipoise Single-pointed concentration on a virtuous object such as emptiness. See *Ocean of Nectar*.

Mental factor A cognizer that principally apprehends a particular attribute of an object. There are fifty-one specific mental factors. Each moment of mind comprises a primary mind and various mental factors. See *Understanding the Mind*.

Mental stabilization Generally, the terms 'mental stabilization' and 'concentration' are interchangeable. More specifically, the term 'concentration' is used to refer to the nature of concentration, which is single-pointedness, and the term 'mental stabilization' is used to refer to the function of concentration, which is stability.

Merit The good fortune created by virtuous actions. It is the potential power to increase our good qualities and produce happiness.

Middle way The correct view of emptiness avoids both extremes and therefore emptiness is called the 'middle way'. See also *Madhyamika*.

Milarepa (AD 1040-1123) A great Tibetan Buddhist meditator and disciple of Marpa, celebrated for his beautiful songs of realization.

Mindfulness A mental factor that functions not to forget the object realized by the primary mind. See *Understanding the Mind* and *Clear Light of Bliss*.

Mount Meru According to Buddhist cosmology, a divine mountain that stands at the centre of the universe. See *Great Treasury of Merit*.

Mundane paths Contaminated actions that lead to samsaric rebirth. There are two types: the ten non-virtuous actions that lead to the lower realms, and the ten virtuous actions and contaminated concentrations that lead to the higher realms.

Naga A non-human being not normally visible to human beings. Their upper half is said to be human, their lower half serpent. Nagas usually live in the oceans of the world but they sometimes inhabit land in the region of rocks and trees. They are very powerful, some being benevolent and some malevolent. Many diseases, known as 'naga diseases', are caused by nagas and can only be cured through performing certain naga rituals.

Nagarjuna A great Indian Buddhist scholar and meditation master who revived the Mahayana in the first century AD by bringing to light the teachings on the *Perfection of Wisdom Sutras*. See *Ocean of Nectar*.

Naropa (AD 1016-1100) An Indian Buddhist Mahasiddha. See *Guide to Dakini Land*.

Negative phenomenon An object that is realized through the mind explicitly eliminating a negated object. Emptiness is an example of a negative phenomenon because it is realized by a mind that directly negates inherent existence, which is its negated object. There are two types of negative phenomenon: affirming negatives and non-affirming negatives. An affirming negative is a negative phenomenon realized by a mind that eliminates its negated object while realizing another phenomenon. A non-affirming negative is a negative phenomenon realized by a mind that merely eliminates its negated object without realizing another phenomenon. See *Heart of Wisdom* and *Ocean of Nectar*.

New Kadampa Tradition (NKT) The union of Kadampa Buddhist Centres, an international association of study and meditation centres that follow the pure tradition of Mahayana Buddhism derived from the Buddhist meditator and scholar Je Tsongkhapa, introduced into the West by the Buddhist teacher Venerable Geshe Kelsang Gyatso.

Non-virtue A phenomenon that functions as a main cause of suffering. It can refer to non-virtuous minds, non-virtuous actions, non-virtuous imprints, or the ultimate non-virtue of samsara. See *Understanding the Mind*.

Object to be abandoned Any object that is the principal cause of suffering, such as ignorance, other delusions, or non-virtuous actions.

Observed object Any object upon which the mind is focused. See *Understanding the Mind*.

Offering to the Spiritual Guide *Lama Chöpa* in Tibetan. A special Guru yoga of Je Tsongkhapa, in which our Spiritual Guide is visualized in the aspect of Lama Losang Tubwang Dorjechang. The instruction for this practice was revealed by Buddha Manjushri in the *Kadam Emanation Scripture* and written down by the first Panchen Lama (AD 1569-1662). It is an essential preliminary practice for Vajrayana Mahamudra. See also *Lama Losang Tubwang Dorjechang*. For a full commentary, see *Great Treasury of Merit*.

Oral transmission The granting of blessings through verbal instruction. Receiving these blessings is essential for gaining authentic realizations. All the root texts and their commentaries have been passed down in a pure, unbroken lineage from Teacher to disciple from the time of Buddha Shakyamuni down to the present day. It is customary at the end of a teaching for the Teacher to recite all the words of the text, just as he or she heard them from his or her own Teacher. A disciple is not considered to have received a teaching until he or she has heard all the words from the mouth of a qualified Spiritual Guide. A teaching that has been received in this way is completely pure, and it carries the blessing of all the lineage Gurus who transmitted the same teachings in the past.

Ordinary appearance and *ordinary conception* Ordinary appearance is any appearance that is due to an impure mind, and ordinary conception is any mind that conceives things as ordinary. According to Tantra, ordinary appearances are obstructions to omniscience and ordinary conceptions are obstructions to liberation. See *Tantric Grounds and Paths, Mahamudra Tantra* and *Guide to Dakini Land*.

Ordinary being Anyone who has not realized emptiness directly.

Path/Spiritual path An exalted awareness conjoined with non-fabricated, or spontaneous, renunciation. Spiritual path, spiritual ground, spiritual vehicle, and exalted awareness are synonyms. See also *Ground/Spiritual ground*. See *Tantric Grounds and Paths* and *Ocean of Nectar*.

Permanent phenomenon Phenomena are either permanent or impermanent. A permanent phenomenon is a phenomenon that does not depend upon causes and that does not disintegrate moment by moment.

Pratimoksha Sanskrit word for 'personal liberation'. See *The Bodhisattva Vow*.

Primary mind A cognizer that principally apprehends the mere entity of an object. Synonymous with consciousness. There are six primary minds: eye consciousness, ear consciousness, nose consciousness, tongue consciousness, body consciousness, and mental consciousness. Each moment of mind comprises a primary mind and various mental factors. A primary mind and its accompanying mental factors are the same entity but have different functions. See *Understanding the Mind*.

Pure Land A pure environment in which there are no true sufferings. There are many Pure Lands. For example, Tushita is the Pure Land of Buddha Maitreya; Sukhavati is the Pure Land of Buddha Amitabha; and Dakini Land, or Keajra, is the Pure Land of Buddha Vajrayogini and Buddha Heruka. See *Living Meaningfully, Dying Joyfully*.

Root Guru The principal Spiritual Guide from whom we have received the empowerments, instructions, and oral transmissions of our main practice. See *Great Treasury of Merit* and *Heart Jewel*.

Sadhana A ritual that is a method for attaining spiritual realizations. It can be associated with Sutra or Tantra.

Sautrantika The higher of the two schools of Hinayana tenets. This school accepts both self-cognizers and external objects to be truly existent. See *Meaningful to Behold* and *Ocean of Nectar*.

Schools of Buddhist tenets Four philosophical views taught by Buddha according to the inclinations and dispositions of disciples. They are the Vaibhashika, Sautrantika, Chittamatra, and Madhyamika schools. The first two are Hinayana schools and the second two are Mahayana schools. They are studied in sequence, the lower tenets being the means by which the higher ones are understood. See *Meaningful to Behold* and *Ocean of Nectar*.

Secret Mantra Synonymous with Tantra. Secret Mantra teachings are distinguished from Sutra teachings in that they reveal methods for training the mind by bringing the future result, or Buddhahood, into the present path. Secret Mantra is the supreme path to full enlightenment. The term 'Mantra' indicates that it is Buddha's special instruction for protecting our mind from ordinary appearances and conceptions. Practitioners of Secret Mantra overcome ordinary appearances and conceptions by visualizing their body, environment, enjoyments, and deeds as those of a Buddha. The term 'Secret' indicates that the practices are to be done in private, and that they can be practised only by those who have received a Tantric empowerment. See *Tantric Grounds and Paths*.

Seed-letter The sacred letter from which a Deity is generated. Each Deity has a particular seed-letter. For example, the seed-letter of Manjushri is DHI, of Tara is TAM, of Vajrayogini is BAM, and of Heruka is HUM. To accomplish Tantric realizations, we need to recognize that Deities and their seed-letters are the same nature.

Sense of shame A mental factor that functions to avoid inappropriate actions for reasons that concern oneself. See *Understanding the Mind*.

Sense power An inner power located in the very centre of a sense organ that functions directly to produce a sense awareness. There are five sense powers, one for each type of sense awareness – the eye awareness and so forth. They are sometimes known as 'sense powers possessing form'. See *Understanding the Mind*.

Sentient being 'Sem chen' in Tibetan. Any being who possesses a mind that is contaminated by delusions or their imprints. Both 'sentient being' and 'living being' are terms used to distinguish beings whose minds are contaminated by either of these two obstructions from Buddhas, whose minds are completely free from these obstructions.

Shantideva (AD 687-763) A great Indian Buddhist scholar and meditation master. He composed *Guide to the Bodhisattva's Way of Life*. See *Meaningful to Behold*.

Solitary peace A Hinayana nirvana.

Solitary Realizer One of two types of Hinayana practitioner. Also known as 'Solitary Conqueror'. See also *Hearer*.

Spiritual Guide 'Guru' in Sanskrit, 'Lama' in Tibetan. A Teacher who guides us along the spiritual path. See *Great Treasury of Merit*.

Spontaneous great bliss A special bliss that is produced by the drops melting inside the central channel. It is attained by gaining control over the inner winds. See *Clear Light of Bliss* and *Tantric Grounds and Paths*.

Subtle mind There are different levels of mind: gross, subtle, and very subtle. Subtle minds manifest when the inner winds gather and dissolve within the central channel. See *Clear Light of Bliss*.

Superior being 'Arya' in Sanskrit. A being who has a direct realization of emptiness. There are Hinayana Superiors and Mahayana Superiors.

Supramundane path Any path leading to liberation or enlightenment – for example, the realizations of renunciation, bodhichitta, and the correct view of emptiness. Strictly speaking, only Superior beings possess supramundane paths. See *Tantric Grounds and Paths*.

Sutra The teachings of Buddha that are open to everyone to practise without the need for empowerment. These include Buddha's teachings of the three turnings of the Wheel of Dharma.

Tantra See *Secret Mantra*.

Tara A female Buddha who is a manifestation of the ultimate wisdom of all the Buddhas. 'Tara' means 'Rescuer'. Since she is a wisdom Buddha, and since she is a manifestation of the completely purified wind element, Tara is able to help us very quickly.

Tathagata The Sanskrit word for 'A Being Gone Beyond', which is another term for Buddha.

Ten directions The four cardinal directions, the four intermediate directions, and the directions above and below.

Tenets See *Schools of Buddhist tenets*.

Thirty-five Confession Buddhas Thirty-five Buddhas who have special powers to purify negativities and downfalls in those who recite their names with faith. See *The Bodhisattva Vow*.

Thirty-seven realizations conducive to enlightenment Any spiritual path that leads to enlightenment. See *Ocean of Nectar*.

Thirty-two major signs Sometimes called the 'major marks'. Special characteristics of a Buddha's form. Examples are the sign of the wheel on the palms of the hands and the soles of the feet. The eighty indications, sometimes called the 'minor marks', include signs such as copper-coloured nails.

Three realms The three levels within samsara: the desire realm, the form realm, and the formless realm. Beings of the desire realm have powerful delusions, beings of the form realm have more subtle delusions, and beings of the formless realm have very subtle delusions. See also *Desire realm*, *Form realm*, and *Formless realm*.

Three times, the Past, present, and future. See *Ocean of Nectar*.

Training the Mind in Seven Points A commentary to *Eight Verses of Training the Mind*, composed by Bodhisattva Chekhawa. For a full commentary, see *Universal Compassion*.

Transference of consciousness 'Powa' in Tibetan. A practice for transferring the consciousness to a Pure Land at the time of death. See *Living Meaningfully, Dying Joyfully*.

Trijang Rinpoche (AD 1901-1981) A special Tibetan Lama of the twentieth century who was an emanation of Buddha Shakyamuni, Heruka, Atisha, Amitabha, and Je Tsongkhapa. Also known as 'Trijang Dorjechang' and 'Losang Yeshe'.

Twelve sources The six powers (the eye sense power and so forth) and the six objects of those powers (visual forms and so forth). See *Heart of Wisdom*.

Two truths Conventional truth and ultimate truth. See *Meaningful to Behold* and *Ocean of Nectar*.

Ultimate truth The ultimate nature of all phenomena, emptiness. See *Heart of Wisdom, Meaningful to Behold*, and *Ocean of Nectar*.

Vaibhashika The lower of the two schools of Hinayana tenets. This school does not accept self-cognizers and asserts external objects to be truly existent. See *Meaningful to Behold* and *Ocean of Nectar*.

Vairochana The manifestation of the aggregate of form of all Buddhas. He has a white-coloured body.

Vajra Generally, the Sanskrit word 'vajra' means indestructible like a diamond and powerful like a thunderbolt. In the context of Secret Mantra, it can mean the indivisibility of method and wisdom, omniscient great wisdom, or spontaneous great bliss. It is also the name given to a metal ritual object. See *Tantric Grounds and Paths*.

Vajra body Generally, the channels, drops, and inner winds. More specifically, the pure illusory body. The body of a Buddha is known as the 'resultant vajra body'. See *Clear Light of Bliss*.

Vajradhara The founder of Vajrayana, or Tantra. He is the same mental continuum as Buddha Shakyamuni but displays a different aspect. Buddha Shakyamuni appears in the aspect of an Emanation Body, and Conqueror Vajradhara appears in the aspect of an Enjoyment Body. See *Great Treasury of Merit*.

Vajrayana The Secret Mantra vehicle. See also *Secret Mantra*. See *Tantric Grounds and Paths*.

Vajrayogini A female Highest Yoga Tantra Deity who is the embodiment of indivisible bliss and emptiness. She is the same nature as Heruka. See *Guide to Dakini Land*.

Vinaya Sutras Sutras in which Buddha principally explains the practice of moral discipline, and in particular the Pratimoksha moral discipline.

Virtue A phenomenon that functions as a main cause of happiness. It can refer to virtuous minds, virtuous actions, virtuous imprints, or the ultimate virtue of nirvana. See *Understanding the Mind*.

Vow A virtuous determination to abandon particular faults that is generated in conjunction with a traditional ritual. The three sets of vows are the Pratimoksha vows of individual liberation, the Bodhisattva vows, and the Secret Mantra vows. See *The Bodhisattva Vow* and *Tantric Grounds and Paths*.

Wheel of Dharma Buddha gave his teachings in three main phases, which are known as 'the three turnings of the Wheel of Dharma'. During the first Wheel he taught the four noble truths, during the second he taught the *Perfection of Wisdom Sutras* and revealed the Madhyamika-Prasangika view, and during the third he taught the Chittamatra view. These teachings were given according to the inclinations and dispositions of his disciples. Buddha's final view is that of the second Wheel. Dharma is compared to the precious wheel, one of the possessions of a legendary chakravatin king. This wheel could transport the king across great distances in a very short time, and it is said that wherever the precious wheel travelled the king reigned. In a similar way, when Buddha revealed the path to enlightenment he was said to have 'turned the Wheel of Dharma' because, wherever these teachings are present, deluded minds are brought under control.

Winds See *Inner winds*.

Wisdom being An actual Buddha, especially one who is invited to unite with a visualized commitment being.

Wishfulfilling jewel A legendary jewel that, like Aladdin's lamp, grants whatever is wished for.

Yama See *Lord of Death*.

Yidam See *Deity*.

Yoga A term used for various spiritual practices that entail maintaining a special view, such as Guru yoga and the yogas of eating, sleeping, dreaming, and waking. 'Yoga' also refers to 'union', such as the union of tranquil abiding and superior seeing. See *Guide to Dakini Land*.

Yogi/Yogini Sanskrit words usually referring to a male or a female meditator who has attained the union of tranquil abiding and superior seeing.

Bibliography

Geshe Kelsang Gyatso is a highly respected meditation master and scholar of the Mahayana Buddhist tradition founded by Je Tsongkhapa. Since arriving in the West in 1977, Geshe Kelsang has worked tirelessly to establish pure Buddhadharma throughout the world. Over this period he has given extensive teachings on the major scriptures of the Mahayana. These teachings are currently being published and provide a comprehensive presentation of the essential Sutra and Tantra practices of Mahayana Buddhism.

Books

The following books by Geshe Kelsang are all published by Tharpa Publications.

The Bodhisattva Vow. A practical guide to helping others. (2nd. edn., 1995)

Clear Light of Bliss. A Tantric meditation manual. (2nd. edn., 1992)

Eight Steps to Happiness. The Buddhist way of loving kindness. (2000)

Essence of Vajrayana. The Highest Yoga Tantra practice of Heruka body mandala. (1997)

Great Treasury of Merit. The practice of relying upon a Spiritual Guide. (1992)

Guide to Dakini Land. The Highest Yoga Tantra practice of Buddha Vajrayogini. (2nd. edn., 1996)

Guide to the Bodhisattva's Way of Life. How to enjoy a life of great meaning and altruism. (A translation of Shantideva's famous verse masterpiece.) (2002)

Heart Jewel. The essential practices of Kadampa Buddhism. (2nd. edn., 1997)

Heart of Wisdom. An explanation of the *Heart Sutra*. (4th. edn., 2001)

How to Solve Our Human Problems. The four noble truths. (2005)

Introduction to Buddhism. An explanation of the Buddhist way of life. (2nd. edn., 2001)

Joyful Path of Good Fortune. The complete Buddhist path to enlightenment. (2nd. edn., 1995)

Living Meaningfully, Dying Joyfully. The profound practice of transference of consciousness. (1999)

Mahamudra Tantra. The supreme Heart Jewel nectar. (2005)
Meaningful to Behold. The Bodhisattva's way of life. (4th. edn., 1994)
The New Meditation Handbook. Meditations to make our life happy and meaningful. (2003)
Ocean of Nectar. The true nature of all things. (1995)
Tantric Grounds and Paths. How to enter, progress on, and complete the Vajrayana path. (1994)
Transform Your Life. A blissful journey. (2001)
Understanding the Mind. The nature and power of the mind. (2nd. edn., 1997)
Universal Compassion. Inspiring solutions for difficult times. (4th. edn., 2002)

Sadhanas

Geshe Kelsang has also supervised the translation of a collection of essential sadhanas, or prayer booklets.

Avalokiteshvara Sadhana. Prayers and requests to the Buddha of Compassion.
The Bodhisattva's Confession of Moral Downfalls. The purification practice of the *Mahayana Sutra of the Three Superior Heaps.*
Condensed Essence of Vajrayana. Condensed Heruka body mandala self-generation sadhana.
Dakini Yoga. Six-session Guru yoga combined with self-generation as Vajrayogini.
Drop of Essential Nectar. A special fasting and purification practice in conjunction with Eleven-faced Avalokiteshvara.
Essence of Good Fortune. Prayers for the six preparatory practices for meditation on the stages of the path to enlightenment.
Essence of Vajrayana. Heruka body mandala self-generation sadhana according to the system of Mahasiddha Ghantapa.
Feast of Great Bliss. Vajrayogini self-initiation sadhana.
Great Compassionate Mother. The sadhana of Arya Tara.
Great Liberation of the Father. Preliminary prayers for Mahamudra meditation in conjunction with Heruka practice.
Great Liberation of the Mother. Preliminary prayers for Mahamudra meditation in conjunction with Vajrayogini practice.
The Great Mother. A method to overcome hindrances and obstacles by reciting the *Essence of Wisdom Sutra* (the *Heart Sutra*).
Heartfelt Prayers. Funeral service for cremations and burials.
Heart Jewel. The Guru yoga of Je Tsongkhapa combined with the condensed sadhana of his Dharma Protector.
The Kadampa Way of Life. The essential practice of Kadam Lamrim.
Liberation from Sorrow. Praises and requests to the Twenty-one Taras.

Mahayana Refuge Ceremony and Bodhisattva Vow Ceremony.

Medicine Buddha Sadhana. The method for making requests to the Assembly of Seven Medicine Buddhas.

Meditation and Recitation of Solitary Vajrasattva.

Melodious Drum Victorious in all Directions. The extensive fulfilling and restoring ritual of the Dharma Protector, the great king Dorje Shugden, in conjunction with Mahakala, Kalarupa, Kalindewi, and other Dharma Protectors.

Offering to the Spiritual Guide (Lama Chopa). A special way of relying upon a Spiritual Guide.

Path of Compassion for the Deceased. Powa sadhana for the benefit of the deceased.

Pathway to the Pure Land. Training in powa – the transference of consciousness.

Powa Ceremony. Transference of consciousness for the deceased.

Prayers for Meditation. Brief preparatory prayers for meditation.

A Pure Life. The practice of taking and keeping the eight Mahayana precepts.

Quick Path to Great Bliss. Vajrayogini self-generation sadhana.

Treasury of Wisdom. The sadhana of Venerable Manjushri.

Union of No More Learning. Heruka body mandala self-initiation sadhana.

Vajra Hero Yoga. A brief essential practice of Heruka body mandala self-generation, and condensed six-session yoga.

The Vows and Commitments of Kadampa Buddhism.

Wishfulfilling Jewel. The Guru yoga of Je Tsongkhapa combined with the sadhana of his Dharma Protector.

The Yoga of Buddha Amitayus. A special method for increasing lifespan, wisdom, and merit.

The Yoga of Buddha Vajrapani. The self-generation sadhana of Buddha Vajrapani.

The Yoga of White Tara, Buddha of Long Life.

To order any of our publications, or to
receive a catalogue, please contact:

Tharpa Publications
Conishead Priory
Ulverston
Cumbria, LA12 9QQ
England

Tel: 01229-588599
Fax: 01229-483919

Email: tharpa@tharpa.com
Website: www.tharpa.com

or

Tharpa Publications USA
47 Sweeney Road
P.O. Box 430
Glen Spey, NY 12737
USA

Tel: 845-856-5102 or
888-741-3475 (toll free)
Fax: 845-856-2110

Email: tharpa-us@tharpa.com
Website: www.tharpa.com

or

Tharpa Publications Canada
1155 Indian Road
Mississauga, ON
L5H 1RB
Canada

Tel: 905-274-1842
Fax: 905-274-1714

Email: info@tharpa.ca
Website: www.tharpa.ca

Study Programmes of Kadampa Buddhism

Kadampa Buddhism is a Mahayana Buddhist school founded by the great Indian Buddhist Master Atisha (AD 982-1054). His followers are known as 'Kadampas'. 'Ka' means 'word' and refers to Buddha's teachings, and 'dam' refers to Atisha's special Lamrim instructions known as 'the stages of the path to enlightenment'. By integrating their knowledge of all Buddha's teachings into their practice of Lamrim, and by integrating this into their everyday lives, Kadampa Buddhists are encouraged to use Buddha's teachings as practical methods for transforming daily activities into the path to enlightenment. The great Kadampa Teachers are famous not only for being great scholars but also for being spiritual practitioners of immense purity and sincerity.

The lineage of these teachings, both their oral transmission and blessings, was then passed from Teacher to disciple, spreading throughout much of Asia, and now to many countries throughout the Western world. Buddha's teachings, which are known as 'Dharma', are likened to a wheel that moves from country to country in accordance with changing conditions and people's karmic inclinations. The external forms of presenting Buddhism may change as it meets with different cultures and societies, but its essential authenticity is ensured through the continuation of an unbroken lineage of realized practitioners.

Kadampa Buddhism was first introduced into the West in 1977 by the renowned Buddhist Master, Venerable Geshe Kelsang Gyatso. Since that time, he has worked tirelessly to spread Kadampa Buddhism throughout the world by giving extensive teachings, writing many profound texts on Kadampa Buddhism, and founding the New Kadampa Tradition – International Kadampa Buddhist Union (NKT-IKBU), which now has over nine hundred Kadampa Buddhist Centres worldwide. Each Centre offers study programmes on Buddhist psychology, philosophy, and meditation instruction, as well as retreats for all levels of practitioner. The emphasis is on integrating Buddha's teachings into daily life to solve our human problems and to spread lasting peace and happiness throughout the world.

The Kadampa Buddhism of the NKT-IKBU is an entirely independent Buddhist tradition and has no political affiliations. It is an association of Buddhist Centres and practitioners that derive their inspiration and guidance from the example of the ancient Kadampa Buddhist Masters and their teachings, as presented by Geshe Kelsang.

There are three reasons why we need to study and practise the teachings of Buddha: to develop our wisdom, to cultivate a good heart, and to maintain a peaceful state of mind. If we do not strive to develop our wisdom, we will always remain ignorant of ultimate truth – the true nature of reality. Although we wish for happiness, our ignorance leads us to engage in non-virtuous actions, which are the main cause of all our suffering. If we do not cultivate a good heart, our selfish motivation destroys harmony and good relationships with others. We have no peace, and no chance to gain pure happiness. Without inner peace, outer peace is impossible. If we do not maintain a peaceful state of mind, we are not happy even if we have ideal conditions. On the other hand, when our mind is peaceful, we are happy, even if our external conditions are unpleasant. Therefore, the development of these qualities is of utmost importance for our daily happiness.

Geshe Kelsang Gyatso, or 'Geshe-la' as he is affectionately called by his students, has designed three special spiritual programmes for the systematic study and practice of Kadampa Buddhism that are especially suited to the modern world – the General Programme (GP), the Foundation Programme (FP), and the Teacher Training Programme (TTP).

GENERAL PROGRAMME

The General Programme provides a basic introduction to Buddhist view, meditation, and practice that is suitable for beginners. It also includes advanced teachings and practice from both Sutra and Tantra.

FOUNDATION PROGRAMME

The Foundation Programme provides an opportunity to deepen our understanding and experience of Buddhism through a systematic study of six texts:

1 *Joyful Path of Good Fortune* – a commentary to Atisha's Lamrim instructions, the stages of the path to enlightenment.
2 *Universal Compassion* – a commentary to Bodhisattva Chekhawa's *Training the Mind in Seven Points*.
3 *Eight Steps to Happiness* – a commentary to Bodhisattva Langri Tangpa's *Eight Verses of Training the Mind*.
4 *Heart of Wisdom* – a commentary to the *Heart Sutra*.
5 *Meaningful to Behold* – a commentary to Bodhisattva Shantideva's *Guide to the Bodhisattva's Way of Life*.
6 *Understanding the Mind* – a detailed explanation of the mind, based on the works of the Buddhist scholars Dharmakirti and Dignaga.

The benefits of studying and practising these texts are as follows:

(1) *Joyful Path of Good Fortune* – we gain the ability to put all Buddha's teachings of both Sutra and Tantra into practice. We can easily make progress on, and complete, the stages of the path to the supreme happiness of enlightenment. From a practical point of view, Lamrim is the main body of Buddha's teachings, and the other teachings are like its limbs.

(2) and (3) *Universal Compassion* and *Eight Steps to Happiness* – we gain the ability to integrate Buddha's teachings into our daily life and solve all our human problems.

(4) *Heart of Wisdom* – we gain a realization of the ultimate nature of reality. By gaining this realization, we can eliminate the ignorance of self-grasping, which is the root of all our suffering.

(5) *Meaningful to Behold* – we transform our daily activities into the Bodhisattva's way of life, thereby making every moment of our human life meaningful.

(6) *Understanding the Mind* – we understand the relationship between our mind and its external objects. If we understand that objects depend upon the subjective mind, we can change the way objects appear to us by changing our own mind. Gradually, we will gain the ability to control our mind and in this way solve all our problems.

TEACHER TRAINING PROGRAMME

The Teacher Training Programme is designed for people who wish to train as authentic Dharma Teachers. In addition to completing the study of fourteen texts of Sutra and Tantra, which include the six texts mentioned above, the student is required to observe certain commitments with regard to behaviour and way of life, and to complete a number of meditation retreats.

All Kadampa Buddhist Centres are open to the public. Every year we celebrate Festivals in many countries throughout the world, including two in England, where people gather from around the world to receive special teachings and empowerments and to enjoy a spiritual holiday. Please feel free to visit us at any time!

For further information, please contact:

NKT-IKBU Central Office
Conishead Priory
Ulverston
Cumbria LA12 9QQ
England

Tel: 01229-588533
Fax: 01229-587775

Email: info@kadampa.org
Website: www.kadampa.org

or

US NKT-IKBU Office
Kadampa Meditation Center
47 Sweeney Road, P.O. Box 447
Glen Spey, NY 12737, USA

Tel: 845-856-9000
Fax: 845-856-2110

Email: info@kadampacenter.org
Website: www.kadampacenter.org

Index

The letter 'g' indicates an entry in the glossary.

Further Reading

If you have enjoyed reading this book and would like to find out more about Buddhist thought and practice, here are some other books by Geshe Kelsang Gyatso that you might like to read. They are all available from Tharpa Publications.

THE NEW MEDITATION HANDBOOK
Meditations to make our life happy and meaningful

This popular and practical best-selling manual, now revised to make it even more accessible to the general reader, is the quintessence of all the teachings explained in *Joyful Path of Good Fortune*. The author guides us through all the twenty-one meditations on the stages of the path to enlightenment, enabling us to discover for ourselves the increasingly peaceful, positive, and blissful states of mind that come from Lamrim meditation.

'One can instantly sense its value ... this book shines.' *The New Humanity*.

MEANINGFUL TO BEHOLD
The Bodhisattva's way of life

Many people have the compassionate wish to benefit others, but few understand how to make this wish effective in their daily life. In this highly acclaimed commentary to the great Buddhist classic *Guide to the Bodhisattva's Way of Life*, the author shows how we can engage in the actual methods that lead to lasting benefit for ourself and others.

'An indispensable Buddhist work – no serious student of Buddhism can afford to be without it.' *John Blofeld*.

EIGHT STEPS TO HAPPINESS
The Buddhist way of loving kindness

This inspiring book reveals deeply transforming, yet practical methods to enable a powerful opening of the heart, the source of all true happiness. It explains how to meditate on eight beautiful verses that comprise one of Buddhism's best-loved and most enduring teachings, *Eight Verses of Training the Mind*.

' ... induces calmness and compassion into one's being.' *New Humanity Journal*.

To order any of our publications, or to receive a catalogue, please contact:

Tharpa Publications
Conishead Priory
Ulverston
Cumbria, LA12 9QQ
England

Tel: 01229-588599
Fax: 01229-483919

E-mail: tharpa@tharpa.com
Website: www.tharpa.com

or

Tharpa Publications USA
47 Sweeney Road
P.O. Box 430
Glen Spey, NY 12737
USA

Tel: 845-856-5102 or
888-741-3475 (toll free)
Fax: 845-856-2110

Email: tharpa-us@tharpa.com
Website: www.tharpa.com